Principles of Management
for the Hospitality Industry

Principles of Management for the Hospitality Industry

Dana Tesone

Rosen College of Hospitality Management,
University of Central Florida

ELSEVIER

AMSTERDAM • BOSTON • HEIDELBERG • LONDON • NEW YORK • OXFORD
PARIS • SAN DIEGO • SAN FRANCISCO • SINGAPORE • SYDNEY • TOKYO
Butterworth-Heinemann is an imprint of Elsevier

Butterworth-Heinemann is an imprint of Elsevier
Linacre House, Jordan Hill, Oxford OX2 8DP, UK
30 Corporate Drive, Suite 400, Burlington, MA 01803, USA

First edition 2010

British Library Cataloguing in Publication Data
A catalogue record for this book is available from the British Library

Library of Congress Cataloging-in-Publication Data
A catalog record for this book is available from the Library of Congress

ISBN: 978-1-85617-799-3

For information on all Butterworth-Heinemann publications
visit our website at www.books.elsevier.com

Printed and bound in Great Britain

10 11 12   10 9 8 7 6 5 4 3 2 1

Working together to grow
libraries in developing countries

www.elsevier.com | www.bookaid.org | www.sabre.org

ELSEVIER   BOOK AID International   Sabre Foundation

Contents

Preface

This book is designed to provide the readers with the planning, organizing, influencing, and control functions associated with management in service enterprises, especially with hospitality organizations. It is presented from the standpoint of a practitioner's perspective, which means it is applicable to the actual tasks, duties and responsibilities that are performed by line and staff managers alike. The book may be used for educational programs in any service industry, but is particularly focused on managing hospitality organizations. The information that is presented includes all of the activities performed by management practitioners.

The objective of the manager in the hospitality service industries is to learn the practice of professional management. This practice includes building a solid foundation of management and leadership knowledge, the development of appropriate skills, and the reflection and self-awareness of personal attitudes about management and leadership. The operating manager who is in possession of this knowledge and these skills will benefit in three ways. First, the operating manager who has a thorough knowledge of professional management and leadership concepts has a foundation on which to develop his or her skills. Second, this combination of knowledge and skills better prepares the operations manager to successfully run, grow and fix any operation within any enterprise. Third, the operations manager who possesses this knowledge and these skills, and who regularly contemplates how his or her actions and behaviors reveal his or her attitudes about management and leadership is more likely to enjoy a rapidly progressive career. In essence, this person will be a better manager for any organization.

This book is written in a straightforward and condensed manner designed to provide the reader with an inclusive, yet precise presentation of the material. The intention is to virtually place the reader in the imaginary workplace to work through items of discussion in each chapter. At the beginning of each chapter, a vignette entitled *IN THE REAL WORLD...* sets the stage for the reader to embark on a given topic. The chapter then concludes with the outcome of the applied role-play with the vignette called *IN THE REAL WORLD...(Continued)*, to provide reinforcement of the material absorbed through reading the chapter.

A section called *Discussion Questions* appears after each vignette to provide thoughtful consideration of the topics presented in each chapter. The questions are arranged in variable formats ranging from open-ended to specific right and wrong answers. *Marginal Definitions* are included throughout each chapter to reinforce the vocabulary of terms associated with professional management practices. A *Glossary of Terms* provides an alphabetical listing of vocabulary and definitions.

The book consists of seventeen chapters, arranged within five parts. The figure below shows a diagram of the relationships and rationale for the book.

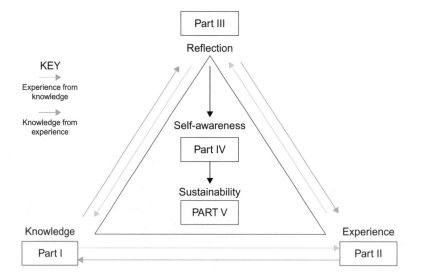

The chapters in Part I of the book focus on the evolution of management and general descriptions of management functions, strategies and activities.

Chapter 1 provides an overview of service enterprise management and provides comparisons and contrasts between service and other industries. Chapter 2 walks us through a historical evolution of management practices and theories to demonstrate the use of all previously discovered ways of managing enterprises in current practice. There is also an inclusive discussion of management and business ethics toward the end of the chapter. Chapter 3 presents a thorough discussion of procedures used for enterprise strategic planning, problem solving and management decisions used to proactively and reactively manage operations. Chapter 4 addresses service enterprise systems, development and structures for the purpose of establishing a foundation through which managers may view the operations within service enterprises.

At this point in the book, we have established a foundation of management knowledge that will be applied throughout the remainder of the text. The reader is now prepared to enter Part II of the book.

Part II contains chapters that present the reader with a snapshot of duties and responsibilities associated with the practice of professional management. There is a thorough discussion of productivity models and the practice of value-added management in Chapter 5. Chapter 6 walks us through the functions associated with organizing resources, structures and systems within the service enterprise. An overview of the human resource management function is the topic of discussion in Chapter 7 of the text. Chapter 8 presents management practices associated with information technology applications and marketing systems. Chapter 9 addresses management accounting and financial control functions within service enterprises. At this stage we have absorbed a combination of knowledge and practices that will prepare us to experience management diagnostics and interventions used to perform tactical strategies.

Part III demonstrates applied strategies and tactics required for effective strategic management. In these chapters, we will reflect on our existing foundations of knowledge and practice to enact management interventions in three major categories. Chapter 10 begins with an overview of strategic diagnostics and interventions and concludes with a demonstration of productivity enhancement tactics that result in value-added management practices. We engage in discussions of corporate and property level growth strategies in Chapter 11 of the text. Chapter 12 provides the reader with practices used to turnaround under performing departments within a service enterprise. At this point, we have accumulated and reflected upon a holistic blend of management knowledge, practices and experiences. We are now ready to enter an examination of ourselves for the purpose of learning how managers may become leaders.

Part IV covers the theories, practices and development aspects of leadership in organizations. Chapter 13 provides an in-depth discussion of leadership awareness for the reader. We convert that knowledge into leadership practices in Chapter 14 of the text. We use our powers of reflection and self-awareness to generate strategies for personal leadership development in Chapter 15. Part V presents information concerning sustainable competitive advantage from both marketing and human resource management perspectives. As we near the completion of the final chapter, we reflect upon all we learn by reframing a summary of major knowledge and experiences presented throughout the text.

It is recommended that readers reflect on actual scenarios in the workplace or classroom role-play while digesting the content of this book. If the book is being used as part of a college course, the facilitator may encourage discussions of actual events to bring each topic to life. The reader is encouraged to convert the knowledge from this book into actual skills to be applied in the workplace. This may be accomplished through two activities. First, apply the knowledge immediately. Turning knowledge into skills requires practice. Practice the knowledge within 24 to 48 hours after reading it. Second, teach these concepts to someone else. We learn through teaching. As one presents this new information to another person, the exchange process will reinforce the knowledge and that 'teacher' will be better prepared to use the knowledge in the workplace. Like the first suggestion, this technique should be applied within 24 to 48 hours after reading and discussing the information.

PART 1

Management Knowledge

CHAPTER 1

Managing Service Enterprises

REAL WORLD EXPERIENCES

It has been a long time since you and your friends started attending classes at the College of Hospitality Management. Finally, you are all taking courses in the final semester of your senior year. While talking with some friends, the topic of postgraduation plans comes up.

Many of your friends are sharing concerns about leaving school to enter the real world. While the prospect seems scary, it also appears to be an exciting time for all of you. The conversation turns toward different opinions concerning the 'ideal job' after graduation.

To be continued...

INTRODUCTION

This chapter provides us with an overview of management and leadership in hospitality enterprises. We will discuss the nature of services provided to customers, guests and clients, and how we may learn the skills required to effectively manage these services. Why do we need to know about management? The answer to this question comes from the career opportunities that exist for college graduates and entry-level employees. Where are the higher paying jobs? In our business, all of these jobs have title of 'manager' attached to the position description.

Some individuals may intend to pursue careers in service operations such as restaurant, lodging, recreation, entertainment, events and other sectors. In this case, the objective would be to become an operations manager. Others may prefer to work in human resources, marketing, sales, accounting, finance or information technology specializations. The best jobs in these areas include titles of manager, director or vice president. So we can see that careers in hospitality, tourism or other service industries will inevitably involve being promoted into management positions.

Many service enterprises do not provide thorough training for management knowledge, skills and abilities. Their expectation is for individuals to enter the workforce with this level of training from universities, colleges, schools and vocational institutions. In most cases, an individual will be promoted from a service or production position into management. But without proper training that person will be unlikely to become a successful manager. The reason this is so is that service jobs and management are two different practices. Service jobs require technical skills to perform job functions. When we become managers, however, we are responsible for other people who perform these functions. This is a totally different skills set and one that every service enterprise worker needs to learn in order to enjoy a successful career. Even if you do not want to manage large groups of people, the success of your career will rely on your ability to manage yourself and administrative assistants.

This chapter begins our journey of attaining knowledge, skills and abilities in service management. It provides an overview of services and the management of those services that will become the template for exploration in every aspect of becoming a manager and a leader in service enterprises.

What is Service?

If someone were to ask the question 'what is service'? The manager's initial answer would be to say, 'it depends…' In this case, it would depend on the nature of the industry providing the service. Most businesses focus on the distribution of products to customers. So in manufacturing, wholesale, and retail sales, customer service is ensuring product delivery to the customer and handling any problems that may arise with the performance of the product. This is not the case in the service sector of business. In this sector, the physical product is really a by-product of the services being rendered. For instance, in a quick service restaurant (QSR), the product is the meal provided. The service consists of those interactions and transactions that occur between the customer and members of the staff from the time of entry to the restaurant through the time of departure from the restaurant. Hence, service consists of interactions and transactions that result in relationships among customers and staff members, which is called *customer relationships*. Hospitality service enterprises are organizations that regularly engage in customer relationships.

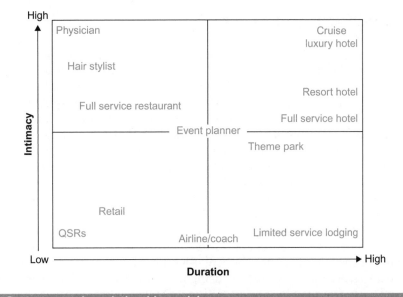

FIGURE 1.1   Customer service relationship model

Customer relationships may be measured by two factors. The first is the *intimacy* or the intensity of the interactions. For instance, a QSR or retail worker merely takes the order and packages the product, so the intimacy with the customer is limited. However, a physician or a luxury hotel operator must know every detail about the client to provide the expected levels of service; thus a high level of intimacy exists with the customer during these interactions.

The second factor used to measure the level of customer service is *duration* of time spent with the customer. The customer spends a few minutes with the QSR or retail worker, while she or he spends 30 minutes or so with a physician or a tax accountant, spends hours in an airplane or full-service restaurant and perhaps days in a luxury hotel. Figure 1.1 demonstrates examples of customer interactions in terms of intimacy and duration.

THE HOSPITALITY INDUSTRY

While all service enterprises focus on service as the main product, the epitome of a service operation falls within the domain of the hospitality industry. The hospitality industry includes services in the areas of lodging, food service, travel, tourism, recreation, entertainment, personal health and fitness, attractions, social events, meetings and conventions. The complexity of these services is quite high in both intimacy and duration levels relative to the interaction with the customer (who is referred to as a 'guest') in this industry. While the information in this book prepares all service industry personnel to practice effective management and leadership, the examples presented in it are taken from the hospitality industry. This is because a person with the ability to manage in this industry is capable of effective management in any industry of choice.

COMMITMENT TO SERVICE

Workers in any industry are famous for slogans and campaigns claiming quality service. The focus is usually on customer service. Very little emphasis seems to be placed on services provided to members of other *stakeholder groups* (shareholders, employees, the community). Interestingly, some hospitality/tourism organizations that claim high levels of customer service provide the exact opposite to their employees. Managers in some firms say they focus on the worker as an *internal customer*.[1] Closer inspection of these companies often reveals unrealistically limited resources, antiquated systems and stagnating bureaucracy. In fact, one of the incentives for promotion in some organizations is the opportunity to escape the customer by dwelling in offices and managing reports. Reports and forms, while necessary to some degree, serve as diversions from the 'business of the business', which is to provide service to internal and *external customers*.[2]

In some cases, reports and forms are used to feed an already bloated corporate bureaucracy that is upheld by senior-level managers. As the bureaucracy grows, the business becomes inverted, focusing inward toward the senior management group and away from the customers and other stakeholders. Because these organizations are out of touch with the stakeholder groups, they are reactive to changes in the external environment (factors outside the organization). This is contrary to the *proactive* approach of healthier competitors. Fortunately, this scenario is becoming more and more the exception to the rule; ...or is it? You decide the answer based on your own customer service and work-related experiences.

SERVICE VERSUS SERVITUDE

One term used to describe the services provided by leaders is called 'stewardship'.[3] Stewardship describes the intrinsic duty of leaders to provide services to their followers every day without being asked for assistance. They do this because they are truly concerned with the welfare of those individuals with whom they interact. In the hospitality/tourism industry, we are trained to anticipate the needs of our guests (customers) and proactively act to satisfy those needs.[4] We don't do this because we 'have to' do it; we do it because we personally and professionally enjoy the challenge of creating memorable experiences for our guests. That is why we hire new people for 'attitude' in our industry. We seek those individuals who genuinely like other people enough to engage in providing them with intimate levels of service for long durations of time. These individuals possess the security within their being to recognize the difference between making a professional choice to serve others, as opposed to an insecure attitude of being in a position of servitude, in which they feel they 'have to' serve others. The difference is a mental paradigm of personal security versus personal insecurity. The insecure individuals will move toward bureaucratic industries and positions that are mostly self-serving, as they pursue their careers.

Think for a moment about the great leaders in history throughout the world. Without exception, they all practiced 'servant leadership,'[5] regardless of their specific calling. Now think about those not-so-great names in history. Were they individuals who provided services primarily for the benefit of others or just themselves? Those who choose to provide service to others have chosen the highest path to self-fulfillment. They join the ranks of the likes of Buddha, Tao, Christ, Gandhi, Mohammad, Abraham, Socrates and others. Consider the status of current day professions; the physician provides service by touching sick people in peculiar places; the teacher is a servant of knowledge; the architect creates aesthetic structures for peoples' enjoyment, while ensuring their safety and so on. A path of service is a choice we make, while one of servitude is forced upon us.

WHAT IS MANAGEMENT?

Simply defined, *management* is the accomplishment of an organization's objectives through the activities of others. This leads us to ask the question, 'What is an organization?' An *organization* is a collection of individuals brought together to achieve a common set of goals or objectives, which for our purposes mean the same thing. An organization is made up of people, who provide goods and services to customers. These people perform their job functions in physical locations such as offices, lodging facilities, restaurants and storefronts.

When groups of people work together in an organization, there are certain expectations for behavior and thinking. The *organizational culture* consists of the shared values, attitudes and beliefs of workers within a specific organization. These shared values, attitudes and beliefs cause workers to engage in behaviors that are consistent with the expectations or 'norms' of that organization. You may identify the nature of an organizational culture by observing the staff members while they are at work. The way they present themselves, their attire, interactions, work habits, and treatment of the customers or guests are all telltale signs of the unwritten codes for behavior that come naturally to the staff members. Other factors that impact the culture are the traditions, historical stories and leadership styles of corporate figureheads. For instance, the *Ritz-Carlton* hotel chain embodies a strong guest service culture that is evident in the saying, 'We are ladies and gentlemen serving ladies and gentlemen.' The majority of employees at these properties take great pride in the culture of the organization. The opinions of individuals concerning the organizational culture are called *organizational climate*. In the case of *Ritz-Carlton*, the climate seems quite positive, with many staff members indicating they are proud to be associated with that service philosophy. Negative perceptions of the culture within other service enterprises would indicate the need for management diagnostics and problem-solving interventions.

When you become a staff member of a service enterprise, you occupy a job, which is really referred to as a position. For each position, there are *tasks*, *duties*, and *responsibilities*, which are items that are listed in a job description to articulate the activities of individuals within that job classification. These become the expectations for the job holder's performance. There are two broad categories of employees in service enterprises called *line* and *staff* workers. Line workers produce products and/or services (chefs and front desk agents, for instance) and/or directly generate revenues (hotel sales personnel, for instance). Staff workers perform tasks, duties and responsibilities intended to support the line workers (accounting, human resources and purchasing personnel, for instance). Management positions also fall within the classifications of line and staff. Line managers work in operations or sales, while staff managers oversee functions that support the line positions.

Regardless of whether a person is a line or staff manager, all managers are expected to professionally manage the service enterprise. We recall that management is defined as the accomplishment of the organization's objectives through the activities of others. *Mismanagement* occurs when managers prove to be negligent in managing the enterprise to a reasonable standard. Different managers subscribe to various styles of decision-making activities. Managers who believe in highly centralized decision-making without seeking input from others in the organization are practicing *autocratic management*. Most autocratic managers are advocates of *classical management* thinking that embraces early engineering approaches of managing organizations that did not consider the human factors involved with work.

Service enterprises, in particular those in the hospitality and tourism industries, are quite labor intensive, meaning they employ large numbers of line and staff employees. Managers who fail to focus on the human aspects of work tend to overlook the needs of employees. This can be costly in labor-intensive businesses and usually results in high levels of *employee turnover*. Employee turnover consists of the total number of individuals who voluntarily (resignation) or involuntarily (discharge) separate from employment in an organization over the course of a year. Employee turnover is usually measured as a percentage of the total employment population within the enterprise. So a turnover rate of 100% means that the equivalent of every position in the company has had to be replaced over the past year. The opposite of employee turnover is called *employee retention*, which describes those employees who remain with the company over a period of one year. If an organization has a turnover rate of 60%, then the employee retention rate would be 40%. The combined turnover and retention percentages will always equal 100%, which represents the total employee population. High rates of employee turnover are costly to the organization, because each person who leaves the company must be replaced with another person to fill the vacated position. Human resource activities to attract and hire applicants for positions are called *recruitment* and *selection*. These activities are expensive and time consuming. Also, during the time that a position remains vacant, waiting to be filled, there will be shortfalls in *worker outputs*. Worker outputs are units of production completed by each worker. When a worker is missing, the associated outputs will be missed and in most cases, will have to be made up by remaining workers, which places a burden on those staff members. Most organizations also measure *management turnover* which is represented by the percentage of managers who voluntarily or involuntarily separate from their positions with an organization relative to the total number of management jobs over a period of one year. The cost of management turnover is quite high in most service enterprises.

One goal of professional management is to increase employee retention rates to a predetermined acceptable level. In order to do this, managers must decrease turnover rates to an appropriate level. Sound human relations skills contribute to enhanced employee retention and decreased turnover in organizations. The ultimate human relations skill is the ability to influence others to willingly follow the manager toward accomplishing the objectives of the organization. This practice is called *leadership*.

Leadership comprises a number of influencing skills that contribute to the power base of the professional manager, which is an important topic area addressed in Part IV of this book. Managers must be trained in organizational diagnostics to identify the health of each work unit. They do this by comparing actual performance levels to standards for performance. When a negative gap exists between actual performance and standards, a *problem* exists in the organization. Managers must possess the ability to identify symptoms in an organization to determine the nature of significant problems – a process called *management diagnosis*. Managers continually diagnose the health of the organization by wandering around, observing performance and conducting *diagnostic interviews*, which are discussions with individuals to identify symptoms of potential problems. Once the manager believes a problem exists, he or she would engage in a practice called *problem analysis* to identify causal relationships involving symptoms that will lead to *problem identification*, which indicates the real problem at hand. Finally, the manager will identify a group of alternative problem solutions and choose one for implementation – a process called *decision-making*.

MANAGEMENT FUNCTIONS

So far we have discussed management activities, which are narrower in scope than management functions. There are four functions of management. They are planning, organizing, influence and control. All managers at all levels of a service enterprise perform all of the management functions. However, the majority of time spent performing certain functions will vary with the level of management within the organization. Figure 1.2 describes the levels of management.

The pyramid shows us that three basic levels of management exist within the service enterprise. The supervisory level is considered to be junior-level management in which the *supervisor, lead* or *assistant manager* actually oversees a group of line or staff workers. For instance, a *dining room supervisor* will be responsible for ensuring that the service staff performs to the standards established for that area of a restaurant. The positions being supervised in this case would include job titles such as *server, busser, host, bartender* and *bar-back*.

The supervisor mostly performs a *control function*, since he or she is responsible for making sure the actual performance of every person in the dining room meets the established standards for performance. In order to do this, the supervisor or lead

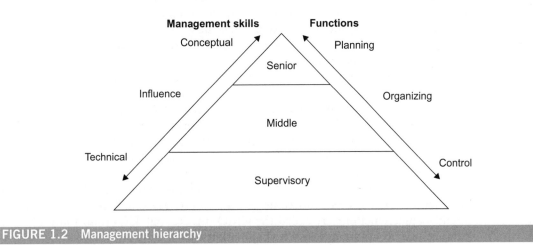

FIGURE 1.2 Management hierarchy

must possess the actual skills required of servers, bussers, hosts and bartenders. These are called *technical skills*, which are the actual skills required to perform a line or staff function. But technical skills are not enough for effective supervision. As we have already discussed, there are people skills required of this job. So the supervisor or lead must possess both technical skills and effective *staff relations skills*, which means the ability to influence the staff to meet performance standards. When a supervisor performs well in this capacity, she or he may eventually be considered for promotion to a middle management position.

Middle-level managers are usually responsible for the function of a sizeable work unit, called a *department, division* or *store* in the case of chain restaurants. Middle managers continue to supervise junior-level managers, supervisors and leads, who in turn supervise the line or staff employees. Consider, for instance, the lobby area of a full-service hotel. The *front-office manager* is the department leader for most services that occur in and around the lobby. These services might include bell staff, front desk agents, reservations agents (sometimes they report to the *sales and marketing director*), concierges, door staff, PBX operators and valet employees. We can see that this is a large area of responsibility, which means it would not be feasible for a front-office manager to directly supervise each position. Instead there are managers and supervisors for each of these areas who report directly to the front-office manager.

The front-office manager has a limited number of *direct reports* who supervise the rest of the staff. So what does the front-office manager do most of the time? She or he does what all middle managers do – organize activities among other departments. The middle manager spends most of the time performing the *organizing function* of management, in which the manager coordinates activities within and outside the department. In addition to the skills associated with supervisory work, the middle manager must establish strong relationships with peers who hold similar level positions in different departments. In our front-office manager scenario, key department managers who will influence the success of the front office include those in the areas of housekeeping, engineering, accounting, sales and marketing, and food and beverage. So we can see that the job of a supervisor is very different from the job of a middle manager. The same is true when one is promoted to a senior-level management position.

Senior-level managers occupy the top positions within a service enterprise. In the hotel business, the senior management team is called the *executive committee*. Members of this committee usually include the *general manager, assistant general manager* (or *rooms division manager), controller* (accounting), *human resources director, chief engineer, food and beverage director,* and the *sales and marketing director*. Depending on the nature of a resort, other executive committee managers may also include *director of security, director of sports and recreation, director of retail, director of information technology, director of entertainment* and other specialized managers. The general manager is the chief operating officer (COO) of hotel and resort properties. If the hotel is part of a chain, there will be a corporate executive committee comprised of vice presidents for each of the areas represented by the executive committee at the property level. The corporate president is the chief executive officer (CEO) of the chain. Individuals who occupy the highest positions within management functions could also possess 'chief officer' titles. These might include chief officers called the CMO (marketing), CIO (information), CFO (finance), CHRO (human resources) and others.

Senior managers are usually promoted from middle management positions. When this happens, their management focus will change from performing mostly organizing activities to engaging mostly in the function of strategic *planning*. Planning is a strategic approach used to achieve future objectives. While senior-level managers will continue to engage in the functions of control, organizing and influence, these individuals spend most of their time focusing on the future direction and objectives of the organization. The most important people skills set for these managers are called *conceptual skills*. These skills provide the senior manager with the ability to articulate and influence workers toward achieving the mission and vision of the organization.

Managers at all levels of the organization have the authority to make decisions aimed at solving problems and contributing to the strategic direction of the work unit. A manager's span of authority will usually increase with each promotion into higher levels of management. *Management responsibility* involves assuming responsibility for an area of authority. Managers should be empowered with balanced levels of authority and responsibility. This means that managers should not delegate decision-making responsibility without granting the authority associated with the job. When it comes to making decisions, there is an element of *management risk* as the manager will be held responsible for the outcomes of each specific decision. Management risk, then, occurs when managers engage in behaviors that may be detrimental to a manager's standing in an organization. Management decision-making is one such behavior.

How Do I Become a Manager?

Management is a practice, not an academic discipline. People with manager titles are expected to become management practitioners. As we already discussed, mismanagement occurs when managers fail to manage their work units in a professional manner. How does this happen? Well, in many service enterprises, the best technical workers are usually promoted to supervisory and ultimately management positions. However, some organizations fail to provide the appropriate skills, knowledge and abilities required of performing management functions. When this happens, the manager will either learn these skills through trial and error, which is a time-consuming and costly process, or that manager will not learn these skills and mismanage the work unit. This results in bad managers occupying positions of authority in service enterprises.

Professional management requires *management training*. Management training imparts skills in the functions of planning, organizing, influence and control. Managers spend a good deal of time solving *problems* that exist within certain work units. In organizations, a problem is defined as a negative gap between actual performance and performance standards. As we already know, the symptoms of a potential problem become diagnosed through the performance of the control function of management, which is really supervision. Management training should provide skills in *intervention planning*, which is a strategic problem-solving approach used by professional managers. The goal of intervention planning is for the manager to generate decisions aimed at *solution optimization*, which provides the best possible solution to a problem through management decision-making activities.

Since management is a practice, the most effective management training programs permit new managers to 'practice' their newly forming management skills. Unlike many academic disciplines, management skills may not be learned in a laboratory. The best way to learn management skills is to mentally rehearse or physically practice management practitioner techniques in the workplace. There are three techniques for providing management training practice to individuals. These are *trial-and-error*, *modeling* and *mentoring* activities. Trial-and-error practice is the least efficient way to learn management and involves learning from actual mistakes and successful outcomes from management scenarios. Modeling involves emulating the visible behaviors of professional managers. Mentoring consists of coaching relationships between mentors (experienced professional managers) and protégés (learners of management) aimed at developing management skills. This is the most effective learning technique for management development. Sound learning programs will include all three of these techniques within the training activities. All of these techniques reinforce the skills of new managers. *Training reinforcement* is intended to habituate new behaviors resulting from training. The goal of all training is to create new habits, which are behaviors that individuals do naturally without consciously thinking about them. The goal of management training is to provide knowledge that is continuously practiced, which results in experiences. It is the blend of knowledge and experience that habituates professional management practices.

THE ROLE OF THE SERVICE SUPERVISOR

The first management position we are likely to occupy will be within the supervisory ranks. These positions normally use titles such as *supervisor*, *lead* or *assistant* manager. We have discovered that service consists of interactions that create relationships with customers (both internal and external). So what is the role of the service supervisor? At first glance it would appear that these individuals ensure positive interactions that result in positive customer relationships. But how do they do that? To answer this, we must consider the nature of supervision and management.

We already know that supervision is the first level of management that oversees the work being performed by line and staff workers. As a person moves up the ladder, she or he spends less time supervising the performance of others and more time engaged in planning and organizing activities. However, all managers must practice supervision at every level of the corporate hierarchy when dealing with individuals with whom they have direct reporting relationships.

Managers and supervisors are primarily responsible for achieving the objectives of the organization through the activities of others. So what is an *objective*? An objective is a target for performance. It is something you want to accomplish for yourself, a department or an organization. For instance, the marketing objective for a hospitality/tourism organization could be 'the acquisition and maintenance of guests'.[6] In other words, every worker in the organization wants to keep the guests to come back, while taking steps to acquire new guests to add to the overall pool of guests who frequent the establishment. In the process of accomplishing this objective, supervisors and managers ensure that actual performance levels are consistent with established standards for performance. Notice that objectives drive a number of activities in Figure 1.3.

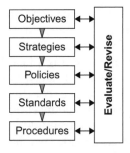

FIGURE 1.3   Objectives and strategies

STRATEGIES AND TACTICS

The objectives for the hospitality/tourism organization are executed through action steps designed to reach the targeted goals (objectives). Broad range action steps are called *strategies*, which are mostly practiced by senior and middle-level managers in the company. Supervisors are responsible for executing these strategies on a daily, weekly, monthly and annual basis through narrow action steps called *tactics*. So objectives drive strategies, which may be broad (strategic) or narrow (tactical) in scope.

Strategies evolve into corporate *policies*, which are broad guidelines for performance throughout the organization. Supervisors convert these policies into *standards*, or expectations for performance and *procedures*, which are daily action steps used by all staff members to meet the standards. For each performance standard, there is a list of procedures that show the workers how to meet that standard. The next step is for the supervisor to compile standard operating procedure (SOP) documents for the department and job lists for each position in the department that specify each standard for performance and the procedures for meeting each standard. Finally, the supervisor observes the staff members to ensure that actual performance is consistent with the standards and procedures for the operation. This process is called *performance assessment* or *evaluation*, which compares actual performance with standards and procedures for performance.

TOOLS FOR PRACTICING MANAGEMENT

So far it has been established that managers achieve objectives and ensure the practice of procedures designed to meet the standards for performance in the department. The next step is to describe the tools used by managers to influence staff members to make these things happen. Managers use their influencing skills to maximize the performance of staff members. These influencing skills are essential for the practice of successful management.

Perhaps the most important tool for supervisors is the ability to effectively communicate with workers, peers and other managers. Communication involves active listening, verbal and written expression skills and the interpretation of non-verbal cues. One example of communication is the establishment of standards and procedures, as well as job lists to guide worker performance.

Managers must be adept at identifying and resolving conflicts in the workplace. It is the job of the supervisor to maintain a work environment that is fair, uniform and consistent for the workers. The ability to handle staff member complaints and grievances is essential to maintaining a healthy work environment.

Also, managers must establish leadership roles with the staff members concerning every aspect of job performance. For this reason, supervisors must possess solid skills in the areas of coaching, counseling and discipline. These techniques are required for effective motivation, training, teambuilding and leadership in the workplace. Skills for management practice will be discussed thoroughly in Chapter 2.

SUMMARY

This chapter began with a discussion of service. We recognized that service consists of customer relationships. Perhaps the most intimate customer relationships exist within the many sectors of the hospitality and tourism industry, which provides many examples to be used throughout the text. We went on to discuss service commitments, as well as intrinsic service attitudes. We learned that the desire to provide service is the foundation of leadership.

We then moved into an overview discussion of management. We described the practice and functions of management in this section. We identified the hierarchy of management positions for both line and staff departments within a typical service enterprise. We recognized the responsibility to practice certain influencing skills in order to enhance employee retention and reduce employee turnover in our labor-intensive organizations. We went on to describe specific practices of professional management aimed at effective decision-making and problem-solving activities.

Our discussions concluded with an overview of how to become a manager. These included functional knowledge, skills and abilities, as well as tools for the effective supervision of staff members.

DISCUSSION QUESTIONS

1. Consider the customer relationship model presented in Figure 1.1. Think about the operations within a luxury resort to include front office, food and beverage outlets, meetings facilities and banquets. What aspects of supervision do you think would be important to ensure proper customer relationships with guests in each of these areas?
2. Consider the management hierarch pyramid described in Figure 1.2. Try to identify the titles of all the managers who might reside in each of the three layers for a full-service convention resort with two golf courses. Which of those managers would be line and staff managers? Describe how the jobs of these managers change with each increased level in the management pyramid.
3. Assume that you are responsible for management training for a restaurant chain. What methods might you use to teach managers about the functions

and practices of management? What would you do to reinforce that training? How would the trainees have converted professional management practices into habits?

4. Consider the information presented in Figure 1.3. Describe the differences and relationships between objectives, strategies, policies, standards and procedures. Describe how you would go about establishing standards and procedures for the service staff in a full-service restaurant.

REAL WORLD EXPERIENCES (CONTINUED)

All of you have completed your required industry internships as part of your program. Monica mentions that she is being considered for a full-time position with a meeting planning company. George reports that the restaurant he has been working at for the past three years is willing to put him through the chain's management in training (MIT) program. Tara is nervous about an upcoming interview for a few cherished MIT openings with a large hotel chain.

Eventually, the conversation focuses on the mixed reactions from a recent career fair held at the school. Some of your friends express disappointment that most of the companies were seeking applicants for line jobs, such as front desk agents and restaurant servers. Your best friend, Alexis, tells everyone that she thought that was true as well, but mentions that she ran into a contact she had met during a guest lecture series who invited her to apply for a supervisory position at the local convention center.

After awhile, you start to notice that those classmates with work experience and networks of contacts seem to be getting better job offers than your friends with no work experience. You think to yourself, 'Boy, I am lucky to have two job offers to become an assistant manager in my sector.' You continue to think, 'I guess that job experience and networking is really paying off.'

CASE STUDY

You are a supervisor for a small work unit consisting of five workers. The previous two supervisors were fired for poor performance. Needless to say, the workers are doubtful about whether you will be any more successful than your predecessors. It is interesting that the work group has sort of bonded as a result of poor leadership and is pretty self-sufficient when it comes to doing the job. You know that the first thing you must do is to earn their respect. Once this is done, you will want to build a team.

Question

How will you earn their respect and then build a team?

Hint

Setting a good example and demonstrating stewardship could help with both objectives.

ENDNOTES

1. Albrecht, B., 2003. Professor finds faith along rural highways with theme parks and sites inspired by God [Final Edition]. The Plain Dealer, Cleveland, OH, p. E.1.
2. *Ibid*.
3. DePree, 1986. Leadership Is an Art, Doubleday, NY.
4. *Ibid*.
5. *Ibid*.
6. Wexler, P. 1986. *Marketing Driven Management*. Penguin Publishing, NY.

CHAPTER 2

Management Practice, Evolution and Ethics

In this chapter you will learn to:

1. Identify the stages and contributions of management evolution.
2. Apply ethical tests to management decision-making activities.
3. Describe an overview of managerial communications, change, behavioral management and stress management.

REAL-WORLD EXPERIENCES

You have been working part-time as a front-desk agent at a local resort for a few months. When you first started the job, you were told to shadow an experienced worker to learn how to perform front-desk transactions. Most of the managers and supervisors were promoted through the ranks at the resort. The front desk gets very busy at times. When this happens, the managers are usually not available for help. The desk area continuously seems disorganized and coworkers often miss their scheduled shifts. After work, it is common for the managers to socialize with the hourly workers. There seems to be favoritism between managers and certain staff members who have become friends.

While you have become proficient in your job duties, you begin to wonder if all resorts are run this way. It just seems to you that everyone's job is harder than it needs to be.

To be continued...

INTRODUCTION

Chapter 1 provided us with an overview of management and service enterprises. In this chapter, we take a closer look at management practices, as well as the evolution and ethical concerns for professional managers. We have already learned that there are two types of managers – those who practice professional management and those who mismanage organizations.

This chapter will provide a snapshot of the practices associated with professional management in service enterprises. Our current practices have evolved over many years of scientific inquiry concerning management practices. We will chart the progress of management evolution that has led to current managerial practices. As we already know, managers make decisions that impact large numbers of individuals. The effect of those decisions may be beneficial or harmful. Professional managers temper their decisions by evaluating how those choices may impact other individuals. The means for evaluating the correctness of decisions falls within the domain of management ethics, a topic we will discuss as we work through the chapter. Toward the end of the chapter, we will engage in discussion of management competencies, such as managing behaviors, communication, change and stress management.

MANAGEMENT PRACTICE

Management skills go beyond those used in supervision to include planning, and organizing functions. Also, influence functions for managers who get promoted beyond the supervisory ranks. We learned in Chapter 1 that there are three management levels within organizations. We also know that the emphasis of management skills and functions change as we progress to each level of the management hierarchy, as shown in Figure 2.1.

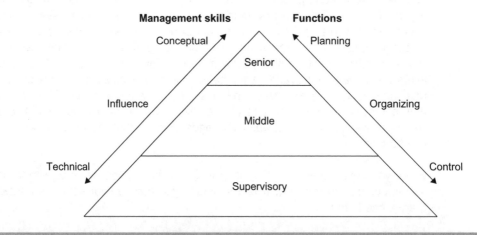

FIGURE 2.1 Management hierarchy

We know that technical skills are those skills required of workers to provide interactions and transactions with internal and external customers. First line supervisors use these skills the most. Middle managers spend most of their time coordinating activities (organizing function) and thus rely mostly on people (or influencing) skills. Executive managers spend most of their time in planning mode and must be cognizant of the big picture for the organization in the present and the future. Thus, they mostly use conceptual skills.

Management universality is the premise that management is an art and a science that has applications across all industrial boundaries. That is why programs of study in business management exist in institutions of higher learning. Programs that offer applied management skills in specific technical environments are specialized management disciplines. For example, Hospitality Management programs apply management principles to the technical aspects of hospitality and tourism enterprises.

Management is a science in the sense that we use specific models for the functions of planning, organizing and control. The art of management lies in those practices that comprise the influencing function of management. The influencing function of management is based on knowledge from the fields of applied psychology, sociology, cultural anthropology and organization theory. Collectively, these fields provide academics and practitioners with a body of knowledge known as **organizational behavior**. Organizational Behavior is the study of individual and group behaviors within organizations. Historically, the practice of management was viewed from the perspective of science and engineering. It was not until the latter stages in the development of management thinking that the influencing function or behavioral aspects of managing organizations were identified. The merging of behavioral and scientific processes is what makes management both an art and a science in current practice. It would be appropriate for us to view the historical evolution of management thinking to appreciate the holistic state of our current practices.

MANAGEMENT EVOLUTION

It serves us to consider the history of management, as collectively it contains the big picture of all aspects related to implementing conceptual, influence and technical skills within the functions of planning, organizing, influencing and control. As academic disciplines, management and psychology are relatively young sciences, beginning with studies in the early 1900s. The evolution of management takes a timeline approach in which the management theories unfolded as distinct approaches. All of these pose merit for today's managerial practice. Figure 2.2 provides a timeline of the historical evolution that occurred from the 1900s through the current time.

Management history is broken into five categories, starting with *Scientific Management* and ending with *Systems Management*. Each category will serve as a heading for the approaches that were developed chronologically. It is important to keep in mind that management started as a very narrow science and has developed into a broad interdisciplinary field of study. Therefore, each of the categories in the history provides a piece of the picture to use in the practice of management today.

1900s–40s	1940s	1950s–70s	1980s	1990s–2000s
Scientific management	Management science	Human relations	Human resource management	Systems management
Hawthorne studies		Leadership	Situational leadership	

FIGURE 2.2   Evolution of management

CLASSICAL APPROACH (SCIENTIFIC MANAGEMENT)

Scientific Management focused exclusively on line supervision as opposed to the overall organization. The goal of Scientific Management was to find the *one best way* to do work. The goal of Scientific Management was to determine the most efficient methods for performing tasks, duties and responsibilities. **Efficiency** results when outputs are achieved using fewer inputs. Another way to define efficiency is a process of *doing things right*. This approach to management did not include consideration of effectiveness issues. **Effectiveness** is the process of enhancing the quality and/or quantity of produced outputs. Some say that effectiveness is *doing the right things*. We should commend Scientific Management for introducing efficiency studies. However, we must realize that it is one-dimensional in that it does not consider effectiveness issues.

Frederick Taylor is considered the Father of Scientific Management. He was an engineer by training and used time and motion studies to identify the most efficient way to do work[1]. We know that Scientific Management is solely focused on enhanced efficiency. The particular area of interest was in the area of reducing labor costs. Taylor would observe workers using various tools and time their movements. One study focused on ditch diggers. Taylor timed their movements using different-size shovels to determine the most efficient shovel for the work. Since his studies focused on time and motion, the method became appropriately known as *Time and Motion Studies*. Taylor also introduced **piece-rate compensation**. Piece-rate compensation provides pay per unit of work produced (outputs).

Frank and Lillian Gilbreth were a husband-and-wife team of scientific management researchers. They were also concerned with identifying *the one best way* to do work. There is a movie about their life and work called *Cheaper by the Dozen* (they had 12 children)[2]. The movie illustrates how their studies influenced their home life, a highly efficient household. In one study, they worked with brick layers and found that efficiency could be greatly improved by placing bricks on an adjustable plank to be raised to the level that at which the brick layers were working. Lillian outlived Frank and continued their work until her death in 1972.

Henry Gantt created a zero-based approach to scheduling project activities using horizontal bar graphs to represent time and vertical lines to represent resource allocation. While Gantt was a proponent of Scientific Management, his project charts were later embraced by Management Scientists in the 1940s, long after Henry Gantt's death in 1919. These became known as Gantt charts and are still used by management scientists today. Gantt also established bonus systems for overproduction.

The French scientist Henri Fayol pioneered administrative management theory. He was responsible for establishing a Comprehensive View of management in organizations. He established a popular management edict called *Fayol's Fourteen Points*. These general principles included themes of authority, unity, centralization, remuneration, equity, stability, initiative and harmony. Another pioneer of administrative management was the researcher Max Weber, who is considered to be the Father of Administrative Management. His work involved the separation of line and staff employee functions. He was responsible for creating specialized departments within organizations on the basis of job functions. This resulted in the **functional organizational structure**, in which departments and reporting relationships are categorized by functions (accounting, operations, marketing etc.). Most service enterprises use functional organizational structures at the business-unit level in current practice.

Scientific Management was the first movement to contribute to the development of management models to be applied in various organizational settings. The limitation of Scientific Management is that it was purely efficiency-based and focused solely on front-line supervision, until the comprehensive models of Fayol and Weber. Also, emphasis was on the one best way to do work. While the Comprehensive View took a more holistic approach to administration, it was also efficiency-based and like Scientific Management did not focus on human variables associated with work. Scientific Management, Administrative Management and the Comprehensive View all fall within the category of Classical Management approaches.

EARLY BEHAVIORAL STUDIES

Elton Mayo was the first to discover that human factors influence production. This finding occurred by accident while conducting a funded scientific study. His research was known as the *Hawthorne Studies*. One study took place in a relay switch production room. The hypothesis was to develop a positive correlation to the amount of lighting in the room and increased production (outputs). It was determined that production increased when the lights were made brighter and continued to increase when the lights were dimmed. Thus, there was no direct correlation between work performance and the lighting. This was an unfortunate finding for Mayo, since the research was being sponsored by a lighting company. It was later discovered that the attention paid to the workers by the researchers was the basis of the enhanced production. The supervisors were removed, which left the workers to perform freely without fear, they started to enjoy their work and the group began to psychologically bond. In this case, group cohesiveness and freedom from controlled supervision resulted in increased production.

Another experiment took place in a wiring room at a bank. As part of this study, individual pay incentives were offered to workers to increase personal production. It was discovered that peer pressure from the group would motivate workers to overlook personal monetary gain to preserve worker solidarity. This was contrary to the expectations of the study. The Hawthorne Studies were conducted between 1924 and 1932 and were the first attempt to view the behavioral aspects of management.

While Mayo's work was quantum leap in his time, the mainstream management research community was not receptive to behavioral aspects of management. This may be due to the dominance in the field by engineers at that time. Behavioral science did not become popular among management scholars until 20 years after the completion of the Hawthorne Studies. When researchers finally embraced the behavioral science aspect of management, Mayo was credited with performing the groundbreaking studies in that area of management.

HUMAN RELATIONS MOVEMENT

The first school of thought in the behavioral science approach to management was called the *Human Relations* movement. The Hawthorne Studies paved the way for the development of the Human Relations movement, which ultimately became the Human Resource discipline of today. This movement focuses on human inter-action and its impact on organization success. Human relations skills are used to enhance productivity using people (influencing) skills. The Human Relations movement was driven by psychologists who sought to understand drivers of behav-iors in the workplace.

In the decade prior to the discovery of transpersonal psychology, Abraham Maslow was responsible for popularizing humanistic psychology, which became prominent in 1954. The *Journal of Humanistic Psychology* was established in 1958, result-ing in the formulation of the American Association for Humanistic Psychology in 1964[3]. The *personal growth* and *potentiality* focus of humanistic psychology was a broad departure from previous paradigms (psychoanalysis and behavioralism) that were preoccupied with pathology. Humanism was based on the assumption that individuals possess a propensity toward self-actualization that could be achieved through experience and reflective practice, as opposed to therapies aimed at cor-recting pathological behaviors through logical analysis or behavior modification[4]. Humanistic thinking spawned numerous studies in the late 1960s, which resulted in popularizing broad interests concerning states of human consciousness among behavioral scholars and practitioners for many years[5]. In more recent times, con-sciousness studies have been embraced by some researchers within the domains of neuroscience and physics[6]. Today, the human relations aspect of management falls within the categories of leadership and human resource management.

MANAGEMENT SCIENCE

Management Science is not the same as Scientific Management. Management Science uses the scientific method and mathematics to improve organization per-formance. The steps in scientific method are: observation, model construction, deduction of hypotheses, hypothesis testing and conclusions. This method is mostly used in large organizations for complex and quantitatively oriented decisions. The type of research employed in the decision-making process is called Operations Research (OR). Management science became popular when the US military sought the assistance of quantitative researchers from universities to create models for strategic initiatives that drove the allied forces during World War II. Management Science models are applied to inventory control models and probability models are applied to economic decision-making practices.

The major contribution of Management Science is its focus on decision-making effectiveness, not simply efficiency, which is the emphasis of Scientific Management. The strategic planning model that is a topic of discussion in Chapter 3 of the text is based on Management Science theoretical constructs. Service enterprise managers, especially those in complex environments like hospitality, use a form of Management Science called **action research** to solve organizational problems. Action research consists of an informal process of data collection, analysis, alternative solution generation, intervention selection, implementation and evaluation aimed at solving problems in the organization. Since management is a practice, we call these steps *diagnostics*, *interventions* and *assessment*, which is a shortened version of the action research model used by managers to solve problems – a topic of thorough discussion in Chapter 3.

Contingency Approach (Situational Leadership)

This method is commonly known as Situational Leadership. Situational leadership considers leaders, followers and the environment as variables for making management decisions. The assumption is that the situation (environment) influences management behavior. This has applications to each of the four functions of management and falls within the Transactional Leadership category of leadership practices, which will be discussed thoroughly in Chapter 14 of the text.

Systems Management

General systems theory provides the grounding for the **Systems Management** viewpoint of organizations. Systems Management views the organization as an entity that consists of interdependent relationships with internal and external subsystems. This is a view of 'wholeness' in which the organization is considered to be a microcosm that exists within an interdependent macrocosm. Systems thinkers realize that the interdependent relationships of subsystems requires 'big picture' thinking, since a change made in a subsystem will have an effect on the larger system. A small number of scholars have applied quantum theories to organizational systems thinking – an approach that could be called **New Science Management**. We will discuss systems thinking for management in more detail in Chapter 4 of the text.

Portions of the current management puzzle have been constructed over many years. Each major breakthrough in management thinking and inquiry has rendered an aspect of management that has implications for current-day practice, as Figure 2.3 demonstrates.

The value of management practices are currently defined by the efficiency and effectiveness of outputs, which are goods and services that result from the transformation of inputs (resources). We will investigate the relationship of inputs, transformation processes and outputs thoroughly in Chapter 5 of the text. The triangular

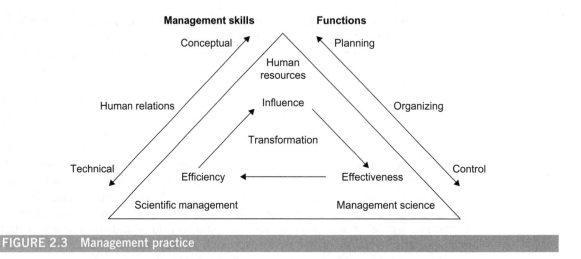

FIGURE 2.3 Management practice

flow of management practice is the combination of applications from the Classical, Behavioral and Management Science contributions from management history. These practices are contained by the microcosm of the organization, which resides in relationships to a dynamic macrocosm of external environments. Parts of the organization are subsystems of a larger system and the organization itself is a sub-system of an even larger system, as we will discuss in Chapter 4 of the text.

MANAGING INDIVIDUAL PERFORMANCE

JOB DESIGN, RESPONSIBILITY AND AUTHORITY

In order to effectively manage the implementation of plans, we must consider the responsibility and **authority** aspects of organization design. The key point to remember is that a balance between the two should exist in equal proportions. Many organizations blatantly violate this premise by delegating responsibility without granting authority to its managers. We know from Chapter 1 that responsibility is defined as the obligation to perform assigned activities. Authority is the right to perform or delegate tasks, duties and responsibilities. General and specific tasks and duties are outlined in a document called the **job description**, which also describes work environment, levels of legal accommodation, and should include specifically how performance will be measured. Job descriptions evolve from an activity called **job analysis**, which is part of the job design process. Job analysis identifies tasks, duties, responsibilities, work environment and confidentiality requirements associated with a position of employment.

While job descriptions are used as documents of expectations for workers, job specifications are documents that list the knowledge, skills, attitudes and abilities required to perform a position. This document is used by human resources practitioners as a hiring guideline for each position in the organization. Figure 2.4

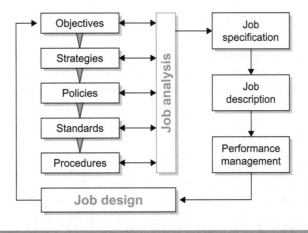

FIGURE 2.4   Job design drivers

demonstrates the relationship between objectives with job analysis used to yield job specifications, job descriptions and performance measurement.

Objectives drive required activities; these drive job design, which drives the measurement of performance. A combination of approaches should be taken during this activity on the basis of the nature of the organization and industry. For service enterprises, these include observation, questionnaires, interviews and environmental audits.

Some managers refer to the document articulating management responsibilities as responsibility reference guides. In actual practice, the document is known as a **manager's handbook**, which unfortunately is not widely available in some organizations. We know that authority is defined as the right to perform or delegate. So, here is the key concept of this section – managers are responsible for achieving the objectives of the organization through the activities of others. They should be granted a proportionally equal amount of resources and influence to get this job done. Authority in and of itself will not necessarily be accepted by workers. The manager must earn the workers' respect for his/her levels of authority. **Line authority** is the right to direct operational activities that generate products or services or revenue. **Staff authority** is the right to advise members of the organization. For instance, the controller is a financial advisor to the organization, therefore he/she has staff authority. The restaurant manager creates and sells products and services, thus he/she has line authority.

Performance with regard to use of authority and living up to levels of responsibility are measured by **accountability**. The manager is held accountable for his/her performance through a control mechanism called the **performance appraisal**. This compares actual performance to established standards for performance. There can only be three outcomes. The manager meets, exceeds or does not meet standards in each category. **Delegation** is the process of assigning both authority and responsibility to individuals within the organization. A decentralized organization is high in delegation, while a centralized company is low. A common mistake among managers is the tendency to delegate responsibility and accountability without granting equal levels of authority.

MANAGING GROUP PERFORMANCE

This section addresses individuals as they interact in groups. Group interaction brings about an added dimension to those aspects already discussed concerning individual behavior. This aspect of behavior is called *group dynamics*. There are two types of groups in organizations – **formal groups** and **informal groups**. Formal groups are those established by the organization (departments, divisions, stores, quality teams etc.). Informal groups are those groups that naturally develop without organization design (social groups, bowling leagues, coffee clutches etc.). Both types of groups evolve through membership in an organization.

There are various types of formal groups. An organization chart is a document that depicts command groups, those that fall within the corporate hierarchy. Task groups are those that are brought together to accomplish nonroutine tasks or projects. This group is sometimes referred to as a task force. Members of a task group may come from various departments and levels in the organization. A task group that is formed to make decisions concerning policy issues is called a *committee*. A steering committee would oversee activities concerning a project. Ethics committees are formed to develop codes of ethics and review compliance with the code. Committees are not necessarily the most efficient means to making decisions, as there are many people involved in the process. However, they can be effective. Positive outcomes associated with committees include participation, representation of varied interests, open-expression forums and quality-level decisions. There are considerations to be made in developing effective committees. There should be specific goals for performance and levels of authority should be specified. A chair should be appointed who possesses effective meeting skills. Each meeting should follow a prepared agenda and should be conducted in a timely fashion.

Sometimes groups become too cohesive. When a group begins to believe it is invincible and members stop questioning processes and decisions, a phenomenon called **groupthink** occurs. This causes bad decisions to be made. Many of the decisions made by the Enron executives concerning auditing practices had disastrous results. This was the groupthink phenomenon at work.

All groups are not teams. A **team** is a group of individuals who orchestrate activities in a manner that yields outcomes greater than the sum of the parts. In other words, a team consisting of four members will achieve more with less than a similar group. This type of outcome is called *synergy*. Synergy is the only reason for developing teams. In sports, we see champion teams that seem to effortlessly overcome challengers. This is the result of each person performing the right function in the right manner at the right time to gain synergistic outcomes.

There seems to be a trend toward the development of self-directed work teams in service enterprises. These are teams of 5–15 people who are self-managed by peers in the group. These teams are suited to certain types of tasks, usually those that require flexibility and creativity. Self-directed work teams do not work well with dull or mundane activities. The real motivators for self-directed work teams are: (i) challenging tasks and (ii) recognition for contributions to the team.

There are stages in the development of formal groups[7]. The first stage is called the acceptance stage in which members are getting to know each other and are somewhat mistrustful. The communication stage is where members become familiar with each other through group decision-making activities. The solidarity stage is that point in which the individuals are comfortable in respective group roles. The control stage is where the group has become a cohesive functioning unit.

Individuals are brought together through the organization and develop friendships and affiliations. We now know that these are called informal groups. An informal group could consist of individuals from many areas and levels in the organization. Informal group interactions satisfy social needs of individuals. Informal groups may be formed on a common interest level, like a bowling league. Informal groups are mostly healthy for organizations by adding a social component to the workplace. Misdirected informal groups can become destructive to the organization.

Just as there are stages in the development of groups, there are also stages in team development[8]. The first stage is the Forming stage, in which members are brought together. Then conflict arises among members, this is called the Storming stage. Next, members assimilate into specific roles as part of the team. This is called the Norming stage. When the team is ready to perform, it is in the Performing stage. And, as is the case with all teams, the group will eventually break up, this is the Adjourning stage. There are three factors to consider with regard to team effectiveness: the people, the organization and the tasks.

MANAGING THE SERVICE ENTERPRISE CULTURE

There is an amazing phenomenon in organizations called the *corporate culture*. Researchers Boulton and Deal do some nice work in this area[9]. Corporate culture is the shared values, attitudes and beliefs within the organization. Just as there are shared values, attitudes and beliefs within a society, the same is true for organizations. These factors influence the behaviors and perceptions of the members of the organization. To diagnose a culture, one must observe many factors, as the cultural values are not written, but they are just understood and agreed to in a subconscious manner.

Symbols are one symptom of the corporate culture. If we were to go to *IBM* headquarters 15 years ago, we would see everyone dressed in dark blue suits with red ties. Today, IBMers dress casually, like people did at *Apple Computers*. Dress is one type of symbol. Others include pins, plaques, trophies, certificates, banners, posters etc. Status symbols are those related to position within the organization. Examples are office layout and furniture, preferred parking spaces etc.

The corporate culture is developed and maintained by the history and traditions of the organization. The older the organization, the more established its culture. Some managers believe that the evolution of organizations in this millennium will severely mutter stayed traditional cultures, as newer organizations have weaker cultures for the most part. On the other hand, there are those who believe that commonly held values and traditions will become more important to workers as time moves forward. Individuals assume informal roles in maintaining the traditions of the culture. Some are storytellers, others are priests or counselors, and some are curators. Visit *Walt Disney World* in Orlando, Florida. If you were to visit their training facility (*Disney University*), you would swear that Walt is still alive. In fact, the orientation sessions for new *cast members* (employees) is called *Traditions*.

The physical environment of a property gives us clues concerning the corporate culture, such as location, layout, neatness, furnishing, signage etc. It is important to diagnose the culture of an organization before taking a position. One would want a culture that does not clash with one's personal values, attitudes and beliefs. A bizarre, creative, chaotic, maverick manager would not do well in a button-down culture. For instance, we do not see many *Marriott* managers leaving the company to work for *Hard Rock Hotel* properties. The leadership styles of an organization are influenced by its culture. Top-priority issues, crises management, training, coaching, role modeling, rewards, status, recruitment, selection, promotion, retirement are all influenced by the corporate culture.

As we discussed earlier in this chapter, values are core philosophies. They are the essence of who we are. Values are mostly formulated during childhood and adolescent development. The only thing that can cause a value shift in an adult is a life-altering event, like a near-death experience. Beliefs are those convictions that arise from past experiences compared with our value system. These are changeable, as long as the person chooses a path of personal evolution. Attitudes are directly related to current experiences and are subject to change. They are our current perceptions of external stimuli and determine our reaction to a newer specific stimulus. Thus, behavior is closely correlated with attitude. However, they are separate issues. Attitude is not behavior. When someone says, 'You have a bad attitude,' he is making a judgment statement about what he thinks, that a person's attitude is based on behavior. With the exception of recruitment and selection, managers should not address attitude, only behaviors, which may be empirically observed.

Some managers suggest that job design approaches may be used to alter attitudes. This is a very difficult endeavor. One would have to understand the personal aspirations of individuals and groups, and then be able to design work to suit those aspirations. This is the stuff of transformational leadership, which is a topic of discussion in Chapter 15 of the text. Another approach to attitude adjustment is training. This is another difficult task. This type of training seeks 'affective' or emotionally changed outcomes, which are the hardest to achieve in a learning environment. Why? Because attitude is just like motivation, actually they are close cousins. We cannot change someone's attitude. But, if we have a working knowledge of applied psychology and learning theory, we can convince someone to change his/her attitude. This will only occur if we are able to reinforce the learning with environmental factors. Thus, we would be able to attain affective outcomes through this type of training.

Managing Behaviors

All things are created twice. Every behavior begins as a thought or an instinct. The thought is converted into intentionality, which causes the behavior. Have you ever heard someone say, 'I could have, I should have ____?' Those are thoughts without intention. Intention is the gap that causes action, which is equal to behavior. Attitude surveys are conducted by human resource practitioners to gauge employee morale. There are two dangers to conducting these surveys. First, many surveys are not statistically valid and reliable. Second, if we ask the questions, we must address the issues of concern according to the responses. For instance, if we ask about the employee cafeteria and the employees say it is horrible, we would have to fix the cafeteria. Otherwise, morale goes lower than if you had not asked in the first place. Symptoms of poor morale run in stages: distrust, discontent, fear, anger, sabotage (of corporate property) and finally apathy. When people just do not care, there is a serious morale problem that requires a professional intervention, which will likely include a good deal of attrition.

Attitude is the cause of learned defense mechanisms and explanations for behavior. Perception is the filter through which we view the world as interpreted by our attitudes. When someone says, 'You have a bad attitude,' that is attribution that suggests a cause for a given behavior. Stereotypes are fixed generalizations about people or groups. Halo effect is focus on one aspect of behavior, instead of all critical behaviors. Projection is assignment of one's own traits onto others. Selective perception filters out incongruent stimuli. Procedural justice is the perception of fair treatment of employees. This is why every organization should have an effective due process procedure to guarantee that employees are treated in a fair, uniform and consistent manner.

MANAGEMENT ETHICS

Managers are responsible and accountable to four distinct stakeholder groups. They are shareholders, customers, employees and the community. These are presented in Figure 2.5.

Proactive managers realize that the interests of all the stakeholder groups are vital to the long-term success of the organization, as well as their managerial careers. There is currently a level of distrust regarding the practices of business owners and managers among the members of American society. This level of distrust might be

FIGURE 2.5 The diamond service model

warranted given the activities of early industrialists and corporations throughout the last century and into this one. The reason this attitude is significant is that the people of this society empower legislators to regulate business enterprises. To paraphrase the words of Patrick Henry, 'when we fail to govern our freedom wisely, we lose our liberties.' Hence, businesses have lost the liberty to do business that was once enjoyed in this 'free enterprise' economic system.

Since managers are employees of the organization, they are members of at least one stakeholder group within that company. Perhaps, they may also be customers or shareholder, in which case they represent more than one stakeholder group. As such, they have personal 'buy-in' to the welfare of the organization in addition to their own career aspirations. Hence, unethical activities may have adverse impacts on these managers on both personal and professional levels.

Most managers are motivated to some degree by status and prosperity. The old sayings, 'what goes around, comes around' and 'live by the sword, die by the sword' are too longstanding to not have some validity. By enhancing the practice of a manager to a professional level, managers enhance their own status and prosperity.

The trade media frequently identify segments of the hospitality industry that produce lackluster financial performance. Further investigations of these segments often reveal incidents of mismanagement, shareholder greed, employee dissention and community mistrust. Proactive organizations seem to have the ability to do well even during difficult times for their particular segment. These organizations also seem to display fewer cases of the negative symptoms associated with this discussion. Hence, we may conclude that proactive organizations are economically healthy entities that are capable of weathering difficult financial events. If this is true, proactive management must make good business sense.

In the broadest sense, managers are members of society. They are also moral beings. Some believe that otherwise morally sound and contributing members of society become amoral individuals when acting in business management capacities. These amoral beings emerge from the workplace each day to resume their roles as responsible citizens. Managers who subscribe to amoral professional practices are really cheating themselves. Since managers are motivated by challenging and meaningful work, it is natural for them to practice in a manner that contributes to the social standing of their respective organizations. This is one reason why when proactive managers are running organizations, those firms seem to reap higher levels of success than their competitors. At the highest level, the manager is a human entity. There are five aspects to the human composite: the physical, the spiritual, the mental, the emotional and the social realms. Self-actualized individuals seek balance among these aspects of the composite[10]. The proactive manager is a balanced individual who is passionate about the challenges and meaning of his/her work. These are the qualities that make his/her a respected leader.

AWARENESS AND PARADIGM SHIFTS

One aspect of management ethics training is to generate awareness of ethical issues and responsibilities associated with managerial decision-making activities. Once this awareness is created, managers sometimes choose to enact shifts in their own management *paradigm*. A paradigm is a model of a principle. For instance, consider a paradigm of public welfare that advocates providing assistance to those members of society who are in need by providing food and shelter. Now consider a second paradigm of job service, in which persons in need are provided with training to become self-supporting. This second paradigm makes no sense in the absence of the first. The first one provides a foundation (food and shelter) that permits the implementation of the second paradigm (self-sufficiency training). An awareness of the first paradigm is required before the second one may be realized. This is a *paradigm shift*. The first paradigm may be illustrated by the proverb 'Give a person a fish and feed him for a day.' The second paradigm might be stated this way, 'Teach him how to fish and feed him for a lifetime.' Awareness of the first proverb gives credence to the consideration of a shift into the second one. In management application, the 'awareness' consists of who we are today and the 'shift' consists of who we want to be tomorrow.

Why should there be paradigm shifts? The simple answer would be that we work and live in an evolutionary world. It is apparent that managers are faced with new problems that require creative solutions. For instance, the mentality that prevailed among managers and venture capitalists during the 1990s, and certainly during the 1980s, is no longer acceptable business practice in this society. At the same time, the policies and practices that existed during those times continue to be used in organizations today. In some cases, the thinking in the hospitality industry has not changed in 50 years. The current environment is changing dynamically. Proactive organizations are rethinking, restructuring and revitalizing operations in efforts to respond to changes that exist in the environment[11]. These activities require major paradigm shifts to establish new principles to guide the changes in organizations. To paraphrase Albert Einstein, 'significant problems in current day cannot be solved with the same level of thinking that existed when the problems were created.' This helps to explain the reason for adopting new paradigms for proactive hospitality and tourism management.

On a universal level, there must be a shift from traditional to modern management thinking in hospitality organizations. In order to do this, managers must shift from crisis management to mission-driven management. Next, managers should shift from checklist management to strategic thinking. This will require managers to shift from 'talk' mode to 'listen' mode in their communication styles. Another shift for managers is from win-lose to win-win outcomes[12]. Also, managers must shift from individual productivity to team-oriented productivity to attain outcomes that are greater than the sum of the parts. Finally, managers must shift from stress inducement to stress management mode to maintain employee energy levels. Are proactive managers ethical managers? Table 2.1 provides a moral evaluation of proactive managers to help you answer this question.

Business ethics are components of the decision-making process that consider the welfare of each of the four stakeholder groups. Advantages of ethical business practices are listed in Table 2.2.

Codes of ethics are formal statements providing guidelines for ethical behavior on the part of managers and other professionals. **Ethics Committees** are composed of employees from multiple departments who create and maintain the codes of ethics for organizations. Sometimes, they act as hearing boards for ethical complaints from stakeholder groups. Ethical conduct should be included in commonly distributed documents such as manager's manuals, standard operating procedures (SOP), employee handbooks and employment agreements.

TABLE 2.1	Proactive Managers
1.	Take charge of personal and professional destiny – they are not victims.
2.	Are mission driven to align their personal goals with organizational goals.
3.	Seek long-term outcomes, not short-term profits or other forms of gratification.
4.	Are empathetic listeners who care about the needs of others, especially their staff.
5.	Seek win/win/win for others, themselves and the organization.
6.	Are synergistic by being team stewards.
7.	Are spiritually, mentally, physically, emotionally, and socially balanced – hence they are holistic beings in search of self-actualization.

TABLE 2.2	Advantages of Ethical Business Practices
Improved productivity, or at least, improved morale on part of employees who are treated with respect and dignity.	
Positive overall stakeholder relations.	
Lessen the perceived need for society to create additional government regulations of business.	

SOCIAL RESPONSIBILITY

Corporate Social Responsibility is defined as the management obligation to take action to protect and improve the welfare of society, as well as the interests of the organization. We already know that social responsibility is our duty to the community stakeholder group, which includes suppliers, neighbors, our industry and society at large. There are various philosophies concerning social responsibility that range from no social obligation to extremely proactive duties to contribute to the welfare of society. In fact, these two views became evident in historical arguments concerning the legal status of corporations.

A definition of the American corporation was established in the landmark US Supreme Court case of *Dartmouth College vs. Woodward*[13]. In an opinion, the then Chief Justice, Thurgood Marshall wrote, '…the corporation is an artificial being, invisible, intangible, existing only in contemplation of Law.'

There are two legal views of corporations. One is called the Legal Creation view and the other is the Legal Recognition view. The Legal Creation view states that the corporation is created by the state (government). The state and law are created by society. Therefore, the corporation is created by society to serve society. When the corporation ceases to benefit society, society may destroy the corporation, according to this viewpoint.

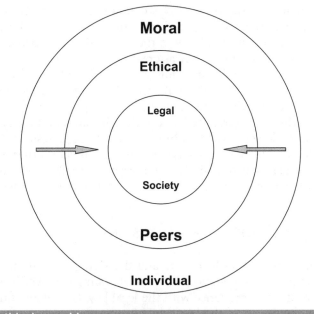

FIGURE 2.6 Legal, ethical, moral laws

The Legal Recognition view notes that the corporation is a free entity. The state (government) merely registers the corporation. The corporation is not a state creation. Therefore, the existence of a corporation is not to serve the needs of society.

The two views represent extremes in philosophies concerning corporations. The Legal Recognition view is a conservative approach to define the corporation. It is in line with the free enterprise system. As a result, individuals who embrace the doctrine of capitalism would subscribe to this viewpoint. Republican Party members would have a tendency to view businesses and corporations from this frame of reference. On the other hand, the Legal Creation view is a liberal interpretation of the status of corporations. Socialistic or highly liberal Democratic Party members might subscribe to this theory of corporations. The Legal Creation philosophy contains the type of thinking that contributes to the current trend of business regulation, which some individuals refer to as the 'corporatization of society,' indicating that government places the burden of curing social problems on the business entity through regulation.

Social responsibility has also been a matter of debate among philosophical scholars. One model suggests that organizations possess social power and hence are responsible to provide disclosure concerning business practices and to consider social costs in the course of doing business[14]. The antithesis of this philosophy is one provided by economist Milton Friedman, who claimed that corporations have no duty to society. Friedman suggests that the only requirement of business is to obey the law and pay taxes and that society should create laws to prevent businesses from doing harm to society[15].

We can see that ethical behaviors are topics of interest from social, legal as well as moral perspectives. In fact, Figure 2.6 provides a depiction of the relationship of these three aspects of morality.

The smallest of the three circles contains the legal law, which consists of codified behaviors prescribed by the legislature, which is empowered by society in theory. The focus of the legal law is the prevention and penalization of pathological behaviors as defined by society as creating social harm.

Ethics are broad guidelines for behaviors established by a group of peers. For instance, codes of ethics for managers are established by professional association, which is true for other practitioners, such as physicians, architects and attorneys. Codes of ethics are above the letter of the legal law and include provisions to prevent harm and to do some good within the context of professional practice. The highest law is the moral law that is based on individual values that drive a person's professional and personal behaviors. A manager who subscribes to high levels of moral values will demonstrate behaviors that are above the legal laws and ethical codes.

TESTING BEHAVIORS AND DECISIONS

Techniques for testing behaviors and decisions range from very simple to somewhat complex. For instance, it would be simple to verify whether a manager's behaviors are in compliance with the legal law. One would only have to be familiar with the provisions of the law, which sometimes seem complicated, but once this knowledge is established, it is a pretty straightforward process to interpret one's behavior as being either legal or illegal. Professional panels may be assembled to interpret whether a person's behaviors have violated an existing code of ethics. This process is also somewhat straightforward.

When we attempt to interpret the morality of a decision or behavior, the process becomes complicated. Two means of evaluating management decisions come from the Consequentialist and Formalist schools of normative philosophy. Consequentialist philosophers are concerned with the consequences of an action as determined through Utilitarian testing, which weighs the good and harm of that an action creates.

For example, let us say that a manager transfers all of the nonperforming employees in a work unit to other departments within an organization. What are the consequences of this action? The manager gets rid of bad performers without having to fire them, so he/she is happy. However, all the managers of the other departments have inherited poor performers. They would not have permitted these transfers if they knew the performance levels of these workers. Each of those managers has incurred harm from this action and the only person to benefit is the manager who encouraged the transfers. Since this action creates more harm to more people than good, the action fails the Utilitarian ethical test. When we review a future decision from this perspective, we ask, 'Does this decision result in the greatest good for the largest number of people?' If not, it is probably an unethical decision.

Another way to test decisions is by using a Formalist approach. Formalist philosophers are not concerned with the consequences of an action. They evaluate the 'form' of the action. A prominent Formalist philosopher was Emmanuel Kant, who provided a three-part test used to evaluate the form of an action. The test is described in Table 2.3.

The test is called the Categorical Imperative. It has three categories of testing and if the action fails just one test, it is considered to be immoral and unethical. Let

TABLE 2.3	A Listing of the Sections of the Categorical Imperative
Test 1 – Universality	The action must be universal, which means if everyone were to do this action, the action would continue infinitely and would not self-destruct.
Test 2 – Beings as ends	The action must respect all rationale beings as ends unto themselves. Therefore, the action may not treat beings as mere means to an ulterior end.
Test 3 – Autonomy	The action must be acceptable to all rationale beings, regardless of their involvement with the action.

us apply the categories to the manager who transfers problem employees. If every manager were to transfer problem employees, would this action continue forever or would it self-destruct? It would self-destruct because no manager would accept the risk of accepting transfer employees. Hence, it fails the Universality test. Does the action of transferring problem employees show respect for all the people involved in this activity? No, it treats people as a means to an end. The manager wants to get rid of bad performers, so he/she convinces other managers to take them into their departments. This manager is treating everyone as means to his/her own end. This behavior fails the Beings as Ends test. Finally, would anyone viewing this behavior think it is the right thing to do, regardless of their involvement with the activity? No rationale person would condone this behavior. Thus, it fails the Autonomy test of the Categorical Imperative. In this case, the practice of transferring problem employees fails all three categories of the test. But even if it had failed only one category, the behavior would be deemed to be immoral and unethical. Since we have learned that transferring our problem employees fails both Formalist and Consequentialist tests, we should be advised to refrain from engaging in this practice. However, we would not need to look far to find managers who regularly engage in that precise practice. These managers are behaving in an unprofessional manner.

Proactive corporations sometimes choose to include moral and social audits as part of the strategic planning process. A moral audit reviews the internal decision-making behaviors of managers and supervisors within the organization and compares those with existing ethical codes. A social audit reviews the morality and ethics of dealings with external stakeholder groups in the course of doing business.

MANAGERIAL COMMUNICATIONS

Managerial communications is the number one skill for all practicing managers. There are four vital competencies that organizations seek in managers: computation (math) skills, computer skills and written and verbal communication skills. Verbal skills range from one-on-one interactions to large-scale group presentations. Many corporate careers have been limited owing to peoples' fear of public speaking. This is probably why colleges require public communications courses and classroom presentations. Many schools also provide courses in managerial or organizational communications to prepare graduates for future management careers.

Management practitioners must become effective communicators in order to influence other individuals to accomplish the objectives of the organization. Effective communications competencies empower managers to perform the planning, organizing, influence and control functions of management. Figure 2.7 provides a depiction of the communications process.

Communication is defined as sharing information and meaning with other individuals. Consider the communication model presented in Figure 2.7. A person generates an idea, which is really an electrochemical reaction. The idea must be coded into symbols (words, gestures, facial expressions, tonality) in order to be sent to another person. At the point of coding, the person with the idea becomes the source of the coded version of that idea, which is now called a message. The encoded message is sent through a transmission (medium) in the direction of a destination (receiver). Media include phone, fax, modem, print, verbalizing, visual cues, anything that carries a message. The receiver now decodes the message to determine its meaning. A feedback loop is sent back to the source for message verification and any other response. At this point, the receiver becomes the source of a new message. The system continues in a loop between the two people. If the receiver understands the intent of the source's message, a successful communication interaction (effective) has occurred.

The problem with effective communication is the significant amount of barriers that exist that influence successful encoding and decoding of messages. Macrobarriers refer to those barriers outside of the communication model that influence effectiveness. These include: information overload, complexity of the environment, multiple languages and the limited time available for communicating activities.

Microbarriers to effective communication are those that exist within the communication model. These include attitude, perception, mood, noise and semantics. Perception is defined as interpretation of a message by a person. Noise is any

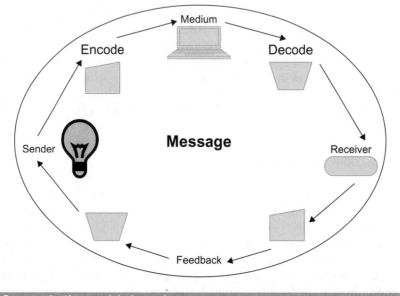

FIGURE 2.7 Communication model channel

distraction and does not have to be physical sound. Thirty people in a room that seats 20 for a meeting has a noise problem. Shuffling papers when someone is trying to talk with you at your desk is a form of noise. Any distraction is considered to be communication noise. Semantics refer to the meaning of words. The English language has numerous cases in which a single word has many meanings.

Communication feedback is achieved through the use of verbal and nonverbal cues. Only 7% of a total face-to-face message is comprehended by what is being said. The other 93% comes from body language and vocal tone/inflection[16]. Therefore, nonverbal cues are very important. Picture a man, standing in a rigid state, nervously tapping one foot, arms folded tight, facial frown, teeth clenched, face is flushed and breathing is rapid and shallow. His significant other approaches and says, 'Honey, what's wrong?' He growls in his lowest voice, 'Nothing!' Does she believe him? Not really. His 7% 'nothing' is not convincing, when compared to all of his nonverbal cues.

The most used, yet least taught, communication skill for managers is active listening skills. Executive managers spend as much as 85% of their communicating time listening to others[17].

One researcher provides the following advice for developing listening skills[18]: Practice active listening. Devote total attention to the speaker. Paraphrase to ensure understanding of the messages. Lean in to the person with posture. Remove physical barriers between you and the speaker if in an informal setting. Make frequent eye contact, but do not stare at the person. Use body language such as nodding to indicate understanding of messages. Use verbal feedback like, 'uh-huh, I see' to show interest.

Organization communication is the practice of communicating throughout the organization. Figure 2.8 describes directional flows. Communication direction is mapped on the organization chart as directives. Upward communication flows from bottom to top, usually in the form of reports. Lateral are communications are those that are horizontal on the organizational chart.

Downward communications flow from top to bottom, usually sideways for the purpose of organizing activities. Diagonal are sideways and up or down across

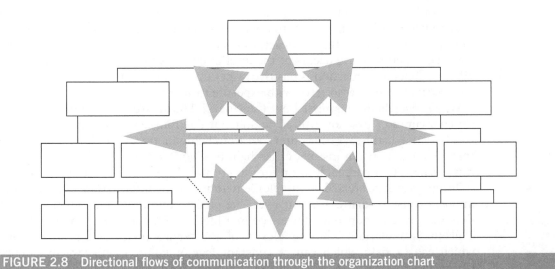

FIGURE 2.8 Directional flows of communication through the organization chart

departments. These are the directions of formal communications or those recognized as part of doing business in the company. **Informal communications** occur among individuals outside the business purpose. A common form of informal communication is the **grapevine**, which is the rumor mill. Studies show an inverse correlation between the effectiveness of formal communications and the accuracy and timeliness of the grapevine.

ORGANIZATIONAL CHANGE

Effective managerial communications are required to enact organizational change. **Organization Development** (OD) is a process of systematic change aimed at continuous organization renewal (adaptation)[19]. The OD practitioner will become the hero of the millennium. The OD practitioner is referred to as a change agent – one who enacts change in an organization. **Internal change agents** are those who work as managers within the company, while **external change agents** are brought in from outside the organization (consultants). All change agents must be sure to demonstrate a balance of people-oriented and production-oriented management styles.

The greatest behavioral barrier to enacting change is peoples' resistance to change. The change agent must be aware of the human variables. The cause of resistance is uncertainty. The change agent takes steps to reduce levels of doubt by providing information about the change before implementing the change. High levels of communication and honesty are required before the change process begins. Field theory proponents call this stage the unfreezing stage[20]. The interventionist is unfreezing current behavior through enhanced awareness concerning the change. The Changing stage is when the change is implemented. The Refreezing stage consists of 21 days of daily evaluation and reinforcement of the change. Since individuals are habitual, changing environments are perceived as stressful by most workers.

MANAGING WORKPLACE STRESS

The word stress is better stated as **distress**. Distress is when a person reacts adversely to variables in the environment that the person considers to be stressors. **Eustress** is still stress. But the reaction is positive in terms of enhanced performance. Peak performance occurs at the level of eustress just below the threshold of distress. Whether a reaction is positive or negative, there are physiological and psychological outcomes associated with exposure to stress.

Why is everybody so stressed-out these days? The answer is that our physiological configuration has not evolved to suit our environment. We were designed to handle acute distress. A bear jumps out from behind a tree. Our kidneys produce a rush of adrenaline. An instinct called fight or flight kicks in. We choose flight and run to safety. Our adrenal levels return to normal. That is acute distress.

Technology has created a complex environment of information overload that imposes constant distress in our lives. We process more information in one year than our great grandparents processed in a lifetime. Our senses are barraged with constant stimulation. The complexity of the environment causes uncertainty, which causes risk, which causes constant fear of failure. Thus, we experience chronic distress.

In times of distress, we are producing massive quantities of adrenaline, which shuts down the autoimmune system and causes us to get physically ill. The chemical imbalance causes us to get emotionally or psychologically ill. In times of eustress, we produce endorphins, which contain the cancer-fighting chemical, interleukin II. Picture someone at a theme park who is about to visit a thrill ride. One person will produce adrenaline, if this is not his/her idea of fun. Someone else will produce endorphins. So, you see that it is all subjective. How do we cope with this chronic infusion of stressors? The answer is balance and coping behaviors. We can choose to reframe those stressors in ways that remove their negativity. This is called becoming proactive versus reactive[21]. The balance part includes exercise, relaxation, meditation, spirituality, rest, nutrition and relatedness to other people who are close to us. Also, getting a job that you love is a big help. Chronic reactions to distress cause disease. This is why some business schools offer elective courses in stress management.

SUMMARY

We began our discussion in this chapter by looking at the organizational behavior aspects of management. We then reviewed the five-phase evolution of management history. We concluded from this that each new school of management thought throughout the last century has contributed to current management thinking and practice. Part of the practice includes managing workplace behaviors.

We learned that professional managers manage both individual and group behaviors. Our discussion in these areas touched upon the applied psychology that empowers managers to perform these practices. From the individual perspective, managers must establish expectations for performance and then ensure that the actual performance meets those standards. We shared many techniques and documents that are used for this purpose. We also learned that group dynamics influence individual behaviors. Professional managers use this knowledge to build effective workgroups and teams when appropriate.

We know that a major individual driver of normative behavior in the service enterprise is called the organizational culture. We looked at how the cultures impact performance levels through behaviors. We used this knowledge to further discuss performance management in service enterprises.

We now know that managers possess a duty to all constituencies. These are called stakeholder groups. Managers possess the duty to make decisions and manage individuals in an ethical manner. As we continued this discussion, we realized that managers may use tests to determine the legal, ethical and moral aspects of decisions.

We then shared the knowledge that professional management practice will require us to develop our own base of knowledge, skills and abilities. We recognized that professional managers engage in a paradigm shift from reactive to proactive thinking processes.

As we moved toward the end of the chapter, we considered specific management practices employed by the professional manager. These discussions included managerial communications, organizational development and managing workplace stress.

REAL-WORLD EXPERIENCES (CONTINUED)

One day you come into work at the front desk only to learn that the front-office manager has been replaced with someone from another hotel. You are not sure why this happened and assume that the front desk will continue to run the way it always had in the past. But, you are surprised that things begin to change almost immediately.

The managers and supervisors start working side by side with the hourly agents. The front-office manager always seems to be around. When he first started in the position, he had private discussions with every staff member. Now there are daily preshift meetings to apprise every one of the challenges awaiting each shift. Staff favoritism in terms of days-off and schedules have completely stopped. There is no more fraternization between managers and staff members that you are aware of.

Over time, the front-office manager introduces training programs and standard operating procedures. All staff members are required to demonstrate the ability to meet the standards. Some of your coworkers are retrained in their jobs. Some of the former managers leave the resort over the months. When this happens, both internal and outside competent candidates are invited to apply for these jobs. It seems that life at the front desk just gets better every day. All the managers seem to be very consistent in their management practices.

One day, the front-office manager announces a train-the-trainer program for high-level performers. You are invited to become a trainer for future front-desk agents. You think to yourself, 'This would have never happened under the old manager. What a difference professional management makes in an operation.'

DISCUSSION QUESTIONS

1. It has been stated that management is both an art and a science. Using the stages of management evolution as a foundation, describe how this statement might be true. Give examples of each stage in current-day practice.
2. Using the illustration in Figure 2.3, describe how managers influence individual and group behaviors in real-world practice. Use as many examples as you can.
3. Using information from the In the Real World vignette, describe how the behaviors of the original managers may be contrary to the authority, responsibility and accountability factors of professional management. Be specific in your response.
4. Think about a hospitality operation and identify at least one example of a formal group and informal group.
5. We use the word 'team' in our industry to excess. Describe a workgroup and determine whether it operates as a real team.

6. It has been stated that communication is the manager's number one tool. How is this so? Please use specific examples of good and poor management communications.

CASE STUDY

A Comparison of Management Styles

You work as a security officer at a large resort. Because of your classes at the university, you work an overlapping shift between the day and early night shift. There is a security manager who supervises each shift. You work four hours with the Alpha shift manager (Brad) and four hours with the Beta shift manager (Sharon). Both managers are former police officers and are very proficient in safety and security procedures. The difference between these two individuals as managers, however, is like day and night (no pun intended).

Brad is a micromanager who does not believe in employee empowerment. He commonly casts blame on the officers for their mistakes; but he is the first to take credit for the ideas of others. He is a stickler for policies and procedures, even when it seems there should be exceptions based on a set of circumstances. He tends to have 'favorites' on his shift who receive preferential treatment over some of the other, harder-working officers. The officers do not complain about Brad to the Director because Brad seems intimidating. Brad often berates the officers in front of their peers and the guests.

Preliminary Questions

1. Are you or someone you know familiar with this type of manager?
2. Provide a specific example of just such a manager, without naming that person.

Conclusion

Sharon, on the other hand, is every bit as proficient as Brad in the technical aspects of security, but she is also respected as a leader among the officers on her shift. As a matter of fact, most of the officers in the department request transfers to her shift when there are open positions. She is considered to be firm, but fair in her approach with the officers. She often takes the blame for things that go wrong, even if it was caused by one of her officers. She always listens to the staff for new ideas to improve performance and takes action to implement good ideas. She is quick to give credit to her officers for their contributions to the shift. She is always available to assist the officers, but lets them handle incidents and make decisions. She always coaches them in private after an incident that could have been handled better. Most of her officers are good performers and she will go out of her way to take care of them.

As a matter of fact, that is how you ended up with your split shift. She knew you were a good performer and that you took morning classes at the university. She is the one who arranged your schedule to accommodate your school activities.

Conclusion Questions

1. What can be specifically learned from the examples of both Brad and Sharon?
2. How do you think Sharon learned to adopt this management style? Is the same true for Brad? If not, how is Brad's training different?
3. What can you take away from this story for current or future use?

ENDNOTES

1. Maslow, A., 1962. Toward a Psychogy of Being. John Wiley and Sons, Inc., Hoboken.
2. Gilbreth, L., 1928. Living with Our Children. WW Norton and Company.
3. Boss, M., 1980. Transpersonal psychotherapy. In: Walsh, R., Vaughan, F. (Eds.), Beyond Ego: Transpersonal Dimensions in Psychology, Tarcher, Los Angeles: pp. 161–164.
4. Bugental, T.F.J., 1965. First invitational conference on humanistic psychology. J. Humani. Psychol. 5, pp. 180–181.
5. Chasse, J.D., 1997. The transaction in a many language hypothesis. J. Econ. Iss. 31 (2), 375–383.
6. Zohar, D., Marshall, I., 2000. SQ: Connecting with Our Spiritual Intelligence. Bloomsbury, New York.
7. Tuckman, B., 2008. Development sequence in small groups. Psychological Bulletin. 63 (6), 384–399.
8. *Ibid.*
9. *Ibid.*
10. Hyman, M.R., 2000. The volitionist's Manifesto. J. Bus. Ethics, 23 (3), 323, 15.
11. McKee, L., 2002. Theory of devolution. Library J. 127 (16), 100.
12. Farrell, B., 1999. Living the 7 habits: stories of courage and inspiration. Library J. 124 (20), 209, 1.
13. Paterson, F.R.A., 2000. 'Supreme Court: enemy of freedom?': constitutional law in Christian school textbooks. J. Law Edu. 29 (4), 405, 27.
14. Davis, K., 1975. 'Five Propositions for social responsibility.' Busi. Horizons, 9–24.
15. Friedman M., 1994. 'The social responsibility of business is to increase its profits,' In: Wines A.W., Stevens A. (Eds.), Readings in Business Ethics and Social Responsibility. Kendall and Hunt Publishing, Iowa, pp. 137–141.
16. Nichols, R.G., 1960. Learning by listening. The Supervisor's Handbook. 22 (1).
17. *Ibid.*
18. Gibson, J.W., Hodgetts, R.M. 1982. Organizational Communication. Prentice Hall, NY.
19. *Ibid.*
20. *Ibid.*
21. *Ibid.*

CHAPTER 3

Strategic Planning, Problem Solving and Decisions

In this chapter you will learn to:

1. Identify the steps in the strategic planning process.
2. Produce a strategic plan.
3. Identify the steps used for problem solving and decision-making activities.

REAL-WORLD EXPERIENCES

You have been working part-time at a chain restaurant near the campus while attending school for the past two years. When you started there, you noticed that the managers and staff socialized with each other quite a bit. While you were friendly with your coworkers, you did not let the job become a major part of your social life. You noticed right from the beginning that the managers played favorites with their friends when it came to schedules and station assignments. This did not really affect you since you were hired to work on specific days of the weekends.

You noticed that things at the restaurant had recently gone downhill. Staff turnover was high, new hires were not very experienced, guest complaints had increased and business had decreased. On a few occasions, you were called in to work extra shifts, which caused you to miss classes. About six months ago, a new general manager, Dave, was brought into your store from the corporate office. After a short time, he began to make serious changes to the operation. Most people hated the new manager at first. He replaced most of the assistant managers and hired many new servers. He implemented controls and service standards for all staff members. He demanded actual performance to the new standards and took progressive disciplinary action when these were not met. At first, you thought he was shaking up the whole restaurant. But over time you realized that your job was becoming easier to perform, your tips have increased and your new coworkers seem to be more professional.

To be continued...

INTRODUCTION

This chapter considers aspects of planning, the first of the four functions of management. The information presented in the chapter prepares us for the practice of implementing tactical strategies as managers within a service organization.

We know from our discussion in Chapter 1 that planning is a strategic approach for achieving future objectives. Senior-level managers spend most of their time in planning mode, which means that their primary focus is on the future direction of the service enterprise. Middle managers also do a good deal of planning as part of the process of organizing activities within the department and among other work units. The purpose of these planning sessions is to accomplish departmental objectives. Planning at the supervisory level of management is usually focused on daily, weekly and monthly activities of work unit staff members. The purpose of these plans is to ensure that actual performance levels meet established standards, which is a control function of management. So, **strategic planning** is the process of attaching **strategies** and **tactics** to each objective set for the organization.

STRATEGIC PLANNING COMPONENTS

The **mission** of an organization describes its current purpose and values. It is why the organization exists. The mission of an organization should be audited on an annual basis. The **organizational vision** describes the potential purpose and values of the organization at some point in the future. The mission or purpose of an organization deals with the present, while the vision is concerned with the future direction of the firm. The mission is articulated via the mission statement – a printed paragraph or so depicting the purpose of the organization. It is an appropriate practice for an organization to be mission-driven. This means that every decision should ask the question, 'Will this activity help to fulfill the mission?' If the answer is, 'yes,' then it is an important decision. The mission should drive each of the objectives for the organization. **Long-term objectives (LTOs)** are those goals for the organization that will take more than one year to accomplish. **Short-term objectives (STOs)** are those that may be achieved within one year or less time. Figure 3.1 describes one version of the strategic planning process.

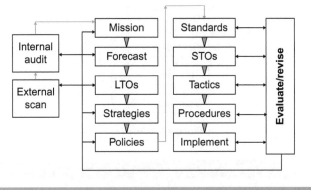

FIGURE 3.1   Strategic planning process

ENVIRONMENTAL SCANNING

Environmental Scanning represents two activities. First, we perform an **External Scan**, which focuses on situations outside of the organization. Next, we complete an **Internal Audit**, which looks inside the organization. Once the factors are identified, they are analyzed. Internal factors are categorized as falling into one of the two categories, **Strengths** (things done well) and **Weaknesses** (things that could be done better). The **external forces** are categorized as **Opportunities** (things with a potential positive impact) and **Threats** (things with a possible negative impact). Why do we use different terms for internal and external factors? The internal factors are within the control of the organization. Therefore, they are done well or not so well. External forces are beyond the control of the organization, therefore they pose opportunities or threats. The total analysis is called **SWOT** (Strengths, Weaknesses, Opportunities and Threats) **analysis**. Its purpose is to develop strategies to convert Weaknesses into Strengths and Threats into Opportunities. SWOT analysis is one form of **situational analysis**, which is the most important part of the strategic planning process.

STRATEGY FORMULATION

The next category is called Strategy Formulation, which is a planning process. The first step is to audit the mission and vision for the organization. These provide the purpose, philosophy and core reasons for existence of the firm in its current form. The question asked here is whether or not it still makes sense to be in this business? Managers use this information to **forecast** the future of the organization. Next, long-term objectives (one to five years) and short-term objectives (less than one year) are formulated. **Objectives** are targets for performance. They are passive and just sit there waiting to be accomplished. They need action steps to be achieved. Strategies are the action steps to achieve long-term objectives. Tactics are the action steps used to accomplish short-term objectives. These result in policies, which are broad guidelines that set standards for decision making and performance.

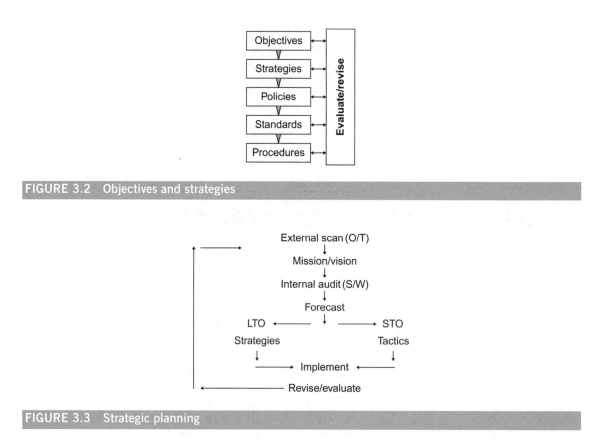

FIGURE 3.2 Objectives and strategies

FIGURE 3.3 Strategic planning

Next is the **implementation** phase. This includes more tactical activities such as programs, budgets, procedures and rules. Finally, it is time to compare actual performance with standards for performance in the final phase called **Evaluation and Revision**. The Feedback/Learning loop provides for continuous evaluation and revision of the entire strategic plan. The implementation steps are described in Figure 3.2.

HOW TO PRODUCE A STRATEGIC PLAN

We have already talked about the components in the strategic planning process. Now, we put them together to produce a strategic plan. This is a powerful tool that has applications for professional planning that range from charting the direction for entire organizations to the development of your own personal career plans. Figure 3.3 takes us through the steps of producing a strategic plan for your work unit or your own career.

The first thing we want to do is to conduct a scan of the external environment. We consider all factors outside the organization that impact it. We have no control over these factors. Thus, we analyze them in terms of opportunities and threats. For an organization, these forces might include technological, economic, political/legal, competitive and other outside factors. For an individual career path, some of the same factors may be forces of influence as well as labor market conditions, industry growth and employer expectations.

We discussed mission – the purpose and philosophy of the organization in its current state. We audit the mission to ensure that it is relevant on an annual basis. We also review the vision for the firm to ensure that it is leading us in the appropriate future direction. These elements will drive the entire strategic plan. Individuals should also be aware of their professional missions when planning a career. Why do we exist? What is our life purpose? Questions like these may be used to audit the missions for individuals.

Next, we look inside the organization for strengths and weaknesses (limitations). We do this by function or department. We combine the external scan information with the internal audit information and conduct a strengths/weaknesses, opportunities/threats or SWOT analysis. The purpose of this type of situational analysis is to convert weaknesses into strengths and threats into opportunities. A career plan would consider an individual's knowledge, skills, attitudes and abilities from an internal perspective and compare those with the outside forces mentioned above.

Now, we attempt to forecast the future (usually one to five years, these days). On the basis of the forecast, the scan, the internal audit, the mission and vision, we set long-term and short-term objectives. You may recall that long-term objectives are greater than or equal to one year in length and short-term objectives are less than one year. Have you written down your professional goals for one to five years?

For each objective, we establish a list of action plans. Strategies are attached to each long-term objective. Tactics are attached to short-term objectives. These are listed in chronological order of completion to achieve each goal. For instance, your goal may be to be hired in a management-level job upon college graduation. If this is the case, you would establish strategies aimed at acquiring technical skills while in school, network with sources of employment and establish an inventory of management skills and abilities.

Finally, we implement the plan, which simply puts the plan into action. Next is the most important part. We continually (at least once per month) evaluate actual performance to the standards (objectives) set by the plan. We revise as necessary because stuff happens. This is the feedback loop for strategic planning (evaluate and revise). Many organizations set the plan and look at it for the first time at the end of the year and wonder why they did not accomplish their objectives. Remember the words of Tom Peters, 'Feedback is the breakfast of champions.[1]'

How to Establish Objectives and Strategies

Objectives – targets – for performance are driven by the mission of the organization. They become the guidelines for decision making, effectiveness, efficiency, consistency and evaluation of individual and team performance. Goals (objectives) are integrated with individual, group and overall organizational performance. As stated before, short-term objectives are goals for less than one year. Long-term objectives are goals for one year or longer. Older approaches to strategic planning used to cite intermediate objectives (those between one and five years in length), but these goals have been outdated by the complex nature of the external environment, which makes it unrealistic to plan for more than five years. All objectives should contribute to the mission. All decisions should contribute to the accomplishment of objectives. Objectives are established for various aspects of the operation. Financial objectives address fiscal performance. Product-market mix objectives identify service and product goals. Functional objectives are based on individual departments or divisions and feed into overall financial and product-market mix goals. There is a hierarchy of objectives from overall goals to individual goals. Suboptimization occurs when there are conflicts between smaller goals and larger goals.

GUIDELINES FOR SETTING OBJECTIVES

* Individuals should participate in determining objectives. Also, personal objectives of workers should be considered within the context of organization objectives.
* Objectives should be stated simply and specifically with established due dates for accomplishment.
* Objectives should be challenging, yet attainable. A common symptom of new managers is that they tend to set lofty goals with unrealistic due dates.
* All objectives should feed into the mission of the organization.

Management by Objectives (MBO) is a process of top/down, bottom/up shared goal setting. The boss sets his/her objectives and shares them with those below him/her. They set objectives to feed into the boss's objectives. They discuss and revise these. They send their objectives to the next layer and the process is repeated throughout the organization. Once objectives are established, actual performance should be continuously monitored to standards set by the objectives. This is called **working the plan**, in which we make the components of the strategic plan key drivers of performance in the organization. Revision should occur on a frequent basis, as contingencies are part of organizational life.

STRATEGIES

Broad strategies for the overall organization are labeled as **Corporate Strategies**. Strategies initiated by specific business units are known as **Business Strategies**. Those that are implemented by functional units are called **Functional Strategies**. For instance, a strategy to develop a multinational corporate presence would be referred to as a Corporate Strategy. One that would expand a product line for a unit would be referred to as a Business Strategy. One that would be applied to Human Resource practices would be known as a Functional Strategy. Divisions within a corporation are referred to as **Strategic Business Units (SBUs)**, thus all divisional strategies are considered to be Business Strategies.

STRATEGIC PLANNING AND BUSINESS CYCLE PHASES

Service enterprises, their brands and corporations all exist at various stages of business life cycles. When a new firm is established, it is considered to be in the introduction phase of the life cycle. Businesses in this mode are considered to be 'start-up' enterprises. If we were to open a new restaurant, for example, that enterprise would be considered to be in the introduction phase for the first two years of its existence. In fact, we would have drafted a business plan in order to secure financing prior to opening the restaurant. During this time, our primary focus would be placed on the financial viability to get the restaurant opened and to keep it in business, as well as to provide the investors with a return on investment (ROI). At this stage, all strategic plans are concerned with the finances of the operation, or a timeframe we might call the *basic financial planning* phase.

As our restaurant becomes more successful and our original financial obligations have been met, we would consider growing the operation, which tells us we are in the growth phase of the business life cycle. We may be considering opening new stores or expanding the capacity of the current restaurant. At this point, annual budgets become less important as we enter into longer-range planning activities. At this point, our restaurant is becoming more future oriented, whereas in the last phase we were totally focused on the present nature of our day-to-day business finances. We could say that our introduction phase was totally tactical (day-to-day activities), while in our new phase we are becoming more strategic. The strategic mode we are in at this stage might be called a forecast-based planning model.

As we spend a few years in the growth phase, our restaurant has evolved into a restaurant company with multiple stores. We now have a senior level of management to oversee a regional operation. At this stage, senior managers begin to take control of the strategic planning process. The forces within the external environment are now very important to the senior managers who develop more strategic approaches to interact with this environment. At this point, we are becoming a real strategically oriented company. We could call this the externally oriented planning phase of our organization.

Finally, perhaps five years or so after our original introduction, we are becoming a mature organization. At this point, the senior managers of our firm have learned to let go of the exclusive control of the strategic planning process. This occurs when they acknowledge that strategic planning in the absence of inputs from lower-level managers is a somewhat useless endeavor in terms of efficiency and effectiveness. At this stage, the strategic planning activities start to be practiced throughout the organization. Organization-wide planning activities start to include brainstorming sessions at all levels of the hierarchy. Techniques such as MBO begin to be implemented. The senior managers of the organization finally embrace the saying that goes, 'None of us is smarter than all of us.' This mode requires creativity and innovation that can only come from the total participation of all managers and staff members. At this point, the organization has finally reached what might be referred to as the strategic management stage of development.

If you are asking why it took so long for our restaurant company to become strategic, you have made a keen observation. The likely answer is that a small enterprise is usually introduced by an entrepreneur. Entrepreneurs, by nature, are great visionaries, but are not always professional managers. The exception might be in the case where an entrepreneur was trained in professional management. In the absence of this, however, it will take a number of years before a small enterprise will be able to afford the talents of professional managers. Once these individuals become attracted to the organization, it quickly evolves into a strategically managed service enterprise. You will possess the knowledge, skills and abilities at the completion of your program.

Advantages and Disadvantages of Strategic Management

Benefits from Strategic Management

The key advantage of strategic management is the establishment of a mission-driven organization. Strategic planning is mission/vision-based. Every component of the process is designed to feed into the organization's mission. Objectives, strategies, tactics, policies, standards, procedures and rules are all established to accommodate the mission. Hence, strategic planning is the only known means to develop a mission-driven service enterprise.

Another benefit of strategic planning is that it provides a clear sense of the strategic vision for the future of the service enterprise. In our restaurant example, it was certainly important for us to focus on daily (tactical) survival. But, if we began with the strategic end in mind (vision), we would have taken steps toward the evolution of the organization at the same time. This was not the case in our example because we did not approach our business from a strategic perspective until a few years later.

A final and perhaps the most persuasive benefit of strategic management is that it fosters an understanding of the forces that exist in the dynamic external environment. As we already know, the environment outside of our enterprise poses opportunities and threats to the business. Those enterprises that fail to manage strategically will tend to operate as 'closed systems,' which is the illusion that the external environment does not impact the financial success of our firm. This was the way management was practiced up until the early 1960s. Back then, businesses could afford to ignore the external environment because of its static nature. This is not the case today. Today's external environment changes rapidly, which is what makes it a dynamic environment. In fact, thanks to technology developments, we have difficulty even tracking the changes in this environment. When outside forces are dynamic, they can create a threat or opportunity overnight. Can you think of a restaurant that did not change menus in response to the low-carbohydrate-diet craze? Do the majority of full-service hotels find it unnecessary to provide broadband access to guests? Can airlines afford to not have interactive websites? All of these demands from the external environment seemingly occurred overnight, or at least within a couple of years. This is the power of the forces that the external environment poses for service enterprises.

Limitations Surrounding Strategic Management

There are a few limitations associated with the strategic planning process. Actually, there is one limitation that poses a few managerial problems. The strategic planning model is a linear process, which means it moves in a sequential manner from Step 1 to Step 2 and so on. This suggests that strategic thinking is a serial-processing scheme, which is not really true. Strategic planning requires people in the organization to engage in behaviors. As we know, human behaviors are not always logical and sequential. The strategic planning process is presented in linear fashion because it helps us to comprehend the steps required for planning and implementation. However, the nature of strategic thinking is to foster leadership interactions aimed at creating an environment of interdependent behaviors within a complex organization in order to achieve common objectives. We saw evidence of interdependent behaviors in our restaurant example during our discussion of strategic phases.

Individuals who work in a single store or outlet that is part of a corporation will tend to focus on internal tactical issues of guest services. A regional manager who oversees a few stores will tend to manage from a broader and more strategic perspective. At the same time, the senior managers at corporate headquarters will be operating from a 'big picture' point of view, with a focus on the overall strategic direction of the brand or organization. We can see that there are three different perspectives from three levels of management in the organization. As the company becomes more strategic, it will invite participation from all corporate levels in the planning and management processes. This requires balance among the tactical, regional and corporate directions for the firm. It would be disastrous to lose sight of any single perspective, yet we need to get all the managers to participate in all three perspectives of the firm at the same time. We can see that this is a complex scenario of three levels being integrated interdependently, with each level assuming primary responsibility for one perspective while keeping the other perspectives in mind. So, we used a linear stepwise process to create a strategic direction that requires nonlinear behaviors on the part of everyone within the organization. Many managers fail to see this behavioral dynamic because the linear strategic planning process appears to be deceivingly simple in its linear format.

TACTICAL STRATEGIES

Tactical strategy development procedures are the same as those used at the corporate level, with the exception that they focus on the direct operation of a business. In the service industry, the business of our business is to attract and retain clients/customers/guests. The tactical strategies occur at the property level for resorts, hotels, lodging facilities, restaurants, theme parks, attractions, entertainment complexes, airlines, convention and conference centers, vacation ownership clubs, country clubs, yacht clubs, ski resorts, sports clubs, casinos, night clubs, marinas, cruise ships and any other service entity where the guests are invited to experience services at a location. What makes these strategies tactical is that the strategic plan filters from the executive level throughout the organization to eventually impact the day-to-day service operations.

Think about a luxury resort hotel property. The strategic planning process at the executive committee level would consist of a thorough examination of the external factors impacting the resort (these would include the corporate governance). Executives would identify each external variable as an opportunity, a threat or possibly both in reference to the potential impact on the performance of the resort. Next, they would prioritize each external factor from the greatest potential impact to the least potential impact on the resort. You may want to refer to Figure 3.3 to review the outline of this process.

Now, there is a list of items marked with an 'O' for opportunity and a list of items marked with a 'T' for threat. Remember, the same item may be listed as both O and T. After identifying Os and Ts, the executives audit the mission for the resort. Chances are it is similar to, but more specific than the corporate mission. If the mission statement is drafted correctly, then it is short, simple and fits on the back of a business card. As a matter of fact, managers at this resort do have the mission statement printed on the rear of their business cards, which is probably a nice touch. The mission audit is just a review of the statement to see if it requires any revisions. Most of the time, this will not be the case. And so, it is this time the executives decide that the mission for the resort still makes sense and requires no revision.

The next step involves a process where the executive committee sits in a conference room and reviews each operating area of the resort. Since the resort appears to have a functional design, the executives review each functional division (accounting, rooms division, human resources etc.). This session starts with the division executive for the area being reviewed. That director will present an honest account of strengths and weaknesses for each operating area in the division to his/her peers and the general manager (GM). The others are only allowed to listen to the presentation. Afterward, they have the floor to share their views of strengths and weaknesses for the operating areas. This is a brutal process for the presenter and requires thick skin on his/her part. Finally, a list of strengths and weaknesses are established for each division and each operating area within the division. Each strong point is listed with an 'S' next to it and each weakness appears with a 'W' next to it. The group has just completed a SWOT analysis, which has resulted in a comprehensive list of Strengths, Weaknesses, Opportunities and Threats that may impact the performance of the resort. A summary is included for each operating area, with broad statements on how to convert Ws into Ss, and Ts into Os (if possible).

Now, the executive group uses the SWOT information to forecast general business trends that may be expected over the coming year. The forecast answers questions such as:

What will be the trends in tourism development?
What economic issues will change?
What changes are likely in the legal environment?
How will foreign policy influence currency exchange rates?
Will there be changes in the political climate in areas such as room tax?
What will be the state of the labor market?
Are there available technologies that will improve our services?
And so on…

These forecast statements will be converted into a general narrative about the expectations for the upcoming year, which will include remarks concerning sales, revenues, pricing, market niches, labor acquisition, repeat guests, business volume fluctuations, new revenue opportunities, cost projections, returns on capital investment, guest expectations, technology implementation and so on.

Given the forecast information, the executive committee members will establish a grand strategy, which is simply the year's mission focus. Next, they will develop long-term objectives for the resort operation as a whole. These objectives will be specific, measurable, attainable but challenging, have realistic timelines with specific due dates or attainment and identify who is primarily responsible for the goal (this may be a good time to review the section on How to Establish Objectives and Strategies). From the resort objectives, the executives will determine division objectives that will feed into the resort objectives.

After a review of the section on Objectives, we remember that objectives are simply passive targets for performance that require action steps for accomplishment. So, while the executive team looks proudly at the list of goals for the year, they now must develop 3–5 action steps (strategies) to achieve each objective. Figure 3.4 describes a document stating each objective and its related strategies.

The executives would generate documents for each objective and list the strategies required to achieve that objective. Notice the use of specific language within the document and the due dates that are printed for each action step. In this case, the person responsible for each strategy would be the director of sales and marketing. Next, the executives would plot all the objectives and strategies on a critical path timeline chart to visually monitor progress for each strategy and objective. This is referred to as the Critical Path Method (CPM). Each column represents the months of a given year and each bar represents the start and completion of each action step. In this example, the objective is to be reached by December 1, with the last strategy to be in place by the end of October. Strategies 1 and 2 will commence at the same time and be performed concurrently. Strategy 1 will be completed by mid-April, with Strategy 2 continuing until September. Strategy 3 will commence in August and be completed in October. The CPM provides a picture of the consecutive and concurrent strategies that will take place to achieve an objective. This provides flexibility so that due dates may be adjusted for exceeding or lagging schedules of accomplishment.

Now, it is time for the executive committee to roll out the strategic plan for the managers and hourly staff at the resort. There are various methods of doing this

Objectives/strategies　　　　　　　　　　　　CPM

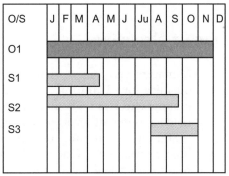

Hotel California—*Such a lovely place!*

Objective: Increase sales by 25% over last year in all revenue operating areas by 1 December 2004.

S1　Direct marketing project through E-Commerce system by 1 April 2003.

S2　Complete rooms, retail, recreation, and F&B upsell program by 30 September 2003.

S3　Roll-out sales commission plan by 20 October 2003.

FIGURE 3.4　CPM of strategic planning

from all-employee high-energy meetings to divisional presentations. There is no one right way to do this, as it depends on the culture of the organization.

After the roll-out sessions, each executive director will meet with department managers to share his/her goals and ask the department heads to develop goals on their level to feed into the goals. The department manager will present his/her goals; there will be discussion and revision, and finally agreement on the goals.

The department manager will do the same process with assistant managers and supervisors. The assistants and supervisors will to the same process with line workers. The end result will be shared goal setting from the top of the organization to the front lines, which will become the standards for performance at every level. This process is referred to as management by objectives (MBO). CPM charts are posted in the work areas and over the next year, the managers and hourly workers will monitor goal attainment performance and revise the due dates where necessary.

The staff members at the resort are now the proud participants in a mission-driven operation in which all members have participated in the goal setting process and have full buy-in to the standards for performance. This completes the proactive strategic planning process. However, things will happen over the next year, which will call for tactical intervention strategies on the part of the department managers. During the initial planning stages, smart managers will engage in 'what-if' analysis to anticipate future scenarios that could impact the effectiveness and efficiency of the plan. They might choose to preplan interventions at this time, a process called **contingency planning**. Disaster plans are examples of contingency plans. A disaster plan will lay out the actions to be taken before, during and after a natural disaster – hurricanes, for instance.

MANAGEMENT DECISIONS

Managers are paid to make decisions that will enhance the productivity of the organization. Planning, organizing, influencing and control all require skills in making effective and efficient decisions. Figure 3.5 describes the types of decisions made at different levels of management.

Some decisions are routine. These are called **programmed decisions** and are highly structured. One-of-a-kind decisions that lack formal structure are called **nonprogrammed decisions**. All decisions impact the system of the organization. Some decisions are far-reaching with great impact. These have a broad scope as opposed to those that have more limited scopes of influence. As a manager assumes more responsibility, his/her scope of decision making increases and its impact on other individuals will increase.

At the supervisory level of management, most decisions are programmed decisions. Let us say for instance you are a front-desk manager at a hotel and you notice that the check lines are getting long. You may choose to take over a terminal and perform a few check-ins or you may request a few cross-trained reservations agents to help out on the front desk. If you are a restaurant supervisor, you may reconfigure service stations when to accommodate a server shortage. Or, you may choose to use a 'crash kit' or manual system when the point of sale computers crash. If there is a rush at the bar, you may choose to prepare drinks or let a veteran barback do so. All

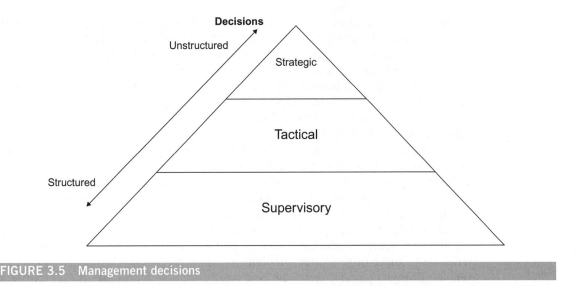

FIGURE 3.5   Management decisions

of these are linear 'if-then' decisions made by supervisors every day. The supervisor thinks, 'If this happens, I have been trained to do that.'

As we get promoted to higher management positions within the hierarchy, we are faced with more unique situations; many of these do not follow a precedent from past occurrences. Since routine (programmed) decisions are handled by the supervisors and assistant manager who report to us, we are faced with handling more difficult nonprogrammed decisions at the middle- or senior-management level. The implications of these decisions will impact larger numbers of people, since we are responsible for wider **spans of authority** at higher management levels. The span of authority considers the number of individuals directly and indirectly reporting to a manager. So, decisions at higher levels of management require more thinking and creativity than those made at the supervisory level of management.

PROBLEM SOLVING

Most decision making is aimed at solving problems. A problem is defined as a negative gap between actual performance and standards for performance. The toughest part of decision making is identifying the problem. Managers will often see symptoms and assume that they are problems. Symptoms often appear to be problems. However, they may be caused by some other less obvious factor. If this is the case, the symptom is not a problem because the cause of the symptom is the real problem. Solve the problem and the symptom will disappear.

Managers must evaluate symptoms and their causes to identify an actual problem. Once the problem is correctly identified, the manager considers alternative actions that might be implemented to solve the problem. At least three alternatives should be generated in most situations. Then, the manager analyzes each of the alternatives in terms of efficiency and effectiveness. In many cases, the optimum alternative is not the best selection due to being cost-prohibitive. Thus, the manager would select the next best alternative. The manager implements the alternative and monitors for effectiveness and efficiency. This last part is the feedback loop that belongs with every model in the field of management.

There are two interrelated conditions in making nonprogrammed decisions. One is **complexity** and the other is **uncertainty**. Complexity occurs when a large number of variables influence the problem. High levels of complexity create limited amounts of total information, or uncertainty. Higher levels of uncertainty create greater levels of risk when making decisions. Also, the scope or impact of the decision will add to the level of risk.

It is appropriate for managers to make decisions by themselves in many situations. At other times, managers may choose to invite participative decision-making activities to generate highly innovative decisions, particularly those with far-reaching implications. There are various formats for group decision-making activities. **Brainstorming** is a group activity used to generate creative ideas to solve problems. In this activity, participants are encouraged to share any idea that comes to mind. All ideas are accepted without criticism and listed for further analysis. The result will be a number of generated problem solution alternatives based on group consensus. This is a creative, yet time-consuming activity. **Nominal group technique** is a form of brainstorming that assures all participants equal participation in decision making by consensus meeting. One method for brainstorming and nominal group technique is to set up a network laptop computers attached to a server. Each participant could concurrently type ideas that show in list format on an overhead projector. **The Delphi technique** uses the distribution of questionnaires to panels of experts (consultants, for instance) who respond to questions anonymously. The responses are continuously recycled until eventual consensus is reached.

STRATEGIC INITIATIVES

We know that senior-level managers spend most of their time focusing on strategic initiatives aimed at the future direction of the organization relative to the mission and vision statements. Tactical strategies are more focused on the current performance levels of the enterprise at the current time. This is the mandate for middle-level managers. Junior-level managers (assistant managers, leads, supervisors) assist the middle-level managers with the implementation of tactical strategies.

Middle- and junior-level managers should constantly be engaged in the planning and implementation of some form of tactical strategy. The appropriate strategy will be dictated by the current circumstances that exist within the enterprise. There are three main categories of tactical strategies. A **run strategy** is used to enhance productivity levels within a department that is meeting standards for performance. A **growth strategy** is implemented when a perceived opportunity for expansion exists. Finally, a **fix strategy** is a tactic intended to turnaround an underperforming department.

Note that each of the three tactical strategies are proactive and dynamic, which means they are intended as interventions to improve the current status of a department. Run strategies are implemented in small steps to improve productivity levels in a department on a daily basis. These strategies are discussed in detail in Chapter 5 of the text. Growth strategies are appropriate for expanding operations to include enhancing existing facilities or adding new stores or outlets. The restaurant example noted earlier is an example of this strategy in action. Growth strategies are discussed in

Chapter 4 of the text. Since fix strategies focus exclusively on employing problem-solving techniques, we will conclude this chapter's discussion with these tactics.

FIX STRATEGIES

Contrary to a run strategy, a fix strategy is warranted when the organization is not pleased with the current performance of an operation. Fix strategies require sound problem-solving diagnostic, implementation and follow-up skills. A person who specializes in this type of operations management is known as a **troubleshooter**. Troubleshooters are individuals who exclusively implement **turnaround strategies**, in which the performance of an operating area must be completely fixed. Fix strategies are the most challenging for a manager, as they involve conflict, change agentry, human emotions, difficult decision-making scenarios and a definite need for an impartial strategic mind-set on the part of the manager. Operational 'chess players' are most suited for this type of work, which requires the planning and execution of operational interventions. The good news is that troubleshooters are among the highest-paid operational managers and some individuals really enjoy 'fixing' operations from an intrinsic aspect. The diagram presented in Figure 3.6 will serve us well here.

The first step in performing a fix strategy is to diagnose the situation within the department. It is likely that the manager appointed to conduct a fix strategy will be new to the department, since the previous manager apparently could not fix it, or he/she would still be there. Also, timing is of the essence in a fix strategy. The new manager should be prepared to work many hours until the 'fix' is complete. The manager will notice some obvious symptoms and will have to use experience and intuition to detect those symptoms that are not obvious (remember that a fix manager is viewed by the existing staff as a threat, so they will try to hide things from him/her). The manager will place symptoms in one of three categories: people, materials and systems (a single symptom can be placed in all the categories in some cases). When the symptoms are categorized, the manager then determines

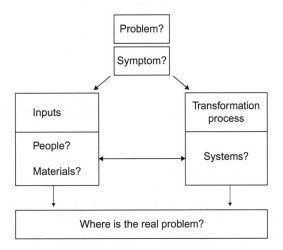

FIGURE 3.6 System investigation

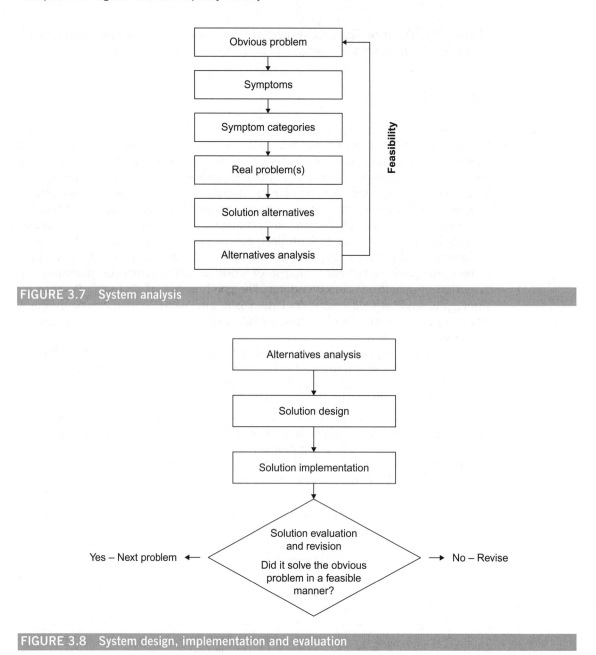

FIGURE 3.7   System analysis

FIGURE 3.8   System design, implementation and evaluation

where the real problems are and prioritizes those in order of importance to the operation, as shown in Figure 3.7.

Next, the manager will establish alternative solutions for the problems and analyze each one to determine the most feasible action to take, as shown in Figure 3.8.

Now, the manager has completed the solution analysis and selection process for each of the problems identified in the operation. The manager lists the solutions in order of implementation for the fix intervention. The manager would use a CPM chart to map out the timelines for the intervention, as shown in Figure 3.9.

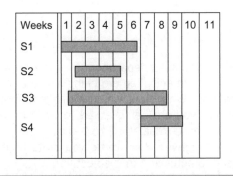

Weeks	1	2	3	4	5	6	7	8	9	10	11
S1											
S2											
S3											
S4											

FIGURE 3.9   Turnaround intervention: CPM

If a fix strategy involves reworking the department, it is considered to be a turnaround strategy. For instance, if the only problem is the lack of training for assistant managers, this would be a quick-fix intervention by providing training for those individuals. In most cases, however, by the time the troubleshooting manager is called in, the little problems would have escalated to complicated problems. For instance, if the manager does not provide training for the assistants, then communication problems start to arise. Next, organizing activities start to fail and staff schedules become a mess. Then customer complaints start to increase. After a while, employee morale starts to suffer. Now, some of the more experienced hourly staff start to take advantage of the untrained assistants, by upwardly delegating their work to the managers. Soon, the good hourly staff members start to quit and the new hires are friends of those same hourlies who take advantage of the managers and so on until the manager gets fired or quits and the organization hires a troubleshooter.

SUMMARY

We learned that different levels of management contribute in various ways to the development of strategic plans in this chapter. We defined the strategic planning process and then learned the specific steps to be taken to produce our own strategic plan. As part of the process, we learned how to establish objectives and strategies for performance. We further discussed the MBO process to facilitate feedback from all levels of the organization as part of the planning process.

After discussing the various phases of strategic development that occur during a service enterprise life cycle, we turned our attention toward a discussion of the benefits and limitation of strategic planning and thinking. We also discovered the processes used to solve organizational problems and to make effective decisions. We concluded the chapter with a presentation of tactical strategies, which are commonly executed by middle- and junior-level managers. Discussion of run and growth strategies were introduced as segues to more thorough discussions reserved for other chapters in the text. Finally, we learned the basics of conducting a fix strategy designed to turnaround a poorly performing department, division or organization.

DISCUSSION QUESTIONS

1. Assume that you are a department manager for a full-service resort (choose your own department). You are being asked to develop a strategic plan for your work unit. What steps would you take to formulate such a plan?
2. Assume that you are being asked to write an objective that indicates a targeted increase in sales of 15% over a period of time. How would you state the objective? How would you state at least three strategies that might lead to achieving that objective?
3. Assume that you have received a directive to implement MBO within your department. What information would you need from the level of management above you to do this? What specific sequential steps would you take to implement MBO in your department?
4. Please take the answers you provided in response to Question 2 above and plot them on a CPM.
5. If you were a manager conducting a fix strategy, would you place your symptoms and problems into categories? What categories would you use?

REAL-WORLD EXPERIENCES (CONTINUED)

One night you were closing out with one of the new assistant managers, Kelly. As you worked through the procedures, you mentioned to Kelly that you thought she was the best assistant manager you have ever worked with. This began a conversation. Kelly responded, 'Don't you think the other AMs are pretty good too?' You said, 'Yes, they are all really experienced and helpful.' Kelly smiles and says, 'This is no mistake, it was all part of Dave's plan before he came here.' 'What do you mean?' you ask, perplexed.

Kelly laughs, as she says, 'Dave is a troubleshooter. He fixes broken stores for the chain.' She continues, 'I met him at the last store he fixed.' You ask, 'Were you an assistant manager there, too?' 'No,' she says, 'I was a lead and a trainer.' She continues, 'Dave came in and shook the place up, just like he did here. He brought in some experienced AMs and one of them became my mentor.' 'Wow,' you reply. Kelly continues, 'Yup, the experienced AM took me under his wing and taught me the ins and outs of management. After watching my performance, Dave invited me to join his next team. That's how I got promoted.'

You inquire of Kelly, 'Will Dave be at this store much longer?' Kelly smirks and says, 'No, his job is almost done here. He is prepping Allison (a senior assistant manager) to become GM here.' Kelly reflects for a moment and says, 'She will probably take over in another three months and Dave will move on to another store.' 'Really?' you say, 'I thought she seemed a little too experienced to not be a GM.' Kelly replies, 'That's how Dave operates.' 'By the way,' she smiles as she mentions, 'He wants to know what your plans are after graduation.'

CASE STUDY

Employee Productivity and Value-added Management

You are a newly hired assistant manager in the Food & Beverage department of a large resort. The F&B Director holds monthly strategy meetings with all the managers in the department for the purpose of devising new ways of enhancing departmental productivity. At this, your first meeting, the F&B Director has invited the Controller and Marketing Director to participate in the meeting. You walk in with your manager, grab a cup of coffee and take a seat. Since you are new to this operation, you observe the dynamics of the following conversations closely:

The F&B Director starts things off, 'Ladies and gentlemen, I have invited Sheila the Controller and Mark the Marketing Director to help us with our productivity enhancement initiative. They will provide us with some new ways of looking at our operation.' After a preliminary overview of the current status of the initiative, Mark starts to comment, 'Look,' he says, 'You got to spend money to make money. If you want to enhance productivity, you need to drive revenues. The only way to drive revenues is to invest in advertising and pro- motional activities to increase business.' Sheila jumps in, 'Hold on there, Mark. The budget is the budget. You don't enhance productivity by over- running your expense budgets. That's ludicrous,' she says. Mark retorts, 'Oh Sheila, not this again. Quite frankly, if you had your way, you would be on the floor with a stop watch conducting time and motion studies to reduce labor.' She defensively replies, 'You bet I would! Efficiency is the key to every opera- tion. Our biggest single expense is labor dollars. So, it makes sense to reduce those expenditures as much as possible.' Mark cajoles, 'Increasing revenues is dollar wise and cutting costs is penny foolish. Put more bucks on the top line and that will take care of the bottom line,' he says. Sheila replies, 'Mark, apparently you were asleep when they talked about scientific management in your school. If you had your way, we would be out of business.'

This discussion continues to go back and forth for quite some time. After awhile, you decide to go get another cup of coffee...

Preliminary Questions

1. How would you describe Sheila's approach to managing resources?
2. How would you describe Mark's approach to managing resources?

3. What thoughts are going on in the minds of the F&B managers as they listen to this argument?
4. Do you tend to agree more with Mark or Sheila? Why?

Conclusion

As you sit down with your second cup of coffee, you begin to realize that this meeting is getting out of control and that this is not the first time that Sheila and Mark have had this argument. The F&B Director just rolls his eyes as the two continue to go back and forth with their managerial philosophies. You realize from your training that both Mark and Sheila are correct in their philosophies and that they simply need to put the two concepts together.

Since this is your first meeting, you are a little shy. But after this elongated debate, you finally say, 'Couldn't we reduce labor costs and increase revenues by developing the talents of our people?' A hush fills the room as everyone turns to stare at you. 'Well,' you continue, 'that would be the human resource approach to enhancing productivity.' The F&B Director smiles at you with approval. 'Next week,' he jokes, 'we will invite Sheila, Mark, and the HR Director to be their referee.'

Conclusion Questions

1. How would you describe the human resource management approach to productivity?
2. Why would a human resource manager tend to be more balanced than the average marketing or accounting manager?
3. What are the pros and cons of Sheila's and Mark's philosophies on productivity?

ENDNOTE

1. Peters, T., 1993. Liberation Management: Necessary Disorganization for the Nano-second Nineties. Hawthorn.

CHAPTER 4

Systems, Development and Structures

OBJECTIVES

In this chapter you will learn to:

1. Describe relationships among systems and subsystems.
2. Describe global, organizational and individual learning systems and career development.
3. Describe organizational and departmental structures.

REAL-WORLD EXPERIENCES

You have been doing an internship with a resort hotel for a few months. You have worked at a number of restaurant outlets at the hotel. One of the restaurant managers named Dave took a special interest in mentoring you and has been meeting with you for coffee regularly to hear your impressions and to answer questions.

Today, you are having coffee as usual and you share this insight with the manager. You start by saying, 'You know, Dave, I have done work in most of the outlets by now. I notice that while the theme and purpose of each restaurant is different, the consistency of policies and standards are the same.' Dave smiles at you and says, 'Yes, that is by design.' You reply, 'Do you mean everyone has the same training?' Dave mentions, 'Well, that's part of it, but that is not the whole picture.'

To be continued...

INTRODUCTION

This chapter provides discussion about service enterprise systems, structure and the career development of managers and staff members. We will learn about the relationships among individuals, work units, the enterprise and its external environment in the following sections. Next, we will learn about our own career development and the stages of human evolution that give us clues concerning the motivational keys of staff members. Finally, we will take a look at the organizational structure of service enterprises. We will use a typical resort hotel as an example to demonstrate organizational structure.

WHAT IS SYSTEMS THINKING?

This section introduces the concept of systems thinking as applied to managing service enterprises. It is important for hospitality managers to understand the broad realm of systems thinking and how it is applied to all functions and practices of management. This overview of systems theory is the foundation for understanding everything there is to know about management and service organizations. A **system** is a network of relationships. All systems contain smaller systems called **subsystems**. All systems also exist within a larger external environment or **macrosystem**. Systems thinking provides templates that permit us to take apparently complicated concepts and simplify them. For this reason, it is in every hospitality manager's interest to understand systems thinking. Figure 4.1 shows the relationships of these three systems levels for a service enterprise.

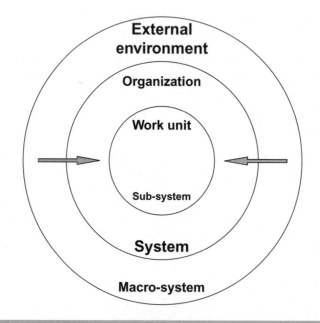

FIGURE 4.1   Linear systems

The service enterprise is an organization, which as we know is a group of people brought together for a common purpose. The enterprise is a system and the work units (departments) within the organization are subsystems of the organization. The organization is also a subsystem of its external environment (a macrosystem). For instance, the enterprise could be a hotel, which is a subsystem of the lodging industry, which is a subsystem of the hospitality industry, which is a subsystem of the tourism industry, which is a subsystem of industry in general. As we learned in Chapter 3, the external environment consists of many factors such as industries, governments, social factors, economics and many more. These are all macrosystems from the perspective of a service enterprise.

Before discussing systems theory, it would be appropriate to identify the role of a few components that will continuously appear in the text. They are: **theories, practices** and **tools**. A theory is an underlying principle or explanation of something scientific or philosophical[1]. For instance, it answers the question of why things happen. A practice is based on a set of theories. So, a practice consists of how to do things, based on why things happen. A tool is something used to perform a practice. Thus, a tool is something we use to do things, while those things we do are based on why things happen. Table 4.1 will help to clarify this relationship between theory, practice and tools.

So, theories drive practices and practices use tools. Thus, philosophy and science give us management principles, which guide us in the practice of management. Management practices require the use of tools, such as technology. Therefore, management is a practice, not an academic discipline as some may have us believe. Further, there are tools to help managers practice management. **Systems thinking** is a practice related to theories from science and philosophy that describe patterns of collaborative energy called relationships[2]. More specifically, the theory is based on the findings of the hard sciences in areas such as physics, biology and neurosciences[3].

We discussed an example of the relationship between theory, practice and tools in Chapter 2 of the text. Recall that we pieced together all of the theoretical categories from the evolution of management thinking over the past century. We learned that the theories comprising scientific management, behavioral science and management science drive current management practices. For instance, we may apply scientific management to improving efficiency or use management science techniques to enhance effectiveness within an enterprise. We always use the findings of behavioral science when performing the influencing management functions. The management tools used as part of these practices would be communication, symptoms diagnostics and management problem-solving skills. So, management skills are tools used to practice management in a manner that is consistent with

TABLE 4.1 **Examples of Relationships Among Theories Practice and Tools**

Why things happen	How things happen	What I need to make things happen
Theory	Practice	Tools
Science/philosophy	Management	Technology

our theoretical knowledge. Systems thinking is a practice that comes from theories that require us to view the enterprise and its people as subsystems within systems. We use our management skills (tools) to perform diagnostic and decision-making practices from a systems perspective (theory).

SYSTEMS THEORY IN GENERAL

On the basis of general systems theory, the management systems approach views every entity as a system with interdependent parts that function as a whole[4]. The key component is the **interdependency** of subsystems. Interdependency is a state of mutual dependence and independence existing at the same time. Consider an example of a small child or infant within a family. During the early formative years, the child is in a state of dependency relative to parents or caregivers. During adolescence, the person may seek independence from parents and authority figures only to become dependent on peers. Later in adult life, an emotionally mature individual develops interdependent relationships with family members and friends. In these relationships, people are not totally dependent or independent to spouses, family members and friends. At the same time, they are a little of both as part of each relationship. The result of these relationships (networks) is a holistic identity of self as an individual and a relater. This reality of human relations is also true among organizational entities.

In an organization, each individual is a member of an entity called a work unit. That work unit is also a subsystem in relation to some larger system, called the organization. That organization is a subsystem of external macrosystems. **Closed systems** are not influenced by the outside environment. Machines operate as closed systems as long as they are not networked with other machines. The only effect of the external environment on free-standing machines is wear and tear of the machines' parts over time.

The external environment of the world influences service organizations, which are **open systems**. These organizations must constantly interact with the external environment for survival and evolution in order to keep up with the changes in the world around them. For instance, the Internet revolution that exists in today's environment influences hospitality organizations to create systems to permit electronic entry by potential guests and customers, something that was not a concern 20 years ago. Hospitality organizations that fail to respond to this situation in the external environment will find themselves at a competitive disadvantage.

A person is a biological system, as are trees, plants and animals, since they all interact with the universal laws for biology that come from the environment. If a person is a system and that person is a member of a family, then the system called 'that person' is a subsystem of the family. The person is a unique and whole system, but when interacting with other people in the family unit, that relationship makes each person a subsystem of the family system. The same is true for organizations, which are really composed of people, each one being a biological system. When the people in an organization interact with others, they become subsystems of the organization that are divided by work units, departments, divisions and so on. The organization may be one unit in a chain of organizations, which makes it a subsystem of that chain. If the chain is in the business of providing hospitality services, then that chain is part of a larger system called the hospitality industry.

WHAT IS THE DIFFERENCE BETWEEN MECHANISTIC AND ORGANIC SYSTEMS?

Subsystems, which are all interrelated and reflect the whole system, influence other subsystems, as well as the big system. Each subsystem plays a role relevant to the general system. Therefore, each part is interrelated and requires consideration of the impact of change on other subsystems and the whole system. Since all subsystems are integrated to collectively represent the general system, interdependence is a key factor in analysis and decision making when planning management strategies[5].

Mechanistic systems are closed systems with definitive life spans and continuously atrophy into nonexistence. An electronic computer for instance will eventually burn out and stop working. Environmental factors may quicken the process. For instance, remove the fan from a computer unit and place it in a very hot room. That computer will die a premature death. Keep the computer fan working and place it in a cool room, and the computer will eventually stop working owing to wear and tear over time (normal life span of a machine). We may use some of its components for spare parts and will probably haul the rest of the computer to the junkyard. If the computer parts are not biodegradable, they will simply exist as rusty junk. Because a computer is a machine (mechanistic), it does not have the capacity to adapt to environmental changes. In a hostile environment, it will wear out quickly and in a compatible environment it will wear out slowly, but it will wear out and stop working. Also, owing to the rapidly developing nature of computer technology, a machine will be likely to become outdated before it ceases to operate. The concept of wearing out is perfectly explained by the laws of Newtonian physics[6]. Since energy creates heat, an extreme environmental change will cause the entity to throw off more energy than it can generate until it has no more energy left (entropy). Once it runs out of energy, the parts stop working and the entity stops doing things (dies).

Organic systems have the capacity for infinite life because of the ability to evolve. For instance, a biological plant or animal will generate offspring during its life, and when it dies it will feed the earth. During its life span, the animal or plant will adapt to the environment for survival. It will pass the genetic adaptive code to the next generation, which will begin its new life as an evolved entity. The plant or animal will know that it is time to evolve when it becomes uncomfortable owing to the changes in the environment. This escalating level of discomfort will cause confusion and energy dissipation (anxiety) on the part of the plant or animal. If minor adaptations do not work, it will experience more anxiety until it thinks it is going to die. At that (bifurcation) point, the plant or animal must escape the discomfort imposed by the environment. It has two choices: Stay the way it is and give away the rest of its energy (entropy) or mutate into some other life form (evolve). Scientists call this environmentally induced anxiety 'chaos[7].' Now we have conflicting conclusions – a paradox between two scientific theories.

One scientific theory supports entropy (death) and the other supports evolution (mutation). Which one is it? One scientist eventually came along to settle this paradox. His solution was that both death and evolution were true as a result of chaos[8].

Here is the explanation. All matter, regardless of density, is composed of energy[9]. As the environment becomes more complex, mechanistic entities give off more energy than can be generated and thus atrophy into oblivion (like the overheated computer). When organic systems enter into chaos, they could expend all of their energy on managing the chaos, or they could apply some of the energy into an evolutionary escape (negentropy)[10]. In the first scenario, the organic system would eventually use up all of its energy and die as a result of the stress from the chaotic event. However, in the second scenario, the organic system has a chance to escape with some of its energy. Once the organic system does escape the chaos, it may begin to replenish its energy. However, in order to do this, the entity ceases to be what it once was, as it takes on a new form of 'life.' Either way, the plant or animal ceases to exist in its original form. It has been changed forever. If the plant or animal is able to mutate, the scientists would say that it created 'new order' out of 'disorder,' and as a result it could be said that it died and survived at the same time.

For example, let us say that there is a certain type of lizard who scurries on the ground and likes to eat things found on the ground. All of a sudden, another animal develops a taste for eating these colorful. The lizard-eating animal is fat and slow, but quick enough to catch a lizard. The next thing you know, most of the lizards in the forest are disappearing. Needless to say, the remaining lizards would be very stressed out. One lizard learns to climb trees and adapts its diet to things that may be found in those trees. A few other lizards witness this behavior and replicate it. Eventually, the remaining lizards on the ground will be eaten and the animals will have to find something else to eat, because they are not physically able to adapt to tree-climbing behavior. A group of scientists walk into the forest and quickly determine that the ground lizards are extinct. They discover, however, a new breed of tree lizard that is very similar to the species that used to live on the ground. While the scientists believe that the ground lizards have died, nature knows that they have only died in their role as ground lizards and that those same lizards have evolved into tree lizards. So, they are dead, yet still alive. The paradox between the second law of thermodynamics and chaos theory has been solved.

What does this have to do with management systems? Well, at this point, let us just say that what is good for the lizard is good for the person. And since organizations are made up of people, they are organic systems. Since managers manage organizations, which are organic systems that use machines as tools, it is good for them to know how toads evolve, so they can use the tools to do the same thing for organizations during times of chaos, which will be imposed on them from the dynamic (quickly changing) external environment[11].

WHAT ARE LINEAR SYSTEMS?

Empirically, we are taught to believe what we can see. So, most systems that are taught to us are linear in nature, which means they are two-dimensional, with a start point on the left side and an end point on the right side. Figure 4.2 shows a linear process for management processes.

The management perspective described by the figure is quite broad, while the systems perspective is somewhat narrow. Management inputs include all resources that are used to create a product or service. These could be material resources, human resources, financial resources and technology resources. The people, equipment, technology and machines convert the raw materials during the transformation process. The final product or service is the output that resulted from that

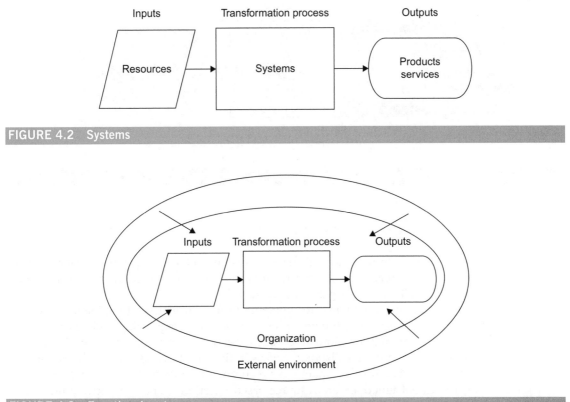

FIGURE 4.2   Systems

FIGURE 4.3   Functional systems

process. The output function is always directly interfaced with a customer or guest. An internal customer would be someone who is providing a service for a guest. The external customer is the guest. So, a worker who provides products and services to another employee is serving the internal customer and one who provides those to the guest is serving the external customer. Everyone in the organization is serving someone either internally or externally.

WHAT ARE NONLINEAR SYSTEMS?

Since all service enterprise systems are open systems, they are surrounded by boundaries to the external environment, which influence the production system. Figure 4.3 shows a description of this interface

Linear transformation processes occur within every work unit of the service enterprise continuously. Some processes serve internal customers while others serve guests and clients (external customers). The organization influences the management of these linear processes through decisions to determine objectives, strategies, policies, standards, procedures and rules for the workplace. The organization is considered to be the internal environment of the workplace. The outside environment influences the entire organization, hence the outside environment influences management and linear transformation processes.

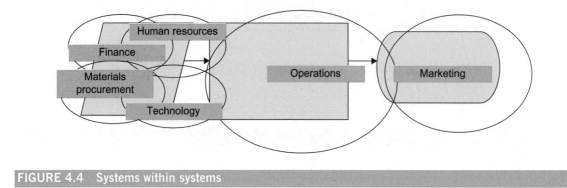

FIGURE 4.4   Systems within systems

WHAT ARE FUNCTIONAL SYSTEMS?

Just as the meaning and learning systems impact the linear production process, there are functional systems that identify the contributions of various work units to that process. These are depicted in Figure 4.4.

Organizational functions are different from management functions. We already know that management functions include planning, organizing, influence and control. Organizational functions represent areas of business specialization. Notice that four functions appear collaboratively over the input section of the linear production process. The finance, materials procurement, human resources and technology organizational functions are resource-based functions. They collectively provide all of the inputs into the transformation process function, which is called operations. Marketing and sales functions deal exclusively with the output portion of the production process, which consists of products and services. Notice that the operations bubble overlaps with the marketing bubble, since operations personnel actually deliver the products and services to the guests and clients. The role of marketing has more to do with the development, placement, pricing and promotion of products.

WHAT ARE INVISIBLE NONLINEAR ORGANIZATION SYSTEMS?

There are invisible nonlinear systems that exist within the organization that influence the linear transformation processes. These are described in Figure 4.5.

The **Meaning System** consists of the organizational culture to include variables such as values, attitudes and beliefs of shareholders, employees and guests that comprise the unwritten norms for behavior within the organization[12]. The **Learning System** is a feedback loop that converts shared experiences into knowledge that is used to further enhance production. Figure 4.5 describes the learning process that takes place in the minds of every individual within the organization. If a formal process is in place to accumulate and disseminate what is learned throughout the organization, that process would be called a **Knowledge Management System (KMS)**[13] (Figure 4.6).

Individuals learn management in the exact same way they do through an organization's learning system. We already know that management theory presents the knowledge component. When we practice management, we gain experiences from

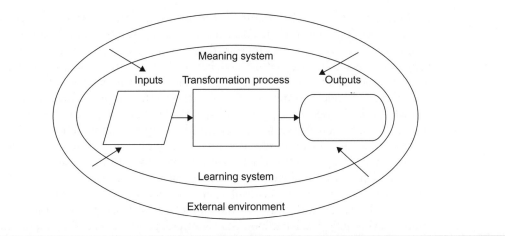

FIGURE 4.5 Non-linear organization systems

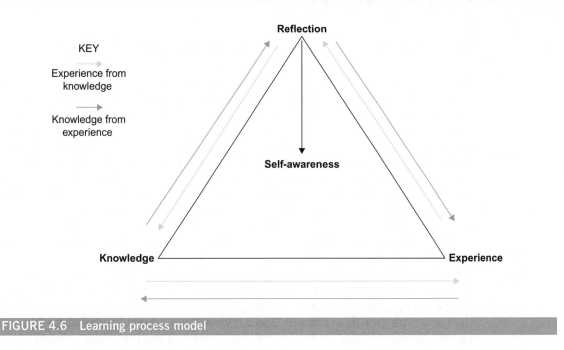

FIGURE 4.6 Learning process model

using the management tools (skills). The way to learn management is to practice it and to reflect on the blend of knowledge and experiences. That reflection should enhance our levels of self-awareness as practicing managers. We discuss this in more detail in the leadership chapters toward the end of the text.

WHAT ARE LEARNING ORGANIZATIONS?

For the reasons cited in the section above, people within organizations must now rapidly assimilate information, alter behaviors, share knowledge and modify cognitive processes to remain in synchronization with the dynamic and global external environment. This is the nature of the Learning Organization[14]. Large organizations are developing Knowledge Base Management Systems (KBMS) for this purpose. These systems bring in information that is converted to knowledge and then disseminate the knowledge within and beyond the organization for the purposes of decision making that will react to rapid changes in the external environment. The use of the Internet, intranets and extranets facilitate rapid knowledge deployment. Knowledge is defined as a process of using cognitive ability to simulate situations that have not been physically experienced through mental rehearsal. This is the premise that underlies the reflective process described in Figure 4.5. In the learning organization, individuals transfer cognitive processes to others in the organization for shared learning. Individuals in these organizations generate continuous cycle that processes knowledge accumulation, knowledge cognition, knowledge transfer, new knowledge generation, finally returning to knowledge accumulation. It is a continuous cybernetic feedback loop that is interdependent, and thus represents global computer networks. The exception is that the 'servers' reside in the human cognitive frontal lobes of the brain.

WHAT ARE GLOBAL LEARNING ORGANIZATIONS?

We have already learned that technology is a key driving force in all societies. Networked technology has created the global village that we fantasized about just a decade ago. The global network is now expanding exponentially. With this expansion, organizations inherit the freedom to seamlessly expand beyond national boundaries. At the same time, the interconnectivity of global networks also creates a form of restriction to organizations. For example, the Asian economic crisis of 1997 started a snowballing impact on all world markets. The analysts could not figure out which market was impacting all the others. At first they thought the Asian market was impacting the Unites States. They then thought the opposite was true, only to reverse this position to their original thinking. What was really happening was a string of interdependent impacts that operated in numerous cycles. There is a fable that a butterfly flaps its wings in South Africa and that the universal response is a tornado in Oklahoma. This is called the 'butterfly effect' that describes the interdependency of networked systems. A subtle change to a small subsystem will generate grand-scale alterations of the landscape of larger systems in the network. This is the state of the global community. Linear systems are incapable of identifying cause-and-effect explanations of interdependent, nonlinear events. Thus, organizations are experiencing rapidly increased impacts from the development of the 'uncertainty factor.'[15] The global nature of business is so interconnected that it is impossible to predict the future. This creates a major limitation with regard to the linear strategic planning and management models.

WHAT IS LIFELONG INDIVIDUAL LEARNING?

We now know that individuals within organizations engage in continuous learning at the local and global levels. They do this to continually adapt to the conditions imposed from the dynamic external environment surrounding service enterprises. So, people learn to adapt and change. In fact, one definition of **learning** is to enact permanent change within an individual[16]. This is what the Learning Process Model demonstrates. It is a process for changing a person's levels of self-awareness as a manager, leader, staff member and an individual.

If learning is the enactment of change, and we are changing from something we already are, then that change must take us to a higher level in terms of our personal evolution through development. Hence, learning provides development. And reflection upon that development transforms us from who we were before the learning process to who we are after the learning process. Thus, we have participated in the process of personal and professional **transformation**, or permanent change toward personal growth. Those of us who choose paths of lifelong learning are engaged in continuous personal and professional transformation. One by-product of this process is the path of career development.

LIFELONG LEARNING AND CAREER DEVELOPMENT

Just as we progress on a journey of biological maturity from birth through death, we also pursue a path of 'work life maturity' or career development. Figure 4.7 depicts the stages of work life development. Each stage in the model represents an escalated maturity plateau that is reached by some, but not all workers seeking career progression.

Primary and secondary research, as well as anecdotal observation in hospitality organizations has resulted in the construction of the *Work Life Development* Model for workers in these organizations[17]. The model is based on development theories of researchers to include Kohlberg[18], Dewey[19], Piaget[20], Maslow[21], Shea[22] and Perkins-Reed[23]. The Work Life Development model is based on the assumption that the mental, social, emotional and spiritual development of the full-time worker is influenced to some degree by work experiences, just as these areas of

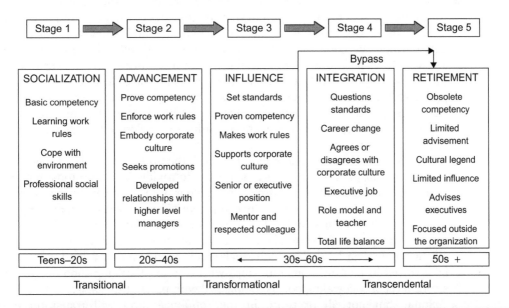

FIGURE 4.7   The work life development model

personal development are partially shaped by childhood and adult living experiences. While most adults reach full biological maturity, this is not the case for everyone. The same is true for Work Life Development. Most, but not all workers reach at least four of the five stages.

Why should managers be familiar with stages of career growth? There are two reasons to gain this knowledge. The first is that to effectively identify individual workplace motivators, the manager must be familiar with each staff member's mentality. The motivational mind-set of a person may be determined by identifying the stages of professional maturity. The second reason is that managers should be engaged in a process of lifelong personal and professional growth through enhanced levels of self-awareness. An understanding of one's place in a career life cycle will serve as a guide for personal evolution. So we enhance the performance of ourselves and others through an awareness of life-cycle development.

THE FIVE STAGES OF DEVELOPMENT

There are five stages of development for workers in service-based organizations. The first stage is called the *Assimilation* stage. New entrants to the workforce are members of this group. Workers in their late teens through middle-20s are usually represented in this range. During *Assimilation*, the worker possesses basic levels of competency. The worker often feels unsure concerning the direction of career progression. In this stage, the worker is learning to assimilate work with other aspects of life. The worker is in the process of learning the rules and policies in the workplace, as well as coping with the corporate environment. In this stage, workers often move laterally to other positions inside an organization or with other organizations to gain different experiences. Also, the worker begins to develop social skills with peers and supervisors during this stage.

A second stage of worker development is called the *Advancement* stage. Individuals at this level are often in their middle-20s to early 30s and have had from 5–10 years of work experience, or a college degree and a few years of experience. These people are concerned with demonstrating work-related competency. Workers are usually in positions to enforce the work rules and possess a clear understanding of the corporate culture. Often, these workers have decided on a basic career path and have been promoted at least once to supervisory or management positions. At this stage, there are usually strong peer affiliations with other managers and supervisors. Workers at this level are beginning to develop comfortable relations with senior-level managers.

The third stage of development is called the *Influence* stage. People begin to become members of this group in their early- to middle-30s, with most remaining at this stage into their 60s or the time of retirement from the organization. In this stage, a person is recognized as being fully competent. This person is usually in a position to make the work rules and policies and is a symbol of the organization's cultural values. This person will often be in a senior line or staff management position, usually at the director level. The individual who is at the *Influence* level will sometimes be involved in mentoring relationships with certain promising subordinates. Also, a strong level of collegial rapport is established with peers at this stage.

Some, but not all of those in the *Influence* level will transition into the *Integration* (fourth level) stage. The remaining individuals will move directly from the *Influence* stage into the *Retirement*, or the fifth and final stage of Work Life Development. Members of the *Integration* stage will almost identically resemble those at the upper end of the *Influence* level, with one exception. While the Influencer has transformed within the organization, the Integrator has transcended beyond a specific organization. Balance for the Influencer means doing whatever it takes to maintain the corporate position, regardless of time requirements and value conflicts. The Integrator, however, is in need of total life balance and is not willing to compromise personal values for professional positions.

Sometimes, an individual in the *Influence* stage will experience a critical shift from egoistic (status) principles to esoteric (self-fulfillment) principles. When this happens, the individual is entering the *Integration* phase or Stage 4 of Work Life Development. As a person makes this transition, a feeling of balance among all aspects of the self begins to emerge, in which the individual now has the desire to perform professional work that provides balance or *Integration* with the other components of self-awareness or identification.

The Integrator is highly energized as a result of the intrinsic meaning of the work. This person exhibits passion, self-mission, vision and dedication to the work itself. This person is highly motivated, yet not consumed with work. It is the nature of the work itself and the perception of the work by the individual that cause these characteristics to become evident. A person in this stage is relentless in the pursuit of meaningful contributions to others resulting from their work. This individual rises as an inspiring leader, mentor, teacher, cheerleader and steward. The question that arises is whether the Integrator will do these things in his or her current organization, or will she or he pursue a career change? The answer depends on the congruence between the organizational culture and the need for the Integrator to perform self-fulfilling work.

How many people actually experience the *Integration* stage before they retire? The answer to this question is unknown. It is likely that a small number of total workers reach this stage before retirement, with a larger number engaging in the experience during retirement. If there is any truth to the evolution of newer generations, we may expect larger numbers of people to reach the *Integration* stage at younger ages than those who chronologically came before them.

The fifth and final stage of the Work Life Development life cycle is called *Retirement*. As was stated previously, not all individuals experience every development stage, but all do eventually retire from the workplace. *Retirement* may be voluntary (the decision to stop working) or involuntary (the occurrence of traumatic disability or biological death) on the part of the worker. Some workers choose to 'mentally' retire (stop being productive) before they physically retire (actually leave the workforce).

Some individuals never get past the *Assimilation* stage and retire after a career of chronic unemployment. Others get stuck in the *Advancement* stage even though they have attained senior-level positions, but do not possess the ability to be a source of influence in the organization. Most individuals who reach the *Influence* stage of the life cycle wait until *Retirement* to pursue integrated activities. Preretirement individuals in the *Integration* stage usually choose to retire when their 'work is done' and they have groomed a talented individual to replace them in the organization. For the Integrators, retirement usually means a new form of personally meaningful work. While most individuals who advance in the Work Life Development cycle do hold senior-level corporate positions, this is not a requisite for moving into advanced stages. Any experienced hospitality worker can recall examples of highly developed people who chose to work in lower-level positions in the organizational hierarchy. As is the case with all individuals, appearances may very well be deceiving.

When it comes to career development, there are no 'right/wrong,' 'good/bad' decisions. Therefore, a person can offer another person very limited advice on the matter. One 'rule of thumb' is for us to do the work we love at the salary we want to earn, in a location where we want to be. These things in addition to a path of lifelong learning will result in contentment, prosperity and personal/professional growth. Some people are not sure what they want to do for a career. One approach to overcoming this barrier is to eliminate those types of things we do not want to do until just a few things are left.

There is a parable about a man who climbed a mountain[24]. He put all his energy to pulling himself up the steep slope. With the last of his strength, he finally reached the top of the mountain. He stood there, feeling exhausted and looked out at the scenery, only to find he had climbed the wrong mountain. Choose your own mountain. Do not climb mountains that someone else wants you to climb.

It has been said that we have a choice in life that will occur 20 years from now. We could end up with 20 years of experience or one year of experience 20 times[25]. The difference lies in what we choose to do with our experiences. If we choose to learn and grow each year, we will be sure to eventually possess 20 years of experience, or we may choose to maintain the same mind-set over the years. Neither choice is 'right' or 'wrong,' they are just choices that are available to us. However, it has been said that the definition of 'insanity' is to repeat the same behaviors with the expectation for a different outcome[26]. Others claim upon reflection to have 'failed their way to success.'[27] And Aldous Huxley proclaims, '...it is not what happens to you in this world, but instead what you do with it[28].' So, we have choices in this life. We could choose to remain the same as we are now, or we could choose to learn and grow every year. Some leaders recommend that we totally reinvent ourselves every year, which may be good advice given the nature of the dynamic environment that surrounds us[29].

SERVICE ENTERPRISE STRATEGIES AND STRUCTURE

There are two levels of strategies in service organizations. The first is at the corporate level, which is heavily influenced by the shareholders of the organization. Some individuals place this level of planning into three strategic categories referred to as directional, portfolio and corporate parenting[30]. Planning at this level is usually removed by some distance from actual business operations. In large organizations, the structure consists of strategic business units (SBU) that comprise another corporate level that produces strategic plans in response to the mandates of the parental corporate entity and so on, until the planning process finally reaches a single operation.

This structure works well for manufacturing organizations and those with diversified product distribution channels for tangible goods. But we already know that the service industry is much more intimate at the customer/guest level of interaction. These enterprises require unique strategies at points of guest interface, sometimes called 'touch points.' For this reason, output portion of the linear production process goes beyond the simple distribution of a manufactured product at the business level.

The *Marriott* organization, for instance, is a conglomerate hospitality corporation that is involved in many businesses that include real estate, construction, mass food product distribution, institutional foodservice providers, assisted living facilities, vacation ownership properties, franchising, contracted management services, various categories of lodging facilities and other business units. The general public believes that Marriott is in the full-service hotel business, which was its core business for many years, and still prominently displays the Marriott brand at the property level. Recognizing this factor, the organization established a separate corporate identity for its hotel division at the top of its structure, where corporate direction is handled somewhat differently than with the divisions that are less reliant on service standards at the guest level.

Most business schools provide courses in strategy and policy for their students toward the end of their programs. The purpose of these courses is to impart analytical skills in the planning and execution of strategies from a corporate perspective. This is sound reasoning, as most industries are supply chain providers with customer sales representatives merely taking orders, processing payment and providing for distribution of products. In the service industry, we call these people 'cashiers.' In other industries 'Customer Service' departments are usually in the business of listening to complaints and handling breakdowns in the billing and distribution processes for most organizations. These positions are deemed by those corporations to be so insignificant that companies continuously develop technologies to replace them, leaving customers to follow phone instructions or press buttons at a kiosk to handle their transactions. With this in mind, it would seem reasonable to focus managerial talent toward the point of product manufacture and distribution in these industries, with corporate strategies used to drive those functions along with portfolio and acquisition/divestiture programs. However, service industries require management talent at the point of interface with the client/customer/guest because that interface is the product, called service, which results in favorable emotional experiences (magical moments) and translates into fond memories for the departing client/customer/guest.

While corporate direction is important from the business perspective in the service industry, managers overseeing the guest/client/customer interactions are just as important. Thus, they must practice management by strategic thinking in order to ensure that the enterprise delivers magical moments while enhancing productivity on a daily basis. With this in mind, let us take a look at a typical organizational structure for a single full-service resort hotel of medium size (500 or so guestrooms) that represents a single-service enterprise SBU. Figure 4.8 shows us the senior-level management team that would be typical for this type of operation.

Hotels are typically designed with functional structures, which means the senior-level managers possess responsibility for specific organizational functions, as described

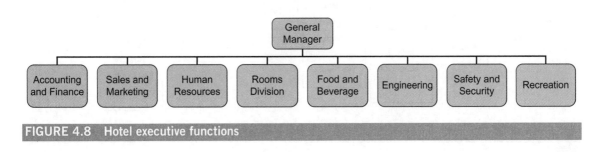

FIGURE 4.8 Hotel executive functions

earlier in the chapter. As we learned earlier in Chapter 1 of the text, the general manager is the Chief Operating Officer (COO) for the hotel, which is commonly referred to as 'the property.' Executives who possess ultimate functional responsibility and authority at the property report directly to the general manager. The actual titles for each of these executives are included in Figure 4.9.

Collectively, the group of executives is called the executive committee. As we learned in Chapter 3, this committee is primarily responsible for the planning and implementation of the property's strategic direction. Most of the senior-level managers hold the title of 'director.' Exceptions to this would be the general manager, rooms division manager (sometimes called the assistant general manager), financial controller (accounting and finance) and the chief engineer (repairs and maintenance). The areas of responsibility and authority for each organizational function are listed in Figure 4.10.

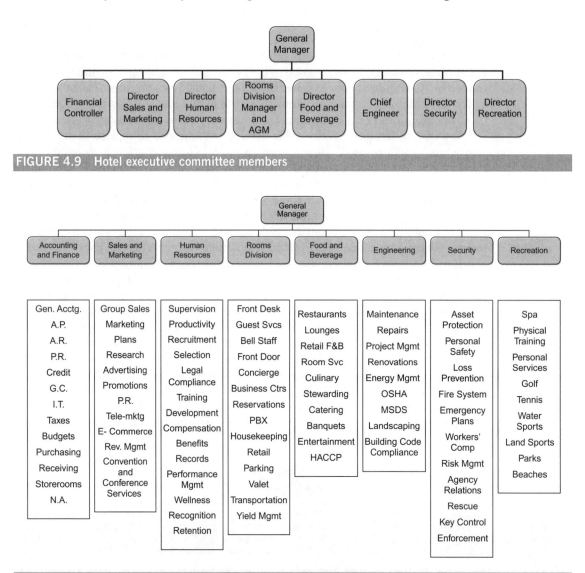

FIGURE 4.9   Hotel executive committee members

FIGURE 4.10   Hotel functions by department

Notice that there are eight functional divisions at the property. Three of them are line divisions (rooms, food and beverage, recreation) and four are staff divisions (accounting and finance, human resources, engineering, security), as we know from Chapter 1. One division, Sales and Marketing, is both line and staff. The sales employees are line workers, while the marketing personnel are staff workers. The areas of responsibility and authority for the financial controller are described in Figure 4.11.

The accounting department is responsible for allocating financial resources and reporting on the financial health of the property. Sometimes, the controller will report to the general manager, and in some organizations this position will report to a corporate chief financial officer. Most of the positions in an accounting office are separated by major general ledger accounts. These include accounts payable, accounts receivable, payroll, credit and cash handling. Additional functions that sometimes fall under the controller could be information technology (IT), purchasing, receiving, storerooms and night audit. The primary focus of a property controller is to ensure efficient use of resources. The opposite of this function is the marketing function, which provides exclusive emphasis on effectiveness levels as measured by the quality and quantity of outputs. The sales and marketing functions are depicted in Figure 4.12.

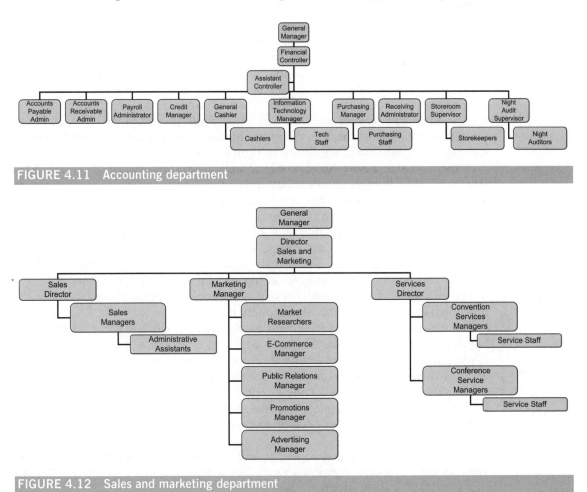

FIGURE 4.11   Accounting department

FIGURE 4.12   Sales and marketing department

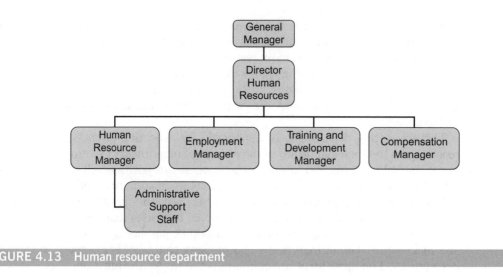

FIGURE 4.13   Human resource department

There are three categories of activities that fall within a Sales and Marketing department. One category is called sales, which has to do with prospecting new clients and closing group sales. The next category is marketing, which includes promotions, public relations, research, e-commerce and advertising. Sometimes, there will be services departments that may fall within the marketing department. These positions would include conference service managers and convention services managers, depending on the size of space available for group meetings and events. Sales and services are line functions, while marketing activities are staff functions that support the line. All of the human resource management functions are staff functions. These are shown in Figure 4.13.

A medium-size resort hotel would usually contain between 800 and 2000 employees. The human resource (HR) director often has at least four managers as direct reports. The human resource manager is a generalist who is usually primarily responsible for employee relations as well as other functions. The other three managers are specialists in the areas of training and development, employment (recruitment and selection) and compensation and benefits. The human resource director is also a generalist and usually assumes primary responsibility for legal compliance and resolution, in addition to performing other HR functions.

The engineering department is responsible for the physical plant aspects of the property. Figure 4.14 describes these functions.

The majority of positions in the engineering department are occupied by trades' journeymen. These include plumbers, painters, electricians, carpenters, masons, HVAC, air conditioning and refrigeration technicians. These skilled trades' people along with apprentices and maintenance personnel perform repair and preventative maintenance functions for the physical plant. Outside grounds are developed and maintained by landscaping personnel. Some engineering departments will also have project managers who oversee property renovations and risk management projects.

The size of a recreation department will vary by the recreation amenities provided at each property. Figure 4.15 provides a depiction of the recreation department for a full-scale destination resort.

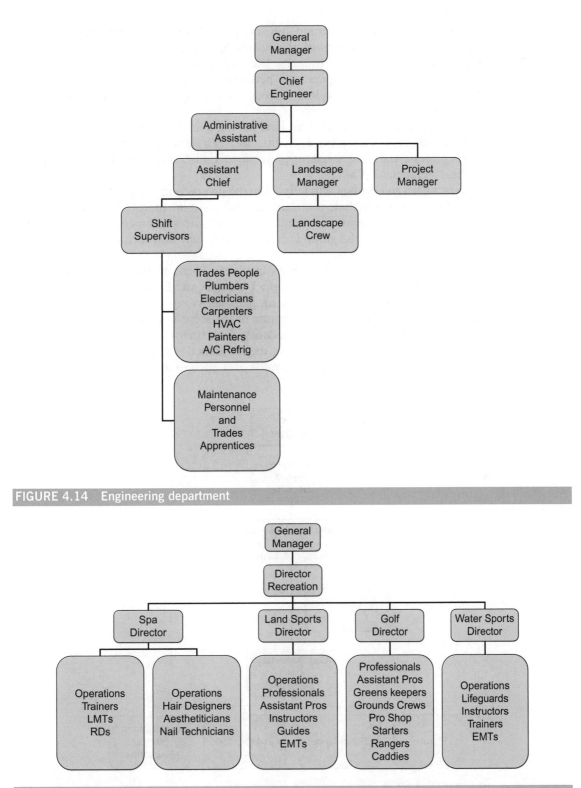

FIGURE 4.14   Engineering department

FIGURE 4.15   Recreation department

Many modern resorts contain full-service spas that provide wellness and personal services to the guests of the resort. Spa practitioners are mostly licensed in their fields and include trainers, licensed massage therapists (LMT) and registered dieticians (RD). Operations personnel are also required to maintain the spa. Personal service providers include hair designers, aestheticians and nail technicians.

If a resort contains facilities for land sports, such as skiing, there will be a specialized staff to provide services in this area. These include operations personnel, sports professionals and assistant professionals, instructors, guides and emergency medical technicians (EMT).

Resorts with golf courses will fall within the jurisdiction of a golf director. Providers for golf courses will include professionals and assistant professionals as well as pro shop operators. The course is maintained under the supervision of a greenskeeper who is responsible for the grounds crew. Courses may also include starters, caddies, golf concierges and rangers.

Some resorts contain water sports facilities. These require the services of lifeguards, instructors, operations personnel, trainers and EMTs.

Lodging properties are responsible for personal safety and the security of physical assets. Figure 4.16 provides a description of the security department functions.

The primary directive for the security department is the physical protection of all guests, employees and visitors to the property. These are life/safety issues. These include security dispatch, patrols and surveillance. All properties contain

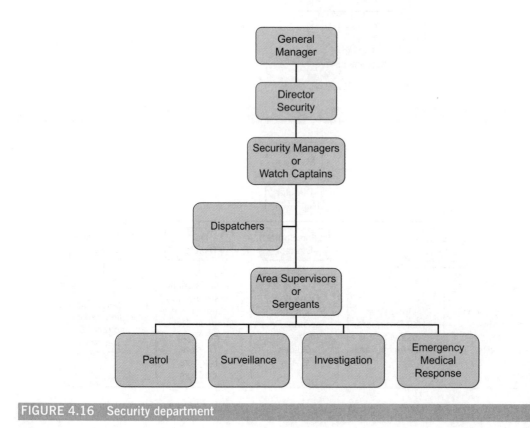

FIGURE 4.16   Security department

sophisticated fire panels and disaster-evacuation procedures. Security practitioners often include EMTs and investigators who file incident reports.

The secondary task of the security department is the protection of physical assets. This function is sometimes called loss prevention. Loss-prevention activities include security systems to prevent thefts, safety programs to prevent accidents and illness (risk management) and background investigations to protect the property shareholders from certain liabilities.

The two largest and most popular operating areas of a hotel are the Rooms Division and the Food and Beverage Department. Depictions of these structures are contained in Figures 4.17 and 4.18 respectively.

The Rooms Division is sometimes referred to as the Rooms and Related Division because it often includes retail operations. For the most part, rooms' functions pertain to the lodging aspect of the property. Rooms' personnel provide the first and last touch points of the guest experience. The Guest Services function contains concierges, bell staff and parking and transportation personnel. Front desk, Reservations and Public Branch Exchange (PBX) operations usually fall with the Front Office operation. Occasionally, the reservations unit will report to the sales and marketing department. But most properties prefer to keep the reservations personnel within the rooms division. The Housekeeping department takes care of cleaning guestrooms

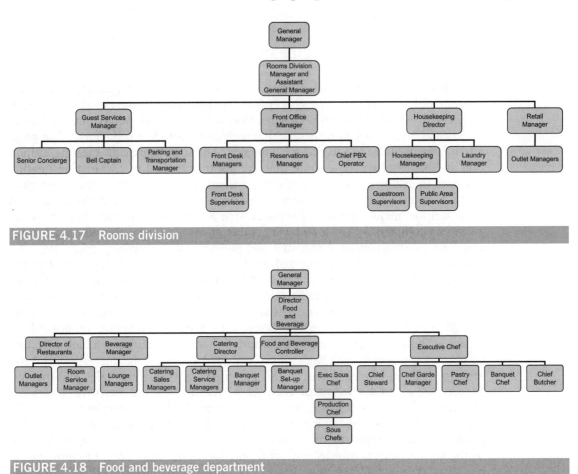

FIGURE 4.17   Rooms division

FIGURE 4.18   Food and beverage department

and public areas throughout the property. Finally, retail operations include stores and gift shops that are located at the property.

Food and beverage operations can be quite complex, depending on the number of restaurants and lounges (outlets) that are available throughout the property. Most medium-size resorts have at least four restaurant outlets that include a signature restaurant, an all-purpose dining room, room service and a coffee shop. Some properties have additional outlets. The same is true for beverage outlets. Most properties will at least have a lobby lounge, a pool bar and an entertainment lounge. But many have additional outlets such as theme and sports bars. Restaurant and beverage outlets serve the needs of guests of the hotel, as well as the general public. Catering facilities consist of meeting rooms, banquet rooms and ballrooms. Group meal functions are booked by catering sales managers and managed by catering service managers. Actual meal services are provided by the banquet staff.

Contrary to free-standing restaurants, the culinary staff for all hotel F&B outlets is centralized under one department. The leader of this department is called the executive chef. Sous chefs are culinary line supervisors. Other work units of the culinary department may include banquet, production, garde-manger, butchery, pastry chefs and cooks. The stewarding department is responsible for kitchen, china, glass and silver sanitation and inventories.

PUTTING SYSTEMS AND STRUCTURE INTO ACTION

Now that we know about systems and structure, let us use an example of a single-service enterprise to bring these concepts to life. Let us say the service entity is a full-service luxury resort hotel with 800 guestrooms, 11 food and beverage outlets, 4 retail outlets and a full-range of recreational amenities to include a golf course. The property has the facilities to serve as a conference hotel with significant meeting, exhibition and ballroom space. Assume that the resort is located in a tourist destination city surrounded by a number of top-brand theme parks that are in close proximity to the hotel's location. The property is a chain hotel with a brand identification that is known for unique specialized services with a boutique European flair. Transient guests are composed of top-level business executives, professionals and upscale tourists. Group clients consist of executive and professional conference participants.

Consistent with the corporate policy, the property is a wage/salary leader in the area and attracts upper levels of the applicant pool for hourly and managerial positions. Also, the property attracts talented managers within the corporation who are seeking career advancement. All staff members complete rigorous orientation and guest service training programs before they may work 'on stage' or 'behind the scenes.' The executive committee comprises a general manager (chief operating officer), rooms division manager, director of food and beverage, recreation director, security director, human resource director, engineering director, sales and marketing director, controller and retail manager. All members of the executive committee are seasoned veterans of hospitality management. At the department level, middle managers range from highly experienced to newly promoted individuals. The same is true for outlet assistant managers and supervisors at the property. As a result of the compensation strategy and work environment, there are large numbers of hourly workers with 10 or more years of seniority at the property. The median age for the employee population is 33.5 years, somewhat older than the industry average of 28.2 years for the location. This is probably due to the longevity of many hourly workers and managers with higher-than-average years of experience. There is a strong organizational culture that emphasizes superlative levels of service and professionalism among the workforce due to the traditions of the chain affiliate and the individual property. As a result, most employees possess high levels of pride in being members of the staff at the hotel.

From a management perspective, there are equally distributed levels of responsibility and authority for the accomplishment of the property's objectives at all levels of the organization. The executive committee members engage in annual strategic planning processes that follow the steps identified in Chapter 3. Once the analysis is complete, they agree on the long-term objectives (LTOs) for the property, with each division articulating its contributions by establishing divisional goals consistent with the overall objectives. The management team practices MBO, after establishing the LTOs. The MBO process follows the Objectives and Strategies outline presented in Chapter 3.

The overall financial picture is favorable for the property, although there are areas that could improve financial contributions. ADR (average daily rate) is very strong and REVPAR (revenue per available room) shows annual percentages that surpass industry increases, as well as increases beyond the local market. Resource allocation is fairly distributed to those departments that demonstrate proficiency in efficiency measures. Capital expenditures are also fairly allocated, allowing staff members to work with state-of-the-art technologies and durable assets in an environment that exceeds industry standards for renovation cycles.

From a sales and marketing standpoint, the property is an 'easy sell' as it is the destination of choice in the local vicinity for clients in the target markets. Discounting is a rare occurrence, since the clientele are willing to pay the price required for the status of staying at the property and hosting conferences there.

While there are rigorous standards for guest services, managers enjoy a good amount of autonomy in directing the activities of their divisions and departments. The entrepreneurial manager is nicely rewarded through generous bonus programs on the basis of unit performance. The culture among managers is a 'maverick leader' style, in which the individuals on the management team are confident and sometimes cocky people, who rebel against any form of micromanagement from above, as well as incompetence from peer managers.

WHAT MIGHT WE LEARN FROM THIS EXAMPLE?

If we were managers charged with diagnosing the efficiency and effectiveness of the operation described in this example, we might observe a number of management symptoms. For instance, we will immediately notice that the property caters to specific niche of clientele. We would also deduce that the property is food and beverage–intensive, with 11 outlets and just 800 guestrooms.

We will note that the property caters to upscale transient and group clientele and is a self-contained conference facility. We may deduce from the style of service that the property is similar to those that carry the *Ritz Carlton* or *Four Seasons* brands.

It appears as though the property believes strongly in long-term human resource management strategies, based on our observations of the compensation, recruitment, selection and training standards. There is evidence of high levels of employee retention, as well as the ability to attract highly talented professional managers. We may also note the presence of a very strong organizational culture at the property.

There is evidence that the property is professionally managed in terms of equal distributions of responsibility, authority, accountability and autonomy. It appears as though the managers practice strategic planning and thinking at all levels of the organization to include the use of MBO.

The property apparently serves its stakeholder groups well by providing uncompromised guest services, sound employment strategies and strong financial performance for the shareholders. At the same time, it appears that resource allocation and use of technology are strategically disseminated to operating departments. In essence, we might conclude that this property is an example of professional management in practice that is consistent with our discussions in Chapters 1–4.

SUMMARY

We began the chapter with a discussion of systems thinking. We recognized that most things are systems and that all systems are subsystems of larger systems. We also realized that systems consist of patterns of networked relationships. Since this is so, a change made to one subsystem will influence other parts of related systems.

We had previously learned that management is a practice. In this chapter, we also realized that the practices of management are based on theories and that we use managerial tools to ply our practice. We learned that general systems theory comes from science and philosophy that help us to identify the systemic nature of the service enterprise. The types of relationships that exist within systems are interdependent in nature, which we identified as being dependent and independent at the same time. This brought us to a discussion of organic systems. We realized that people and organizations are organic systems.

At this point, we took a look at various types of systems from very small to large entities. Linear systems describe production processes and we realized that practically all linear systems are surrounded by nonlinear systems. Next, we identified the functional systems that surround linear production systems. Our discussion of learning systems led us to look at learning processes and to define learning organizations, which we expanded to the global arena. This led us back to discussions of individual learning and resulted in us learning about the work life development of people we will work with and manage. We concluded this section with the reasons for pursuing evolutionary paths of lifelong learning.

Having completed our discussions around systems, we moved into the topic of organizational structure. We started this with a comparison of service enterprise structures to those within other industries. Next, we walked through the organizational charts used by a typical resort hotel to highlight every department from the executive level through the operating levels in the organization. After a brief discussion of each department, we used an example to bring our new knowledge of systems, structure and other topics learned in Chapters 1–3 to life. We completed the chapter with a review of lessons learned up until this point.

1. We discussed that subsystems have interdependent relationships with other subsystems and the larger system of the organization, which is a subsystem of the external environment. Please give an example of this in practice.
2. What is the relationship among linear systems and nonlinear systems in service enterprises? Please use an example to articulate your response.
3. Please describe the learning system as it applies to organizations, work units and individual managers. Be complete with your answer.
4. Consider the Work Life Development model listed in the chapter. Can you think of people that you know who are in each stage? What behaviors or thinking do they demonstrate? What stage are you currently in? Do you think that will change? When?
5. Why do managers need to know the current level of worker development?
6. We discussed functional organizational structures. What does this mean? What functions would be represented by an executive committee for a full-service resort hotel?
7. Identify the titles of at least five middle-level managers from the organization charts presented in the chapter. What position does each report to? What positions report to the middle-management position?
8. Consider the example of the resort hotel under the section Putting Systems and Structure into Action. Would you like to work for that hotel? Identify at least five things about the hotel that you find appealing or unappealing to you.

REAL-WORLD EXPERIENCES (CONTINUED)

You sit back as Dave begins his explanation of the big picture. He starts by saying, 'This hotel is big, it is like a big system with lots of littler systems inside and an even bigger one outside.' He continues, 'But for now, let's just look at the inside systems. Every restaurant is a small subsystem of the F&B Department, which is a subsystem of the hotel. You may remember from your employee orientation that the COO of this hotel is the GM.' He smiles, 'The buck stops there. He is like the leader of the big system.' He looks for your nod of understanding and continues, 'The executive for our system is the F&B Director. He also has a big job. He must bring together restaurants, beverage, catering, culinary, sanitation and financial controls for the department.' You nod and Dave says, 'The leader for restaurant outlets is the Director of Restaurants. It is her job to ensure that each restaurant outlet understands its role within the big picture of the guest experience.' He goes on, 'The illusion we create for the guests is that they are having a different dining experience in each of our outlets, but they also notice that each outlet is held to the same general service standards.' Dave finishes, 'This can only happen if the F&B Director ensures that each work unit does its part to make that happen and the Director of Restaurants makes sure all the restaurants work together to provide consistent service standards.'

Dave sits back and stares while you ponder this information. Finally you say, 'I get it. It's like running the Titanic. Everything must come together to make the magic for the guests.' 'Right,' Dave replies. You continue, 'So the systems and the structure provide the communication of the objectives, strategies, policies, standards and procedures that translate into services that are consistent in every area of the property.' Dave looks surprised and exclaims, 'Brilliant deduction! I couldn't have said it better myself.' You both chuckle and Dave says, 'You'll make a great GM someday.'

CASE STUDY

It was a muggy and hot afternoon in this large, culturally diverse Southeastern city. Jason was delighted to have been asked to serve as a meeting planner for one of the country's largest office supply company's annual meeting for its store managers. The hotel was a 4-diamond deluxe property and the level of quality provided by the meeting planner company was exceptional. Jason had the pleasure to work for this specific event three years in a row. As such, he had much more responsibility this year than simply meeting and greeting at the airport or driving the spouses and significant others of delegates to the mall for an afternoon of shopping.

This year would be different. On day #2 of the five-day meeting, Jason was scheduled to take his own VIP motorcoach with the President, CEO, CFO and all of the company's vice presidents to a three-hour morning of tennis. Mini-tournaments had been arranged and it was to be a morning of fun and bonding for all of these top executives. The motorcoach was well-maintained and had just had a thorough washing of its exterior. The interior had been decorated with ribbons, flyers, posters etc. All the signage indicated what a fantastic year Print & Paper, Inc. had just past. They recently opened their 500th store on the Isle of Lower Goldfish Ridge and the stock values continually were improving.

Jason arrived to the motorcoach at 6:30 a.m., even though the departure time was not until 8:00 a.m. He wanted to meet the driver, make sure the vehicle was clean and had a full tank of gas. He verified name cards placed at each seat. He tested the on-vehicle microphone so he could animate the tour of the city as they drove to the resort for the tennis tournaments. He called the catering manager on duty to make sure that the continental breakfast was set up outside the bus and that there were napkins, plastic silverware and other containers to take onboard. And, of course, he made sure that the coffee was going to be hot and fresh! After all, these were the VIPs of an already VIP group!

At 7:30, the first set of VIPs arrived. They were warmly welcomed, given a printed itinerary and served their continental breakfast. By 7:52 a.m., all of the 37 VIPs were ready to go and loaded onto the motorcoach. There were cheers, applause and lots of smiles as Jason closed the door and took the microphone.

'Good morning ladies and gentlemen!' he bantered. It is a pleasure to be your escort on this morning's VIP tennis outing. We will be leaving downtown Nice City, USA for a 35-minute ride to our destination. On the way, I'll be giving you some information about our beautiful city and also providing you information about the tennis tournaments and team preparation. Racquets, hand towels, tennis balls and any other necessary equipment will be provided at Sunny Resort. We will return to the bus at 11:00 a.m. for our drive back to the hotel, with enough time for you to shower, change and get ready for our delicious 1:00 p.m. luncheon and entertainment hosted by none other than the fabulous Ms. Raz-a-Ma-Taz.

And so, they were off. Happy people. Many eating their muffins, chatting, drinking coffee and seeing the wonderful sights of a wonderful city on a wonderful, sunny morning.

About 20 minutes into the drive, there appeared to be a traffic jam. Up ahead on the four-lane road, there was a railroad crossing. Neither the driver nor Jason noticed that the crossing gates were down. However, the traffic was at a complete standstill. 5 minutes, 8 minutes, people became edgy. Jason said, with a cheerful demeanor, 'I'm sure you all know about traffic in large metropolitan cities... I guess everyone is on his or her way to buy office supplies at one of your stores.' With that, people laughed and resumed their conversation. Jason took the opportunity to step down off the stairs and walk ahead into the traffic. What he saw stunned him.

About a block down, just across the railroad tracks, was an adjacent north/south street which was completely covered with marathon racers. On the sidelines were tables with cold refreshments, cheering fans and announcers with loudspeakers. It appeared that unbeknownst to Jason and/or the motorcoach driver the group was now immersed in the middle of the once-a-year NICEVILLE, USA MARATHON. 'Stay calm,' thought Jason to himself, 'runners do just that – they run – these people will be passed quickly.'

The story would not unfold so nicely. Indeed, 500 registered marathon racers had started four miles prior to the previous point where Jason and his entourage had come to a complete halt. Jason was instructed by city police that all streets leading to Sunny Resort would be blocked for at least 60–90 minutes. 'This could not have happened!' Jason yelled out loud. He slowly walked back to the motorcoach and motioned for the driver to meet him outside. By this time, several of the meeting attendees had stepped off the bus to either have a cigarette, get fresh air or just see what was going on.

After describing the hopeless situation to the driver, the driver said, 'No one at the main post told me anything about marathon. They usually fill me in on such details. But, you know, young man, wouldn't have mattered anyway, it's darn blocked this entire region of Niceville.'

As a meeting planner with only four large groups worth of experience under his belt, Jason stood stunned. 'What should I do?' he thought. He immediately pulled himself together. First, he looked around to see what available stores, restaurants etc. were within walking distance. Right next to the motorcoach was a large discount retail store. He checked to make sure that he had a company credit card with him – he remembered in training, 'All good meeting planners are prepared for any sudden change of events.'

Jason approached Mr. Bigtime CEO and asked if he could have a word with him. Of course, Mr. CEO already knew something was wrong by the look on Jason's face and the somewhat trembling sound in his voice. 'Mr. Bigtime CEO,' he managed to get out, 'Um... it looks like no one could have forecast this city-wide event, sir, but we're going to be stuck for a long while...' Before he could say another word, Mr. CEO yelled back, 'Son, I'll have you fired if you don't get me and my people to Sunny Resort! Don't tell *ME* that no one could have predicted this event – every one in the Southeastern United States knows there's a big marathon race here today! How could you do this to me... to us! Don't you know that Print & Paper, Inc. is paying more than one million dollars for this meeting! I'll have your butt fired in a minute – get me your supervisor on the phone!'

'Please, Mr. Bigtime CEO, let me offer something to you,' responded Jason. 'I know I'm young, a recent college graduate, but I've worked large conventions and meetings for three years now – both as a student and for the past year as an employee of ACME Meeting Company. We've never let Print & Paper, Inc. down on anything, and I'm not about to start a new trend. Just please give me a few minutes.'

With that, Jason went over to the large discount retailer. To his delight, he found tennis racquets and tennis balls as well as souvenir white hand towels (perfect for tennis) that had a bright, yellow sun and the words NICEVILLE, USA printed in bright blue color. He also found plastic cups, ice, snacks and a host of other fun 'items' that could be used as prizes. These included souvenirs from the city, fun gifts for both males and females and some delicious, locally made chocolates.

After spending over $572.00, Jason reboarded the bus. Luckily, the driver had the common sense to keep the motor running so it was nice and cool inside. The faces Jason saw, however, looked somewhat 'heated' from their frustration. By now, they had been waiting over 40 minutes in one spot – with no tennis courts in site.

Jason asked everyone to return to reboard the bus and return to their seats (including Mr. Bigtime CEO). Confidently, he took the microphone and proudly stated, 'We have a surprise for you today. No, no one knew we would run into a world-class marathon. And no one knew that this world-class marathon would come head-to-head with a world-class office supply company's annual meeting. So, instead of acting like babies, we're gonna' set up shop *right here* and have our own tennis tournament in the parking lot of this retail store.' Sure enough, the parking lot was empty as no one could get down the street to park and visit the store because of the marathon.

At first unhappily, everyone exited the bus. Soon smiles came on their faces as they saw the quality (very low indeed) of the tennis racquets and balls that Jason had purchased. The hand towels became a big hit as souvenirs. The teams took turns and the scoring methods were shortened to allow faster passage of one team to the next. Soon, the VIPs were sitting on lounge chairs that Jason had purchased and drinking the cold beverages. Laughter was heard and one VIP even shouted, 'Tom, I'll kick your butt here on this asphalt and prove that I can beat you at tennis ANYwhere!'

Some people who had become bored with the marathon now gathered in the parking lot and were placing cash bets on which team would win. The Vice President of Sales wound up talking to a gentleman who owned a rather large law firm nearby and was convincing him to have a Print & Paper, Inc. sales representative switch them from their competitor office supply company.

Before long, no one realized that the marathon had passed and the street was clear. There, in NICEVILLE, USA, sat a parked motorcoach, pulled up as close to the curb as possible, with its hazard lights on. And, there were probably 37 of the highest-paid corporate executives playing a tennis tournament in a store parking lot.

Team #3, the 'Jetsons' as they called themselves, won the tournament. Jason proudly gave out their prizes, as the bus turned back toward the hotel. Marie won a bottle of $8.99 perfume, which she said smelled like something her grandmother used to wear. John, the Vice President of Finance, won a lounge chair, which he proudly said he would use the day after the conference at his pool to relax and regroup from his physically tiring tennis tournament. And, Cherie won a two-pound box of chocolate, which appeared to already have become one pound lighter.

On the way back, Mr. Bigtime CEO pulled Jason aside and said, 'Young man... what you just did was save a meeting. You did it with ease, with no 'how to' manual, and you made it look easy. Just tell me what you would have done if we were stuck in a neighborhood with no Bobby's Discount Store, though.' Smiling, Jason said, 'Um... sir, I'm not really sure, but why don't you have a piece of this here delicious chocolate.'

Questions:

* Did Jason do the right thing by making such an impulse decision? Why or why not?
* How could the client have responded to Jason's actions?
* Give an example of an instance within a hospitality setting where you think 'risk taking' such as that used by Jason would also be appropriate.
* Should meeting planners have a backup plan for every event? If so, who should decide what that backup plan will be? How should it be communicated to staff?
* If you were Jason's boss, how would you treat him upon return? Should Jason have phoned his boss before making this decision – or any large decision, for that matter?

ENDNOTES

1. Zukav, G., 1979. The Dancing Wu Li Masters: An Overview of the New Physics. Bantam Books.
2. *Ibid.*
3. Tesone, D.V., 2000. Leadership from the sciences. *Journal of Leadership Studies*.
4. Senge, P., 2006. The Fifth Discipline: The Art and Practice of the Learning Organization. Business and Ecomics.
5. *Ibid.*
6. LePage, D., 2008. Evolution myths: Evolution defies the second law of thermodynamics. *New Scientist*.
7. *Ibid.*
8. Bailey, K., 1990. Social Entropy Theory. State University of New York Press.
9. Mitchel, E., 1996. The Way of the Explorer. Putnam.
10. Zukav, G., 1979. The Dancing Wu Li Masters: An Overview of the New Physics. Bantam Books.
11. Wheatly, M., 2006. Leadership and the New Science: Discovering Order in a Chaotic World. Berrett-Koehler Publishers, Inc.
12. *Ibid.*
13. Tesone, D.V., 2002. Handbook of Hospitality Resources. Pearson: Boston.
14. Senge, P., 2006. The Fifth Discipline: The Art and Practice of Organizational Learning. Business and Economics.
15. *Ibid.*
16. *Ibid.*
17. *Ibid.*

18. Kohlberg, L., 1973. 'The Claim to Moral Adequacy of a Highest Stage of Moral Judgment'. *Journal of Philosophy* 70, 630–646.
19. Sidorsky, D., 1977. John Dewey: The Essential Writings. New York: Harper & Row.
20. Piaget, J., 1932. The Moral Judgment of the Child. London: Kegan Paul, Trench, Trubner and Co.
21. Maslow, A.H., 1970. Motivation and Personality. Harper-Rowe.
22. Shea, G.F., 1986. How to Develop Effective Mentoring. Crisp.
23. *Ibid.*
24. Tesone, D.V. Hospitality Information Systems and E-Commerce. Wiley.
25. Endnote
26. Endnote
27. Ash, M.K.
28. Huxley, A.
29. Tesone.
30. Hunger, D.L., Wheelen, T.L., 2001.

PART 2

Management Functions

CHAPTER 5

Productivity and Value-Added Management Practices

In this chapter you will learn to:

1. Describe value-added management.
2. Identify five service enterprise production systems.
3. Describe how to manage resources, systems and outputs for enhanced productivity.

REAL-WORLD EXPERIENCES

You are an intern working alongside a room service manager, Peter, at a resort hotel. The busiest time for the room service department is in the early morning when many guests call in continental breakfast orders between 7 and 9 a.m. The standard for these order deliveries is 35 minutes or less. You remember a time when this standard was not being met when the hotel had full occupancy. But you watched as Peter implemented systems to overcome the problem of timely order delivery.

This morning Peter approaches you with what he calls 'a challenge and opportunity.' He has a gleam in his eye as he says, 'Okay, are you ready for your first systems challenge?' You smile and say, 'I guess so.' 'Here's the situation,' he says, 'We solved the problem of delivery times, but our new opportunity is to develop systems for more efficient tray and table retrieval.'

He continues, 'You see, we are running out of trays during the morning rush and when we sweep the corridors for trays after the rush, we are spending too much time getting our china, glass and silver back.' He smiles at you and says, 'You want to take a crack at solving this one?' You reply, 'I'll give it a shot.'

To be continued...

INTRODUCTION

This chapter will begin with a description of value-added management (VAM), which is a basic *run* strategy in which managers enhance productivity levels in small increments each working day. We will take our first look at the productivity model to identify its three main components and define related terminology. Next, we will consider five production systems that exist in service enterprises. We will note their relationships to each other and then discuss the production sequences for each of the five systems. Next, we will look at productivity systems from a senior-management perspective to understand how to manage inputs, transformation processes and outputs. Finally, we will discuss how you can become a value-added manager for a service enterprise.

WHAT IS VALUE-ADDED MANAGEMENT?

We already know that the job of managers is to accomplish the objectives of the organization through the activities of others. All objectives are in some way related to productivity enhancement. **Value-added managers** (VAMs) add value to the organization through their area of responsibility by enhancing productivity in small increments every day.

All objectives, strategies, policies, standards and procedures should be designed with productivity enhancement in mind. So, what is **productivity**? Productivity is a linear system that consists of inputs that feed a transformation process, which yields outcomes in the form of products and services. The linear process is surrounded by nonlinear, invisible factors to include meaning and learning systems, which serve as dynamic feedback loops. This should sound familiar to those of us who reviewed Chapter 4. Figure 5.1 provides a depiction of the linear and nonlinear productivity systems.

We referred to the model as a production system in Chapter 4 of the text. In this chapter, we are primarily focused on the relationship of each component of the model, which is the productivity view of production systems. As managers, we must never consider production without thinking of it from a productivity perspective. This perspective requires us to track activities from input through output stages to improve the learning and meaning systems that surround the linear model. This is called the **productivity process**. The objective of using the productivity process is

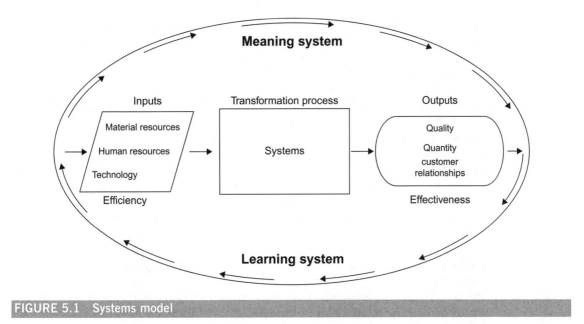

FIGURE 5.1   Systems model

to create **process improvement**, which requires us to dissect and revise subroutines to improve overall processes.

From an engineering perspective, the focus is totally on the linear equation of inputs, transformation process and outputs. This was the approach of scientific management practitioners in the early twentieth century. We already know that managers must also include management science, human behavior and systems thinking strategies in the practice of professional management. We know from Chapter 4 that two dominant nonlinear systems drive worker performance. These are called the meaning and learning systems within work units and service enterprise organizations. We might recall that the meaning system is based on individual and organizational values, attitudes and beliefs (culture) and that learning systems comprise the intellectual capital (knowledge) of workers as individuals and groups.

SERVICE ENTERPRISE PRODUCTION SYSTEMS

We learned in Chapter 1 about the generic differences between service enterprises and general commerce. In Chapter 3, we found that service organizations are much more complex than other industries in terms of strategic direction and problem solving. Chapter 4 reinforced this complexity from the perspective of systems and structures that drive service enterprises. Service organizations also operate with more production systems than standard manufacturing and distribution firms.

The majority of commercial enterprises subscribe to a **supply chain** approach to management. The supply chain is a continuum of steps that occur in manufacturing and distribution of products that ranges from the original point of manufacture to the end user (customer). For instance, a vehicle manufacturing company will require various material resources to be assembled into a car. These products are manufactured in various parts of the world and shipped to other varied assembly companies. The assembly companies will combine these parts into components of a car and ship them to the car assembly plant. The plant will assemble the vehicle and ship it to a distribution center. The distribution center will ship the vehicle to an auto dealership (retailer) for sale to the consumer (customer). In this case, the supply chain begins with plastics, metals and electronics used to assemble parts. The parts are assembled and shipped to the auto manufacturer and the finished product (car) is shipped to an intermediary (distribution center). It is then shipped to the dealer and ultimately purchased by the customer. This is a chain of product manufacturing and distribution. It is linear line of assembly and distribution from start to finish. The supply chain approach of product assembly and distribution is a very small component of service organizations.

Most service enterprises operate five types of production systems concurrently and repetitively within a single physical plant. These include: service transaction systems, maintenance systems, repair systems, distribution systems and product production systems. Each of these systems is directly related to serving external customers (guests, clients) or internal customers (individuals serving guests and clients). This is the key point that differentiates service enterprises from manufacturing firms. The relationships of the five types of production systems are depicted in Figure 5.2.

Notice from the figure that the products are being consumed at the same time the production systems are in operation. This is the antithesis of supply chain firms that move products sequentially through a linear process one step at a time. Simultaneous production and consumption is a nonlinear process. This is evident in the interdependency of all of the five production systems. The Service Transaction system is the hub of all the other systems. As we know from Chapter 4, this means

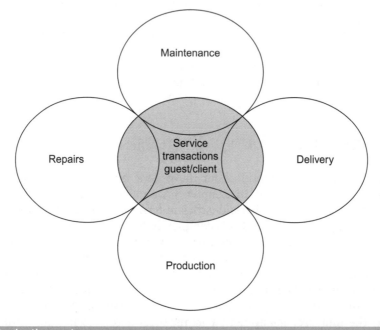

FIGURE 5.2 Production systems

100

that the Maintenance, Repair, Product and Distribution systems are subsystems of the Service Transaction system, which provides the guest/client experiences. Hence, service transactions are the outputs that result from each of the four subsystem inputs and transformation processes. Also notice that all of the five systems are *production systems*, in that they each produce an outcome for the guests/clients or internal customers. However, the only production system that produces actual products is the *product production system*. Let us take a look at what this all means.

The service transaction system is in operation during any touch point with a guest/client or internal customer in which there is a conversion process. In a lodging facility, the act of guestroom check-in is a conversion process from a vacant to an occupied room. When a concierge provides tickets to a show, the conversion process is the possession of those tickets by the guest. When an inquisitive guest is escorted to the spa, the conversion process is guest knowledge about the location and services available within that amenity. When an airline agent changes a seat assignment, the conversion process is a new seat. When a door attendant flags a taxi, the conversion process is transportation for the guest. We can now see that all service transactions result in some form of conversion from one state to another, which could be intangible (knowledge of location and amenities) or tangible (a guestroom, ticket or transportation). Service transactions comprise the majority of transactions within a service enterprise; and we can see that thousands of these occur in many establishments every day.

Maintenance production systems convert unusable space into usable space. In a lodging facility, this would pertain to public areas and guestrooms. In order for a guestroom to be placed into available inventory, it must be vacant and clean. Lobby areas and public walkways must be clean and orderly. Banquet and meeting rooms must be set to the specifications of the banquet event order. Grounds must be groomed and free of debris. Vehicles and aircraft must be prepared for guest embarkation. Maintenance production systems consist of activities of continuous restoration of physical space to standards for guest/client use.

Repair production systems convert inoperable physical property and equipment into working order. This is the work of trades' people such as carpenters, mechanics, technicians, painters, plumbers and others. In lodging facilities, guestrooms needing repairs are placed on *out-of-order* status, which removes them from available inventories. Public areas also require constant repairs, which is also true of *back-of-the-house* areas and equipment. Frequent preventative maintenance and repairs are also required for aircraft, ground transportation vehicles, attractions, cruise ships, golf courses, recreation facilities, clubhouses and other entities. Repair production systems also apply to recreation professionals and technicians who repair personal equipment used by guests, such as golf clubs, tennis racquets, sailboats and the like.

Product production systems apply mostly to foodservice sectors of the services industry. Free standing and chain restaurants usually come to mind when we mention foodservice operations. But we must also include the F&B divisions of full-service lodging establishments, airline and institutional catering entities, as well as cruise line F&B providers. We learned about the complexity of foodservice operations through our examination of hotel F&B operations in Chapter 4. The aspect that sets product production systems apart from the other four is the conversion of *raw materials* into finished products. The conversion processes in service transactions, maintenance, repairs (with some exceptions, such as carpentry) and distribution do not include raw materials. The product production unit in the foodservice sector is called the culinary department. Culinarians produce finished plates from raw ingredients to be consumed by guests. The distribution points for these finished products may be to dining rooms, cafes, guestrooms, aircraft and retail centers. Also, bartenders produce finished beverage products from raw ingredients for consumption at bars, lounges, guestrooms, dining rooms and cafes.

The conversion process of a distribution production system consists of movement of physical items or information from one point to another. Again, foodservice sectors provide us with examples of the distribution of plates to diners. In a restaurant or dining room service, personnel perform the distribution process. Room service personnel distribute food and beverage products to guestrooms in lodging establishments. Banquet servers and off-site catering servers distribute quantity products for functions. However, distribution production systems are not the exclusive domain of foodservice sectors.

In a full-service lodging facility, the bell staff distributes luggage, newspapers, faxes, dry cleaning and other items to-and-from guestrooms and other areas of the hotel. Housekeeping personnel distribute linens and amenities to guestrooms. Guestroom attendants distribute linens and supplies to housekeepers. Public area cleaners distribute paper goods and linens to guest facilities. Laundry personnel distribute linens to restaurant outlets and health spa facilities. Night auditors distribute guest folios and daily reports. Concierges distribute tickets and tour information. Security officers distribute safety information. Receiving agents distribute purchased items to storerooms. Storeroom personnel distribute requisitioned items to work units. Kitchen stewards distribute china, glass and silver to outlets. Information systems distribute reports to operating and administrative areas. And so on. In fact, a hotel is a network of distribution production systems in which individuals, items and information travel across the property many times every day.

WHAT ARE THE SEQUENTIAL STEPS IN PRODUCTION SYSTEMS?

We already know that there are three phases to each production system to include inputs, transformation processes and outputs. The three phases may be applied to each of the five production systems – service transactions, maintenance, repairs, product and distribution. Figure 5.3 will serve as a visual guide for us to examine the processes for each of the production systems.

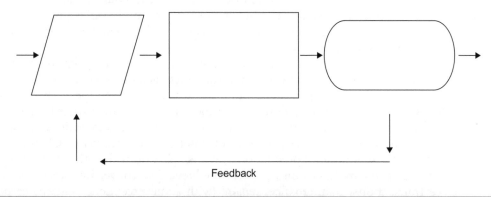

Feedback

FIGURE 5.3 Productivity model

The vast majority of service transactions use human resources as the primary input in the form of front-line service personnel or those who support front-line service personnel. In fact, a number of service transactions occur between guests and service personnel without the use of any material resources. Examples would include sharing information or escorting the guest to a location. In many other cases, the transaction will require the use of supplies and equipment, such as a computer to perform a check-in procedure. A small, but growing number of service transactions are automated, such as check-in kiosks and Internet property tours. In such cases, the major input is technology. If we were to view the total number of service transactions, we would determine that the highest-level input is human resources and the second highest is technology, with the lowest-level input being equipment and supplies. The transaction process includes time spent with the guest and the sequence of steps in the transaction process. The outcome is the status of the guest – checked-in, informed, transported, accommodated etc. All transformation processes include timing and sequencing of the process to create an output.

Since maintenance production systems are cyclical processes, there are three steps taken to complete each conversion. These are prepreparation, processing and postpreparation. The prepreparation phase requires human resources, equipment and supplies to be available to the maintenance provider. The transformation process includes the steps required to convert the facility from dirty to clean. The postpreparation phase is to prepare for the next cleaning phase, such as restocking a housekeeping cart for use the next day. Maintenance production systems are intensive in terms of human, equipment and supply resources. A facility that is ready for guest/client use is the output associated with this process.

The three steps in the repairs production process include diagnostics, intervention and testing. A plumber may inspect a malfunctioning toilet and determine that the ball fitting needs to be replaced. A replacement part should be on hand and the transformation process will be to install that new part. The plumber will then test the equipment for functionality. Repair production processes are just as intensive as maintenance processes in terms of human, equipment and supply resources. Although there are fewer repair workers than maintenance personnel, trades' people earn higher rates of pay, which inflates the cost of labor for repairs. The outputs consist of operating equipment and facilities, which is necessary to put them back in available inventory.

The inputs for product production systems are quite high relative to the profit margins of food and beverage revenues. Once the raw materials are available in working storage, the culinary team takes steps to convert those materials into finished plates. This is an expensive transformation process that requires significant levels of human, equipment and supply resources to produce outputs. The sanitation (maintenance production) costs associated with food production are also high. As we discussed, the service staff handles the timely and accurate distribution of products to the guests.

Human resource inputs are primary to the distribution function. As is the case with certain service transaction processes, information distribution is becoming more automated. In these situations, technology is the primary input for information dissemination. In some cases, physical distribution may require equipment such as hand trucks, dollies, carts or trays. The transformation process involves moving items or information from one point to another in a timely and accurate fashion. When this is accomplished, a favorable output is the result.

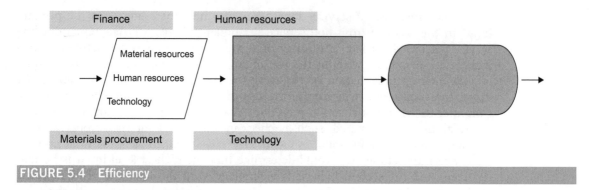

FIGURE 5.4 Efficiency

THREE ASPECTS OF THE PRODUCTIVITY MODEL

INPUTS

Let us take a separate look at each of the three components of the productivity model to further understand its role in productivity enhancement. Figure 5.4 shows the input component.

At this point, we will view each component of the productivity model from the perspective of the total service enterprise. Later, in Chapter 10, we will bring our viewpoint to the tactical approach of managing specific work units. As a senior-level manager, we view the acquisition and allocation of resources (inputs) from a conceptual viewpoint. We learned in Chapter 1 of the text that conceptual (seeing the big picture) skills are primary for practicing senior managers.

HOW DO WE MANAGE MATERIAL RESOURCES?

The first category of resources is referred to as material resources. These include raw materials, equipment and supplies. We must spend money to acquire these resources and in fact, cash and credit are considered to be financial resources used to acquire all other resources. Most equipment is considered to be a capital expenditure with a payback period of many years. Supplies fall within the operating expenses category of a financial budget for a service enterprise. Material resources are attained through a procurement or purchasing process. Individuals responsible for material resource acquisition contribute to the productivity model by procuring quality materials at reasonable prices. Some untrained managers believe that the objective of purchasing materials is simply buying at the lowest price. This is a mistake from a productivity perspective, as inferior quality of materials will actually drive up expenses owing to premature replacement. The same is true for the procurement of raw materials. Raw materials are unfinished goods that must be converted into finished goods. Culinary teams for instance will use ingredients (raw materials) to produce plates (finished goods) in a restaurant. Poor-quality meats, fish and produce may become costly owing to poor yields of useable products. For instance, a case of lettuce usually contains 24 heads and the total weight should be at least 45 pounds. If the lettuce is of poor quality, culinarians must discard inferior portions of each head, which will drive up overall food costs. Yield from meat products depends on postpreparation shrinkage, which will decrease finished portions and also increase overall costs of goods sold.

At the time of delivery, the purchased materials go through a receiving process in which the items are inspected relative to quality and quantity specifications. Items that pass this process will be placed in inventory. Most service enterprises divide inventory into two categories. *Storeroom inventory* contains items that are available for production systems usage. Workers from production units will order items from the storeroom inventories through a requisition process. When the requisitioned materials are delivered to the work units, those items become *working inventory* (materials that will be placed into the production process in a short period of time).

Storeroom inventories are crucial to the resource side of cash flow for the service enterprise. This is why inventories must be managed in order to enhance overall productivity levels. As is the case with all management practices, inventory management requires balance. There must be sufficient inventories to fill all work unit requisitions, yet a surplus of items in storeroom inventory costs the organization money. Par levels, the amount of materials that should be on hand determine the appropriate amount of items in storeroom inventory. The difference between on-hand inventory and par levels will become the order volume for the purchasing department. When those items are received, the inventory volume goes back to par levels that are available for requisitions from the work units.

Successful inventory management is measured by the aging of inventories. Each storeroom has an objective for moving the dollar value of total storage during various time frames depending on the type of stock. When the total dollar value of a storeroom is moved, we can say that we *turned over (storeroom turnover)* that storeroom one time. For instance, a beverage storeroom will house spirits, wine, beer and mixers. An aggressive turnover objective would be *one turn* every 30 days. That would mean that work units would have requisitioned the dollar value of the entire stock in a period of about one month. How does this impact productivity enhancement? When you move all storeroom inventories to working inventories, those items will be quickly sold at a markup to generate revenues and profits. This will more than pay the accounts payable invoices incurred when the items were purchased and received into inventory. If the enterprise does not move the inventory, then dollars in the form of 'paid for products' remain sitting on the shelves and collecting dust. Hence, the cost of inputs is increased and overall enterprise productivity declines. The more times we turnover storeroom inventories, the more we are enhancing overall enterprise productivity. Using our beverage storeroom scenario, if we were to increase our rate to 1 turnover every 28 days, our turnover rate would increase from 1.0 to 1.07 per month. This would be a 0.07 productivity enhancement for the enterprise through sound inventory management practices.

How Do We Manage Human Resources?

We know that the higher the turnover for material resources, the more productive we are being. The opposite is true when it comes to managing human resources. In order to enhance productivity, we should minimize employee turnover. Employee turnover consists of individuals who leave the service enterprise either voluntarily (resignation) or involuntarily (discharge). It is measured as a ratio that compares the number of exiting employees to the total employment population within an organization.

For instance, if a small company with 100 employees incurs 50 vacated positions, the employee turnover rate for that year will be 50%. If 10 employees leave, the turnover rate will be 10% and if 100 employees leave the employment turnover rate will be 100%. There are varying reports about average employee turnover in our industry. Most organizations strive to achieve a turnover rate of less than 60% each year.

How does employee turnover affect productivity? Well, we hire people for knowledge, skills, abilities and attitudes (KSAAs). These KSAAs produce products and services within the service enterprise. KSAAs are the inputs of human talents that perform transformation processes that yield outputs (products and services). In an ideal labor market, we would be able to hire as many people as we need with required KSAAs. But unfortunately, this is seldom the case in the 'real world;' so in our industry, we usually hire for attitudes and train for knowledge, skills and abilities. This training is an investment in our workers. When we invest in the development of our workers, we are treating them as **human capital**, which is the crux of human resource management thinking. Like any capital investment, we expect a return for our invested dollars. Our return from the workers begins when they have acquired the KSAAs to contribute to productivity. At this point, each worker is an asset to the organization. When we lose one of those workers, we lose productivity and have wasted our invested dollars.

Let us consider a small example of worker productivity. We are going to open a restaurant with 100 front and back employees. We conduct a hiring blitz and prescreen every applicant. We narrow the applicant pool down and conduct further screening processes. We end up with 120 new workers who will go through our preopening training program. At the end of the program, 110 workers are left as we open the restaurant. We overstaff the restaurant with these workers and start a new recruitment and selection process. Within one month, 10 employees leave – some quit and others were discharged, so we are down to 100 employees. We have 10 new workers ready to replace them. Now we are back to 110 employees. Over the next six months, we wind down to 100 workers, just the right number for our restaurant. Of course, we continue our recruitment and selection processes for future replacements. As we approach our first year in business, we have only replaced 10 more workers at the restaurant. During our first year of business, our employee turnover rate is 30% (30 employees out of an average of 100). Our replacement strategies minimized the time and money required to replace those 30 workers. We did a good job of managing our human resources by reporting a very low turnover rate for this sector of our industry and minimizing replacement time. With 100 fully trained workers, we are in a position to continuously enhance our productivity levels.

How do we manage human resources for productivity enhancement? We cannot even think about doing that until the critical mass of employees in the work unit have attained the status of assets (appropriate levels of KSAAs). Once this is accomplished, we begin to execute productivity enhancement strategies in small increments by looking for ways to improve inputs and transformation processes. We remember that there are four functions of management – planning, organizing, influence and control. All of these functions are important for enhancing productivity in general, but managing human resources is mostly a matter of using our influencing or leadership skills. We know from Chapter 4 that invisible Meaning and Learning systems surround the linear production process. Both of these systems require managers to use their influencing skills to encourage workers to take steps to enhance the productivity of a work unit and ultimately the entire service enterprise. As we will learn in Part IV of the text, leadership is all about motivation on the part of leaders as well as followers.

How Do We Manage Technology?

Technology is partly a material resource from the standpoint of electronic hardware components. It is also intangible from the view of software used to drive the technology to perform production tasks. When we combine hardware and software, we get Information Technology (IT). When we network IT among nodes, we are dealing with Information Systems (IS). In their current state, IT and IS are used to automate transactions that were previously performed through manual means. All of the stakeholder groups are impacted by IT and IS in service enterprises.

Customers, guests and clients use electronic means to access product, pricing, placement and promotion aspects of the service enterprise through the Internet. Employees use networks to automatically perform tabulation, reservations, requisitions, billing, check-ins/outs and settlement transactions. Shareholders monitor the financial performance of service enterprises through electronic networks. Suppliers, competitors and other community entities use intranets and extranets to interface with organizations.

Managers in service enterprises must become familiar with the language of IT and IS in order to make sound decisions concerning hardware and software procurement, network configurations, as well as systems implementation and evaluation. Technology can be used as a productivity enhancement tool by automating certain transformation processes. However, misapplications of technology may interfere with productivity enhancement strategies. This is particularly true in service enterprises where the creation of magical memories through face-to-face interaction is the main product. Managers who do not familiarize themselves with IT and IS knowledge may end up with technologies that negatively impact the quantity and quality of products and services, which is the antithesis of productivity enhancement. Smart technology decision making on the part of managers may greatly enhance productivity, as we will learn in Chapter 8 of the text.

What Is the Objective of Managing Resources (Inputs)?

In a word, **efficiency** is the objective of resource management. As we learned in Chapter 2, efficiency can be phrased as doing things right. More specifically, efficiency consists of the metrics used to evaluate inputs in terms of costs of goods sold. There are costs associated with financial, material, human and technological resources. There are additional costs associated with the transformation processes used to render outputs. The price charged to customers, guests or clients should be higher than these combined costs. The difference between costs and revenues is called profit.

Efficiency is measured in total costs of goods and services sold. Productivity enhancement from a resource perspective will yield lower overall costs. As we continue to improve efficiency, costs will continue to decrease or we will be able to render higher levels of outputs with the same costs by making changes in the **transformation process**. The transformation process is a linear process that converts

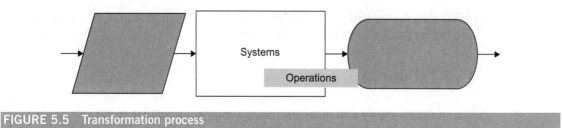

FIGURE 5.5 Transformation process

materials, human capital and technology into products and services for customers, guests and clients.

TRANSFORMATION PROCESSES

When we speak of transformation processes in service enterprises, we are really talking about our operations. This is not to suggest operations in the sense of Rooms and F&B divisions versus administrative departments. This use of the term 'operations' applies to the conversion processes in all functions, both line and staff. Figure 5.5 provides a depiction of this use of the word 'operations.'

We already know from discussions in Chapter 4 that transformation means to enact change. The operation of every work unit is to enact changes repeatedly every day. We constantly convert inputs into outputs for each of the five production systems. We could say that the operations or transformation process is the systems aspect of our production system. It encompasses all of the techniques used to transform inputs. Once we convert something, it is changed.

There are two aspects that influence the transformation process. One is called **competencies**, which are the combined knowledge, skills and abilities of our human resources. The second aspect is the **climate** that exists within each work unit contained by the service enterprise. The climate includes present worker attitudes, management proficiency and transformational systems. It is both the human and environmental dimensions of each work unit. We recall from Chapter 3 that the definition of an organizational problem is a negative gap between actual performance and standards for performance. We also know that problems may be categorized as being material resource, human resource (people) or systems problems. We do not know for sure that our human resources possess appropriate competencies until we observe them engaging in the transformation process. If we diagnose the competencies as substandard, we know we have a people problem that must be solved. If competent people are encountering difficulties performing the transformation process, then we know we have a systems problem on our hands. A systems problem is a work unit climate problem. The exact cause could lie in the transformation systems, worker attitudes or managerial proficiency. Let us consider a few examples of these situations in action.

A TRANSFORMATIONAL SYSTEMS PROBLEM

Let us take an example of a front-desk operation at a full-service resort hotel. Lately, there have been complaints from guests about the long check-in lines. In fact, we can see the long lines forming at 3:00 every afternoon. As a new manager, one would want to first see if there were a resource (input) problem at the front desk. The manager notices that there are plenty of computer terminals and each is staffed with a front-desk agent, so there does not appear to be a lack of material resources to do the job. Next, the manager checks on the competencies of the desk agents. The manager observes that each agent quickly processes each computer screen required to check-in a guest. The agents are cordial and friendly as they zip through this process. Apparently, we do not have a competency problem. Next, the manager wonders if the agents are being proficiently managed. The manager observes that all supervisors are proficient in providing support, fixing problems and jumping in to help with check-ins when appropriate. Wondering if there may be negative perceptions among the agents, the manager speaks with each one to determine their attitudes about working at the front desk. During these conversations, the new manager learns that the only complaint among the agents is the new front-office software added to the property management system (PMS) used to check-in guests. The manager learns from the agents that the new system requires five additional steps to complete a check-in. 'Aha,' the manager thinks, 'we have a systems problem here.' The manager meets with the controller who purchased the system to work out a solution. The IT guys write some new code to eliminate the extra steps and the check-in process is reduced by five steps. The check-in process becomes quicker, the lines become shorter, the complaints stop coming in and the desk agents are happier.

PROBLEMS WITH PRESENT WORKER ATTITUDES

There are only two ways for negative worker attitudes to exist in the work unit and both are the responsibility of the managers. The manager could fail to hire people with service enterprise attitudes, which result in poor job/person/environment fit, or the manager permits negative attitudes to evolve over time. Let us look at a restaurant scenario.

A new manager takes over a restaurant. She is immediately confronted with guest complaints about poor service and negative interactions with the service staff. The manager decides to diagnose the real problem. She first decides to speak individually with each assistant manager, lead (supervisor) and worker in the restaurant. She asks a number of pertinent questions of each person. She also observes the staff in action. The manager looks at the point-of-sale system (POS) to see if there are problems with order processing, plate and beverage production, distribution and tendering functions. These all seem fine to her. She checks the inventories of raw materials, equipment and supplies used in the restaurant and these all seem to be up to established pars. Next, she reviews the recruitment and selection procedures, which clearly seem to screen for hospitality attitudes among new hires. She suspects that something is happening that is causing good people to develop negative attitudes about the workplace over time. The manager decides to hire a mystery shopping service for multiple visits to the restaurant during her prearranged absences. The shopper reports come in and her suspicions are confirmed. She has a management problem, which is a people problem. It seems that the managers are competent and diligent when she is at the restaurant. But this is just an act for her benefit. When she is not at the restaurant, the managers are nowhere to be found. This confirms the comments made to the manager during staff interviews – that the managers were not supporting the staff during crucial service periods. It is the job of managers, assistant managers and leads to support the staff at all times. When they fail to live up to this responsibility, the jobs of the staff become harder to perform and resentment will eventually lead to negative attitudes toward the work unit. In this case, the new restaurant manager will need to implement an intervention aimed at redirecting the behavior of existing assistants and leads or managing them out of the organization to be replaced with responsible managers.

WHY ARE ALL ATTITUDE PROBLEMS MANAGEMENT PROBLEMS?

The answer to this question reflects upon our many discussions throughout the first four chapters of the text. We defined management as the accomplishment of the organization's objectives through the activities of others. We also noted that management functions include planning, organizing, influence and control. We recognized that managers should possess equal amounts of responsibility and authority. Finally, we learned that professional management involves articulating and achieving objectives, strategies, policies, standards and procedures.

Professional managers will hire for attitude and train for knowledge, skills and abilities. If they live up to this responsibility, they will enact appropriate recruitment, selection, training and development strategies. Professional managers provide support to the staff members through resource acquisition and allocation, systems designed to achieve standards, and interventions to ensure the flow of transformation processes. Attitudes are mental perceptions based on recent interpretations of experiences by individuals. Managers manage attitudes by managing the work unit climate. If a significant number of individuals possess negative attitudes concerning a work unit, the managers are not competently managing that climate.

OUTPUTS

Outputs are the results that occur from blending inputs with transformation processes. Figure 5.6 provides a depiction of outputs in relationship to inputs and transformation processes.

How do we measure outputs? We first want to be sure that our outputs meet our established standards. Our standards will identify the expectations for the number of outputs produced in a timely manner called **quantity standards**. We will also have **quality standards** that articulate specifications for each service or product we

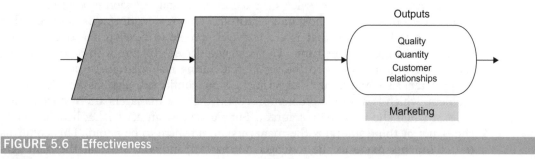

FIGURE 5.6   Effectiveness

provide. For instance, we may have a standard that states we will answer all phone calls within two rings using the scripted salutation. This is an example of a quality standard. A quantity standard for a reservations department might be to handle X number of phone calls per hour and close X number of reservations at or above an established sales rate per shift. **Total Quality Management** is a process of continuously improving inputs and processes used to achieve quality and quantity standards. Value-added management goes one step further by continuously finding ways to achieve quality standards and to increase quantity standards by working smarter, not harder. When our outputs meet the established standards for quality and quantity, we would say the operation is being effective. **Effectiveness** consists of metrics (measurements) used to evaluate outcomes in terms of quantity and quality. As we learned in Chapter 3, we could also say that effectiveness involves *doing the right things*.

For service enterprises, the ultimate outcome resulting from effectiveness is the establishment of **customer relationships**. Customer relationships are continuing patterns of interactions with our new and repeat guests and clients. Effective operations within a service enterprise will support the **marketing** efforts of the organization. Marketing is a function of acquiring and maintaining guests and clients. When we acquire a new guest/client, we are initiating a new customer relationship. When we maintain a guest/client, we are reinforcing our customer relationship with an existing (repeat) guest or client. Effective outcomes reinforce marketing strategies aimed at initiating and maintaining ongoing customer relationships. **Customer loyalty** is a measurement of the strength of an ongoing customer relationship. Smart marketing executives realize the value of lifetime customer relationships, which measures the potential revenues to be realized from a guest or client throughout his or her lifetime through repeat business generated through customer relationships.

How Can You Become a Value-added Manager?

The first step in becoming a value-added manager is to understand all we have discussed in this chapter concerning production systems and productivity enhancement. Figure 5.7 provides an overview of these.

We know that financial investments render material, human and technology resources that serve as inputs into the linear process of production. The resources are converted through a transformation process system to render outputs in the form of services and products. The objective for resource usage is to be as efficient as possible. The objective for outputs is to be as effective as possible. The answer to improving both efficiency and effectiveness often lies within the transformation process. We can reduce resource expenses and increase outputs by streamlining transformation process systems. Another option is to use system improvements to maintain current efficiency levels while increasing outputs. A final value-added strategy would be to reduce the cost of resources while maintaining existing levels of outputs. Any of these three strategies will enhance productivity levels.

A fourth option is to increase costs a little bit to earn a large increase in revenues. When we say that we are running an operation, we mean that we are adding value to that operation through productivity enhancement. Hence, value-added management is a **run strategy**. When we say we add value every day, what we really mean is we

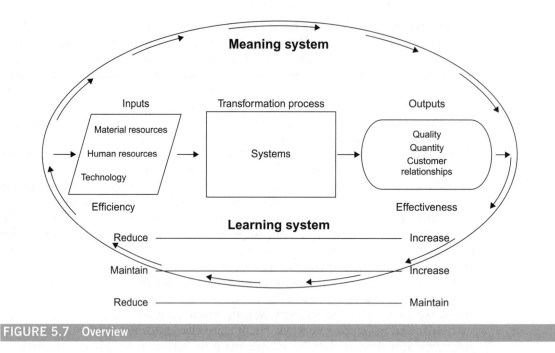

FIGURE 5.7 Overview

take steps to do this every day, so we may not realize the outcome of productivity enhancement daily, but every day we work toward this. So, at the end of the day the boss says to you, 'What have you done for me today?' You say, 'I have devised an upselling program that will start to enhance check averages. I plan to have it in practice within two weeks.' This statement lets the boss know that you are a value-added manager. This is an example of a small increase in costs (incentive payments) for large increases in revenues (increased average checks). However, as a manager, it is not your job to do these things alone.

Since you are a manager, you accomplish the objectives of the organization through the activities of others. This means that you must create value-added workers in order to become a value-added manager. What are **value-added workers** (VAWs)? They are workers engaged in continuous productivity enhancement to add value to the organization and to themselves. How can you do this? You can do this by teaching all of the workers about productivity enhancement. When you teach these techniques to the workers, you are fueling the learning system in your work unit by adding new competencies to staff members. You are also enhancing the meaning system of the work unit by providing meaningful opportunities for workers to contribute to improvements of the work unit.

A run strategy is implemented when the department is operating at a level that is acceptable to the organization. That is, when there are no significant problems in the operation and there are no specific plans for expanding the operation. If a work unit or service enterprise is experiencing significant problems, then a **fix strategy** is in order to conduct an intervention to turn the operation around. Expansion plans call for **growth strategies**. We will discuss these strategies more thoroughly in Chapters 11 and 12.

When a person sends out a resume for a management position, that resume should demonstrate that the potential manager has the skills to perform each of the operational strategies. They include running the operation, fixing the operation and growing the operation. These are the only things for managers to do from an operations standpoint. Productivity enhancement is a 'run' strategy. When we say we are maintaining an operation, that is really not true, we are running it with productivity enhancement in mind.

When an operation is in *run* mode, it is time to become a value-added manager. Balance is the key to VAM. We must always look at both sides of the productivity enhancement model. If we make a decision concerning resource acquisition or allocation, we must look at how that decision will impact the effectiveness of our outputs. If we choose to alter the quality or quantities of outputs, we must consider the impact that decision will have on efficiency. VAM is like a seesaw with efficiency on one side and effectiveness on the other. The transformation process acts as the balancing mechanism.

If we push too hard for efficiency, we may lose effectiveness. For instance, a hotel chooses to lay off many front-desk agents during a period of low occupancies, leaving the desk severely understaffed. Guests are surprised to see only two lines at a front desk with 10 computer terminals. The two harried desk agents do their best to handle the check-ins, but the task is simply too overwhelming. The guests are not happy and start to select other hotels for their next visit to town. In this case, the hotel managers are being very efficient (lower payroll) but are not being effective (losing customer relationships). Recognizing this problem, the front-office manager does a hiring blitz for desk agents. Every terminal is staffed during every shift, even during slow check-in periods. There are no lines at the front desk. Now the front desk is being very effective. But is it being efficient? The guests will ultimately start paying for those extra desk agents through higher room rates, which they might not be willing to pay. What is the answer? The front-office manager should balance efficiency and effectiveness measures with sound staffing guidelines. The manager should also continuously find ways to improve the check-in systems. That is how you enhance productivity and become a value-added manager.

Summary

We began the chapter with a discussion of value-added management, which is the process of adding value to the service enterprise by enhancing productivity in small increments during each working day. We defined productivity as a linear system consisting of inputs, transformation process and outputs. We recognized that this linear process is surrounded by nonlinear systems called meaning and learning systems that influence productivity enhancement. We recognized that productivity enhancement is a continuous practice of process improvements.

We realized that service enterprises possess different production systems than those in manufacturing, which follow a supply chain approach to product development and distribution. This led us to identify five production systems that exist in service enterprises. These are: service transactions, maintenance, repairs, product and distribution systems. We recognized that all five systems take place concurrently and repeatedly throughout the enterprise. We identified service transaction system as the hub of the other four systems. Next, we described the processes contained within each of the five production systems.

We considered the three steps of the productivity model from a senior management point of view. We identified the components that comprise the input, transformation process and output subsystems. We discussed how to manage each aspect of the productivity system to enhance performance. We realized that the transformation processing system is really the operations portion of the system. We recognized the two influencers of that system as being competencies and climate. We further established that this section of the productivity model contains systems problems, which could include sequential processing factors or human factors. We recognized that managers are responsible for managing the systems, competencies and climate of the work unit.

We discussed the measurements of productivity as being efficiency and effectiveness. Efficiency measures resource utilization and effectiveness measures outputs. We concluded the chapter with methods used to become a value-added manager. We recognized that VAMs create value-added workers who participate in the incremental enhancement of productivity by streamlining systems.

REAL-WORLD EXPERIENCES (CONTINUED)

Over the next few mornings, you shadow the servers as they make their deliveries, taking note of the number of trays left outside of rooms each hour. The servers take a service elevator to each floor of the tower. The service elevator leads to an oversized housekeeping foyer behind a service door leading to each corridor. Servers deliver their trays to specified guestrooms and practically run down the halls to the service elevators to keep up with the morning rush. You notice that they walk past used trays in the hallway.

You think to yourself, 'I know they are supposed to bring those trays back with them. But they are so busy I can understand why they don't do that.' In your mind you say to yourself, 'There has to be a better way.' As you return to the room service area, you walk past a pastry chef pushing a sheet pan cart full of pastries to an outlet. This catches your eye.

After the rush is over, Peter approaches you and says, 'Have you solved our little productivity problem yet?' You smile and say, 'As a matter of fact, I have an idea.' Peter smirks, 'I'm all ears.'

You begin, 'Here's the situation. There are plenty of trays in the hallway by 8 a.m., but it is too busy for the servers to stop, pick them up and bring them to the dishroom.' You continue, 'But we have this big housekeeping foyer in front of the service elevator on every floor.' Peter says, 'Yeah, go on.' You continue, 'The banquet department has a bunch of those carts that they don't use in the morning. So I am thinking, we put a cart with sheet pans on every floor. The servers pick up trays on their way back to the elevator. They place the trays on the sheet pans before entering the elevator.' Peter says, 'I'm with you so far.' You continue, 'We have a kitchen steward retrieve nearly full carts and replace them with fresh ones. That way the china, glass and silver go to the dishroom and the trays come back to us.' You complete your discussion with, 'And, I think it will cut our tray pickup time in half.'

At this point, Peter is smiling broadly. He says jokingly, 'Well, rookie, I think you have a plan here. I guess they are teaching you pretty well at that hospitality school of yours.' Peter concludes his joking with, 'Let's do it.'

DISCUSSION QUESTIONS

1. What is value-added management? How would a person become a value-added manager?
2. How do we manage material resources, human resources and technology resources?
3. What factors influence the transformation process? Who is responsible for managing those factors? How do we manage those factors?
4. What are outputs? What is the impact of outputs on the guests/clients?
5. Please describe, compare and contrast each of the five production systems in a service enterprise? Are any of them more important than the others? Why or why not?
6. How do we measure inputs and outputs? Are they the same measurements? Why or why not?
7. Please describe a scenario in which there is a systems problem. How would you go about solving that problem?
8. What is the role of balance in value-added management? Please be precise in your answers.
9. It has been said that value-added management is a *run* strategy. What does this mean? When should we implement productivity enhancement strategies? Are there times when other strategies might be more important? Please describe these.

CASE STUDY

You are a newly hired assistant manager in the Food and Beverage department of a large resort. The F&B Director holds monthly strategy meetings with all the managers in the department for the purpose of devising new ways of enhancing departmental productivity. At this, your first meeting, the F&B Director has invited the Controller and Marketing Director to participate in the meeting. You walk in with your manager, grab a cup of coffee and take a seat. Since you are new to this operation, you observe the dynamics of the following conversations closely:

The F&B Director starts things off, 'Ladies and gentlemen, I have invited Sheila the Controller and Mark the Marketing Director to help us with our productivity enhancement initiative. They will provide us with some new ways of looking at our operation.' After a preliminary overview of the current status of the initiative, Mark starts to comment, 'Look,' he says, 'You got to spend money to make money. If you want to enhance productivity, you need to drive revenues. The only way to drive revenues is to invest in advertising and promotional activities to increase business.' Sheila jumps in, 'Hold on there, Mark. The budget is the budget. You don't enhance productivity by overrunning your expense budgets. That's ludicrous,' she says. Mark retorts, 'Oh Sheila, not this again. Quite frankly, if you had your way, you would be on the floor with a stop watch conducting time and motion studies to reduce labor.' She defensively replies, 'You bet I would! Efficiency is the key to every operation. Our biggest single expense is labor dollars. So, it makes sense to reduce those expenditures as much as possible.' Mark cajoles, 'Increasing revenues is dollar wise and cutting costs is penny foolish. Put more bucks on the top line and that will take care of the bottom line,' he says. Sheila replies, 'Mark, apparently you were asleep when they talked about scientific management in your school. If you had your way, we would be out of business.'

This discussion continues to go back and forth for quite some time. After a while, you decide to go get another cup of coffee...

Preliminary Questions

1. How would you describe Sheila's approach to managing resources?
2. How would you describe Mark's approach to managing resources?
3. What thoughts are going on in the minds of the F&B managers as they listen to this argument?
4. Do you tend to agree more with Mark or Sheila? Why?

Conclusion

As you sit down with your second cup of coffee, you begin to realize that this meeting is getting out of control and that this is not the first time that Sheila and Mark have had this argument. The F&B Director just rolls his eyes as the two continue to go back and forth with their managerial philosophies. You realize from your training that both Mark and Sheila are correct in their philosophies and that they simply need to put the two concepts together.

Since this is your first meeting, you are a little shy. But after this elongated debate, you finally say, 'Couldn't we reduce labor costs and increase revenues by developing the talents of our people?' A hush fills the room as everyone turns to stare at you. 'Well,' you continue, 'that would be the human resource approach to enhancing productivity.' The F&B Director smiles at you with approval. 'Next week,' he jokes, 'we will invite Sheila, Mark and the HR Director to be their referee.'

Conclusion Questions

1. How would you describe the human resource management approach to productivity?
2. Why would a human resource manager tend to be more balanced than the average marketing or accounting manager?
3. What are the pros and cons of Sheila's and Mark's philosophies on productivity?

CHAPTER 6

Organizing Resources, Structure and Systems

OBJECTIVES

In this chapter you will learn to:

1. Understand inter- and intradepartmental organization activities.
2. Identify relationships among inputs, systems and outputs.
3. Recognize the organizing role of various levels of management positions.

REAL-WORLD EXPERIENCES

You have been working as an intern at the front desk of a large resort hotel. You work with front-desk supervisors, who report to a front-desk manager, who reports to the front-office manager. The supervisors and front-desk manager seem to be closeby to where you work during every shift. The front-office manager seems to be there during busy times, but she spends a lot of her time away from the desk. You begin to wonder to yourself, 'I wonder what the front-office manager does, when she isn't near the desk.'

To be continued...

INTRODUCTION

We already know that middle-level managers spend most of their time dealing with the organizing function within and among departments, while senior managers focus mostly on planning and supervisors (leads) are mostly focused on control functions. But all managers must demonstrate the ability to organize resources, systems and outcomes to some extent. As we know, this means coordinating, prioritizing and sequencing activities that occur throughout the linear and nonlinear systems associated with the productivity model. This chapter is about the tasks associated with managing the organization of resources, systems and outputs.

CORPORATE EVOLUTION

If we reflect for a moment on our discussion in Chapter 2, we recall the emergence of classical management during the early years of the management evolution. There were two classical management scholars who were early researchers in the area of organizational functions for corporations. The first was the father of bureaucratic management, Max Weber. The second individual was Henri Fayol, the father of administrative management. There are managers and researchers who still believe in the classical approach to management. As we already mentioned, the advantage associated with management evolution is the ability to use all of the managerial tools and concepts. Most of what was put forward as 'new ideology' by Fayol's famous management recommendations would be considered to be common sense in today's management practice.

As bad of a connotation as bureaucracy has today, there was a time when it was necessary to organize organizations. At first, this aspect of management was overlooked because most organizations of that day were entrepreneurial ventures that were never intended to become large firms in the first place. But eventually, these companies found themselves growing to become large entities requiring the organization of management activities. It is still true today that an entrepreneurial venture may grow into a large entity that will eventually require professional management.

Let us say a person opens a full-service restaurant serving lunch and dinner with a unique theme. Business starts out slow, but word gets around town about the great food and service. In a year, the restaurant has lines of waiting guests out the door, and is doing four turns on a good night. Now, the owner decides to expand with a second unit. How will the owner ensure the same levels of culinary specifications and guest service as experienced at the first restaurant at the new location? The answer is – professional management practices intended to replicate in the new store what the owner's family does in the original store. The second store is a success. Now, the owner is thinking about offering franchises of the concept. How will the owner ensure that the original standards are provided in the franchise units? The answer is – professional management. The first store was an entrepreneurial venture, in which success did not require a good deal of organizing activities. With the second store, and ultimately the franchised stores, the operation becomes complex and requires professional management to organize activities to ensure consistent standards.

This is why the classical managers presented research on administrative and bureaucratic management during times when entrepreneurial start-ups grew to become large businesses. In the practice of management, the scholarly discipline that shows us the techniques for organization and structure comes from a specialized area called Organization Theory.

ORGANIZATIONAL DESIGN AND STRUCTURE

Let us consider organizational design and structure. We recall from Chapter 3 that structure consists of relationships among organizational functions. The organizational chart is a graphic representation of these relationships. Figure 6.1 provides an example of an organizational chart, with arrows demonstrating the flow of information required for the coordination of resource distribution, systems and outcomes.

The middle managers are located in the third line from the top in the figure. Formal structure refers to those relationships designated by the organization (the boxes in the chart). Informal structure refers to those informal relationships established by people within the organization. Pay a visit to the employee cafeteria of a large hotel and watch the middle managers. Notice that they have bonded and sit together talking 'shop' and discussing other things. They have established an informal relationship with each other on the basis of the organizational need to coordinate activities and resources among departments. Now, look around the cafeteria and notice the middle manager eating lunch alone. It is likely that the manager will not be around for long. Why? This is true, because this manager has failed to bond with other middle managers. Middle managers spend most of their time organizing resources and activities with other departments. While that manager occupies a place on the formal organizational chart, the lack of informal relations with other middle managers may adversely affect his/her performance.

Organizational design provides structures that place work areas into departments. The most common structure is called the functional structure, which structures departments by function such as: finance, operations, human resources, sales etc. Some organizations choose to structure by product or services. This would look like: luxury, full-service and limited-service for a hotel chain. Some large and dispersed organizations choose the geographic structure. This would be: Northeast, Southeast and Western regions. Other organizations choose to structure

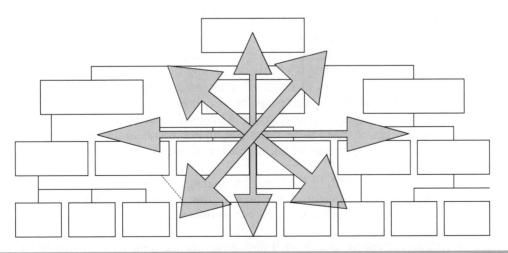

FIGURE 6.1 Directional flows of communication through the organization chart

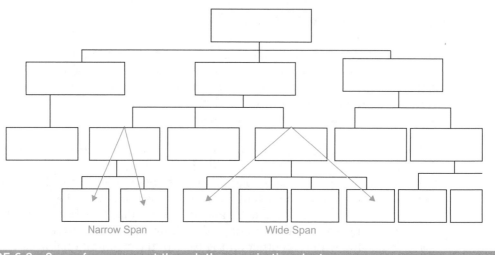

Narrow Span   Wide Span

FIGURE 6.2   Span of management through the organization chart

by customer. An example would be professional, association and government groups for a convention sales management firm.

Division of labor is another aspect of organizational structure. Some managers suggest that specialization is the key to division of labor (highly specialized workers). Others believe workers should be generalists. Actually, division of labor should be designed with the fulfillment of individual workers and the needs of the organization in mind. Most people in today's environment seem to be generalists, the opposite of specialists. We should ask – what can each individual do to contribute to the whole system that is satisfying to him or her, and reasonable in terms of workload? It is this point specifically that causes us to take exception with the classical managers. They would not take individual fulfillment into consideration in the process of organizational design. The aim of classical management is to enhance efficiency. Thus, we have the assembly line, which has people doing mindless work, which gives them time to think about things like labor strikes. Modern managers, instead, create work that is fulfilling to individuals, sacrifice a little efficiency and make up for it on the effectiveness side. This is the systems paradigm discussed earlier in Chapter 1 of the text.

The division of labor is clearly defined by the organizational chart, which provides a representation of spans of management. **Span of management** is measured by the number of direct reports to a single manager. The more direct reports, the wider the span of management. This used to be called as span of control, but the term has changed to be more descriptive by including all of the management functions. Comparisons of narrow and wide spans of management are depicted in Figure 6.2.

The average width of total spans of management within an organization is used to determine the height of the organization's structure. Organizational structure ranges from very tall to very flat across organizations and industries, as shown in Figure 6.3.

The current trend is toward flattening organizations by removing layers of middle management. Taller organizations seem to have more **centralized decision making**, in which decisions are made at the top of the organization and passed

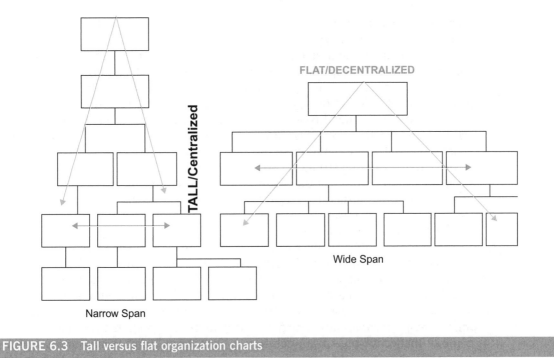

FIGURE 6.3 Tall versus flat organization charts

down. **Decentralized decision making** often occurs in flatter organizations in which individuals share authority and responsibility for decisions. **Scalar relations** identify chain of command. If individuals report to one boss, there is **unity of command**. If middle managers were to follow scalar command chains to implement organizational activities, the process would be from that middle manager to the top of the organization and back down the chain representing another middle manager. If this were the rule, it would take forever to implement an idea. The **gangplank** provides means for individuals to interact laterally across departments without having to run up and down the scalar chain. The sideways arrows across the middle-management positions represent the gangplank relationships. This is the organizing activity that bonds middle managers.

How Do We Create an Organizational Structure?

Organizational structure comes from organizational design activities. The mission, grand strategy, size, scope and services of the enterprise will determine the appropriate design of organizational functions. For instance, a medium-size hotel or resort may create a division called the *Rooms and Related Operations*. A typical rooms division includes front office, PBX, housekeeping and guest services departments. Related operations might include retail, recreation and spa facilities. If these are limited service areas, then it might make sense to house them within the domain of the rooms division. However, if any of these areas are greatly expanded, we might choose to add a member of the executive committee with expertise to oversee these areas. These positions might include directors for retail, recreation or spa operations. In such as case, the rooms division would narrow its scope to include traditional departments and related operations would fall within the scope of management of each appropriate executive.

We learned about job design and job analyses in Chapter 3. These processes are part of the overall organizational design methods used to devise organizational and departmental structures discussed in Chapter 4. This is a scientific process that provides the best design of organizational responsibilities, reporting relationships, authority and accountability for every position contained within each major category of functions and services throughout the enterprise. Once an organizational chart is devised, service enterprise managers should think seriously before making changes to the existing structure. We know from our discussions of systems that a small change to one area of the organizational structure will have a ripple effect on other areas of that structure. Organizational structure is the result of a long-term commitment to the effectiveness and efficiency of the service enterprise, as we discussed in Chapter 5 of the text.

The only times that changes to the organizational chart are appropriate are during phases of growth or reengineering. Organizational growth involves expansion in terms of scale and/or scope of operations. These scenarios could include additional outlets, enlarged existing outlets and new diversified outlets, such as the addition of an all-inclusive health spa to an existing resort. Enterprise reengineering is a major turnaround strategy resulting from poor performance that is an outcome of ineffective organizational design. Both growth and turnaround strategies are costly endeavors that require careful feasibility analyses and *what-if* contingency planning. These activities should be performed by managers with very high levels of expertise in the disciplines of organizational design and development.

How Do We Manage Interdepartmental Organization Activities?

Interdepartmental organization involves prioritizing and coordinating activities between our department and other departments. We learned through earlier discussions in this chapter that the gangplank is a means for managers to interact laterally to organize activities. This is an example of a structural approach to facilitating interdepartmental organization activities. We learned in Chapter 2 that scientific managers were concerned with engineering aspects of work performance with absent consideration of relational skills. We know from the big picture of management evolution that both engineering and relations approaches are required for effective management. As department managers, our influencing skills are crucial to the organization of interdepartmental activities. A department manager does not have authority over managers of other departments. Yet, each department manager does possess interdependent relationships with other managers. An individual department manager relies on those who manage related departments. The performance of each department is dependent upon the performance of other departments. Savvy department managers will establish positive **quid pro quo** relationships with other departments. A quid pro quo relationship exists when something of value is exchanged for something of value. In this case, the valuable exchange occurs in the form of interdepartmental support. So, we manage interdepartmental organizing activities through influencing skills used to establish positive relationships with other departments.

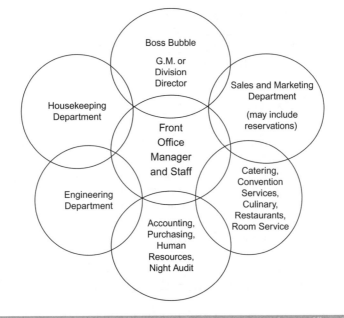

FIGURE 6.4 The Bubble Management Model: an example for a hotel front office department

One author provided us with the 'nucleus theory' of managing interpersonal relations with lateral members of the organizational structure. We could call this the Bubble Theory of managing interpersonal relations.

Imagine yourself and your department as being contained within a bubble. Along the edge of the bubble, there are other bubbles, which represent those departments or individuals who you rely upon to effectively accomplish tasks. A sample Bubble Management Chart is represented in Figure 6.4.

How Do I Practice Bubble Management?

The experienced department manager will view the organizational positioning of the department in a way that is similar to the departments on an organizational chart. The exception to the *bubble* view is that each interdependent department is pictured as a cell that resides on your department's bubble. The manager realizes that the success of the department team depends on linkages with teams in the surrounding bubbles. The manager also recognizes the importance of maintaining working relationships with representatives from these teams. The Boss Bubble includes the senior administrative assistants. While these people have no formal authority over the department manager, they are important links to the president, general manager and executive committee members. Administrative assistants are sometimes referred to as **gatekeepers**. This means they guard access to the executive offices and influence the executives' opinions concerning various department managers. The savvy department manager is cognizant of the importance of administrative assistant personnel due to their professional relationships with the bosses.

While the Boss Bubble may be the most intruding force on the department, it does not require as high a level of maintenance as some of the other bubbles. For instance, the crucial bubbles for a full-service hotel front-office manager would include the housekeeping, engineering and sales functions. These areas require closer linkages than some of the other areas. Thus, these are areas in which more effort is expended to establish and maintain interdepartmental relations.

WHAT ARE ORGANIZATIONAL BANK ACCOUNTS?

Every individual who represents a department in a bubble possesses an organizational bank account with each department on the bubble. The organizational bank account is similar to a financial bank account in that people make deposits and withdrawals. Like a financial bank account, the objective of the organizational bank account is to avoid becoming overdrawn. Ideally, one would want the deposits in the organizational bank account to exceed withdrawals, just like a financial bank account with a positive balance.

WHAT IS MY ORGANIZATIONAL CURRENCY?

While the currency in a personal bank account is money, organizational currency is in the form of 'favors' and 'cooperation' with other department managers. A front-office manager who has done many favors for members of departments on the front-office bubble will maintain a positive balance in the organizational bank account with that department. Also, other department managers learn that they can count on the front-office manager to help out in times of need. This could be called an *organizational credit rating*. A positive bank balance and a high credit rating among comanagers means the front-office manager will receive cooperation from other departments on a regular basis.

While a high interdepartmental credit rating warrants equal levels of cooperation and support from members from other departments, managers with low credit ratings find themselves in positions in which other departments will not be willing to lend support to them or their departments. In the case of the front-office manager, a high credit rating with the housekeeping department (based on a high account balance) will result in fast inventory turns, concise information, cooperative prioritization of preparing rooms for check-in and occasional special favors. If the front-office manager maintains a poor rating with the sales department (low bank account balance), it is likely that group rooming information will be slower and less accurate, rooming blocks will be incomplete, guarantees will not be communicated and contracts or billing information may be unavailable.

A poor credit rating with a single department may cause a ripple effect for the department inside the bubble. For instance, the poor credit rating with the sales department will slow down the flow of group check-in information, which is passed on to other operating departments. Let us say that a group is scheduled to receive amenity fruit baskets, which are prepared by members of the culinary department. The room service department may be responsible for delivering the fruit baskets to the guestrooms. If the sales department releases the group rooming information at the last minute, the amenity orders go to the culinary department at the last minute, and the room service staff will have to deliver the baskets at the last moment. In this case, a poor relationship between front office and sales has created a hardship for the culinary and room service departments. Who gets the blame? The front-office manager and staff. The front-office manager then blames the sales manager, which worsens the front-office manager's credit rating with the sales department.

Some middle managers believe in the misconception that their sole purpose is to make the boss happy. In the pursuit of this quest, they alienate workers and comanagers. They make themselves look good at the expense of their comanagers. They do this by shifting blame to other departments and stealing all the credit for performance success. For a short period of time, these managers establish very 'fat' bank accounts with their bosses, at the expense of their comanagers. Eventually, the boss is faced with the dilemma of supporting the manager who is alienating other departments. An inexperienced boss may decide to declare bankruptcy in all other bank accounts by seeking to replace the other department managers. On the other hand, an experienced boss will recognize that one manager is seeking accolades at the expense of the other managers.

There are five performance criteria when dealing with fellow managers. They are the same criteria used among managers and workers. They include: expectations, procedures, resources, accountability and consequences. A manager must meet the expectations and procedures of the comanagers. The manager must share resources with them. The manager must be accountable for interactions among comanagers. Finally, the manager will receive the consequences of inappropriate actions, not from a boss, but from other managers. Therefore, organizational bank deposits involve interacting with other managers in ways that meet or exceed expectations and procedures while sharing resources and levels of accountability. Conversely, failing to meet expectations – refusal to comply with procedures, hoarding of resources and pointing blame will result in bank account withdrawals. Each bank deposit results in the positive outcome of comanager collaboration. Too many bank withdrawals result in the consequence known as lack of cooperation – maybe even comanager retaliation. Plenty of withdrawals with no deposits results in overdrawn accounts with departments on the bubble. A number of overdrawn accounts will result in departmental bankruptcy. When the department becomes organizationally bankrupt, it goes *out of business* as far as support from lateral departments. Eventually, the bosses in the organization will realize the need to change the management of the overdrawn department. If the entire organization becomes bankrupt, the shareholders will be likely to make the management changes at the top of the organization.

Let us consider how a newly appointed middle manager might use the diagram in Figure 6.4 listed above. When a new middle manager takes over a department, she could place the name of her department in the center bubble. She would then list the names of her bosses in the top bubble and include the names of administrative assistants. Next, she would think about those departments or individuals who have the greatest impact on her and the department. She would list them in the vacant surrounding bubbles. As she reflects on each completed bubble, she might consider what she can do for them, and what they can do for her. She would equate those things she can do for them to potential deposits in her organizational bank account. Things they can do for her would be considered to be potential withdrawals from her department's bank account.

ORGANIZING SYSTEMS

We already know from our Chapter 4 discussions that both linear and nonlinear systems must be managed in service enterprises. We recognize the linear system as containing inputs (resources), transformation processes (systems) and outputs (services and products). We recall that nonlinear systems surround this linear process in the forms of internal meaning and learning systems, as well as external environmental factors. In Chapter 5, we refined our observations to consider the multiple production processes that occur in service enterprises simultaneously. We identified service transactions that are surrounded by maintenance, repair, product and distribution production systems.

First-level managers (assistants, leads, supervisors) organize microsystems, which are those contained within a single work unit. Middle managers are responsible for organizing both departmental and interdepartmental systems. Senior managers organize interdepartmental systems, as well as macrosystems, which are those that comprise the entire service enterprise by participating as members of an executive committee.

WORK UNIT SYSTEMS

When we view the systems within a single work unit, we usually find that they are narrow in scope, but complex in terms of production processes. Consider an example for the culinary work unit within a single restaurant, as depicted in Figure 6.5.

Prior to opening for operation, the back-of-the-house (BOH) staff engages in pre-prep activities by requisitioning raw materials, kitchen sanitation activities and the stocking of supplies at various stations. Materials and supplies preparation constitute distribution production systems, while the sanitation pre-prep is a

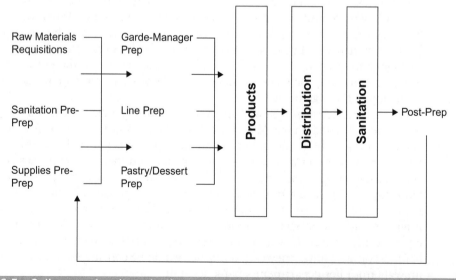

FIGURE 6.5 Culinary work unit production systems

maintenance production system. Once the pre-prep phase is completed, the culinarians begin the preparation phase to supply the cold line (garde-manger), hot line and dessert stations with required items. At this point, the restaurant opens for business and the stations produce products (plates) that are distributed by the service staff to seated guests. During this process, items must be sanitized and replenished into the stations to continue with the product production and distribution processes. At the close of business, certain postpreparation activities take place and the cycle begins again for the next business day or meal period.

Notice that at this microscopic level the systems appear to be linear with the pre-prep phase feeding the prep phase and so on. This would be the systems view of the BOH work unit manager. The front-of-the-house (FOH) manager would have a similar view of that work unit with emphasis on distribution systems, which are the crux of FOH operations.

Department Systems

A middle manager would view these systems more holistically as service transaction, maintenance, product and distribution systems. The middle manager would be additionally concerned with physical plant maintenance and repairs. Figure 6.6 depicts the systems perspective of a restaurant manager who oversees BOH and FOH activities.

The same systems lose the appearance of linear sequential activities as we step further away from a work unit operation by moving into middle-level management. BOH and FOH systems work in linear lockstep from the perspective of work unit managers. The restaurant manager with responsibilities for both sees them in less detail because he/she is viewing the blended operations from a perspective of

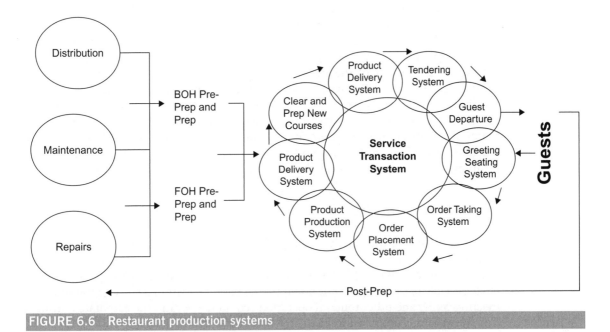

FIGURE 6.6   Restaurant production systems

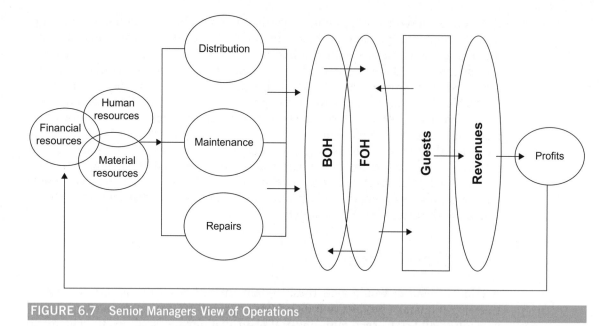

FIGURE 6.7   Senior Managers View of Operations

interdependent relationships. This tells us that activities are linear and interdependent relationships are nonlinear. The restaurant manager views the operation from a 'bigger picture' perspective than the BOH and FOH work unit managers.

Enterprise Systems

Owners and senior-level managers would view the operations of a single restaurant from an even broader perspective than the view of the restaurant manager. This viewpoint is presented in Figure 6.7.

We can see that the viewpoint of a senior-level manager consists of a wider span of the supply chain when compared to the models used by work unit and middle managers. To the left of the model, we consider resource acquisition and allocation. The senior manager will consider revenues and profits on the right side of the model. From this perspective, a portion of the profits are retained to provide future financial resources to support the acquisition and allocation of human and material resources, which are inputs in relation to the operation. As was the case when we compared work unit manager and middle manager perspectives, the senior manager's viewpoint of a single restaurant is broad, yet comprehensive.

Corporate Systems

Chain affiliates are ultimately managed by senior corporate executives. Corporate-level senior managers view each service enterprise from far away within the confines of an off-site corporate office or headquarters. These corporate officers possess the broadest view of each restaurant, hotel, theme park, recreation facility, entertainment/meeting venue and other tourism operations contained within the corporate portfolio. This viewpoint is described in Figure 6.8.

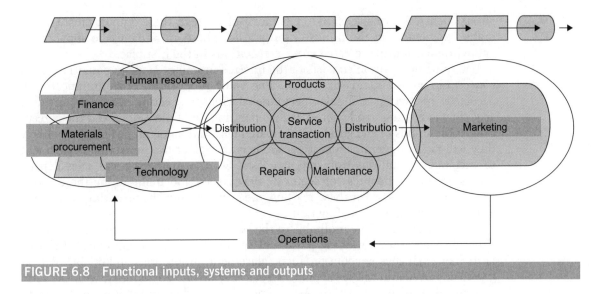

FIGURE 6.8 Functional inputs, systems and outputs

The corporate executives view each enterprise unit from a functional perspective of inputs, systems and outputs that move through the supply chain continuum. We can see from the model that each division of the supply chain follows its own subsystem of inputs, systems and outputs, as noted at the top of the figure.

The four resource functions include Finance, Materials Procurement, Human Resources and Technology. Each of these functions performs sourcing and acquisition of resources. For instance, the finance department will find sources of capital funds and acquire those. Purchasing professionals will source and acquire material products. Human resource practitioners are responsible for sourcing and acquiring workers and technology managers do the same with hardware and software packages. Sourcing (finding) and acquiring (attaining) activities comprise the inputs to the systems for each of the four resource departments.

The transformation processing systems within the four resource departments convert acquired resources into a ready state to be used by the enterprise. Finance personnel will transform bulk investments into allocated funding for various departments within an enterprise. The purchasing unit will divide and place materials into available inventories. Human resource practitioners will process, orient and train newly acquired workers for positions within the organization. Technology modifies and otherwise prepares software and hardware products for end users within the enterprise. These activities comprise the transformation process conversions that take place within each of the four resource provider departments.

The outcomes for all resource provider departments consist of distribution systems. The finance area distributes available funds, while the procurement area creates available inventories for departmental distribution. The human resource office distributes knowledge, skills, attitudes and abilities in the form of talented employees, while the technology personnel distribute ready systems for workers and guests to use. The outputs of resource departments serve as inputs via distribution systems to operating departments.

We have already examined the inputs, systems and outputs of operating units in detail in this chapter. The outputs of these departments serve the needs of guests/clients. As we discussed in Chapter 1 of the text, these outputs create memorable experiences in the minds of our guests. These are intended to support the **value proposition** that created guest expectations in the first place.

The value proposition consists of the inferred promises made to potential guests concerning our standards of service. The value proposition is communicated to guests by marketing and sales personnel during prospecting activities aimed at acquiring new guests and clients. If the operating units meet or exceed the perception in the minds of the guests as compared with our value proposition, it is likely they will visit us again as repeat guests. It is the job of the marketing department to encourage visitations from repeat guests. So, the marketing and sales departments are in the business of acquiring new guests and maintaining the existing level of repeat guests. For these reasons, the outputs from the operating areas serve as inputs to the marketing function.

Repeat guests are more profitable to the service enterprise than first-time guests. This is so because marketing personnel spend money to communicate to prospects (potential guests) about products, placement, promotions and pricing. Repeat guests do not require these expenditures, as they are already familiar with the services provided by the enterprise. As we know from earlier discussions in this chapter, profits are used to provide new financial resources that are invested into the enterprise. The outputs associated with marketing and sales personnel will result in some profits from acquiring new guests and even higher profits from maintaining and expanding the base of repeat guests. Hence, the outputs of the marketing and sales departments become inputs to the financial resource side of the supply chain, which starts the process all over again.

Corporate officers recognize the series of interdependent relationships that exist among all of the functional departments within every enterprise contained within the service portfolio. The resource functions maintain interdependent relationships with internal profits and outside sources from an input perspective. They transform resources and distribute them to the operating areas of the enterprise. The operators use these resources as inputs to transformation processes that generate service transactions, as surrounded by distribution, maintenance, repairs and product production systems. They render guest services as outputs, which serves as inputs to the marketing value proposition used to acquire and maintain guests. The profits generated from the guests serve as new financial resources that regenerate the cycle of interdependent relationships. This composite provides the *big picture* associated with the inputs, systems and outputs contained within every service enterprise, from the smallest operation to the largest conglomerate service industry corporation.

SUMMARY

We began this chapter by recognizing that all managers must perform organizational functions within and among departments. We know that this is one of the primary functions for middle-level managers; however, all managers are organizers to some extent. We learned that managers organize inputs, systems, outputs and structures. Organizational skills require knowledge of scientific and relational aspects of service enterprises.

Toward the beginning of the chapter, we recognized that all of the practices learned in Chapter 2 of the text contribute to our ability to organize activities within and among departments. With these skills in mind, we explored the nature of organizational structure and design. We looked at organizational charts that represent the reporting relationships in organizations. Within this context, we considered the concepts of division of labor and spans of management. We learned that some organizations use tall structures, while others operate with flatter structures. We noticed that tall organizations seem to possess more centralized decision-making activities, while flatter ones shared responsibilities for decisions throughout the organization. We further understood scalar relationships within the hierarchy, as well as gangplank methods used for lateral communications.

Once we understood the nature of organizational structures, we engaged in conversations concerning the design of organizations. We borrowed on our discussions from Chapter 3 concerning job analysis and job design to emphasize these processes. These discussions led us to consider the relational aspects of interdepartmental organizing activities.

We recognized that the interdependent relationships among department managers necessitate the development of collaborative relationships, as emphasized by the Bubble Management process. We went on to discuss the practices associated with interdepartmental relationships and organizing activities. We came to the realization that interdependent relationships exist among systems, as well as managers.

We considered the perspectives of organizational systems to include inputs, transformation processes and outputs from the perspective of managers with varying levels of responsibilities. We first considered the work unit manager perspective using an illustration of a culinary department within a restaurant. We expanded this view with a restaurant manager's perspective of the interdependency of relationships between BOH and FOH. We then elevated the viewpoint to that of an owner or general manager and finally considered the systems perspective from the standpoint of corporate officers.

Once we reached the corporate systems perspective, we were able to witness the interdependent relationships among all of the organizational functions that exist throughout the supply chain. We concluded that this perspective may be applied to small as well as very large service enterprise corporations.

DISCUSSION QUESTIONS

1. We learned in Chapter 2 about the evolution of management, which include scientific management and behavioral approaches to management. How would you apply both of these to the organizing functions of managers at the work unit, department and senior levels of management?

2. Discuss the organizational flows of communication, spans of management, scalar chains, gangplanks and tall versus flat organizational structures. How would you use this knowledge as a practicing manager?

3. From an interpersonal relations perspective, how would you manage organizing activities with members of other departments? Please discuss the specifics of this activity using a typical department management position as an example.
4. Describe your understanding of the similarities and differences among perspectives of inputs, systems and outputs from the perspectives of work unit managers, department managers, owners and general managers, and corporate officers.

REAL-WORLD EXPERIENCES (CONTINUED)

One day you are having lunch with a front-desk supervisor and the front-desk manager. Eventually, the front-office manager, Tiffany, became the topic of discussion. At this time, you mention, 'You know, I have been wondering what she really does. I mean, I see you guys a lot more than I see her during each shift.' Chad, the supervisor, and Brooke, the front-office manager, start to chuckle. 'What did I say?' you respond to them.

Brooke says to you, 'We aren't trying to be rude with our laughter.' She continues, 'It's just that most new people don't understand the nature of the job of a department head.' Brooke paused, and then continued, 'We really run the department and Tiffany takes care of the relationships with the other departments.' You wonder out loud, 'Why would she need to do that?'

Brooke smiles and says, 'Well, let me put it this way – have you had many problems with the housekeeping department during your shifts?' You think for a moment and reply, 'No, not really.' Brooke says, 'How about the engineers?' 'No, they're pretty good, actually,' you reply. Chad chimes in and says, 'Is the sales department pretty good at providing us with room blocks in a timely fashion?' 'Yup,' you reply. Brooke then says, 'Can you think of any department that doesn't cooperate with us?' You think for a moment and say, 'No, I can't think of any.'

They both smile at you and say, 'That is what Tiffany does for us as the front-office manager.' They continue, 'Don't get us wrong, that isn't all she does, she is responsible for all lobby guest areas and is always on hand when we are weeded at the desk.' You think for a moment and finally say, 'I just assumed all departments would naturally want to work together.'

Brooke replies, 'You would think that would be the case. But you should have seen this place before Tiffany took over. We had problem after problem because the last front-office manager just couldn't take care of the other departments.' She finishes, 'Our jobs were not much fun back then... come to think of it, that is probably why the last front-office manager got fired.'

CASE STUDY

You work in a human resource office for a large resort as a management trainee. Lately, you have been assisting the employment relations manager by working as an employee relations representative. In this capacity, you spend most of your day listening to employee complaints about the way their supervisors treat them or interpreting policy issues that they did not bother to look up in their employee handbooks. You find the work to be emotionally draining, since most of the time you are dealing with negative scenarios. However, it is also rewarding from the aspect of being in a position to help solve disputes and answer employee questions.

At about 3:15 p.m., a woman, Bonnie, storms into your office, apparently experiencing a fit of rage. Bonnie works as a dispatcher in the Room Service department on the second shift that begins at 3:00 p.m. She takes over for the morning shift dispatcher, a guy named Bif.

Bonnie slams her hand on your desk and screams, 'I've had it with this job! I'm walking out right now. This Bif is a total idiot and if you don't fire him, I quit! It's him or me, you decide!' she shouts. You look at her calmly and say to her, 'What seems to be the problem?' 'What's the problem, what's the problem?' she blurts, 'I'll tell you the problem, Bif is a creep, a nerd, an SOB, a slob, a derelict, a lazy bum, a stupid idiot and an ugly, egotistical jerk, that's the problem!' She yells at you. Sensing a potential employee personality conflict, you ask Bonnie, 'Have you discussed this with your manager?' She laughs, 'My manager, I haven't even seen my manager in three days... my manager, what a joke!'

'I see,' you say empathetically, 'I'll tell you what, Bif is gone for the day by now. Would you be willing to go back to the Room Service department and start work to give me an opportunity to look into to this for you?' Bonnie replies, 'I'll go back there now, but after tonight I'm outta here if you don't get rid of that bum.' She leaves your office in a huff.

Preliminary Questions

1. Identify at least three of the most important observations in this scenario.
2. At this point, what do you think is the cause of Bonnie's behavior?

Conclusion

As soon as Bonnie leaves you walk into the employment relations manager's office to describe the interaction you just encountered. The wise ER manager says to you, 'So what do you think we are dealing with here?' You say, 'Sounds like a personality conflict to me.' 'Maybe' replies the manager, 'How about the absence of the room service manager during a shift change, what do you think about that?' You reply, 'It seems like an important time for the manager to be around to me, since one shift is closing and another is starting, while the phone keeps ringing. Maybe, the manager was called into a meeting or something.' 'Maybe' says the ER manager, 'But your report says that Bonnie hasn't seen the manager in three days, which tells me he hasn't been available for three consecutive shift changes. What to you think about that?' You jokingly reply, 'I hate it when you make me think.' He chuckles, 'I know, but that's my job in training you.' You say, 'Well, I guess we need to find out why the room service manager hasn't been around for these shift changes.' The ER manager replies, 'Sounds like a good start.'

The ER manager picks up the phone and dials the room service manager. 'Hi Bob, could you stop by here right away? I think there is a situation you should know about.' The room service manager arrives about five minutes later. 'What's up?' he asks. The ER manager explains the situation. After citing all the facts, he finishes with, 'What disturbs me, Bob, is that when we asked if this complaint went to you, we were told you haven't been around during the shift changes, which is contrary to the policy in our managers' manual.' Bob replies, 'Yeah, the F&B director has had me putting together a project for the past couple of weeks and I have gotten so caught up in it that I forgot to check with the dispatchers during the shift change. I know exactly what the problem is and the cause is really not a personality conflict between Bif and Bonnie, it's the overlap situation. Normally I make sure Bif keeps the area neat for Bonnie's arrival. Then I usually have him close out in the service area so he isn't in the booth while she sets up. To give her a hand, I usually handle the phones for her for about 15 minutes. Whenever Bif thinks I'm not watching, he leaves Bonnie a sloppy area and makes snide comments to her during the overlap because he knows she has a 'short fuse.' Bob finishes by saying to both of you, 'I'll take care of this and let you know when it's fixed so you can check back with Bonnie to make sure everything is alright with her.'

'Thanks, Bob' the ER manager says. After Bob departs the office, the ER manager smiles at you and says, 'Another day, another experience.' 'Let me know when you get a tough one,' he jokes with you.

Conclusion Questions

1. Now that you have more information, what would you say if you had to critique the way this situation was handled? Be specific with your comments.
2. If you had to differentiate between symptoms of a problem and an actual problem, how would you analyze this case by listing symptoms and real problems?
3. If you had to place your 'core problem' into categories such as human resources, systems and material resource problems, which categories would apply to the core problem(s) you have already identified?

CHAPTER 7

Human Resource Management and Influence Skills

OBJECTIVES

At the end of this chapter you will learn to:

1. Understand how the function of management influences human behavior.
2. Define the three components of management influence.
3. Describe best practices for managers in a communication process.
4. Explain how managers can influence attitudes and motivate within internal communications systems.

IN THE REAL WORLD

Loren is a friend of yours who graduated college last year. Because she always worked part-time in the industry throughout her school years, she landed an assistant outlet manager job immediately upon graduation. You run into her at the local Starbucks and the two of you decide to catch up on old times.

You say to Loren, 'Wow, you have a great job with a great company, I'm so proud of you.' 'Yeah,' Loren replies, 'But you know my real love is human resource management.' She continues, 'But it seems there are very few jobs out there and when I do apply for one of them, it seems they already know who they are going to hire.' You tell her, 'Yeah, I have heard that from other people. The HR offices use the excuse that applicants don't have actual experience, yet no one will hire them to get some experience. It sounds like a real catch 22 situation.'

To be continued…

INTRODUCTION

It is common knowledge that the practice of **human resource management** (HRM) is prevalent in most organizations ranging from small- to medium- to large-scale corporations. The current-day human resource (HR) manager has direct influence on the strategic direction and thinking of both private and public sector organizations. As a result of this influence, HRM and human resource development (HRD) officers command large salaries that are often in the six-figure range, with some senior practitioners reported to earn annual direct compensation in excess of $250,000[1]. The reason for this is a relatively current shift in organizational thinking. From the time of the industrial revolution through the middle of the twentieth century, workers were considered to be nothing more than expenses for labor that created a financial burden on the profits of their respective companies. Since employees were considered to be expense items, managers believed they were expendable in the same fashion as any material resource used to get the job done, such as a jackhammer or a shovel. When a worker became too tired or ill to do the job, he was replaced with another worker who was willing to take that job. For this reason, scientific managers (who were mostly trained as engineers) espoused supervisory practices that completely overlooked the 'human factor' in worker productivity enhancement[2]. We learned in Chapter 2 that during the early 1960s, a small group of progressive management practitioners changed their thinking about workers from that of 'expense item' to one of **human capital**, which means that an employee is an asset to the organization and is thus worthy of investment and development. The next section of the chapter takes us on the journey from 'then' to 'now.'

A HISTORICAL PERSPECTIVE

Let us look back in the history that occurred during the last few decades of the nineteenth century, just before the commencement of scientific management. An agrarian economy existed at that time in which wealthy landowners employed the services of 10 or more workers who were labeled as slaves, serfs, crop sharers or indentured servants. Unfortunately, these landowners served as 'role models' for the unenlightened managers who ran large factories during the Industrial Revolution.

During the early Industrial Revolution, top managers were usually wealthy factory owners and supervisors were individuals with the ability to coerce and intimidate the workers. History books are rife with examples of factory owners abusing child workers, paying insufficient wages and utilizing the 'my way or the highway' form of motivation. Human resource management was not even a thought that crossed these early managers' minds, much less considered as a viable practice. Employees of those times were considered to be as disposable as tissues.

The fact is that the first corporate HR department is barely 100 years old. When compared with the disciplines of medicine, mathematics and the fine arts, the practice of human resource management may be considered to be in its infancy. For this reason, some managers continue to challenge the viability of human capital investment and development practices that are championed by their HRM peers.

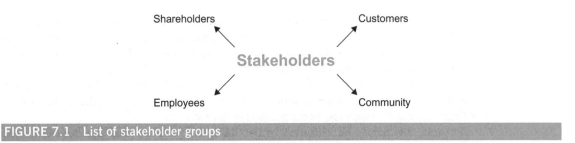

WHO DO CURRENT HR PRACTITIONERS SERVE?

Some of corporate America's current chief executive officers have been accused of providing mere 'lip service' concerning HRM practices[3]. Most annual reports commence with a 'letter to the stockholders,' proclaiming that the workers are the firm's 'most valuable assets.' Some individuals note that this is the only attention paid to the employees throughout a typical fiscal year[4]. While some executives continue to label human resource practices as 'necessary evils,' more proactive managers embrace them as part of the mainstream of corporate strategic planning and direction. Interestingly, many of these firms are those held in good standing among shareholders, customers and the community at large. A proactive CEO will tell you that 'solid HR practices are just good business.'

Who are the stakeholders or 'constituents' served by human resource management practitioners? In actuality, HR practitioners have the same responsibilities in the area of stakeholder service as any other corporate manager. The **stakeholder group** consists of constituents for an organization. Members of the stakeholder group include the categories of **shareholders** (stockholders in publicly traded firms), **employees**, **customers** and the **community**. Shareholders are individuals who are investors or owners of a company. Employees belong to the stakeholder group that consists of the workers for an organization. In service enterprises, we refer to customers as guests and clients who purchase our products and services. Finally, the community consists of outside stakeholders who are not members of the other three stakeholder groups. These could include vendors, neighbors, industry sector colleagues, regulators and others. From a practical perspective, human resource strategies are aimed at balancing the needs of each of the stakeholder groups attached to the service enterprise.

In healthy organizations, the needs of each stakeholder group will be satisfied more or less equally. On the other hand, dysfunctional companies will serve the needs of one stakeholder group (the shareholders, for instance) at the expense of another group (such as the employees). When this happens, the senior HR manager is at odds with the value system of the organization (or at least the CEO) and will attempt to stabilize the imbalance in the interests of both groups. Figure 7.1 provides a description of the stakeholders as the people who the HR practitioner and every other manager in the organization should serve in balanced proportion.

WHAT IS HUMAN RESOURCE MANAGEMENT?

In the current century, there is both good and bad news associated with government regulation of employer/employee relationships. Employment regulation takes place through legislation aimed to protect workers and applicants from unfair and unsafe treatment, as well as providing accommodations for those who have special needs in the workplace. Some consider the regulations to be 'bad news' as there are very high costs associated with legal compliance as determined by the courts. However, certain HR practitioners consider this good news, as the legal environment has created high-level positions in organizations to ensure the protection of a firm's assets through legal compliance strategies.

Human resource practitioners must be proficient in the development and implementation of **legal compliance** strategies in order to protect the assets of the organization from legal damages. For this reason, they are trained to become experts in the areas of legal environments and employment law. It is important for HR practitioners to balance sound managerial practices with legal compliance issues. Hence, HR managers should be highly trained in the practice of professional management. Some individuals incorrectly contend that all that is needed in legal compliance area are the services of a labor attorney. While this person may be well versed in the law, it is likely he/she will not be trained in the field of management. For instance, if you operate in a state in which the courts establish that employee handbooks are construed to be implied-in-fact contracts, an attorney will advise you to refrain from the distribution of the handbooks. Good legal advice, perhaps; but what about your duty as a manager to clearly and effectively articulate the expectations for performance in the organization, as well as identify all terms, conditions and privileges of employment? Human resource practitioners must balance professional management practices with labor law strategies. Some individuals tend to confuse the term **labor law** with another term, **labor relations**. These are two individual concepts. Labor law deals with state and federal legal regulation and tort (common law) doctrines applied to employment relationships. Labor relations law, however, deals with the right of individuals to elect union representation within organizations.

Labor relations is an aspect of the legal environment that is separate from the field of employment law. The field of labor relations identifies the legal rights of workers and organizations concerning the right to organize and engage in collective bargaining processes. As is the case in employment law, strategies are required to assist practitioners in dealing with union as well as nonunion workplace environments. Of course, all of the aspects of the employment legal environment arose from prior practices in organizations that were deemed by society to be detrimental to those engaged in employment relationships. This would lead us to believe that certain managers acted unethically in their dealings with employees in the past, which created the perceived need for the society to protect employees through the actions of the legislature and the courts.

All HR practitioners should become experts in the practices associated with **business ethics**, since it is the role of human resource managers to act as protectors of employee rights as well as those of other stakeholder group members. Business ethics is a branch of normative philosophy applied to business decisions and behaviors. Figure 7.2 shows the relationship of legal and ethical concepts as the 'what' of human resource management.

Now that we know the why and what of human resource management, we could ask the question, 'How do we practice HRM?' This is a crucial element of training for HR practitioners as well as all professional managers.

FIGURE 7.2 The relationship of legal and ethical concepts as the 'what' of human resource management

We learned in Chapter 3 of the text that all managers must be strategic thinkers. The same is true for human resource managers. Every HR function requires taking the steps necessary to develop and implement sound strategies. For instance, HR practitioners will implement strategies for **recruitment** and **selection** practices. Recruitment is the process of generating qualified pools of applicants for each position in the organization. This is different from selection, which is the process of choosing the best applicant for each position. The selection process results in newly hired individuals with the service enterprise. How do we go about giving new and existing employees the knowledge, skills and abilities to do the job? Or, how do we develop employees for the next higher-level position? These fall within the domain of **training** and **development** strategies. Training provides knowledge and skills required for employees to perform in current positions, while development provides abilities required for future promotional opportunities within the organization.

Once we train employees, we would like them to remain with our organization for a reasonable period of time. HR practitioners call this function, employee retention, which is the opposite of employee turnover. **Employee relations** strategies are implemented for service enterprises to retain their best and brightest staff members (employees), which results in lower employee turnover rates. A big part of employee retention comes from clearly established expectations for performance and honest, objective feedback on how well employees meet those expectations, which is a basic aspect of professional management. These components and others are contained within a **performance management system** for an organization.

OTHER HUMAN RESOURCE FUNCTIONS

HUMAN RESOURCE CONTRIBUTIONS TO ESTABLISHING EXPECTATIONS

Since the difference between human resource management and personnel administration is the strategic focus of human capital, the HR manager is an important participant in the entire strategic planning process that includes goals, strategies,

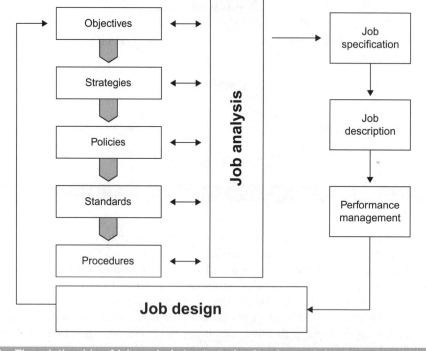

FIGURE 7.3 The relationship of job analysis to strategic planning and development within an organization

policies, standards and procedures. Once these are in place, the human resource manager focuses on job design activities for the organization. Job design is the practice of arranging tasks, duties and responsibilities into positions. Technically, a job consists of the tasks, duties and responsibilities contained within a position. A position consists of the jobs performed by an individual. This is why people refer to their positions as their 'jobs' when speaking in slang terminology.

The primary function in the job design process is called **job analysis**. Job analysis consists of steps taken to identify knowledge, skills, tasks, duties, responsibilities and the working environment for each individual who holds a position. Figure 7.3 demonstrates the relationship of job analysis to strategic planning and development within an organization.

Job analysis activities should take place for every position in the organization at least once per year. Of course, there are many organizations that have never performed job analysis, but this does not mean that the inaction is the correct way of doing business. The first result of job analysis activities is the creation of a document called **job specification**. The job specification (job spec, for short) identifies the knowledge, skills, attitudes and abilities that determine the qualifications for a specific position. These documents are used as part of the recruiting and selection processes. Another document resulting from job analysis is called the **job description**. This document articulates the tasks, duties, responsibilities, reporting relationships and sometimes the criteria for performance evaluation relative to a particular position. So, the job specification identifies the qualifications of a potential employee in specific position, while a job description articulates the activities for the jobholder. The final outcome of the job analysis process is the criteria used to evaluate actual performance as compared to standards, which is part of the performance management system. Evaluations of workplace performance are known as performance appraisals.

Job analysis is a key driver of almost every human resource strategy. For instance, job specs and job descriptions are used to provide qualifications and realistic job previews during recruitment and selection activities. Compensation plans are determined by qualifications and activities of positions as well. Career planning and development activities are also driven by the job analysis function, as well as training, orientation, performance management systems and health/safety plans. Of course, there are safeguards to be taken in the design and implementation of job analysis activities. From a legal perspective, HR practitioners must ensure that any tests used are statistically valid and reliable for job relatedness. Also, the ADA has had an impact on the format of job descriptions, which must include essential duties listed in order of importance. Table 7.1 shows an example of a job description.

A number of methods may be used to collect data for job analyses. These include observation, work sampling, interviewing, questionnaires and combination methods. Work sampling is the collection of statistical samples of work being observed. In most cases, HR practitioners use a combination of observation, questionnaires and interviews for data collection. There are behavioral aspects of job analysis activities that require consideration on the part of participants. Any time an employee is being observed or asked questions about the job, it is a cause for anxiety. People are naturally creatures of habit and they fear those factors that may interrupt their routines by causing schedule changes or additional tasks and duties. Also, it is natural, especially during times of the media reporting corporate downsizing, for employees to be concerned that their jobs will be eliminated. For these reasons, it is essential for the job analysis practitioner to take honest and empathetic approach to collecting the data for analysis. Table 7.2 provides the basic steps involved in the job analysis process.

THE RIGHT OF EMPLOYEES TO KNOW THE EXPECTATIONS FOR PERFORMANCE

The information provided so far in this chapter concerns the primary right of individuals in the workplace. That right is to be professionally managed, which includes the processes presented here. The strategic approach to managing individuals begins with an audit of the corporate mission for the organization. Next, objectives for performance are established. Objectives should be specific, measurable, attainable, challenging and include who is responsible for 'what' is to be accomplished by 'when,' which is the due date for completion of the objective. Each objective requires action steps called strategies. Strategies lead to policies, which are broad guidelines for performance in the organization. From those policies, standards are established to provide clear and objective expectations for performance. For each standard, there is a list of procedures that walk the worker through the process of meeting the standard.

Since the human resource practitioner acts in the capacity of 'managers' manager,' it is incumbent upon the HR manager to ensure that the practices presented so far actually exist and are communicated in every department and work unit in the

TABLE 7.1 Sample Job Description

Position: Executive Administrative Assistant	Reports to: General Manager
Department: Administrative and General	Subordinates: None

Basic Function: Provides administrative support to the General Manager by coordinating calendars, handling correspondence, receiving visitors, screening telephone calls and general filing and administrative area maintenance.

Essential Duties:
1. Arrive at the work area at the scheduled time and prepare the executive offices for business within 30 minutes of arrival.
2. Handle all incoming phone calls using the standards and procedures for telephone etiquette.
3. Collect and distribute incoming mail items, place-outgoing items in the mailroom.
4. Complete correspondence, filing and other administrative tasks within prioritized timelines.
5. Prepare the office for closure at the end of the business day.

Additional Duties (as assigned):
1. Accompany the General Manager to specified meetings and client functions.
2. Make administrative decisions for the administrative staff in the absence of the executives.

Qualifications:
1. Ability to process communications and computations at a level equivalent to the standards for a high-school graduate.
2. Typing speed of at least 70 wpm.
3. Ability to solve administrative problems and prioritize tasks.
4. Diplomacy skills consistent with those required of an executive-level manager.

Working Conditions:
1. Works in an ergonomically designed environment.
2. Eighty percent of working time requires sitting in an upright position.
3. Twenty percent of working time requires mobility to various areas within the organization.

Measures of Effectiveness:
1. Measured to the standards articulated in the Standard Operating Procedures Manual for Executive Administrative Assistants.
2. Demonstrated willingness to make sound administrative decisions and show flexibility in work routine.
3. Demonstrated efficiency and effectiveness in the prioritization and completion of administrative tasks in a timely manner.

TABLE 7.2	Sample of a Job Analysis Process

Job Analysis Process

1. Identify existing positions and review documentation for each job.
2. Explain the job analysis process to subjects and supervisors in areas being analyzed.
3. Conduct the analysis in the most unobtrusive manner possible.
4. Prepare job descriptions and job specifications on the basis of the findings of the analysis.
5. Revise performance management systems to reflect the changes made to job descriptions and job specifications.
6. Maintain and update job descriptions and job specs throughout the period of time until the next job analysis process.

organization. The absence of such practices in an organization is an indicator of mismanagement, which is a breach of management responsibility. Although it is seldom the case that legal challenges occur on the basis of the breach of management responsibility, mismanagement does constitute a form of negligence in an organization.

THE RIGHT OF EMPLOYEES TO KNOW THE RULES AND DISCIPLINE PROCEDURES

While standards and procedures articulate performance expectations, **rules** consist of the codes of behavior within the workplace. Failure to behave within the expectations set by the rules results in misconduct on the part of the worker. In some instances, the behavior may be of such a severe nature as to constitute gross misconduct. An issue of gross misconduct is usually grounds for employee termination from the company resulting from the first incident. So, while the SOP sets the guidelines for performance, the Rules of Conduct set the guidelines for acceptable behavior in the workplace. Once the worker has completed training, failure to meet the conduct or performance standards will result in discipline. Discipline has a negative connotation with most individuals due to its punitive applications. However, the definition of discipline is a form of training that redirects behavior to achieve desired performance and/or conduct. As is the case with all management practices, discipline must be administered in a fair, uniform and consistent manner for all individuals. Also, the organization should have a process of progressive discipline in place. This means that the process requires disciplinary warnings that result in appropriate consequences for repeated undesirable actions. This is where the '3 strikes' analogy in organizations comes from. However, it is not as cut-and-dry as most organizations would like to believe. For instance, some companies have policies that state that the first incident of failure to perform or misconduct results in a verbal warning. This is misleading, as a manager never has a disciplinary interaction with an individual without creating a document of the incident and how it was addressed.

So, in proper practice, there really is no such thing as a verbal warning. Instead, there is a 'first warning,' in which the incident is discussed along with required corrective actions on the part of the employee, ending with a notice that further incidents will result in progressive disciplinary action up to and including involuntary

TABLE 7.3 Sample of a Corrective Interview Form

Corrective Interview	
Employee Name:	Date:
Position:	Supervisor:
Date of Hire:	Date of Incident:

What was done wrong?

What was the adverse effect on the organization or other employees?

What must be done to correct the situation?

Employee Comments:

Note: Any further occurrence of this nature will result in disciplinary action up to and including suspension from duties and/or termination.

Reason for Action	Action Taken
(check below)	(check below)
Violation of policy	Coach and Counsel
Job Performance	Disciplinary Warning 1,2,3
Misconduct or other inappropriate behavior	Suspension (investigation)
Other Just Cause	Termination

Employee Signature/Date	**Witness Signature/Date**
Supervisor Signature/Date	**Executive Signature/Date**
DHR Signature/Date	**GM Signature/Date**

separation from the company. Whenever this type of discussion takes place, it should be done in the privacy of an office and a third party should be present to witness the interaction. Hence, there are three people in the room for a discussion of disciplinary warning, the supervisor, the employee being addressed and a third-party manager to witness the discussion. All parties should sign a printed copy of the warning notice at the conclusion of the conversation. In the event that the employee does not want to sign the notice, the supervisor merely indicates 'Refused to Sign' on the form, which is confirmed by the witnessing manager. Table 7.3 shows an example of a Corrective Interview form used for counseling and discipline discussions.

Notice that the form requires a thorough explanation of exactly what was done wrong, the effect on the organization or other employees, the required corrective action on the part of the employee and a space for the employee to list comments about the situation. You may ask, 'Why have an area for employee comments?' This is a good question about a very important aspect of employee rights.

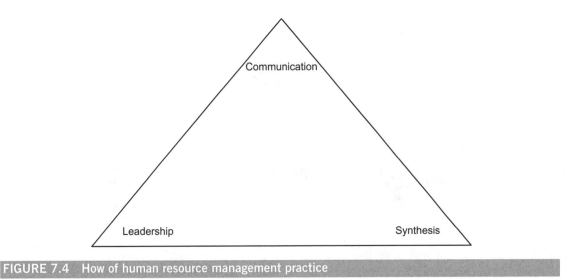

FIGURE 7.4   How of human resource management practice

How Do We Practice Human Resource Management?

All managers, especially HR practitioners, possess expertise in the influencing skills of management. Figure 7.4 depicts the 'how' of human resource management practice.

Now that we know about the constituents and practices of HR professionals, we are ready to engage in the three most important influencing processes (tools) of management. These are **communication**, **leadership** and **synthesis** skills.

The first process is effective communication skills, which are perhaps the manager's most powerful influencing tools. It is possible for a person to know all there is to know about management and yet be unable to perform as an effective manager if he/she lacks the ability to effectively communicate with individuals and groups. Communication processes are used to exchange ideas for the purpose of sharing information and concepts.

There are many definitions of communication in organizations. This section presents a simplified definition for us to use. Communication may be defined as the sharing and understanding of information among individuals[5]. While this sounds simple, the process of engaging in effective communication is really quite complex. This is due to the individuality of people. Individuality impacts personal perception. Each person perceives information in different ways. Therefore, while everyone in a group of people may hear the same message, that message will mean different things to different people. A perfect example of this is the old game of passing a message along a line of people. Each person whispers a message in the ear of the next person in line. At the end, the message repeated by the last person in line is usually very different than the original message. Take this phenomenon and multiply it times the numerous incidents of communication that take place among people in an organization. It becomes evident that organizational communication is a very complicated topic. Consultants tell us that lack of effective communication is the most prominent problem in organizations[6]. A model for organizational communication is presented in Figure 7.5.

Notice that the model starts with the Sender. The Sender thinks of an idea. This idea is merely a thought in the Sender's mind. The Sender must encode the

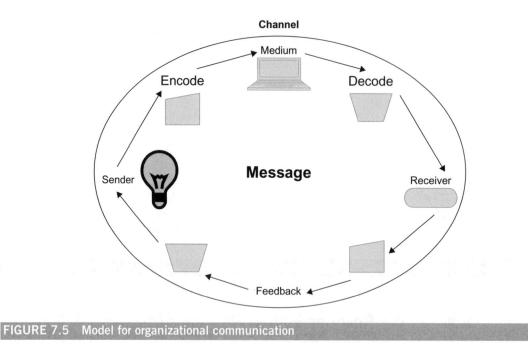

FIGURE 7.5 Model for organizational communication

thought into a message. This means the Sender is using words to symbolize the concepts within the thought. After the Sender identifies the words or symbols to be used to represent the thought, the Sender chooses a Medium for the message. A Medium may be written formats such as memos or letters. A Medium could also be electronic, such as a telephone, intercom or email. A medium could be verbal, such as an interview, a meeting or an informal discussion. All of these examples represent means through which a Sender packages and sends a message. Since the message is packaged for the Receiver of the message, the package is known as the Medium. The Medium is the format used for broadcasting a message to intended Receivers. The medium carries the message to the Receiver, who then must decode the message. The process of encoding into a medium and decoding by the receiver comprises the channel of the message. After the Receiver decodes the message, a Feedback loop is used for the Receiver to respond to the message. The Feedback loop closes the cycle. This permits the process of Sender, Medium and Receiver to begin again.

Consider an example to demonstrate the Communication Model. A manager has decided to enact a change in staff scheduling practices. The manager notices that individuals sometimes prefer specific days off for various reasons. In the interest of fairness, the manager develops an idea that will provide members of the staff to request days off before the schedule is made for the following week. So far, this is just a concept in the mind of the manager. Now, the manager must put the idea into words (encoding). The manager jots down a few notes concerning the idea. Next, the manager must decide on how the message will be sent to the staff. The manager decides to announce the new practice in an upcoming shift meeting and to follow up with a printed notice concerning staff requests. In this case, there are two Mediums: one is the meeting (verbal) and the other is a notice (written). A shift meeting is scheduled for Wednesday. At the meeting, the manager presents the new procedure for requesting days off prior to each week's posting of the schedule. The manager looks at the facial expressions and body language of the participants to ensure that all understand the new procedure (feedback). Finally, the manager asks if anyone has any questions about the procedure (feedback). A member of the staff indicates that she has a question. At this point, the feedback loop is closed and a new communication process is about to begin. The person with the question becomes the Sender. She thinks about what she wants to ask, finds words to encode her message, verbalizes the words in the form of a question (Medium) and watches the manager (Receiver) for a response (Feedback). As the manager decodes the question, the manager prepares a response; thus, the manager is starting a new communication process as the Sender.

This is the Communication Model at work. We communicate so quickly that we do not recognize the steps involved in our communications. We develop ideas, encode them, place them in a medium, send them for decoding, watch or listen for feedback and await a response in fractions of seconds.

WHY ARE COMMUNICATION SKILLS IMPORTANT FOR MANAGERS?

If the practice of management involves accomplishing the objectives of the organization through the activities of others, then it seems that the ability to effectively communicate is crucial for the success of the manager. Imagine knowing all there is to know about the field of management. Also, imagine how effective you would be with that knowledge if you could not talk, write or otherwise communicate with the workers. No matter how much knowledge a person has in the field of management, if that person is unable to communicate with other people, the tasks and goals will not be accomplished. Therefore, that person will not be a successful manager.

LISTENING SKILLS

How well do most people listen? According to some experts, the majority of individuals listen at an effectiveness rate of 25%[7]. Also, the experts indicate that individuals who work in senior management positions spend as much as 85% of their communication time listening to other people[8]. It is a fact that listening skills top the list of effective managerial communication skills. While effective listening is the most important communications skill, it is perhaps the least taught skill.

One reason for possessing effective listening skills is that you, as the manager, will make decisions on the basis of information presented to you. You will be involved in the scenarios listed in Table 7.4.

Each of the activities listed in the table above requires effective listening skills for maximum decision making. Therefore, the smart manager is in the listening business. As managers assume higher levels of responsibility, their listening skills become more important.

BARRIERS TO EFFECTIVE LISTENING

Effective listening requires time, energy, concentration, technique and objectivity. Listening actively actually requires more effort than talking or writing. Many managers

TABLE 7.4 **Management Scenarios**

Item	Scenarios
1.	Problem solving
2.	Conflict resolution
3.	Performance evaluations
4.	Resource allocation
5.	Brain storming
6.	Strategic planning
7.	Organizing departments
8.	Customer satisfaction indicators
9.	Scheduling
10.	Assigning duties
11.	Hiring personnel
12.	Coaching and discipline
13.	Policies and rules
14.	Practices and procedures
15.	Other activities to support your staff members

TABLE 7.5 **Barriers of Effective Listening**

Diverted attention
Mood and experience
Judgmental attitudes
Noise (distractions)
Planning responses
Lack of interest
Failure to ask probing questions

think they are actively listening to people, when they are, in fact, creating barriers to effective listening. Some barriers to effective listening are listed in Table 7.5.

Here are examples of a few typical scenarios:

An individual arranges to meet with the manager. As the individual approaches the manager's office at the appointed time, the manager is on the phone. The manager waves the person into the office without missing any of the phone conversation. The person sits down and waits for the phone conversation to end. Finally, the manager hangs up the phone and addresses the person sitting in the office. As the person begins to speak, the manager shuffles through the papers on the desk. This is an example of diverted attention. The manager is not fully listening to that person, who is likely to feel uncomfortable with the lack of attention.

In another situation, a person may enter the manager's office only to find that the manager is under severe stress. The manager is obviously fatigued and distracted. This is an example of mood as a barrier to effective listening. Perhaps the person wants to talk to the manager about a problem that has been recently addressed by many other workers. Upon hearing the topic of discussion, the manager indicates disinterest in what the person has to say; the manager has already 'heard it all.' This would be an example of experience as a barrier to effective listening.

In another scenario, a person is attempting to explain to the manager the reason that some action was taken. The manager appears to be closed minded. This is an example of judgmental attitude as a barrier to effective listening. In another instance, there is a small meeting with four participants. One participant stands up and gazes out the window. Another person is doodling. Another is tapping a pencil. These are examples of noise as a barrier to effective listening. In this case, noise does not necessarily have to mean noise in the audible sense. Any distraction, even silent distractions, creates a form of distraction called noise.

PLANNING THE RESPONSE

One expert describes the two-person conversation as a Multiple Party Monologue. In this scenario, both parties are concentrating on what it is they want to say. Both start talking, and the first person to draw a breath is declared the listener[9]. However, this person is not really listening. Instead, the person is mentally rehearsing a response to interject when the speaker stops talking.

This is often the case in organizational discussions. Planning the response is a common barrier to effective listening. When this occurs, the speaker should reiterate the message until the listener indicates that it has been heard by responding appropriately. Another technique for overcoming this barrier is to permit the intended listener to talk first. After all has been said, the barrier of mental rehearsal should be overcome.

MOOD AND EXPERIENCE

Most individuals have high and low spans of attention throughout the workday. Some individuals are 'morning people,' others are 'late bloomers.' Peak times are those during which the individual is energized and focused. Since effective listening requires focused energy, it may be appropriate for managers and supervisors to schedule discussions during peak periods. Often, workers will approach the manager during an inconvenient time. The manager now has a dilemma. If the manager takes the time to talk with the worker, it is possible that the manager may be distracted and not listen effectively. On the other hand, if the manager does not talk with the worker, the worker may feel that the manager does not value the worker's existence. Perhaps an appropriate response on the part of the manager would be to reinforce that the worker's feedback is important. However, due to the current level of activities, it may be an inappropriate time for the discussion.

The manager might further state that the discussion should take place when both parties are able to effectively concentrate on the topic. The manager would then proceed to schedule an appointment for the discussion.

LACK OF ATTENTION

In every department, there seems to be one or two workers who spend large amounts of time discussing seemingly unimportant issues with the manager. The manager eventually becomes programmed to believe that these people will waste the manager's time. In these cases, the manager must work to overcome this judgmental barrier. In order to do this, the manager must assume the optimistic view that one of these times, this person is going to focus on an issue of substance. The manager thus expends effort to listen effectively, just in case this becomes that opportunity. A word of caution to the inexperienced manager: Some individuals prefer talking to working. The manager must determine if the worker's visit is a work avoidance tactic. If it is suspected that this is true, the manager should suggest that the worker schedule another time for the discussion.

FORMAL AND INFORMAL COMMUNICATION

Formal communications take place when people are representing the interests of the organization as part of their appointed duties. A manager who conducts a performance appraisal is communicating formally because the manager is acting in an appointed capacity and is engaging in a form of communication that will be documented for the record. Other types of formal communications include, but are not limited to, memos, letters, meetings, bulletin board postings, announcements, policies, procedures, standards and newsletters.

Informal communications exist outside the mainstream of the organization's communications channels. A commonly cited example of informal communications is called the 'grapevine.'[10] Practically, all members of an organization (minus a few senior managers) participate in the grapevine. It is the informal communication process that takes place among people within the organization or industry. Usually, the grapevine consists mostly of rumors, innuendo, speculation and hearsay information. Topics of communication may extend beyond organizational issues into people's personal lives. The grapevine is often labeled as the 'rumor mill' or the 'word on the street.' At times, the grapevine may be a source of accurate information that travels faster than the flow of information in the formal communications process. Regardless of the accuracy of information traveling through the grapevine, managers are advised to pay close attention to what is being communicated. The grapevine is an important source of information concerning the attitudes and morale of workers in an organization. Some studies indicate that the speed and accuracy of information within the grapevine increases significantly in organizations with poor formal communications flow[11]. The opposite seems to be true for organizations with open, honest and free-flowing channels of communication.

Managers also possess opportunities to engage in constructive informal communications with workers. As a matter of fact, experienced managers often report that they get much more done while acting informally than they do through formal communication modes.

Nonverbal Communication

A good deal of information gained during face-to-face interactions comes from nonverbal cues. These include body language, facial expressions, eye contact, posture and gestures. Some research indicates that as much as 75% of information is gained through observing nonverbal cues[12]. Interpreting nonverbal behavior is often subjective. Cultural differences provide varied interpretations associated with nonverbal cues. For instance, for people of western European cultures, lack of eye contact may indicate dishonesty. For individuals from other cultures, the same action may symbolize respect for authority[13].

Choosing Message Media

Recall from the Communication Model that the Sender encodes a message into a Medium for transmission to the Receiver(s). Media may take the form of informal conversations, email, meetings, notes, memos, letters and other forms of transmission. Most forms of media may be classified in one of the two major categories. The first category is written media. This would include electronic media such as email. The second category is verbal interaction.

Like most people, managers have a tendency to avoid confrontation. For this reason, some managers seem to prefer placing messages in written format as opposed to engaging in verbal interaction. In many instances, putting messages into writing may be less constructive than face-to-face interaction. There are many reasons to avoid written forms of communication. Face-to-face interaction provides both parties with opportunities to extract information through nonverbal cues discussed in a previous chapter. Personal interaction often adds to the perception of importance of the topic of communication. Also, people feel important when they are invited to interact with a manager or supervisor. Finally, a familiarity often develops as a result of personal interaction. As long as professional distinctions are maintained, familiarity makes the work environment comfortable. Therefore, it is suggested that managers take every appropriate opportunity to communicate verbally with members of the staff.

There are occasions that call for written communication media. Written messages have posterity; that is, they last for long periods of time and provide future reference materials. Also, written communications provide documentation of an event for future reference or as a matter of record. More formal occasions call for written media. For example, a worker who has demonstrated superior performance may appreciate a formal letter of congratulations from the manager. One recommended technique is to use hand-written thank you notes sent to staff members for appropriate reasons. Of course, any issue that requires documentation requires the use of written communications. Finally, conversations or meetings may be clarified through written follow-up documents.

Managers must decide on the appropriate communication media for each set of circumstances. Whenever possible, it is suggested that personal interaction be chosen as a medium for communication. Some circumstances may warrant verbal interaction with written follow-up correspondence. The problem with overreliance on written communications is the perceived lack of importance of memos and other correspondence in most organizations. This is due to the paper avalanche and information overload associated with written messages in organizations.

DIRECTIONAL FLOWS OF ORGANIZATIONAL COMMUNICATIONS

Recall the communication channels cited in the Communication Model. The Medium is the means of message transmission. The channel is the direction of transmission throughout the organization's hierarchy (organizational chart). Many managers are familiar with the traditional downward direction of communication. The managers send directives downward through the organizational chart, and workers adhere to the directions. Managers should be aware that effective communications require flows of information in multiple directions. Figure 7.6 illustrates the directional flow of communications.

Notice that communications flow in many directions in a healthy organization. Directions include upward, downward, lateral and diagonal flows. Upward flows should include open feedback to managers who support those working on the line. Lateral flows provide organization of tasks among operating departments. Diagonal flows provide support information from higher levels in the organization to line workers. Upward diagonal flows provide feedback to diagonal support networks.

Communication skills are vital to a manager's ability to accomplish the objectives of the organization through the actions of others. Therefore, the responsibility for communicating effectively in all directions lies squarely with the immediate supervisor. Messages must be honest and appeal to the perceptions of others to be effective. While written communications are sometimes appropriate, they are often less effective than verbal interactions. The communications model demonstrates the development of the message by the Sender, the transmission of the message through a Medium, the sending of the message through the Channel, the decoding of the message by the Receiver(s) and the Feedback loop. The Feedback loop

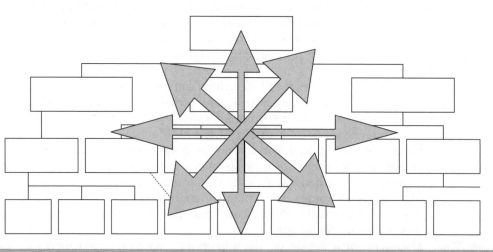

FIGURE 7.6 Directional flows of communication through the organization chart

closes one communications sequence and starts another sequence. Therefore, the Feedback loop goes beyond clarifying the Receiver's interpretation of the message. The grapevine is an example of an informal communication system. In a healthy organization, it is recognized that complaints and grievances are useful and important parts of the communication process.

OTHER INFLUENCING SKILLS

The very best real-world HR practitioners are considered to be 'manager's managers.' This means they are people who show other managers how to be professional managers. It is important for all HR managers to possess thorough knowledge concerning the practice of **leadership** skills, as we will discuss in Part IV of the text. Leadership is the demonstrated ability to influence others to willingly participate in activities. All professional managers must be completely versed in the knowledge and practice of these skills.

All management processes and information are merely academic if we are not able to apply them in real-world settings. We call this ability, **synthesis**. Synthesis is the ability to apply abstract concepts in a realistic setting. We learned about the value of synthesis during our Chapter 4 discussions on learning organizations and will revisit this topic from a leadership perspective in Part IV of the text. Management synthesis requires that we reflect upon combinations of knowledge and experiences. This reflection is how we make sense of professional management, HRM and leadership practices. Figure 7.7 shows the whole picture after we put together the 'who, what and how' of human resource management in service enterprises.

Notice that we begin our discussions with our constituent group, otherwise referred to as the stakeholder group that consists of shareholders, customers, employees and the community. This is represented by the center of the diagram, in which it is our contention that the interests of all parties should be kept in balance.

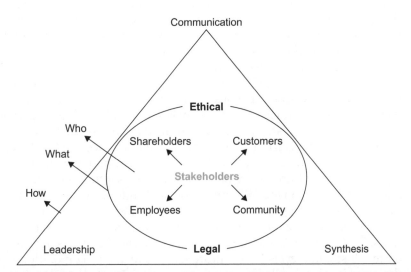

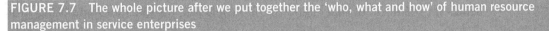

FIGURE 7.7 The whole picture after we put together the 'who, what and how' of human resource management in service enterprises

The eclipse balances the 'what' of our responsibilities to the stakeholder group. We possess the duty, responsibility and accountability to do business in a legal and ethical fashion. In doing so, the HR practitioner protects the long-term interests of the shareholders by protecting the assets of the organization from legal liability. He/she protects the employees by ensuring fair, uniform and consistent management practices, which trickles to the customers, who deserve to be treated in the same manner. Finally, by being legally and ethically responsible, the organization is guaranteed to be a good neighbor to the community in which it does business, which includes vendors, other suppliers, the competition, the general industry, government officials, and neighbors in the vicinity surrounding the physical plant, as well as other members of society.

Finally, we conclude our discussions with sections that present the skills that enable HR practitioners and other managers to make these things happen. The human resource practitioner must be an effective communicator in order to ensure that the organization balances its responsibilities to each of the stakeholder groups. This effort requires leadership capability, which is particularly necessary if the HR practitioner intends to become a 'manager's manager,' as we recommended earlier in the chapter. And, as noted in the cliché, 'It don't mean a thing if you ain't got that swing[14],' we must 'swing' into action as managers by using the skills at each corner of the outer triangle in the figure, which are communication, leadership and synthesis.

CULTURAL DIVERSITY

What is **culture**? The experts provide numerous definitions of this term. One simple definition is the shared values, beliefs and attitudes among a group of people. Usually, we think of cultures as pertaining to ethnic groups or regions of national origin. It is true that regional and ethnic cultures possessing shared values, attitudes and beliefs do exist. The values for one culture may be incongruent with those for another culture. When individuals disagree with or misunderstand the values of other cultures, conflict occurs. Some regions or ethnic backgrounds possess singular or **homogeneous** cultural norms. This occurs in areas that are isolated from external cultural influences.

American culture consists of influences from many races, ethnic backgrounds, communities and global regions. Thus, the American culture may be defined as having multiple influences, which makes this culture **heterogeneous** in nature. The hospitality industry is also heterogeneous and for this reason, individuals in our industry must learn to disregard cultural differences and embrace cultural similarities. This is the essence of cultural diversity training programs.

While social cultures are applicable to entire societies, there are also cultural systems that are established by small groups of individuals who are brought together by some common purpose. For instance, there are cultures for business organizations, social organizations, industry segments, as well as certain types of institutions. These cultural systems are similar to societal cultures; however, they operate on much smaller levels. The culture for a company or corporation is referred to as the **organizational culture**, which is the collection of shared values, attitudes and beliefs for members of that organization. People join organizations and bring with them various backgrounds and cultural ideals. They assimilate into the organization as an employee and begin to understand the unwritten core philosophies and rules for behavior in that organization that are referred to as **norms** or acceptable behaviors. These norms include traditions, rites, rituals, ceremonies and celebrations within the organization. Behaviors including dress codes, formality levels, inside humor, buzzwords, company acronyms and others are symptoms of the organizational culture.

SUMMARY

In this chapter, we have provided an overview of management within organizations as related to the service of the stakeholder groups. After a brief review of historical events in management, we noted that the function of human resource management exists to protect the assets of the organization and to ensure the development of human capital. Then we walked through topics that briefly describe the journey to discover the 'who, what and how' of human resource management and management influence. Finally, we described how we would practice newly formed knowledge and skills in the practice of human resource management.

IN THE REAL WORLD (CONTINUED)

It has been six months since you last talked with your friend, Loren. One day you run into her at the mall. After the usual social exchanges, you ask her if she is still in the same job. Loren says to you, 'I have a great story to tell you. Let's get a latte and talk.'

You are sitting at the coffee shop when Loren starts her story. 'You know,' she said, 'I ran into Katie a few months ago, and she has an HR job with her company.' She continued, 'So, I asked her how she got the job. Katie told me that she was in the same predicament as me about not getting hired for HR jobs, so she volunteered to work one day per week at her property's HR office for free just to get some experience.' Loren went on to say, 'Well, they really liked her, and someone got promoted and she got their job!' 'Wow,' you reply, 'Great strategy.'

'Well,' Loren chimed in, 'I went down to my HR office and offered the same type of volunteer work. The HR director was shocked that I was willing to work for free, but he said okay.' Finally she says, 'I have been doing this for four months and it looks like a new position is going to open up soon. I'm not going to jinx myself, but the director asked me if I might be interested in applying for that full-time position.' You reply, 'Wow! That's great.' 'Yup,' Loren says, 'I should know if I get the job in about a month.' She concludes by saying, 'You know? I'm sure glad I was able to get advice from Katie.'

QUESTIONS FOR DISCUSSION

1. Do you know anyone who works in human resource management? Have they ever talked about their jobs? Is it a 'love/hate' relationship in their view? If so, why?
2. What type of people do you think are attracted to becoming HR practitioners? Why do you think certain types are more prone to do human resource management than others?
3. Do you think operations managers should practice human resource management functions and skills? How would they benefit from such a practice? Do you think this is an area of management that you should be very knowledgeable about when you become a manager? Why or why not?
4. Is there any area in the overview of HR management that you find interesting? Why do you like that area, or why don't you like any of the areas?

CASE STUDY

You are working as a clerical assistant in the human resource office for a large internationally recognized theme park complex. One month ago, there was a terrorist attack in New York City. Since that time, the theme park has been under high alert as a potential terrorist-target zone. The tourism industry in your town relies heavily on visitors that arrive by air travel. Since the attack, flight arrival passenger numbers have declined significantly in your city. As a result of this, visitor volume at the theme parks has dropped by at least 50%. Immediately following the attack, the corporate office issued a freeze on all position requisitions. Since that time, all part-time workers were laid off and full-time workers have had their hours reduced. The big fear among the workers is that a massive layoff of full-time workers might occur.

Preliminary Questions

1. There are two types of approaches to addressing this problem. A reactive approach is one focus that would be on short-term responsive action without concern for long-range complications. Another would be to take a proactive approach that would balance the immediate responses with long-term concerns. Which would you take? Why?
2. The most vulnerable group of people in this situation are the hourly employees. The salaried managers and professional employees are the most costly, however. Would you consider ways to reduce expenses in the hourly and salary categories? What ideas come to your mind to make this happen?

Conclusion

The human resource director called a department meeting first thing this morning. All of the human resource managers and workers were present at the meeting. There is a somber mood, as everyone has an idea of what this meeting will be about. The director starts to address the group, 'Well, guys, as you know, business isn't getting any better. We have tried every trick in the book to retain our full-timers, but we are getting heat from corporate to start downsizing. I was in the president's office all day yesterday, and the bottom line is that we are being told to reduce the full-time hourly and supervisory staff payroll by 5%. I hate the idea of putting our people out on the street, especially now when jobs are so scarce in this town. I called you all together to see if there is some sort of creative solution we could come up with to avoid a massive layoff.'

Everyone in the room is silently thinking about the ramifications of a layoff that include concerns about their own jobs.

After a long pensive silence, the director chimes in with, 'C'mon guys, I know this is not the best of times, but we have a chance to use our talents to do as little harm as possible to our cast members.'

You figure there is nothing to lose, so you speak up, 'I have a friend who works in General Services in the Cruise Division, who tells me that they are recovering quickly from the tragedy and that bookings are going through the roof. I guess the guests who would normally visit our parks are opting for cruises, since they seem to be safe vacation get-away options. The hiring freeze has been lifted over there, so maybe we could shift some parks personnel to shore side and onboard cruise positions.'

'Hmmm,' the director murmurs, 'I didn't even think of the cruise division. I'll bet they are doing more business than before the tragedy.' The employment manager jumps in by saying, 'We can notify everyone of the problem we are facing here in the parks and announce opportunities for temporary placement with cruise operations. I know that they schedule their onboard staff using three-month employment contracts. Usually, they fill the contracts from outside sources. We could offer these contracts to cast members who are flexible enough to work onboard positions. As far as shore-side jobs, they will just have to work in a different location on a temporary basis.'

The compensation manager adds, 'Since the cruise division revenues will be higher than budget, they will be able to afford a few extra benefits. We could outsource some of our janitorial and housekeeping staff to one of our vendors to provide housecleaning and lawn maintenance for those cast members who elect onboard temporary positions and offer that service as a benefit. We can pay for it from one of the benefit accounts, which will be a small amount of the payroll savings due to the outsourcing of our own staff.'

The training manager suggests, 'We can shift our training resources to cruise operations and get everyone prepared with the necessary skills through "crash-course" training programs. Since our cast members already know our service basics, all we have to do is brush up on the technical job aspects. We can have them ready to do new jobs in a flash.'

At this point, everyone is enthusiastically buzzing with great ideas. The director is visibly enthused and says, 'This is a fabulous alternative to layoffs. I'm going to call the cruise division HR director right now.'

Conclusion Questions

1. Do you think it is a good idea to switch workers from the parks division to the cruise division? What are the advantages and disadvantages to this strategy? Be specific.
2. Identify the HR specialists in this scenario and match their ideas to each specialty. Evaluate their contributions to the overall strategy. Explain the value of specialized contributions to general outcomes.

ENDNOTES

1. Anonymous, 2002. Compensation resources IOMA's report on salary surveys. 2 (12), 8, 2.
2. Beigbeder, S., 1999. Disability management – improving employee health and the company bottom line. J. Property Manag. 64 (3), 98, 3.
3. Chaston, I., Badger, B., Sadler-Smith, E. 2000. Organizational learning style and competences. A comparative investigation of relationship and transactionally orientated small UK manufacturing firms. Eur. J. Market. 34 (5/6), 625.
4. Shanoff, B., 2002. Corporate collars climb. Waste Age 33 (7), 30, 2.
5. Gibson, J.W., 1999. The role of management history in the management curriculum: 1997. J. Manag. Hist. 5 (5), 277.
6. Gibson, J.W., 1999. Management history gurus of the 1990s. Their lives, their contributions. J. Manag. Hist. 5 (6), 380.
7. Sobo, E.J., 2002. Improving organizational communication and cohesion in a health care setting through employee–leadership exchange. Hum. Organ. 61 (3), 277, 11.
8. *Ibid.*
9. *Ibid.*
10. Babcock, R.D., 2001. Language-based communication zones in international business communication. J. Bus. Commun. 38 (4), 372, 41.
11. Xu, X.M., 2003. Some UK and US comparisons of executive information systems in practice and theory. J. End User Comput. 15 (1), 1, 19.
12. Park, H.S., 2002. How people really detect lies. Commun. Monogr. 69 (2), 144, 14.
13. Pilcher, J.K., 2002. Authoring social responsibility. Qualitative Inquiry 8 (6), 715, 23.
14. Tesone, D.V. 2003. Management and Technology for the Hospitality Industry: Higher Tech for Higher Touch. Pearson Custom Publishing, Boston, MA, pp. 46–49.

CHAPTER 8

Managing Technology and Marketing Systems

OBJECTIVES

At the end of this chapter you will learn to:

1. **Understand the role of Management Information Systems within enterprises.**
2. **Define basic hardware and software computer components.**
3. **Describe the telecommunication interfaces used for marketing functions.**
4. **Describe enterprise operations information system interfaces.**

IN THE REAL WORLD

You are working as a Manager in Training (MIT) for the Food and Beverage department of a resort. You are assigned to a restaurant outlet. You notice many problems with the point of sale system at the restaurant. It seems that the system frequently crashes, servers are frequently lined up waiting to input orders and the remote printers commonly fail to communicate. It seems that the system goes down at the busiest parts of each shift. When this happens, you must contact a technician and wait to have the systems repaired. It seems that everyone who works in the restaurant is very frustrated with this system.

One Saturday night, the system went down as usual near closing time for the restaurant. You called the technician who arrived just after the restaurant closed for business.

To be continued...

INTRODUCTION

Why do managers need to know about information technology (IT) and information systems (IS)? We learned in Chapter 3 that technology is the key external driver that influences service enterprises. In Chapter 4, we identified technology as a resource used as an input to systems that provide transformation processes. Since managers are responsible for adding value to the linear productivity processes, they must become familiar with IT and IS in order to make sound decisions. From a management perspective, resource acquisition, implementation and evaluation are standard practices. IT and IS are important areas that require a little technical knowledge in order to perform these management practices.

The marketing function of service enterprises has been dramatically altered by developments in IT and IS. Current management practice requires managers to be aware of developments in electronic commerce (E-commerce) and customer relationship management (CRM) systems. In fact, Management Information Systems (MIS) bring together all of the organizational functions to include marketing, human resource management, accounting, finance and operations. All managers must be familiar with the basics of MIS in order to understand the inputs, interfaces and systems of the service enterprise.

Toward the end of the chapter, we will discuss applications of MIS to business operations that provide service transactions, distribution, repair, maintenance and product production outputs within service enterprises. A functional approach is taken in this chapter. We recall that we learned about these production systems in Chapter 5, as well as organizational functions in Chapter 3. The organizational functions mentioned in the chapter include: marketing, human resource management, production operations, finance and accounting. Business processes are supported by cross-functional information systems that handle multiple business functions. The main processes presented in this chapter are Supply Chain Management (SCM) and enterprise resource planning (ERP), which are used to facilitate front- and back-end E-commerce and internal employee application interfaces (EAI).

COMPUTER BASICS

Let us consider a few computer basics to help us understand how information is processed. Input devices are used to put data into the machine. These include keyboard, mouse, touch screens, pen, optical scanner, microphone and camera. Processing is done by the central processing unit (CPU), which performs the functions of the computer. For instance, when we identify CPU chips as being within the 8,600 series through Pentium IV, we are talking about microprocessor specifications.

COMPUTER HARDWARE

There are three major categories of computers: mainframe, midrange and micro. Consider a networking scenario where your micro would be running through a few servers (midrange) to access many databases (mainframes). Mainframe computers are used mostly for data storage and transactions. Midrange computers usually act as servers to some network (including the Internet) or operate as workstations to perform specific functions requiring high-powered calculation and artistic functions. Microcomputers are those used by the end users (desktops, laptops, cell phones, personal digital assistants (PDA)).

It is suggested that we are on the cusp of the fifth generation of computing, which may be true in the R&D laboratories. Actually, most of us use hardware and software that still resembles late-stage Generation 4 computing. Moore's Law is a theory that states that technology doubles every 18 months and markets reach their half-cost in the same period of time[1]. Unfortunately, most of us are about two years behind the current model distribution of hardware and software, and thus we operate in a state of Moore's Inverse[2]. Table 8.1 describes the impact of computing generations for home and office users[3].

Prior to the late-1980s, personal computers were novelty machines that possessed little real utility in terms of application programs. It was the development of the 8,600 series of processor that caused these stand-alone machines to be used in homes and offices. Businesses used mainframe systems with 'dumb terminals' attached to them before this time. It was the 8,600 processor that became the original enabler for end users to become empowered to manipulate their own data via databases, spreadsheets and word processors. Unlike today's generation of computing, the PC user of the first generation needed to be competent in text-based DOS coding to operate these applications.

TABLE 8.1 Evolution of Common Home/Office Technology Used for Online Training

Component	1990	1995	2000	2002–6
Hardware	8,600 series 40 Mb Disk 16 Mb RAM	PentiumI&II 1 Gb Disk 32 Mb RAM	Pentium III 10 Gb Disk 128 Mb RAM	Pentium IV 40 Gb Disk 356 Mb RAM
Software	DOS W3.1 ProComm	W95 ISP Browser	W/ME ISP Browser Video editor	W/XP ISP Browser Video format
Coding	Unix	HTML	Editor/ Courseware	Courseware
Connectivity	9,600 Baud	28 kb/s	56 kb/s	>200 kb/s
Host Server Interface	Unix	Website	Courseware – Platform	Courseware – Platform
Generation/Online	1 G/OL	2 G/OL	3 G/OL	4 G/OL

Source: Tesone, D.V., 2003. Management & Technology for the Hospitality Industry: Higher Tech for Higher Touch. Pearson, Boston, MA.

Personal computers (PCs) are commonly used by most of us. They include desktop, notebook and palm-held models. Handheld versions are called personal digital assistants (PDAs) and are currently used for computing and communications. The future of the PDA will be phenomenal. They will be our major source of communication with most commercial institutions in the next few years. Old PCs were text based, using the operating system called DOS. The launch of computers with the general public was due to the development of graphical user interfaces (GUIs) such as Windows and Apple, which are now the dominant operating systems on the respective makes of machines. The combination of GUIs, advancements in chip technology and telecommunications has created demand for multimedia capabilities. Sound cards and video capture are common on most PCs.

Cameras, video camcorders, DVD /MPEG players and optical scanners are becoming popular peripherals. Some cost-conscious PC users are opting for low-cost network computers (NCs) exclusively designed for use on the Internet. The old 'dumb' terminals hooked to mainframes have been replaced with transaction terminals such as automatic teller machines (ATMs) and point of sale (POS) machines.

Midrange computers serve roles in addition to being network servers. Specialized functions such as computer-aided manufacturing (CAM) and computer-aided design (CAD) are best handled by midrange computers, called workstations.

The power is still in the mainframe computer, which is really what we are accessing when we use the Internet. Most business enterprises have PCs networked with midrange and mainframe computers. State-of-the-art mainframes (used in defense, research and mega corporations) are called supercomputers. They use parallel processing architectures and interconnected microprocessors for phenomenal processing speed. Advances in microprocessor technology are being applied to midrange and microcomputers as well.

Output devices include video display units (monitors), printers, audio output units and others. Storage falls into two categories: primary and secondary. Primary storage is called memory. Read Only Memory (ROM) is coded into the memory chip and runs the computer. Random Access Memory (RAM) operates application programs.

Secondary storage devices include disks, memory sticks and tapes. Peripherals are those items attached to the computer as external devices, such as microphones and printers.

Other input devices include optical scanning using optical character recognition (OCR) technology with handheld wands or desktop scanners. Forms, invoices, credit cards, airline tickets and various other documents are scanned for databases, billing, sorting and other functions. Magnetic stripes are commonly used on POS systems and ATMs. Smart cards contain information embedded on microprocessor chips. Additional input devices include digital cameras and magnetic ink character recognition (MIRC) technology.

The smallest data element is called a bit (binary digit). A byte contains a group of related data in 7- or 8-bit units. Storage capacities are measured in the following hierarchy: kilobytes (KB), megabytes (MB), gigabytes (GB) and terabytes (TB). A metric KB is equal to 1,024 bits, with an MB being about 1 million, GB = 1 billion and TB = 1 trillion bits. Primary media and magnetic disks are considered to be direct access storage devices (DASDs) while other storage media, such as tape, use sequential access.

SOFTWARE

Table 8.2 provides an illustration of system and application software. End users use application software most of the time. As you know, the list of commonly available application programs continues to grow. Notice that there are general and specific application programs. Systems software is used to manage and run utilities and application programs. Most end users refer to systems management programs as operating systems.

The left column of the table displays a list of operating systems. The most commonly known operating systems for PCs are Microsoft Windows and the Microsoft Direct Operating System (MSDOS).Unix is a well-known mainframe operating system (OS). Operating systems perform functions that the end user does not readily notice. The OS manages hardware resources, data and program files, permits the user to multitask (more than one application at a time) and provides support services referred to as utilities (examples include control panel, file manager, setup etc.). Some operating systems are designed for stand-alone (single) machines, while others support networked machines. Systems support programs also include software to monitor usage and performance and security integrity.

Software suites contain multiple applications programs in a single group. Microsoft Office is one popular suite that combines compatible word processor, spreadsheet, presentation and database applications. For Internet users, browser programs provide interfaces for navigation. The two popular browsers are Netscape and Internet Explorer. The browser is launched by the Internet service provider (ISP), which usually provides a suite of applications including email, chat and other applications. A popular ISP for phone modem users is *America Online* (AOL), while cable modem and digital subscriber lines (DSL) work through proprietary Internet service providers, such as cable and telephone companies.

Electronic mail is used for messaging among targeted users. Word processing software provides the ability to create documents to be published in print (hard copy) or electronic media. Desktop publishing facilitates professional documents such as newsletters, brochures and books. Spreadsheets are used for business modeling, planning and calculations. They are arranged in cells that permit the entry

TABLE 8.2   Operating Systems and Applications

System Software	General Use Applications	Specific Use Applications
DOS	Word processors	Computer-aided design
Windows	Spreadsheets	Computer-aided manufacturing
Unix	Databases	Point of sale
Linux	Media players	Property management software
Java	Presentations	Global distribution software

Source: Tesone, D.V., 2003. Management & Technology for the Hospitality Industry: Higher Tech for Higher Touch. Pearson, Boston, MA.

of alphanumeric data or formulas. The power of spreadsheets is the ability to do 'what-if' analysis by having the formulas do multiple calculations. Database programs facilitate the storage and manipulation of large amounts of data. End users often rely on the reporting functions of databases to attain specific information for various business applications. Presentation software provides graphics for professional presentations. Multimedia programs add sound, video, photos and hyperlinks to presentations for more inclusive entertainment and information dynamics. Hyperlinks may include hypertext (linkages to locations containing text) or hypermedia (linkages to multimedia sites). The languages used for this type of programming are Java, Hypertext Markup Language (HTML) and Extensible Markup Language (XML). Today, webpage editor programs are used to invoke HTML codes, precluding the need to learn the specific programming language. With the use of intranets (private Internet-like programs for organizations), groupware applications (shared application programs) are used by many people from remote and local server locations, which results in decreased application software expense. A type of application called the personal information manager (PIM) is one that will dramatically affect the future of commerce. The PIM can load, store and sort information concerning customers, clients and prospects on a PDA machine for future interfaces between customers and organizations.

It is predicted that most individuals will use PIMs that contain all buying preferences to interface with commercial PDAs that will handle most E-commerce transactions in the near future. For instance, if you travel on business, your PIM will contain all travel and lodging preferences for you. Given the specifics of a trip, your PIM will shop the airlines, hotels, car rental companies and restaurants for availability and pricing. It will book all of those arrangements on the basis of your preference for accommodations and pricing heuristics (rules of thumb for how much you are willing to spend). The shopping and arrangements are made between your PDA and the commercial PDAs. Theoretically, there would be no need for human interaction for preliminary transactions. This could free service enterprise workers to interact more effectively with visiting guests on a face-to-face level.

Programming languages contain instructions used to execute programs for users. Code written in binary digits (1s and 0s) is called machine language, which is the most basic level of programming. Assembler languages are also basic and use symbols to relate to binary coded instruction. High-level languages include Cobol, RPG, Fortran, Basic etc. These are procedural rules of code used to program at a level above machine and assembler languages. Fourth generation languages are also known as natural languages. They are results oriented, permitting the machines to determine instructions used to arrive at intended results.

Object-oriented languages (OOP) have become major tools for software development. C++, Visual Basic and Java are examples of these programs. In this type of programming, objects are established that consist of data elements and activities tied together. For example, an object could be set at a value such as a country club member's name and include instructions for member activities such as calculating a perpetual golf handicap on the basis of an array of scores.

Any programming language above machine language requires machine translation. Assemblers translate symbolic codes into binary. Compilers translate high-level languages. Interpreters are specialized compilers that translate program statements one at a time as they are executed.

ENTERPRISE TELECOMMUNICATIONS

Enterprise telecommunications is not a new concept for most of us. Most of us communicate frequently through networked telecommunications from home and work. When we do this, we work with information that is accessed from servers and brought to us via hardwires, wireless routers, telephone or cable lines. This is an example of two-way telecommunications, as you may send and receive information over the lines of communication.

Just as individuals use telecommunications, so do business enterprises. The business uses this medium for collaboration, communication and coordination of activities within an organization and among those stakeholder groups doing business with the organization. Email, video conferencing, chat/discussion groups and multimedia webpages are supported among locations by the Internet, intranets and extranets. Wide area networks (WAN) and metropolitan networks (MAN) may be used to link internal databases within a single organization that would communicate via a local area network (LAN). Wide and metropolitan area networks are called WANs and MANs respectively, referring to distances of a few miles (WAN) to specific metropolitan locations (MANs). A MAN covers a metropolitan area, such as a city. For instance, Philadelphia completed a project where the entire city is available for wireless connectivity. A WAN could be as small as a single organization with various locations over a few miles to the entire Internet. This is misleading, in that WANs can cover a span of a few miles to the entire world. Sometimes, organizational WANs with various locations over a number of miles are considered to be Campus Area Networks (CAN). Anything beyond a LAN falls within the category of a WAN, to include, but not limited to MANs and CANs. Customers link electronically with organizations to view product catalogs and order products or services from inventory and distribution databases. This is called electronic commerce (E-commerce). The strategic advantage of business telecommunications is that organizations may overcome geographical, time, cost and structural barriers to business effectiveness and efficiency. Seamless and rapid telecommunication networks make this possible. Figure 8.1 depicts enterprise collaboration, E-commerce and internal business systems for a typical service enterprise.

For those who follow the stock market, it is common knowledge that technology stocks were 'hot' in the 1990s. Part of the reason is the deregulation of telecommunication organizations. Large corporations and smaller firms are still fiercely competing for market share in wired and wireless telecommunications in the fields of information, communications, entertainment, commerce and education. The stock market began to settle down as *Dot Coms* became known as *Dot Bombs* from financial perspectives. However, the competition is still very strong in the E-commerce field, and many practitioners consider themselves to be E-commerce specialists. In the current environment, there appears to be a blurred definition between E-commerce specialists and Marketing specialists.

What is the reason for the competitive environment among communication organizations? In a word, we could say it is about 'connectivity.' Everyone is racing to be the first and best in the field of connectivity. Thanks to the popularity of the Internet, an open systems approach to telecommunications is driving the competition. Open technology systems are facilitated by standards of compliance for hardware, software,

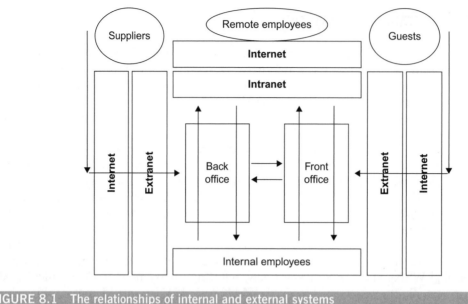

FIGURE 8.1 **The relationships of internal and external systems**
Source: Tesone, D.V., 2003. Management & Technology for the Hospitality Industry: Higher Tech for Higher Touch. Pearson, Boston, MA.

applications and networks. These standards permit connectivity and interoperability among networks on a global level. Examples of standardization include Open Systems Interconnection (OSI) models as established by the International Standards Organization (ISO) and the Internet's TCP/IP file transfer protocol suite. Any chief information officer (CIO) who represents a hospitality organization will tell us that these standards are having a dramatic impact on all service enterprise sectors.

A major influence in telecommunications is the shift from analog transmission to digital network technologies. Digital media transmit data in discrete binary impulses (the same as computers) to provide higher transmission speeds, large amounts of information movement, greater efficiency and much lower error rates. Billions of dollars have been spent by communications and entertainment organizations to replace copper-wire media with fiber optics that transmit data via laser light impulses. Land-based microwave wireless services are being replaced with low-orbit and regular satellite transmitters. Managers must be aware of these core technologies when making investment decisions concerning telecommunications to enhance the strategic positioning of organizations.

As long as the need for digital/analog/digital conversion exists, networks will require the use of telecommunication processors (switches, routers and modems) to link host, server and user computers. The computer transmits to a modem and follows a channel (wire or satellite) to a router and switch for servers and host computers that receive and transmit requested data back to the user. This is the telecommunications process. LANs may be a small as being contained within one room. Wide and metropolitan area networks are called WANs and MANs respectively, referring to distances of a few miles (WAN) to huge expanses of distance (MANs).

Telecommunications channels consist of wired and satellite media. Satellites transmit microwave beams for wireless transmission. Terrestrial microwaves are carried by

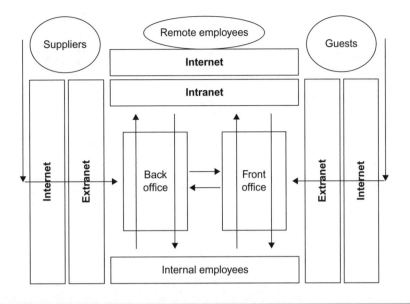

FIGURE 8.2 The relationships of internal and external technology systems for business to employee relationships
Source: Tesone, D.V., 2003. Management & Technology for the Hospitality Industry: Higher Tech for Higher Touch. Pearson, Boston, MA.

antennae on buildings, towers and mountains. Traditional satellites operate as relay stations as they orbit the equator. Large enterprises use very small aperture technology (VSAT) to bypass commercial communication channels. Cellular phones use radio technologies to communicate between cells located on towers. These systems are providing digital transmission with greater efficiency and security. Integration of phone and radio technologies is providing mutliuse 'packet radios' through cell phone carriers. The cost of wiring buildings for LANs is often prohibitive, which causes enterprises to consider wireless LANs that use high frequency, low frequency and infrared beams. Wireless fidelity (WIFI) technology has recently been implemented on a large scale. Modems convert digital to analog to digital to provide communications between computers over analog channels. Multiplexers facilitate many terminals with the ability to communicate over a single line. Bandwidth refers to the speed of transmission over telecommunications channels as measured by bits per second (BPS). High-speed digital channels are referred to as 'broadband,' which use microwave, fiber optic or satellite to transmit at speeds up to several billion BPS.

TELECOMMUNICATIONS FOR BUSINESS MARKETING

The business function of marketing is concerned with planning, promotion and sales of existing or new products in new or existing markets. Figure 8.2 shows information systems and technologies used to support the marketing function. Notice that the same components that support enterprise operations also support the marketing function.

Mass marketing is intended to create a market from the masses of potential consumers. Direct marketing is aimed at a specific niche of consumers. Interactive

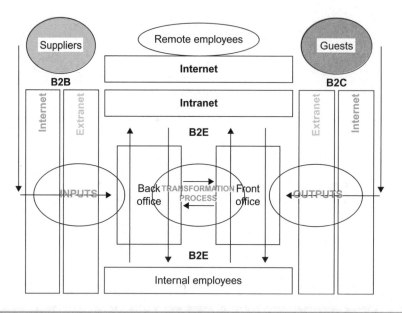

FIGURE 8.3   The inputs, transformation processes and outputs in technology systems
Source: Tesone, D.V., 2003. Management & Technology for the Hospitality Industry: Higher Tech for Higher Touch. Pearson, Boston, MA.

marketing involves interdependent communications with consumers and ultimately customers for a product or service. The Internet makes interactive marketing a common feature in business enterprises including manufacturing and service sectors. Sales force automation provides access to databases and transaction processing from remote locations by members of the sales staff to enhance efficiency and effectiveness of product distribution. Sales and customer relationship management provides analysis and reports of product distribution. The Internet provides enhancements to advertising, promotion and target marketing efforts. Market research and forecasting are assisted with data mining and analysis. Collectively, these functions are known as CRM systems, which is the essence of E-commerce in its current state. Customer relationship management is the essence of service enterprise marketing. We remember from Chapter 1 that there are internal and external customers in service enterprises. Thus, everyone is a customer. The holistic E-commerce model provides for business-to-business (B2B) functions on the supply chain side of the organization (inputs). Business-to-customer (B2C) functions occur on the front end of the organization through outputs. And business-to-employee (B2E) functions enhance productivity by using technology to support workers in the transformation process. Figure 8.3 provides a depiction of these relationships.

The figure demonstrates the relationships among all individuals who interface with a specific service enterprise. Guests and suppliers now interface with the hospitality organization through the Internet, which leads them to the company's extranet and takes them into the back- and front-office operations respectively. Remote employees also use the Internet to access the company's intranet to gain access to front- and back-office operations. Internal employees are those at the worksite who use the intranet to access databases and groupware. Lay a transparency of the productivity process that we discussed in Chapter 4 over top of the figure and we see that the

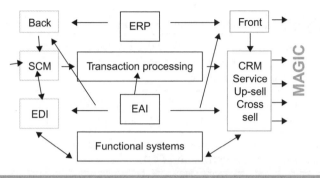

FIGURE 8.4 E-business systems
Source: Tesone, D.V., 2003. Management & Technology for the Hospitality Industry: Higher Tech for Higher Touch. Pearson, Boston, MA.

back end consists of inputs, the middle consists of transformation processes and the front end is the guest interface where the magical memories are created as a result of service transactions that occur through service enterprise outputs. The entire model from left to right provides a comprehensive picture of an ERP process that integrates the entire supply chain for the service organization.

The ERP model typifies the open systems model by permitting electronic access to the hospitality organization from all the stakeholder groups. For instance, a resort hotel would use B2C interfaces to enhance customer relationships by providing direct access to sales and marketing information and parts of the property management system (PMS) such as reservations. B2B functions comprise electronic data interchange (EDI) systems with suppliers that facilitate automated purchasing, inventory process control, just-in-time (JIT) inventories and electronic billing and payment processes. B2E is the newest focus of ERP systems that enhances worker productivity by streamlining the transformation process and providing automated external employee benefit services (such as dry cleaning pickup and delivery) to enhance the quality of life for employees and reduce outside distractions from the workplace. Figure 8.4 highlights the systems used in each section of the supply chain for these purposes.

MANAGEMENT INFORMATION SYSTEMS

The newest wave for MIS is to contribute to the strategic positioning of the hospitality/ tourism organization. We saw this in the 1980s when the personnel department was elevated to the human resource function. We learned in Chapter 7 that the cause of the increased status of human resource management was the strategic approach to HR management recognizing that employees were human capital. The key driver to MIS becoming a strategic business unit is the opportunity for global networking via the Internet, intranets and extranets. There are numerous opportunities to expand the open systems aspect of hospitality corporations. The only limitation for current and future hospitality managers is their imaginations.

Networking capability has broken geographical and time barriers to doing business. Information technology is playing a major role in business reengineering for the improvement of effectiveness and efficiency. Changes in work flows, job requirements and organizational structures are attributable to IT.

TABLE 8.3	Management Standard Reports
Periodic scheduled reports – Standard reports generated on periodic basis. Examples include: night audit reports – daily, MTD budget reports – weekly and variance reports – monthly.	
Exception reports – Produced and distributed when something out of the ordinary occurs. Flash and pop-up reports are examples.	
Demand reports – Sorted and specialized reports available to managers through database report generators and SQL.	
Push reports – Exception information 'pushed' through the network to the workstations of all managers with a need-to-know. Similar to exception reports but distributed to a more specific group of managers.	

Source: Tesone, D.V., 2003. Management & Technology for the Hospitality Industry: Higher Tech for Higher Touch. Pearson, Boston, MA.

Quality processes are greatly enhanced by IT. Continuous improvement processes, mass customization, service levels, costs and customer responsiveness are greatly enhanced from IT applications. The statistical measurement process alone is tedious and time consuming when done manually. Computer computation removes this burden and permits the work units to focus on products and services.

The service enterprise corporation that uses IT capabilities may greatly enhance its competitive edge. Customized solutions, business collaboration, flexible organizational structures all provide what the customer is looking for when doing business with a firm.

As a customer, we often do not realize that other organizations are participating in the development of our products and services, as we may be dealing with a virtual company composed of many firms acting in collaboration. An example in the services sector could be found in major theme parks who are in concession with service providers from myriad provider organizations who interact with guests to provide entertainment and hospitality services.

Information systems are certainly efficient and effective when it comes to management information used to make decisions. Managers have access to automated information that used to take long hours of tedious manual operations to compile. This is one of the intended outputs that drove the developments in the areas of database development and networking (discussed at greater length in another chapter). Table 8.3 lists four types of management reports that are generated from information systems. The periodic reports (daily, weekly, quarterly, annually distributed) are automatically generated and distributed to lists of managers and executives on the basis of need-to-know requirement for the information. Additional reports such as schedules, hours worked, banquet event orders (BEOs), occupancy and others are distributed to the general employee populous, again, on the need-to-know basis of the specific information. Many individuals in organizations are accustomed to these reports being printed on paper and placed in intra-company mailboxes for distribution. More progressive companies, however, use electronic distribution, which is more effective and efficient than printed reports.

TABLE 8.4	Online Analytical Processing (OLAP)
Automated analyses in environments that include data warehouses linked through a DBMS with data mining features.	
Consolidation – Chain home offices providing information by property, by city, by region, by district, by nation.	
Drill-down – The opposite of consolidation. The chain home office can identify top producers at specific properties in ranking order and compare them with regional or national performance.	
Slicing and dicing – Breaking information into segments or niches.	

Source: Tesone, D.V., 2003. Management & Technology for the Hospitality Industry: Higher Tech for Higher Touch. Pearson, Boston, MA.

The other three examples listed in the table include reports that indicate occurrences that are outside of the ordinary business-as-usual scenario. The reports are intended for notification that usually requires some action on the part of the manager.

Reports are generated by queries that order the sorting and combining of various records in the database that are used to provide specific information and analysis. Marketing and project managers are particularly fond of the power associated with online analytical processing (OLAP) procedures available in progressive service enterprise organizations. Table 8.4 provides a listing of this activity.

The information presented in the table is particularly useful for marketing analysis to generate timely and accurate marketing plans. Notice that the data may be arranged from broad volumes to very narrow areas for analysis. This feature provides information for specific analysis used in trend forecasting and single 'snapshots' of individual operations as they relate to the entire organization. This type of analysis is usually performed by chain operations in lodging, restaurants and travel-related organizations. For instance, an airline would use this procedure to view specific flight routes in terms of passenger load and profitability and use the information to redirect, add or cancel segments.

When it comes to strategic planning for all areas of the organization, decision support systems (DSS) provide statistical support to justify or nullify what managers intuitively apply to making decisions. A listing of the statistical analyses is given in Table 8.5. It is important to note that the key word here is 'support.' Some managers confuse the recommendations of these systems with the final decisions. If this was true, there would be little need for thinking managers. Remember, technology is not here to replace people or thinking, but to be used as a tool for people in organizations. Before the development of sophisticated DSS systems, spreadsheet application programs were touted as a manager's greatest tool for 'what-if' analysis. With DSS systems, the what-if aspects go way beyond the figures plugged into a spreadsheet.

Other DSS applications include data mining, executive information systems and enterprise information portals. These functions require data warehousing interfaces to access both internal and external sources of information. More information is provided for these functions in specific technology courses covering E-commerce design and development.

TABLE 8.5	Decision Support Systems (DSS)
Statistical software used to perform complex analysis of multiple variables. An example is a yield management program used to compare variables to enhance revenue management.	
What-if analysis – Considers hypothetical scenarios. For instance, what if a disaster occurred in two major cities that immediately stopped business and leisure destination travel?	
Sensitivity analysis – Specialized what-if analysis. For instance, how would different group profiles impact hotel retail sales?	
Goal-seeking analysis – Referred to as 'how-can' analysis. For example, how can we increase sales by 10% over the same period last year?	
Optimization analysis – Provides templates for decisions to maximize profit or revenues. Again, yield management is a perfect example.	

Source: Tesone, D.V., 2003. Management & Technology for the Hospitality Industry: Higher Tech for Higher Touch. Pearson, Boston, MA.

Data Mining Software – analyzes huge volumes of historical data to identify trends and patterns for current and future use.

Executive Information Systems – formerly used by top-level managers to make long-range strategic decisions. Today, these systems are used by most managers in the strategic planning process.

Enterprise Information Portals – link internal and off-site data warehouses with extranets and intranets to access and analyze data within and outside the organization. When linked with hypermedia databases, the information is converted into business knowledge for current and future use, which is known as a Knowledge Management System (KMS).

ARTIFICIAL INTELLIGENCE

Artificial intelligence (AI) comes from the blended disciplines of computer science, biology, psychology, linguistics, mathematics and engineering. The goal of AI is to create machines with human physical and mental abilities (reasoning, learning and problem solving). AI is not a new technology application, however, it has not been widely used until recently, as cost and machine power limitations prevented the development of its application for practical uses. Some of the aspects of AI are listed below[4]:

- Neural Networks – the closest electrical simulation of an organic system. Composed of networked processors that interact as transponders and have the capacity for learning based on identification of patterns and relationships.
- Fuzzy Logic – Processors that can perform reasoning on the basis of inferences and incomplete data (the opposite of 'crisp data') in response to SQL inquiries.

- Virtual Reality – Computer-simulated reality based on multisensory input and output devices to create undetected simulated environments through telepresence illusions.
- Intelligent Agents – Applets that perform tasks for end users using a built-in knowledge base about processes. Application Wizards are good examples.
- Expert Systems – Knowledge-based system that possesses expertise in a single discipline. Users pose questions and problems and the ES provides solutions.
  - ➤ Knowledge base is the information contained by the system in factual and heuristic form.
  - ➤ Inference engine provides analysis tools for If/Then reasoning and adds experiences to the KB through repetition.
  - ➤ The expert shell is programmed by a knowledge engineer and a logic programmer.
    Source: Tesone, D.V., 2003. Management & Technology for the Hospitality Industry: Higher Tech for Higher Touch. Pearson, Boston, MA.

All of these applications have been available from a technological research and development (R&D) reference since the early 1990s. While chips have been built into commonly used machines and appliances that use some of these technologies (automobiles, for instance), the more powerful applications have been precluded from reaching market places owing to hardware constraints. Today, however, with more powerful microprocessors and lower hardware costs, researchers are considering broad applications of these technologies. The implications for the hospitality/ tourism industry over the next 10 years will only be limited by decision makers' imaginations. This is a wonderful time for service enterprise innovation from the view of these technologies, as they permit the hospitality manager to use creative talents to envision and develop applications in conjunction with technical experts.

So far, we have discussed many of the advancements in technology and information telecommunications that provide the establishment of fully functional marketing and E-commerce systems. These systems infiltrate the interior aspects of the organization and link those to outside sources via the Internet, intranets and extranets. The key driver for these applications is the overall advancement of telecommunications technologies. We have already learned that technology is facilitating new forms of open systems within, between and among the variables that exist in the external environment.

SERVICE ENTERPRISE MANAGEMENT SYSTEMS

At this point, we have enough information about technology to comprehend the interfaces of systems that provide for transaction processing and process control in service enterprise organizations. Building on models that we discussed earlier in the chapter, we will view descriptions of the systems that we work with on a daily basis using a full-service lodging property as our example. Figure 8.5 depicts an information system for the human resource management office. Similar functional systems would be in place for accounting, marketing and other business functions.

The figure provides the description used to demonstrate the hierarchy of data for a Human Resource Information System (HRIS). The data hierarchy structure consists of characters, fields, records and files within a database, which are used

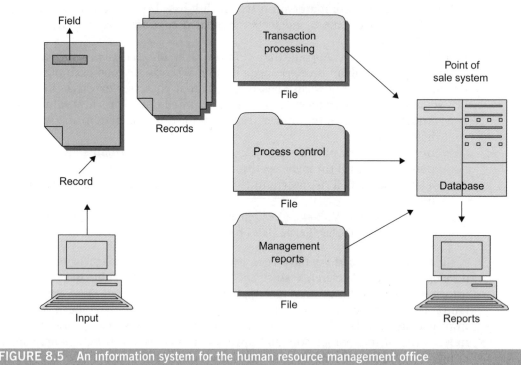

FIGURE 8.5   An information system for the human resource management office
Source: Tesone, D.V., 2003. Management & Technology for the Hospitality Industry: Higher Tech for Higher Touch. Pearson, Boston, MA.

to store, sort, manipulate and query data to produce useful information for management knowledge and decision making. Multiple database interfaces require the services of a database management system (DBMS). These relationships are shown in Figure 8.6.

A collection of databases is interfaced with a DBMS. End users work through each respective database in a work area to input and extract data. Each database interfaces with a central database, the DBMS, which acts as a centralized warehouse for the entire operation, thus the term **Data Warehouse**.

One important database for many service enterprises connects back- and front-office operations. For instance, the central backbone or nervous system of a hotel, convention center, conference facility, catering property, bed-n-breakfast, hostel and other lodging operations is called the property management system (PMS). Figure 8.7 shows how a PMS for a full-service hotel acts as a hub for other aspects of the operation. Most individuals assume that the PMS is only linked to the front-office operations, which used to be true until more expansive interfaces started to become available in mid-1980s.

Figure 8.8 zooms into the front-office operation for a closer inspection of the interfaces relevant to those functions.

Notice that the functions to the left of the front desk are back-office functions (behind the scenes), while those to the right represent front-office (on stage for guests to see) functions. There are three points of guest interface. The first point of interface is by phone or the Internet to the Reservations Department, where guests inquire about availability and pricing to book guestrooms. The room rates quoted by

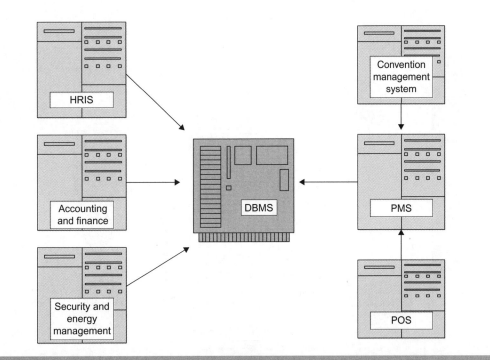

FIGURE 8.6 A database management system
Source: Tesone, D.V., 2003. Management & Technology for the Hospitality Industry: Higher Tech for Higher Touch. Pearson, Boston, MA.

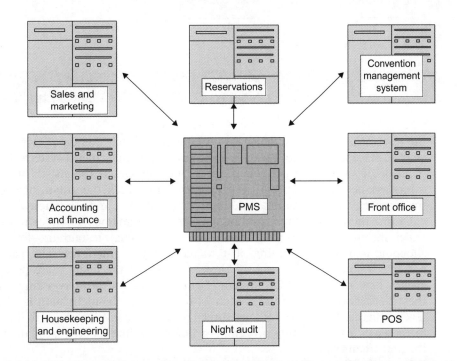

FIGURE 8.7 The property management system
Source: Tesone, D.V., 2003. Management & Technology for the Hospitality Industry: Higher Tech for Higher Touch. Pearson, Boston, MA.

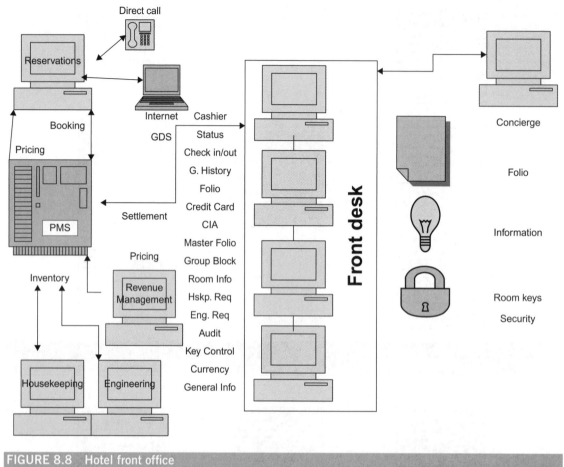

FIGURE 8.8   Hotel front office
Source: Tesone, D.V., 2003. Management & Technology for the Hospitality Industry: Higher Tech for Higher Touch. Pearson, Boston, MA.

the reservations agent will be based on information that was input through the revenue management (sometimes referred to as yield management) system. The second point of guest interface is upon check-in and throughout the guest's stay with the front-desk personnel. During the stay, guests may seek the one-to-one services of the concierge for information, entertainment, child care and other unique needs.

During the guest's stay at the hotel, there are numerous activities to partake in, which include recreation (golf, tennis, water sports etc.), restaurants, lounges, retail shopping and in-room dining, just to name a few amenities. The guest simply presents a smart card at each of these outlets and the charges are posted to the guest's folio through a POS system. Figure 8.9 shows the networking process for these transactions. At the end of each 24-hour period, the night audit team compiles revenue figures from POS data networked through the PMS, along with direct entries to the PMS (room revenue) to generate a daily revenue report that is distributed to the hotel managers.

For each POS icon represented in the figure, there is a separate LAN that handles transaction processing within the respective outlet. The network (subsystem) could be as small as a single terminal for a small gift shop or as wide as multiple

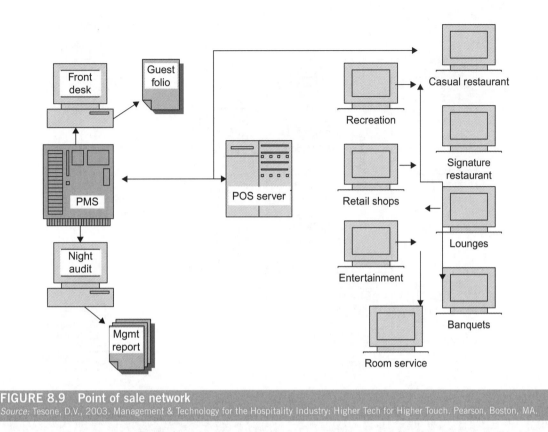

FIGURE 8.9 **Point of sale network**
Source: Tesone, D.V., 2003. Management & Technology for the Hospitality Industry: Higher Tech for Higher Touch. Pearson, Boston, MA.

connections in a restaurant or showroom. The LAN consists of terminals and printers that are arranged in a hub around a master (server) terminal. In a hotel outlet, the master terminal provides the direct connection to the POS server. In a free-standing restaurant, the master terminal may also be the server for the system. Chain restaurants may be connected to a remote server through a WAN or MAN. The master terminal has the ability to collect all the data from the other terminals and produce various reports, such as sales, covers, menu abstracts and others. If the master terminal is connected to a POS server, the reports for all of the outlets are generated from that single server.

Figure 8.10 describes the POS network within a single restaurant. The flow of data originates in the dining room to be placed with the lounge and kitchen areas for production and ultimately service to the restaurant guests seated at the tables. The dining room terminals are located in front-of-the-house service areas. In a short period of time, these will be eliminated with PDAs connected with wireless connections, which will save service steps. The food orders are transmitted to the kitchen production areas for preparation at respective stations behind the culinary line. The food orders are delivered, the remaining steps of service are provided (hopefully in WOW style) and guest checks are tendered.

All of the information from the dining room is 'dumped' into the master terminal, which is usually located in a back-office area of the restaurant. The master terminal has the capacity to generate all of the management reports for the restaurant. The server terminals also generate reports for use by the service staff. In some

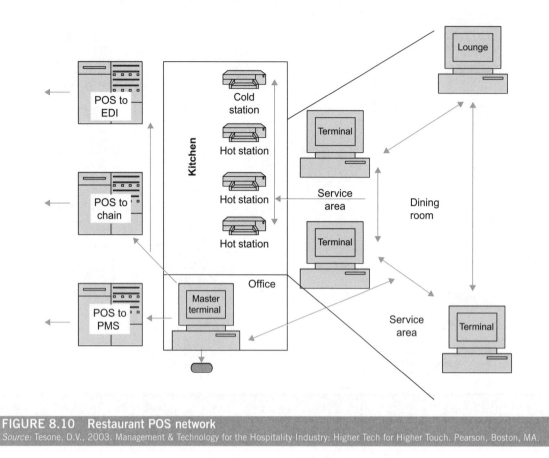

FIGURE 8.10 Restaurant POS network
Source: Tesone, D.V., 2003. Management & Technology for the Hospitality Industry: Higher Tech for Higher Touch. Pearson, Boston, MA.

cases, there are back-of-the-house components to the network to assist with culinary management functions, such as product usage, prepped items on hand etc.

There are four possible options for information flow from the restaurant's master terminal. In a free-standing restaurant, the information flow could terminate at the point of the master dump (symbolized by the green terminator icon in the figure). A hotel restaurant would transmit information from the master terminal to the POS server, which would ultimately transmit the data to the PMS. A chain restaurant might transmit to a regional office or commissary. In the event that an EDI interface is established, information would be transmitted to a purchasing location for comparison to inventories and converted into electronic orders for products from the vendors or commissary.

Regardless of the structure of the business (hotel, free-standing/chain restaurant), Figure 8.11 shows the flows in an EDI system. The master terminals from the outlets connect to the inventory systems in the storerooms. Inventory items were previously requisitioned from the storerooms for use in each outlet. If the requisitions are electronic, then the storerooms have the capacity to maintain a perpetual inventory, meaning they have continuous counts of items requisitioned from stock. The master terminals report the usage of stock items at the end of business to the perpetual inventory. This permits the storerooms to forecast usage for the next business period.

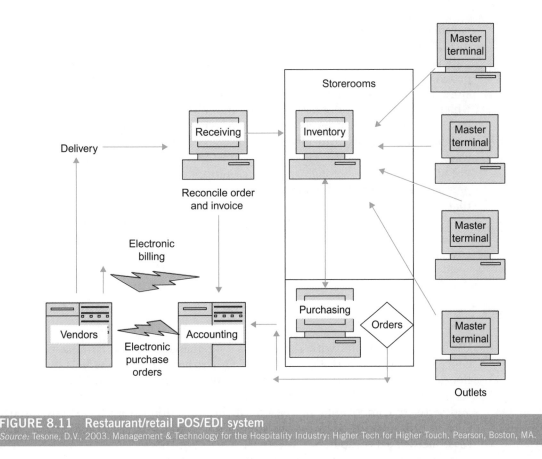

FIGURE 8.11   Restaurant/retail POS/EDI system
Source: Tesone, D.V., 2003. Management & Technology for the Hospitality Industry: Higher Tech for Higher Touch. Pearson, Boston, MA.

The calculation for the storerooms is par stock (standard levels) less requisitions (working stock in the outlets) equal stock on hand. The difference between stock on hand and par stock equals the amount needed to reorder, which the purchasing office would follow in the absence of EDI and perpetual inventory systems. However, with EDI, par levels may be reduced to near zero in some cases, because electronic interchanges with vendors produces JIT inventories. In Figure 10.5, the storerooms know how much stock was requisitioned for the outlets and how much was used in the outlets, indicating the amount of working stock in the outlets for the next business period. On the basis of this information plus the next day demand, the storerooms may forecast the next day's usage and report this to the purchasing department for the placement of stock orders to the vendors. The purchasing director establishes purchase orders (POs) to notify the vendors of each purchase amount. The POs are sent through the Accounting office and electronically transmitted to the vendors.

As we learned in Chapter 5 of the text, the vendors process the orders for delivery to the property. The receiving agent at the property inspects the incoming orders to ensure that they meet the specifications and that the invoice amounts are correct. The stock is then entered into inventory in the storerooms and the invoices are confirmed with the Purchasing and Accounting offices, which notify accounts payable to accept the electronic billing totals from the vendors. Payment is scheduled for electronic distribution to complete the purchasing cycle. Meanwhile, the outlets requisition the materials needed for the new business period and the perpetual cycle continues. The reason for the cycle to include purchasing, accounting, storeroom and receiving as separate functions is to ensure 'checks and balances,' which keeps all parties honest. Also, by monitoring usage versus sales in the outlets, exceptionally high levels of usage will generate exception reports, which are 'red flags' for managers to investigate discrepancies, which may indicate theft or waste at the outlet level.

This section has brought together information from previous sections to present information technology applications in hospitality settings. The examples that were presented are mostly focused on hotel, restaurant and retail systems. However, similar networks are used in other areas of service enterprise operations to enhance efficiency and effectiveness as means to improving productivity levels and positive customer relations programs.

SUMMARY

We began this chapter with the rationale for managers to be familiar with basic concepts associated with IT and IS, which together comprise the field of MIS. We first identified the broadest range of MIS functions to include SCM and ERP systems that result in EAI support functions. We reviewed basic computer hardware and software components and described their evolution from the 1980s through current times. We then turned our attention toward the telecommunications process of networked computers.

We engaged in discussion of enterprise telecommunications to include intranets, extranets and the Internet used to provide communications among suppliers, employees and guests of the service enterprise. This led us to examine the types of networks used for enterprise communications.

We learned that the same systems that drive the enterprise also impact the effectiveness and efficiency of the marketing function within a service enterprise. We identified a few basic marketing strategies and explained how information systems have revolutionized these activities. Next, we imposed the linear productivity model learned from Chapter 3 of the text over the enterprise telecommunications systems interfaces. This model provided us with an understanding of the ability for guests and clients to virtually interface with a service enterprise.

We used the foundation of concepts learned at this point to describe E-business and E-commerce systems. We realized that MIS has recently become firmly entrenched as a strategic enterprise unit within organizations owing to the influence of these systems upon all the business functions. We then investigated various technologies used to manage service enterprises to include DSS, OLAP, AI and others.

Toward the end of the chapter, we described the interfaces associated with the service enterprise operations. We learned about functional IS networks, DBMS, PMS and POS systems. We finally investigated electronic links to back-office operations and supply chain functions such as procurement and inventory management systems.

IN THE REAL WORLD (CONTINUED)

Tom, the technician, finally arrives one hour after the restaurant closes. You had to use manual systems to close out the shift prior to his arrival. You decide to follow him around as he diagnosed the hardware and software problems that caused the crash. You look over his shoulder and ask questions as he works on the machines. It seems to you that he is fixing things that he has already repaired many times.

When the technician finishes, you offer him a cup of coffee and start to ask him about the restaurant system. He says, 'Your outlet is the only one in the hotel with these problems.' You ask, 'Why is that?' Tom replies, 'Well, the hotel controller recently purchased this system on the basis of its low price.' 'That makes sense,' you say. 'Yup,' Tom answers, 'It always seems to make sense if you don't understand systems.' You ask, 'What does that mean?' 'Well,' Tom starts, 'The main problem with your system is that it is incompatible with the hotel's PMS. That's the main reason that it crashes.' 'But why do I have lines of servers waiting to input orders?' You ask. Tom smiles and says, 'That is the extended reporting feature that your controller wanted on these machines. You see, the accounting office wants a lot of detail reports for cost-control purposes. These machines are programmed to force service personnel to enter more details than normal so those reports will be automatically generated.' He looks at you to be sure you are following his logic, as you pour another cup of coffee. Tom continues, 'This means that your servers are filling in additional screens of information that have nothing to do with entering orders. The more screens, the more time it takes to process a transaction.'

'Wow,' you say, 'That is not very guest friendly.' You continue by saying, 'What about the kitchen printers going down all the time?' 'Oh,' Tom replies, 'That is a wiring issue.' You look perplexed as he continues, 'You see, kitchens are hostile environments for electronic interfaces. Your controller chose a lesser-priced wiring scheme to save installation costs.' You ask, 'How would you have wired it, Tom?' Tom says, 'For a kitchen or any high-traffic work area, I would go wireless.'

As Tom packs up his tools and prepares to leave, you ask him how you can learn more about POS machines. Tom tells you to pick up a management information systems book at any store to read up on the systems.

The next day, you meet with the restaurant manager, Erin, and fill her in on what Tom told you. 'Hmm,' Erin says, 'I guess we both need to learn a little about technology basics so we can discuss this situation with the F&B Director and Controller tomorrow.'

DISCUSSION QUESTIONS

1. Consider Table 8.1and describe the specifications you would use to order a set of terminals and processors for a front-desk operation at a medium-size hotel.
2. Identify and describe the functions of the following types of software: operating systems, general applications, specific applications, workstation software.
3. Describe the similarities and differences among LANs, WANs and MANs.
4. What types of clients are served by E-commerce, E-business and ERP systems?
5. Describe the functions of OLAP, DSS and AI. Please give examples of each as they would be used within various sectors of service enterprises.
6. Describe the interfaces among a PMS, POS and EDI systems that might be found in a full-service hotel.

KEY TERMS

Management Information Systems use a number of acronyms to describe electronic functions and processes. Key terms are listed below and should be incorporated into the practicing manager's vocabulary.

Bandwidth

CAD	Computer-aided design
CAM	Computer-aided manufacturing
DASD	Direct access storage device
DSL	Digital subscriber line
DSS	Decision support systems
E-commerce	Electronic commerce
Extranets	Outside access private networks that resemble the Internet
General Use Applications	Software for generic uses such as word processing
GB	Gigabyte
GUI	Graphical user interface
HTML	Hyper Text Markup Language
Intranets	Internal private networks and resemble the Internet
JAVA	Script language for webpages
LAN	Local area network
LINUX	Open access operating system
MB	Megabyte
MAN	Metropolitan area network
MSDOS	Microsoft Direct Operating System

OLAP	Online analytical processing
OS	Operating system
OOP	Object-oriented programming
PDA	Personal digital assistant
POS	Point of sale system
RAM	Random Access Memory
ROM	Read Only Memory
Specific Use Applications	Software for specific functions such as CAD
TB	Terabyte
UNIX	Operating system for mainframe computers
XML	Extensible Markup Language
WAN	Wide area network

ENDNOTES

1. Moore's Law.
2. Tesone.
3. Tesone, D.V., et al., 2002.
4. O'Brien, W., 2001.

Management Control Functions

In this chapter you will learn to:

1. Identify the key aspects of accounting and financial controls.
2. Identify the processes of material resource procurement and distribution.
3. Identify the components and processes contained within a performance management system.

ON THE JOB TRAINING

Your friend Marcy is working with a food and beverage controller for a hotel as part of her school internship. Since Marcy is your roommate, she shares the details of each day of work with you.

After Marcy's first day on the job, she tells you that she is going to have a chance to troubleshoot the controls for the banquet department of a hotel. She admits, 'I don't know what all this will be about, but I'll bet it will give me some insights about how resources are used in a complex environment like a resort hotel.'

To be continued...

INTRODUCTION

In this chapter, we consider the **control** functions of managing service enterprises. The control function of management involves measuring actual occurrences as compared to standards. Managers control tangible items such as resources used as inputs to the transformation process of production systems. They also control intangible items such as performance and processes. As managers, we must control outputs on the basis of quality and quantity standards for products and services.

Control functions exist in every area of the production system to include inputs, transformation processes and outputs.

As we know, the primary focus of front-line service enterprise operations consists of face-to-face interactions with our guests and clients that result in memorable service experiences. During those interactions, we seamlessly perform transaction processing from the first point of contact through the time we bid our guests farewell[1].

Management controls occur in both back- and front-of-the-house operations of the service enterprise. We know from Chapter 1 that back-office staff personnel support line workers in FOH operations. Two-way communication flows between the BOH and FOH operations are required to enact appropriate control functions. BOH and FOH managers collaborate to provide process and performance control functions, as well as those related to tangible resources and outputs.

Managers are responsible for controlling both tangible and intangible resources used for each aspect of production processes. Financial and material resource controls are intended to improve the efficiency of tangible inputs. Human performance requires techniques used to control workplace performance. The control function of management consists of tasks that ensure that actual performance meets established standards for performance.

FINANCIAL CONTROLS

Financial controls must exist at both the operating and corporate levels of the service enterprise. The Accounting Office possesses the primary responsibility for controlling operating revenues and expenses, while corporate finance officers usually take care of capital investments. Both accounting and finance practitioners are responsible for all financial controls.

Accounting Information Systems (AIS) assist those practitioners with financial controls. AIS consist of computer networks used to report business transactions and economic events that occur within a service enterprise. Figure 9.1 provides a description of AIS interfaces.

The AIS is linked with all transaction processes that include a payment component at both ends (back and front) of the organization. The figure demonstrates the locations of these transactions. **Supply Chain Transactions** occur as part of the procurement processes used to acquire material resources for use within the hospitality enterprise. **Sales Transactions** involve payments for products and services rendered by the enterprise. In our business, there are a few variations involving payment portions of sales transactions. **Booking Transactions** reserve space for future use, which may include a confirmation deposit rendered to a hotel or full payment for a cruise or flight at the time the reservation is transacted. **Tendering or Cash Settlement Transactions** involve after-the-fact payment for products and services rendered. Examples of these would be the checkout procedure at a hotel or payment for noninclusive incidentals during a cruise. **Credit Transactions** occur when sales are posted to an account that includes terms and conditions for future cash payment. For instance, clients may have established House Charge accounts at restaurants or City Ledger accounts with hotels. The AIS is automatically linked with any transaction that involves a monetary exchange at both the Supply Chain and Sales ends of the service enterprise[2].

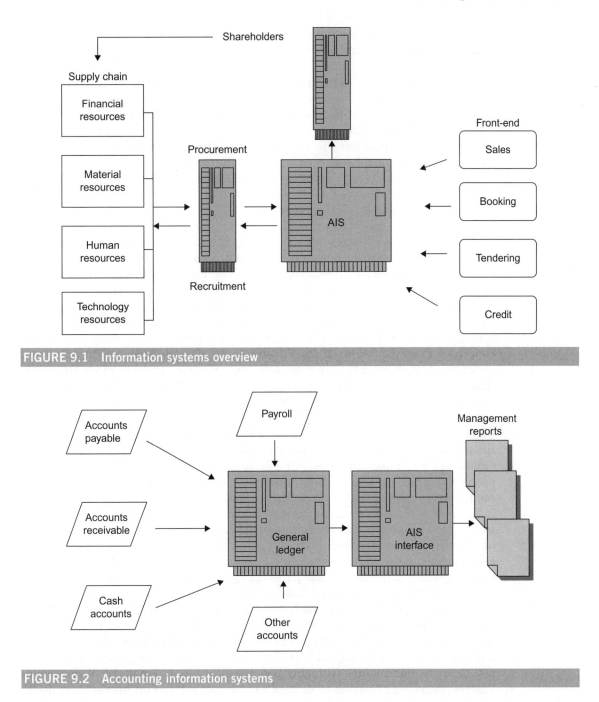

FIGURE 9.1   Information systems overview

FIGURE 9.2   Accounting information systems

The hub of an accounting database is the **General Ledger (GL)**, a journal that consolidates data received from other journals that contain data from specialized accounting functions. Figure 9.2 provides a picture of the journal entries that provide inputs to the General Ledger.

The **Accounts Receivable (AR)** ledger tracks entries pertaining to credit transactions with clients who owe payment to the hospitality enterprise at some future point in time. Sales transactions with hotel guests who have City Ledger accounts would be posted to Accounts Receivable, while noncredit sales are reported as cash settlements of daily revenues. Credit transactions also occur on the Supply Chain end of the hospitality organization with vendors and suppliers. These purchase transactions are recorded in the **Accounts Payable (AP)** ledger to track the payment of bills owed to suppliers of material resources such as goods, equipment and supplies. The **Payroll (PR)** account is used to monitor the payment of salaries and wages, as well as deductions that are placed in accounts to pay federal, state and local payroll taxes and benefit contributions. Accounts Payable and Payroll are examples of expense accounts, while Accounts Receivable is a revenue account. Additional expense accounts include sales tax, debt service and other accounts used to monitor expenses incurred by service enterprises[3].

The majority of sales transactions for hospitality enterprises are considered to be cash transactions, in which most clients pay their bills by cash or credit cards. For the hospitality enterprise, however, this is not a guaranteed form of payment, as credit card companies may not honor payments on certain transactions for a number of reasons. Also, credit card companies charge points for each merchant transaction, which discounts the amount of cash received from each of these sales transactions. Merchant discounts in addition to dishonored settlements will have a negative impact on the cash position of the hospitality enterprise. Cash Management is also concerned about the disbursement of cash reserves through Accounts Payable.

Accounts Payable consists of debit accounts or money owed to other businesses that support the Supply Chain of the hospitality organization. The terms and conditions of these accounts are based on time and money. Terms of payment may include a discount for early payment and interest added for late payments to the supplier. **Cash Management** seeks to maximize the amount of cash on hand by calculating the present and future values of money disbursements used to pay expenses. This calculation determines the most suitable amount of time that should lapse before processing an AP payment. Other financial management strategies include investment management as well as capital and operational budgeting processes.

From an asset management perspective, hospitality organizations are **capital intensive**. This means that large amounts of capital dollars are spent on the assets of the hospitality enterprise. Lodging companies make huge investments in real estate acquisitions, which include the construction and design of quality properties. The same is true for theme parks, along with additional capital investments in state-of-the-art technologies used to provide attractions to entertain guests of the parks. Airlines continuously purchase new aircraft and companies in the cruise business commission new vessels to expand their fleets. The recreation sector invests heavily in the development of clubhouses, golf courses, sports facilities and full-service health and wellness spas. Restaurant chains purchase premium real estate to build stores in highly populated locations. **Financial Management Systems** provide forecasting tools used to calculate returns on investments (ROI), interest rates, asset appreciation and terms of capital financing and amortization.

Hospitality operations are **labor intensive**, which means that payroll expenses are extremely high relative to other service industry providers. This makes sense given that our primary product consists of face-to-face guest interactions. Financial Management Systems (FMS) contain models to perform ratio analysis to measure units of labor expenses to units of production. For instance, hotels will calculate employees per guestroom ratios and restaurants measure labor units per plate production. These and other ratios are used in budget forecasting and planning activities to control labor costs[4].

The role of the accounting and finance departments is simply to record, track and report the status of financial controls. The individuals who actually control expenses and revenues are the operating managers of line and staff departments and divisions. The implementation of financial controls falls within the fiscal responsibility of all managers in the service enterprise.

MATERIAL RESOURCE CONTROL

Material resources are sourced and acquired through the procurement process for distribution through the output portion of the service enterprise supply chain. Controls must be established to monitor the efficiency of material resource usage at every step of the production system process. We learned in Chapter 3 of the text that the objective of efficiency is to maximize the utility of resources use.

PROCUREMENT AND INVENTORY CONTROLS

Procurement systems are used for the purchase of material resources made available through the supply chain of the service enterprise. Most purchasing departments use some form of computer automation to perform certain procurement functions. Figure 9.3 provides a depiction of common procurement systems for hospitality organizations.

Hospitality procurement professionals are usually referred to as **Purchasing Managers** or **Purchasing Agents**. These individuals are responsible for acquiring material resources for the hospitality enterprise in a timely and cost-efficient manner. A process called sourcing is the means by which the purchasing professionals identify vendors that provide the resources that meet the specifications of a specific hospitality organization. The purchaser will determine procurement volumes from operational forecasts used to determine resource usage. Once the volume levels have been determined, the purchaser will secure pricing bids from a number of purveyors (vendors). The purchaser will then issue a **Purchase Order (PO)** to each selected vendor. The PO is an authorization for Accounts Payable to pay for a specific invoice after the goods are received by the hospitality organization. In most cases, the PO is generated electronically from the Accounting Office[5].

The next step in the procurement process is for vendors to deliver the products to the service enterprise. The person in charge of receiving purchased items is usually called a **Receiving Agent**. The Receiving Agent works independently from the Purchasing Agent to ensure **checks and balances**, which is a procedure of separating the order and entry points for purchases. The Receiving Agent verifies counts and quality specifications of items that arrive at the receiving dock and signs invoices for items that meet with these specifications. Once the items are received, the invoice is transmitted to Accounts Payable and the new stock is forwarded to appropriate storage areas and counted as inventory. Operating departments will requisition items from inventory (stock) for use in their areas[6].

There are three aspects in the inventory management process that take place in the storage areas. The established level of inventory on hand for each item is

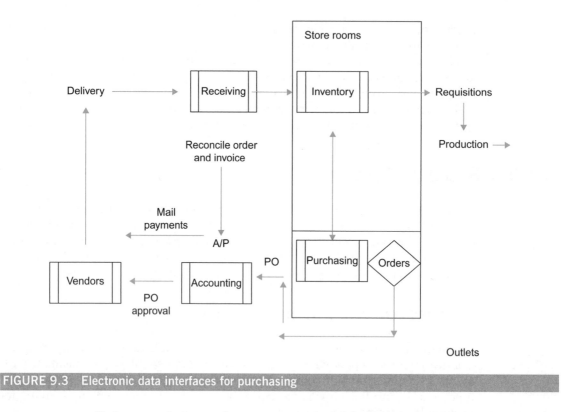

FIGURE 9.3   Electronic data interfaces for purchasing

called par stock. Items that are requisitioned for operating areas are deleted from the par stock. The difference between par stock and items on hand becomes the order amount that is sent to the purchaser. A perpetual inventory is an electronic process of accounting for storeroom transactions in real time. A perpetual inventory will track items that are entered into inventory to reestablish pars. It will also track each requisitioned item and remove it from on-hand inventory, and then calculate order volumes. The order volumes will be electronically distributed to the purchasing office, which begins the procurement process[7].

A perpetual inventory system may also be used to automate the procurement process. As we learned in Chapter 8 of the text, the purchasing office of a service enterprise could establish an Electronic Data Interchange (EDI) interface through an extranet for access by suppliers (vendors). This permits purchasing agents to review electronically generated reorder levels to make additions and deletions on the basis of forecast fluctuations. Once the purchaser is satisfied with reorder levels, the request for bids would be electronically transmitted to selected vendors. Vendors respond with electronic bids, with the best bid receiving an electronic PO from the purchasing agent. Next, the items are delivered and go through the receiving and storage process. Invoices are approved and the Accounts Payable electronically transmits funds to pay the invoices at appropriate times[8].

PRODUCTION CONTROLS

So far in this chapter, we have discussed systems that enable accounting, procurement, receiving and inventory management functions. Many of the items requisitioned from inventories are used as raw materials to produce tangible products. Hence, it makes sense for us to take a look at systems that facilitate the product production process. We learned about the various production systems in Chapter 6 of the text. Now, we will consider each of those systems from the perspective of management control.

We know that Food and Beverage operations produce tangible products that require a product production process performed by culinary practitioners. This could range from quick-service restaurants to fine-dining establishments. Catering and banquet culinary units are in the volume foods production business. Full-service hotels will range from mid-scale to luxury operations, which will reflect the span and scope of food service outlets within a given property. Luxury hotels will house numerous food and beverage outlets that range from casual to fine-dining establishments. A similar range of food service outlets will exist at theme parks, attractions, recreation and social clubs, as well as meeting, entertainment, travel and event venues. Food and beverage services are part of just about every sector of the hospitality industry[9]. We know from Chapter 6 that the product production system converts raw materials in the form of ingredients into finished products, which are consumable food and beverage items. Any tangible item that is produced from raw materials is considered to be a product. We know that product production is just one system contained within a restaurant operation. Food service outlets must also manage maintenance, repair, distribution and service transaction systems. The management of these systems applies to every sector of the service enterprise industry.

The full-service lodging sector provides numerous examples of repair and maintenance production systems. For instance, a hotel guestroom is an existing product. It is taken out of inventory while occupied and replaced into inventory when it is vacant and clean (ready for a check-in). If the shower in a guestroom is malfunctioning, the room is taken out of inventory and labeled as an 'out-of-order' room. It is only when repairs are completed to the shower that the room may be placed back into inventory. Public areas, such as the hotel lobby, are also part of the lodging product and must be kept to the standards expected by guests. The outside grounds of a hotel require cleaning and landscaping, as they exist for the aesthetic enjoyment of the guests. All of these areas require production processes that do not create new products; instead, the processes maintain and repair existing products.

In cases involving lodging, food service, clubhouse, theme parks, attractions, meeting and event venues, there are physical plant facilities and outside areas (grounds) that must be continually maintained and repaired. Air and sea travel organizations must maintain aircraft equipment and vessels, as well as terminal and gate areas. A maintenance production system converts an occupied space into a state of readiness for reoccupation by customers, clients, passengers or guests, while a repair production system converts an 'out-of-order' physical space into one that is ready to be occupied by guests, clients, passengers or customers[10].

HUMAN RESOURCE CONTROL

Material resources include raw materials, tools, equipment and supplies that are used for product conversion. Human resources are inputs of human capital in the form of workers who possess the knowledge, skills and abilities to perform the conversion process. In the case of product production, workers transform raw materials into finished products. Workers may also use raw materials such as replacement parts during the transformation process that occurs during repair production. Maintenance production usually requires the use of tools, equipment and supplies to enact the transformation process to produce outputs. Distribution production systems move items and information from one physical location to another. All of the production systems support service transaction systems, which are the hub of all guest and client interactions. We learned this concept in Chapter 6 of the text. All production systems produce outputs that result from the completion of transformation processes. Outputs are measured in terms of quality and quantity. Quality is measured in terms of compliance with established standards for outputs, while quantity refers to the number of outputs produced per work unit.

HUMAN RESOURCE ACQUISITION

We learned from Chapter 7 of the text that recruitment and selection processes comprise the acquisition of human resources. We recall that recruitment is the process of generating a pool of qualified applicants for a position. The selection process involves choosing the best candidate for a specific position. We also realize that qualifications are determined through demonstrated knowledge, skills, attitudes and abilities (KSAAs). The two documents used to determine KSAAs are called job descriptions and job specifications. We recall that job descriptions list the tasks, duties, responsibilities and reporting relationships for a jobholder. Job specifications list the specific knowledge, skills, attitudes and abilities for a specific position. Both documents arise from the job analysis function, which should be used to update job descriptions and job specifications at least once per year. This policy will ensure current documents to be used to control the qualifications for job applicants.

Once an individual is hired into a position, HR practitioners must determine gaps between required and actual KSAAs of the new hire. This gap will determine the types of training programs used to instill knowledge and skills for each newly hired worker. The evaluation and reinforcement aspects of the training process provide controls used to determine the competency levels of recently trained employees relative to the respective job description and job specification for the position. At this point in time, the newly hired worker has demonstrated the ability to perform the job functions to established standards. The established standards become the benchmarks or controls that will be used to evaluate future performance for each worker. It is the job of professional managers to clearly articulate the expectations for performance via the established performance standards for each position. Figure 9.4 depicts the documents used to communicate standards for performance for each position within a service enterprise.

The figure shows us the familiar progression of objectives to strategies and strategies to policies. We further see the transition of policies into standards and procedures. We recall this model from Chapter 2 of the text. Each of these steps from the strategic planning process discussed in Chapter 3 is converted into various documents that collectively comprise an employee handbook. Employee handbooks are usually distributed to newly hired workers during employee orientation sessions. Professional managers know that new workers will not learn the contents of the handbooks during orientation sessions, so they convert the contents of the handbook into a way of doing daily business in every work unit. This becomes

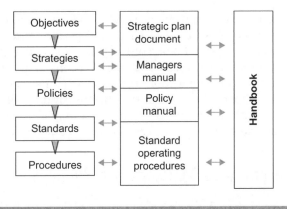

FIGURE 9.4 Human resource document sources

part of the departmental training for every new worker that is reinforced on a daily basis through informal observation and feedback from the manager.

A properly constructed employee handbook will include a number of pertinent sections used to articulate performance standards for workers employed by a service enterprise. These are guidelines that must be combined with the specific set of expectations contained within the job description for each position. Employee handbooks should be updated once per year, with current workers signing receipts for each newly published edition. The documents listed in the figure may be included in all versions of the handbook, or there could be a manager's version and a smaller one for other workers.

The strategic plan document should be a summary of the plan for the current year that includes the service enterprise mission, grand strategy, objectives and specific strategies intended to achieve both long- and short-term objectives. A separate section may be included to articulate the objectives and strategies for a specific department. The managers' manual is a document that identifies the dos and don'ts of professional management practices. A policy manual consists of broad guidelines used to meet performance standards. Finally, a standard operating procedures (SOP) manual provides specific performance standards with stepwise procedures used to achieve each standard. These combined documents are intended to provide objective and clearly articulated performance standards for every worker associated with the service enterprise. As is the case with all management practices, the documents alone will not ensure desired performance levels. It is the job of every manager to reinforce performance standards on a daily basis with the objective of habituating those practices into daily behaviors. The articulation of performance standards is the first step in producing a performance management system within a service enterprise.

PERFORMANCE MANAGEMENT SYSTEMS

Performance management systems take a systems approach to managing desired behaviors in the workplace. A performance management system provides planning, identification, encouragement through the communication of standards as well as evaluations of actual performance, as compared with established performance standards. The purpose of performance measurement is to provide feedback to employees about their performance and to take actions to facilitate improvement, as well as provide recognition of successful performance levels by giving rewards. Actually, this is not a stand-alone process, as some managers would have us believe. Instead, it is a multidisciplinary approach to people management that requires daily observation and communication through coaching, mentoring and disciplinary warnings on the part of the manager. The effectiveness of these practices is related to the levels of awareness on the part of the manager concerning the service perspective, leadership practice, worker motivation and work life development.

THE PERFORMANCE MANAGEMENT PROCESS

The performance management process starts with performance standards, which are simply behavioral goals. Then, job criteria (referred to as job lists) are established, which prioritize the importance of each job function by listing the procedures to meet each standard. The worker exceeds, meets or does not meet each category of performance. Since some aspects of performance are more important than others, we attach mathematical weights (10%, 50% etc.) to each performance category. Next, we multiply the weights (percentages) times each category. The averaged total of performance categories will provide an indication of the overall performance levels. For instance, if the worker exceeds standards for a criterion that is 60% of the job and meets the rest, that worker is above the standards (or an excellent performer, as most managers like to say). The process just described is called a performance appraisal.

PERFORMANCE STANDARDS

What is the basis of performance standards? As we already know, the productivity model, which measures effectiveness and efficiency, is the basis of identifying value-added workers. Customer relationship issues such as service levels and product quality/quantity are measures of effectiveness. Reducing resource expenses is an efficiency measurement. For example, a server in a full-service restaurant provides excellent guest service in a station consisting of 12 covers (seats). That server is being effective. Another server provides the same level of service in a station with 20 covers. That server is both efficient and effective because he/she is meeting the quality standards for eight more guests than the other server. If every server had this ability, there would be fewer servers required to staff the restaurant, which will result in lower payroll costs without comprising service quality. If the manager were to staff the restaurant in stations of 20 covers with the servers providing mediocre service, the restaurant would be efficient, but not effective. Thus, the manager would be meeting only part of his/her performance responsibility.

The holistic approach to management performance responsibility is presented in Figure 9.5.

A performance management system includes every management activity from strategic planning through performance appraisal. The system includes the management functions of planning, organizing, influencing and control. The performance appraisal activity is a control process, in that it compares actual performance with standards for performance, which is what management control is all about.

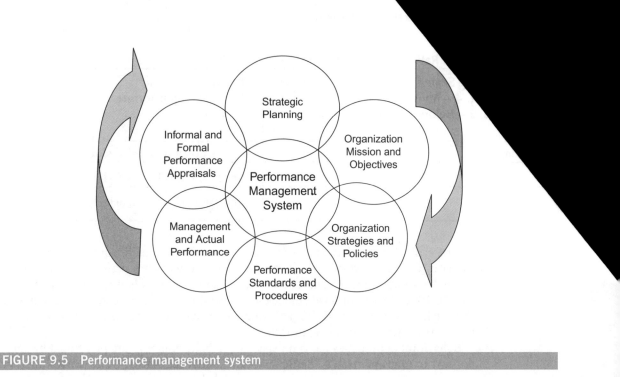

FIGURE 9.5 Performance management system

PERFORMANCE APPRAISALS

There are two types of performance appraisals. One is done daily and is mostly verbal. This is an **informal appraisal**. The **formal appraisal** is written (usually on a performance appraisal form) and occurs on a periodic basis (usually annually). Who appraises whom? Well, managers always appraise their workers, but workers could appraise their supervisors as well; this is called the **180 degrees model**. In some cases, subordinates, supervisors and peers participate in the appraisal process. This is the **360 degrees model**. Peer ratings are becoming popular with the push toward **self-managed teams (SMT)**. Almost all ratings are multisource as they usually include one extra step up in the chain of command. Self-evaluations are good introspection tools. However, most people lack the level of self-awareness to do this function effectively. If we use customer feedback plus all the other ratings mentioned here, we are truly doing a multisource rating.

There are various formal appraisal methods. The most popular is the **Category rating method**, which includes **graphic rating scales** (1–5) and **checklist methods** (check off the statement that applies). Table 9.1 shows examples of graphic rating and checklist methods.

Comparative methods rate employees against each other. The **Ranking method** ranks them from best to worst. A **Forced distribution** approach puts most rated individuals in the middle (average) of a curve and a few at each end (below average to the left, above average to the right of the curve). Narrative methods involve writing reports on the basis of performance observations.

A powerful observation and recording tool is called the **critical incident method** that combines informal observations and feedback sessions with formal reviews. A manager using this method will take notes of objective observations of important (critical) activities (incidents) for each employee. The manager takes five minutes

Performance Appraisals

Rating	Checklist Method (Check the appropriate column)	Check
5	Attends every scheduled shift	X
	Attends most scheduled shifts	
	Attendance is not consistent	

during each shift to place the notes in a file marked for each worker. At the end of the year, we have a year's worth of notes on each worker's performance (a powerful tool). Another written method of performance appraisals is the **essay** appraisal. This is used for senior-level management positions in most cases and includes a thorough written essay on the performance of the executive, which is another format of the narrative report approach.

Behavioral approaches focus on specific job behaviors that are predefined by some document. One approach is the **Behaviorally Anchored Rating Scale (BARS)** method that uses concrete descriptions of expected behaviors in a checklist format similar to the one presented previously in Table 9.1. The BARS method adheres to the Dictionary of Occupational Titles to identify position descriptions. This document is not conducive to most service enterprise positions as it is more geared toward manufacturing and administrative functions. Service industry managers usually generate customized behavioral criteria in order to use this method. As we learned in Chapter 3, **Management by Objectives (MBO)** is both a goal setting activity and a performance appraisal method. It involves top/down, bottom/up goals to be set for every level of the organization on the basis of the mission. Supervisors then review the accomplishment of objectives at some later date. A few organizations have implemented a performance management system known as the **Balanced Scorecard**, which is a method that includes quantitative measurements on one axis and qualitative metrics on the other axis. The purpose of the balanced scorecard is to provide weights for measuring service to all of the stakeholder groups, as opposed to other methods that focus solely on the contributions to the customers and shareholders.

PERFORMANCE APPRAISAL VALIDITY ERRORS

In actual practice, the performance appraisal system will be a hybrid of many methods that have been mentioned in this section. There is a factor known as **rater error** that will invalidate the performance appraisal. One example of rater error consists of **Recency effect**, which occurs when we do not use the critical incident method and can only remember the last few weeks of performance for each worker. **Central tendency** error is the tendency on the part of a manager to try to make everyone average. **Rater bias** occurs when personal issues cloud the objective criteria of the review. **Halo effect** is rating all categories on a single attribute. For instance, a worker may have a problem with chronic tardiness, but performs well in all other aspects of the job. The rater may attribute low scores to every performance category based on the tardiness issue. **Contrast error** occurs when comparisons are made to other workers instead of to objective criteria. We see this problem when untrained managers engage in subjective management practices, which may only occur in the absence of enforcing adherence to established objective performance standards.

PERFORMANCE APPRAISAL INTERVIEWS

The most important part of a formal review is the performance appraisal interview. It should be done in private, be a two-way dialog and only occur after the person being reviewed has had sufficient time to read the completed appraisal document. The worst thing for a supervisor to do is to avoid issues that may be less than positive. People have a tendency to this because we do not like to deliver bad news and prefer to avoid interpersonal conflict. This practice is dishonest on the part of the manager and will ultimately result in negative consequences for both parties. However, in the process of delivering negative information, supervisors are cautioned to always be kind and compassionate with their interactive style.

As far as legal aspects of performance appraisals are concerned, supervisors should remember to be sure the methods used for evaluation are valid, reliable, fair, uniform and consistent. This rule is true for any management practice.

THE FORMAL APPRAISAL PROCESS

The human resource office is responsible for communicating the policy and procedures for formal performance appraisal activities within the organization. The HR practitioners also handle the administrative aspect of appraisal development, distribution and documentation. To ensure fairness, uniformity and consistency, formal appraisals usually require multilevel review and approval and include the approval of the human resource director. Table 9.2 provides a listing of the formal performance appraisal process.

It should be evident from the steps outlined in the table that the formal appraisal process is time consuming. However, the opportunity to provide feedback for an employee's performance is worth the time, effort and expense. Experienced managers recognize the leadership opportunity involved with taking sufficient time to provide feedback to the workers. Poorly trained managers sometimes consider the appraisal process to be a perfunctory process. If those managers were to place themselves in the shoes of the workers, they would realize that performance feedback is vital to sound employee relations.

MANAGEMENT CONTROL AND SUPERVISION

The responsibilities for engaging in the management control function vary among positions at different levels of the service enterprise organization. We learned in Chapter 1 of the text that management levels include senior-, middle- and first-level (supervisors and leads) positions. Senior managers are responsible for establishing the policies that influence the control of financial, material and human resources within the enterprise. This results from the strategic planning activities, which are a primary area of concern for senior-level executives. Middle-level managers

TABLE 9.2	Formal Performance Appraisal Process

1. Human resource office tracks the time period of performance appraisals.

2. Human resource office distributes appraisal instruments 30 days prior to due date.

3. Operating managers complete the appraisal instruments.

4. Operating managers attain approval of the rating from executive and human resource managers.

5. Operating manager establishes a scheduled interview time with the employee.

6. Operating manager gives the employee sufficient time to review the appraisal document.

7. Operating manager conducts the appraisal interview by engaging in dialog with the employee.

8. Employee provides written commentary and signature on the appraisal document.

9. Executive and human resource director signatures indicate approval.

10. The appraisal document is admitted to the employee's personnel file.

11. Human resource office schedules the next periodic appraisal date for trace.

12. Human resource office processes payroll change document in the event of a pay increase.

13. The accounting office processes the payroll change document.

are responsible for establishing and revising standard operating procedures (SOPs) for every work unit contained within the department or division. Both senior- and middle-level managers view management control from broad perspectives.

The first-level managers of the service enterprise are primarily responsible for the management control function. This is the nature of supervision. We know from Chapter 1 that higher-level managers oversee larger numbers of positions, but they rely upon work unit managers, supervisors and leads to perform daily supervision activities. Supervisors spend 90% of their management time performing control tasks by observing the actual performance of workers and comparing those behaviors to standards for performance. The supervisory practices also ensure the efficient use of financial and material resources throughout the production processes for each work unit contained within the service enterprise. First-level supervisors rely upon technical expertise to ensure that performance standards are met. They must also be adept in coaching, training, progressive discipline, conflict resolution, communication, evaluation and leadership skills in order to add value to the production processes within each work unit. The first-level managers and supervisors of the enterprise work most closely with the guests and clients to ensure that they are being served at a standard that is consistent with the value proposition of the service enterprise. In essence, it is the supervisors who make the difference in terms of serving internal and external customers. Just as noncommissioned officers in the military are the backbone of operations, service enterprise supervisors make the guest experiences happen. Those first-level managers who continuously enhance both efficiency and effectiveness of services through management controls are practicing value-added management (VAM).

Summary

We began this chapter by identifying management control practices, which ensure that actual performance levels meet established performance standards. We recognized that managers must control both tangible and intangible resources. Tangible resources comprise financial and material resource control. Intangible control focuses on human performance issues. All controls are aimed at meeting the efficiency objectives of the service enterprise through every aspect of production systems.

Financial controls are currently supported by accounting information systems that assist with tracking various financial transactions. We learned that the hub of the accounts systems is called the general ledger account and that numerous other financial accounts interface with this ledger. Accounting and financial management systems are used to control cash flow, capital and operating expenditures, and labor costs. These funds are used to purchase material resources used for future production systems.

Material resources are sourced and acquired by a purchasing department. Material resource procurement requires both purchasing and inventory control systems that interface with the accounting function. Material resource controls involve checks and balances used to monitor those resources from the point of acquisition through the requisition for use in the production system.

Production system controls monitor the utility of material resource usage at every point of the production system. We reinforced the production systems for service enterprises as consisting of product, maintenance, repair, distribution and service transaction systems. The individuals who use material resources within a production system are referred to as human resources.

Human resources are acquired through the recruitment and selection processes, usually overseen by a human resource department. The value of human resources is based on KSAAs. Newly hired workers go through training to provide additional KSAAs that are listed on job specifications. Part of this training is to learn the expectation for performance contained within the performance management system.

What makes a performance management system a 'system?' The mission for the organization, which is used to develop objective performance standards, drives a performance management system. The standards are broken down into policies and procedures for each task that is driven by these standards. Managers and supervisors symbolize the service perspective in their daily interactions. They are aware of human motivational factors and take a personal interest in the work life development of the staff members. They engage in sound leadership practices, through which they employ effective communication skills used to coach, recognize, evaluate, counsel and use progressive discipline with the staff members in appropriate situations. Managers and supervisors employ the use of the critical incident method to account for all-important aspects of performance. Finally, they provide constructive feedback to the workers through performance appraisal methods, which are used to redirect behaviors below the standards and to develop the careers of workers who meet or exceed the standards.

We concluded the chapter with a discussion of the role of management control among first-level managers. We learned that the supervisory function is a control function. First-level managers are very important for ensuring that actual performance meets standards for performance. Those managers who continually enhance efficiency and effectiveness of production systems are practicing value-added management.

IN THE REAL WORLD (CONTINUED)

A few months have passed since your friend Marcy started her internship. One night you are sitting with a bunch of friends and one of them, Jason, starts talking about the restaurant he is working at. He mentions that the place is a mess, with many servers engaged in theft and the constant lack of materials needed to do the job. You smile and tell everyone, 'Well, Marcy is our resident controller, maybe she can tell you how that problem might be fixed.'

'Well,' Marcy chimes in, 'I'm no expert, but I did have a chance to participate in a controls turnaround as part of my internship at the hotel.' The others look interested and chide, 'Tell us about it, Marcy.'

Marcy begins to tell her tale. She says, 'Well when I started there three months ago, the F&B controller told me I would be in for a real learning experience. I had no idea how bad the controls can get in a poorly managed operation.' She continues, 'In this case, it was the banquet department that had all the problems – very similar to the ones you described, Jason.' This piques Jason's interest.

Marcy continues, 'As it turns out, it was simply a lack of financial and material resource controls.' She said, 'The F&B controller was famous for saying if they steal our stuff, shame on them, if we can't control it, shame on us.' Marcy continued by saying, 'It's all about checks and balances. We implemented controls from inventory requisitioning through the POS system. We placed locks on working inventories that required manager access and we frequently audited their beverage storeroom.' Marcy concluded by saying, 'After about 30 days, all the costs were back in line and we identified a captain who was fired for stealing liquor.'

Jason looked at Marcy and said, 'Wow, you did learn a lot in a short period of time.' Marcy replied, 'Yup, I know exactly what controls to put in place for the future.'

DISCUSSION QUESTIONS

1. There was talk throughout the chapter concerning the enhancement of productivity in hospitality enterprises. How would automated procurement, inventory management and requisitioning activities enhance productivity for operations managers?
2. Some people believe that managers just fill out performance appraisal forms without giving them much thought. Do you think this is true? How would you feel if someone did that to you?
3. Sometimes a manager runs a department and everyone in it is above average. He/she leaves and a new manager takes over. When the new

manager does appraisals, he/she rates everyone as average. How can this be if there has been no change in performance?

4. You sit down with a manager for your performance appraisal interview. The manager starts citing dates and times of specific behaviors performed by you over the past year. Do you think that manager has a photographic memory, or is he/she using some other technique? Would you use such a technique? Why or why not?

CASE STUDY

This hotel was part of a major chain. It was also one of the chain's very successful locations after a major renovation. The staff was quite happy and they were treated well. It was no surprise that guest scores were also quite high in comparison to other locations of the brand.

The general manager was especially proud of his low turnover rate. In an industry with turnover rates that often exceed 100% annually, this property hovered around 40%. The front desk, often a critical spot for turnover, was another bright spot at this property. Six of the 10 full-time front-office staff members had been at the property for over five years – quite an accomplishment in the high-turnover hospitality industry.

Audrey, a full-time front-desk agent, was facing financial problems. A mother of two, she had been divorced three months ago. Although her relationship had been self-described as 'ended years ago,' the official divorce came in the year 2000. Shortly after the divorce, she began dating her immediate supervisor, the front-office manager, Gerald. Dating was discouraged among hotel employees as discussed in the employee handbook. Dating of a supervisor and his or her direct subordinate was prohibited – again, explained clearly in the employee handbook. Gerald and Audrey did a good job of hiding their relationship – as a matter of fact, until this particular incident, no one at the property had figured it out. Considering the usual 'rumor-mill environment' of many hotels, the hidden relationship came as a surprise to those close to the two employees.

The divorce had left Audrey in dire financial straits. It was a true challenge just to make ends meet. She thought of pursuing a second, part-time job in the evenings since she mainly worked the 7:00 a.m.–3:00 p.m. shift at the hotel. Gerald discouraged it and said he would help her out financially. As time went on, he did not fulfill his financial promise to Audrey and she desperately needed money to feed her children, pay her bills and take care of some automobile problems.

In the month of May, the hotel's management company changed its policies on several accounting procedures. One of these new procedures required each front-desk employee to have his or her personal bank audited on a weekly basis. Since Audrey was Gerald's girlfriend, he felt that it was 'okay' to never audit her bank and just made up the correct numbers each week. This proceeded until the date of the incident, July 17, 2000.

During the week of July 15–22, 2000, Gerald took a vacation to visit his parents in North Dakota. During his absence, the general manager, Pablo, took it upon himself to count banks one evening. This was normally not a part of his regular routine, but he was manager on duty and figured it would occupy some of his time. On that particular evening of July 17, 2000, the hotel had a very low occupancy of just 27% and there really was not much else for Pablo to attend to.

While counting banks, he found that Audrey's bank was missing an even amount of $500.00. As per hotel policy, he counted banks with Greyson, the F&B manager, so that there were two people present at all times. Greyson, a member of the executive committee, was indeed permitted to count banks and had done so many times at the hotel. They counted it three times to be certain of the loss as Audrey had never had any such issue before. Confused and upset, Pablo phoned Audrey at home. There was no answer and there was no answering machine or voice mail. It was late, so he figured he would wait until 7:00 a.m. in the morning to confront her.

At 7:00 a.m., he confronted Audrey as she was entering work. Along with the human resources director and controller, they sat Audrey down to discuss the situation. Audrey immediately appeared uncomfortable and upset – she paced and did not want to sit still in the seat. As they pulled out the forms and receipts from the adding machine, Audrey exclaimed, 'I know what this is all about. That jerk has decided to rat on me.' Perplexed, the three managers looked at her. Pablo responded with, 'Audrey, would you please settle down and explain what is going on here.'

The explanation given was that for a period of three months Audrey would take $500.00 out of her bank between paychecks so she could float herself financially. She said that the divorce had left her financially strapped and she just could not make it. She always paid the money back when she could, but it seemed that the situation had become a never-ending cycle. She told the managers that Gerald was indeed her boyfriend and that they had been dating for the past three months. She admitted that she indeed knew this was against company policy, but he said not to worry and that he would 'always cover for her.' She went on to state that they had been fighting rather strongly for the past three weeks and that is why he probably brought the missing money to the general manager's attention. When Pablo explained that he had indeed counted the bank himself, Audrey was at a loss for words.

Audrey began crying hysterically, begging for forgiveness, and mentioning that without work she would be forced to a shelter as she had no family members in the area to provide for her or the children. The human resources director calmed her down somewhat and asked her to sit in the waiting area while the three managers discussed the situation.

In the particular state where this hotel is located, theft of $500.00 or greater is considered a 'felony' according to state law. Further, hotel policies dictate that if an amount greater than $50.00 is missing when a bank is audited of any employee, it is grounds for immediate termination.

Audrey looked sadly through the glass window of the human resources office as the three managers determined her fate.

Questions

- What is the best course of action for the managers?
- Who is the responsible party in this situation? Should Audrey be given a concession since she is a single mother with no other forms of income?
- How does Gerald fit into the situation?
- What legal actions should the hotel take, if any?
- In your opinion, what type of cash drawer policies are appropriate for a hotel? Should employees be permitted to borrow money between pay-checks if, indeed, they fully pay it back by a specified due date?

ENDNOTES

1. Tesone, D.V., 2006. Hospitality Information Systems and E-Commerce. John Wiley & Sons, Hoboken, NJ.
2. *Ibid.*
3. *Ibid.*
4. *Ibid.*
5. *Ibid.*
6. *Ibid.*
7. *Ibid.*
8. *Ibid.*
9. *Ibid.*
10. *Ibid.*

PART 3

Strategic Applications

CHAPTER 10

Tactical Productivity Strategies

OBJECTIVES

In this chapter you will learn to:

1. Identify and explain each of the three tactical strategies.
2. Describe the steps used to conduct managerial diagnosis and intervention implementation.
3. Describe productivity control and output productivity interventions.
4. Describe production systems contained within functional departments.

IN THE REAL WORLD

A friend of yours from school, Kelly, has been engaged in an internship at a theme park for the past three months. She has been working alongside a very experienced manager, Jeremy, who never seems to be satisfied with the current state of his operations.

One day you meet with Kelly at the park for lunch. You ask her how the internship is going. She sighs and begins by saying, 'You know, when I first started working with Jeremy, I thought he was the most negative person I ever met. But over time, I realized he is just into continuous improvement for his operation. The guy is so good at diagnosing and implementing productivity interventions.' You ask her, 'What is that?' Kelly smiles and says, 'It's when you constantly tweak some part of the operation to make it more efficient and effective. Jeremy has shown all sorts of ways to do this. In fact, this Friday we are going to sit down and review our accomplishments. I'm a little nervous about that,' Kelly finishes.

To be continued...

INTRODUCTION

We have already learned a good deal about management knowledge and management functions throughout Parts I and II of the text. Our assimilation of the information from the past nine chapters should position us to consider the overview of tactical strategies from expanded perspectives.

This chapter will revisit some of the information previously presented in Chapter 3 of the text to provide an overview of tactical strategies used by managers at all levels of service enterprise organizations. We will then discuss the skills of performing management diagnostics and interventions. Next, we will consider diagnostics and interventions applied to enhancing productivity. We already know that value-added managers (VAM) are those who enhance productivity levels within work units departments, and divisions of service enterprises. This is done incrementally in small steps taken every day to improve resource utility, streamline transformation processes and improve the quality and quantity of outputs.

AN OVERVIEW OF TACTICAL STRATEGIES

We know that senior-level managers spend most of their time focused on strategic initiatives aimed at the future direction of the organization relative to the mission and vision statements. Tactical strategies are more focused on the current performance levels of the enterprise at the current time. This is the mandate for middle-level managers. Junior-level managers (assistant managers, leads, supervisors) assist the middle-level managers with the implementation of tactical strategies.

Middle- and junior-level managers should be constantly engaged in the planning and implementation of some form of tactical strategy. The appropriate strategy will be dictated by the current circumstances that exist within the enterprise. There are three main categories of tactical strategies. A **run strategy** is used to enhance productivity levels within a department that is meeting standards for performance. A **growth strategy** is implemented when a perceived opportunity for expansion exists. Finally, a **fix strategy** is a tactic intended to turnaround an underperforming department.

Note that each of the three tactical strategies is proactive and dynamic, which means they are intended as interventions to improve the current status of a department. Run strategies are implemented in small steps to improve productivity levels in a department on a daily basis. Growth strategies are appropriate for expanding operations to include enhancing existing facilities or adding new stores or outlets. Fix strategies are the exception to the proactive rule in that they are partially reactive and later become proactive strategies.

MANAGEMENT DIAGNOSTICS

We learned in Chapter 1 of the text that management is a practice. All professional practitioners perform **diagnostics**, which consist of identifying and prioritizing symptoms that ultimately fit into a pattern that defines a problem. Physicians diagnose physiological problems, while attorneys diagnose legal problems. Architects define physical plant structural problems and engineers focus on electronic and

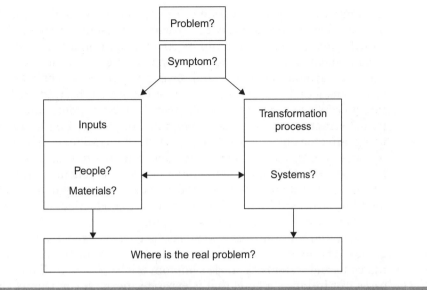

FIGURE 10.1   System investigation

mechanical problems. Each practitioner deals with reactive and proactive problems. A physician is being reactive when he/she heals a sick or injured person and is being proactive when he/she improves the current health of a normal patient. The attorney who protects the existing assets of a client is being proactive, as opposed to defending a client in court (reactive). The architect may be called in to design a new building (proactive) or to fix a structural flaw in an existing property (reactive). And the engineer may be asked to proactively build a better mousetrap or reactively fix a broken one. In management practice, we diagnose problems aimed at improved performance or expanded operations from a proactive perspective. We also perform diagnostics on underperforming work units for the purpose of reactively fixing them; then we proactively make them better than the norm.

We remember that the definition of a problem is a negative gap between actual performance and standards for performance. At this point, our new knowledge leads us to expand this definition by saying that a problem is a negative gap between actual performance and *intended* standards for performance. In the case of an underperforming work unit, the diagnostic phase will render problems that require reactive interventions at first and then transform into proactive interventions during the rebuilding of the work unit. Run and growth strategies are completely proactive in nature, since they seek to improve or expand an operation that is meeting current standards. In these cases, the interventions are designed to 'raise the bar' of existing standards.

Regardless of whether we are performing reactive or proactive diagnoses, the process of identifying symptoms and potential problems are always the same. Figure 10.1 revisits this process.

The first step in performing any tactical strategy is to diagnose the situation within a work unit, department, division or organization. The manager will notice some obvious symptoms and will have to use investigative skills, experience and intuition to detect those symptoms that are not obvious. Most obvious symptoms are found in the outputs section of the production system. For instance, customer demand that exceeds the service capacity of a restaurant could be a symptom of a growth problem. Status quo profits could be an initial symptom of a productivity enhancement problem. Complaints concerning guest services and inferior products could be a symptom of a potential turnaround problem. The manager will trace the symptoms found in the outputs area of the system back through the transformation process and input sections to collect additional information concerning a suspected symptom of a problem. Symptoms of potential problems may be detected using numerous techniques. These include observation, questionnaires, interviews or focus groups, records inspections and listening to casual conversations among guests and employees. If a symptom appears to be generated in the transformation process of a system, it will be labeled as a *systems* symptom. Those symptoms found to be caused by the input section of a production system will be labeled as either material resource or people symptoms.

The objective of the diagnostic phase is to collect and analyze symptoms for root causes. The manager will place symptoms in one of the three categories: people, materials and systems. A single symptom can be placed in all the categories in some cases. For instance, a hotel that is experiencing guest complaints about long check-in lines at the front desk could find multiple causes of this system. If the cause is nonproficient desk agents, there would be a people symptom. The cause may also be an insufficient number of computer terminals, which would be labeled as a material resource symptom. Also, the check-in software may require too many keystrokes, indicating a systems problem. This one symptom could have root causes in all three categories of symptoms, indicating a threefold operations problem.

A material resources symptom would be caused by a shortage in acquisition or allocation of materials, supplies, equipment or technology or the use of defective materials that feed into the transformation process of a production system. Technology factors may also influence systems symptoms. Systems symptoms may also include sequencing, timeliness, accuracy or redundancy flaws within transformation processes of a production system. The most difficult diagnostics fall within the people category of symptoms. While behaviors are observable, other organizational factors such as culture and cognition are not empirical entities. People symptoms could include competencies, staffing levels, supervision, management, leadership, motivation, group dynamics, mental states and other human variables.

When all of the symptoms are categorized, the manager then determines the nature of real existing problems. The manager prioritizes these in order of importance to the operation, as is shown in Figure 10.2.

At first glance, the diagnostician will be presented with an obvious problem by a member of the senior management team. In many cases, senior-level managers do not possess the skills to differentiate between problems and symptoms. The diagnostician initially views this obvious problem as a symptom of a potential problem. The diagnostician will proceed to collect data from the targeted operation, looking for obvious as well as subtle indicators of potential symptoms. Next, the diagnostician will categorize the symptoms and analyze each one to identify patterns of causal relationships that indicate real problems. The final phase of the analysis will be to prioritize the symptoms in order of importance to a potential intervention. The diagnostician will generate solution alternatives and analyze each one from the viewpoint of feasibility. The most feasible alternative solutions will become part of the intended intervention.

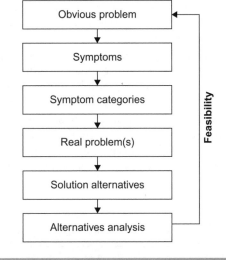

FIGURE 10.2 **System analysis**

MANAGEMENT INTERVENTIONS

Management interventions involve the implementation of problem-solving strategies in a work unit, department, division or organization. All interventions result in two outcomes. First, they solve problems within a targeted area of the service enterprise. Second, they always result in changes to an area of the enterprise. Managers act as change agents when performing diagnostics and interventions. Management interventionists who are employed by the service enterprise are considered to be internal change agents, while those hired on a consulting basis from outside the firm are referred to as external change agents. Individuals who specialize in systemic continuous change aimed at organizational renewal are called **organization development (OD)** practitioners[1]. Anecdotal evidence suggests that the best OD practitioners are those who incorporate change management into their overall management practices. Most managers make small incremental changes to the operations. This is certainly the approach for continuous productivity improvement. Sometimes, when the organization is in a reactive mode, quantum changes become necessary. Fix strategies are examples of quantum changes performed in work units, departments, divisions and organizations. Growth strategies may be performed on a quantum scale, such as adding multiple stores to a chain restaurant over a small period of time. Sometimes, growth strategies are implemented on smaller scales, such as adding a new menu item or expanding the seating capacity of a dining room. The most common behavioral barrier to change implementation is the resistance to change on the part of the workers. Change agents realize that sound communication skills should precede any incremental change to overcome this barrier. In the event of quantum change, the change agent must generate a sense of urgency on the part of employees to overcome resistance. For instance, when a manager performs a turnaround intervention, the staff members learn quickly that failure to change could result in negative career outcomes up to and including possible discharge from employment. Figure 10.3 provides a depiction of the steps used to design and implement a management intervention.

The intervention development process begins with the analysis of alternative solutions. Next, the manager will choose an alternative and design the solution intervention. The smallest incremental changes might require a single solution such as revising the sequence of steps in a transformation process. Most interventions, however, will employ a number of solutions to be implemented in either concurrent or consecutive sequence. In these cases, steps in Figure 10.3 will be replicated one time for each intervention. Managers will plot multiple intervention strategies on a timeline for completion, as shown in Figure 10.4.

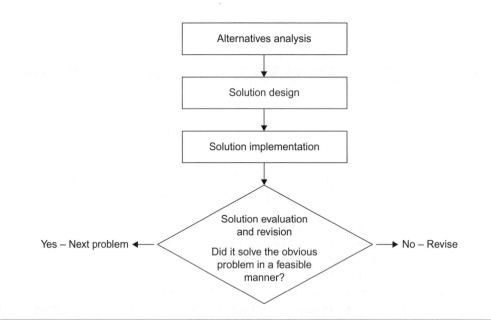

FIGURE 10.3 System design, implementation and evaluation

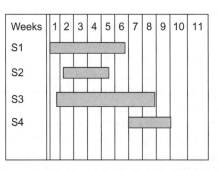

FIGURE 10.4 Intervention strategies

The critical path method (CPM) chart is the tool used to plot the timelines for each intervention strategy. There are four strategies noted in the figure (S1–S4). The numbers at the top of the chart represent Weeks 1 through 11, which tells us that this intervention is expected to occur over 11 weeks. The first intervention strategy commences in Week 1 and should be completed in Week 6. S2 begins in the middle of Week 2 and will finish in the middle of Week 5. S3 runs from the end of Week 1 through Week 8. The final strategy will be implemented from Week 7 through Week 9. We can see that the manager plans to complete the intervention by the end of Week 9, yet the chart shows an 11-week window. This is because situations might occur that will put the interventionist behind schedule, so he/she builds in some cushion time. This in itself is a sound strategy, as he/she will tell the senior managers that the intervention will take 11 weeks to complete and will finish the project ahead of schedule. Savvy managers know how to under-promise and overdeliver. By the middle of Week 2, three of the strategies will be implemented concurrently. We can see that S4 cannot commence until S1 and S2 are completed and S3 is in its fifth week.

DIAGNOSTICS AND INTERVENTIONS

All tactical strategies use the steps outlined in the sections above. Managers who practice these steps frequently begin to perform them unconsciously. This level of practice creates a state of unconscious competence in which the diagnostic and intervention activities are performed without exerting high levels of concentration.

Outside consultants might choose to use a more formal process called action research to diagnose problems and implement interventions. This process is expensive and time consuming. It begins with an initial investigation to collect preliminary data. The data are shared with a formative committee of senior managers. The data are analyzed to determine symptoms and problems. The priorities are determined by committee consensus. A document is created that begins with a Statement of the Problems. Intervention techniques are then designed and implemented. The interventionist meets with a summative committee of senior managers to evaluate and revise the results as the last step of the action research intervention.

The reasons that outside consultants use a more formalized approach is that they need to learn the workings of the service enterprise from scratch. Internal change agents are already familiar with the culture, nuances, policies, processes and practices of an organization. Hence, the data collection process is swift when conducted by a corporate insider. Also, outside consultants are contracted for specific purposes. Practicing managers within an organization usually possess the authority to conduct interventions without seeking approval from upper-level managers.

In fact, experienced managers do much less quantitative work than outside consultants. Our intuition concerning hidden problems grows with our daily experiences from practicing management. This really is not as much a phenomenon as some people think. We log our experiences into the long-term memory portion of our brains. When we find ourselves facing a similar experience in the future, the hippocampus part of the brain will feed those lessons learned into our consciousness. This is called parallel brain processing, which is a topic we will discuss more thoroughly in Chapter 16 of the text. When we experience a situation for the first time, our brain uses serial or sequential logic processing to absorb information and

Productivity = Inputs over outputs

P=1/0

Inputs = Costs of sales = Operating expenses

Outputs = Revenues or income from sales

Productivity = Cost percentages

Lower cost percentages = Higher gross operating margins

FIGURE 10.5   The relationship between costs and sales used to measure productivity

respond. This is much slower than parallel brain processing. When experienced managers claim that they have a 'hunch' about a problem, they are really saying that this situation is similar to others they have experienced in the past.

PRODUCTIVITY ENHANCEMENT STRATEGIES

We know that all production systems consist of three parts. There are (1) inputs that go into a (2) transformation process to render (3) outputs. Inputs consist of resources that must be acquired and allocated into the production system. All resources cost money. Direct costs are considered to be operating expenses or costs. Operating expenses include all resources that are directly used as inputs for a production system. Indirect costs are considered to be capital expenses such as physical plant costs (overhead) and equipment expenses. Outputs consist of services and products that result in sales, which generate revenues or income for the service enterprise. When we view the two ends of the production system, we see costs to the left and sales to the right of the transformation process. Hence, productivity is measured by the costs of sales. Figure 10.5 depicts the relationship between costs and sales used to measure productivity.

We see that productivity equals inputs divided by outputs. In accounting terms, inputs are measured as costs of sales or operating expenses. Outputs are sales that generate revenues or income. When we divide costs by revenues, we get a number that represents a cost percentage of sales. If the percentages decrease, then gross operating profit margins will increase. If the percentages increase, then profits will decrease. So, the measurement of productivity is cost percentages, which are indicators of profit margins. Where do the objectives for productivity come from?

At the senior-management level, the productivity objectives are established as part of the strategic planning process, as we learned in Chapter 3. Those objectives will generate policies, standards and procedures. The accounting office will issue an annual operating budget on the basis of the financial objectives for the service enterprise. The budget lists forecasted operating expenses and revenues for each department or division. If we divide the total operating expenses by the forecasted revenues for each month, we will see the average monthly expectation for productivity.

Managers will track their progress toward meeting the financial productivity goals on a daily basis. Some days they will surpass the average and on other days they may fall below the average forecasted profit margins. If they are conscientious, they will meet the productivity goal by the end of each month or accounting period (some organizations use 28-day accounting periods for budgeting purposes).

PRODUCTIVITY CONTROLS

We learned about the control function of management in Chapter 9 of the text. We know that management control involves the comparison of actual performance to standards for performance. Productivity management involves the control of costs (inputs), processes (transformation) and production (outputs). The operating budget identifies the objectives for cost and production controls. It does not, however, provide information concerning processes implemented within transformation systems.

Managers implement procedures aimed at controlling costs within their departments. The first cost control technique is to establish sound procedures for the sourcing and acquisition (procurement) of raw materials, equipment, supplies and other material resources. These ensure that quality (per established specifications) products are purchased at reasonable prices with timely delivery. Next, inventory management systems are designed to control the storage, distribution and turnover of items in stock. Similar systems exist in each operating area to monitor inventory controls. Collectively, these controls ensure the management of enterprise assets. They are intended to preclude pilferage, waste, shrinkage, breakage and aging of unused inventories. These systems contribute to the overall efficiency of every production system within the service enterprise.

We learned in Chapter 7 of the text that we operate in a very labor-intensive industry. It is important to differentiate between two viewpoints of payroll dollars. We know from Chapter 7 that the human resources side of the supply chain views individuals as human capital. This means that workers are corporate assets worthy of investments intended to add value. We do this by engaging in activities designed to enhance knowledge, skills, attitudes and abilities (KSAAs). So, the first viewpoint is that human capital is a long-term investment in the employees of the service enterprise. The second view is from the standpoint of the budget. The single largest operating expenditure within a service enterprise is the payroll. The payroll consists of salaries, wages, benefits and paid taxes for each employee. When we speak of labor expenses, we are referring to the payroll dollars spent by the enterprise.

Managers must control labor expenses in order to maintain and ultimately enhance productivity measures. We may consider this control function from both quantity and quality perspectives. Quantity approaches focus on numbers of workers, scheduling practices and output per labor hours. We must remember that all of our production systems surround the hub of service transactions. For this reason, managers must be more creative with controlling labor dollars than simply cutting staff hours. Smart managers control their payroll expenses by combining quality and quantity initiatives. For instance, an average broiler or grill cook has the ability to produce approximately 30 plates per hour during peak dining periods. Hence, the labor output for this worker is the revenue from 30 entrees divided by his or her hourly wage. An excellent culinarian at the broiler or grill station can produce about 60 entrees per hour, nearly double the capacity of an average cook. An executive chef could argue that the excellent broiler or grill person is worth a higher hourly wage. We could find after doing the math that we could enhance output per labor hour from that station by paying a fractionally higher wage to an excellent producer. This decision would inflate payroll dollars by a small amount, resulting in much higher revenue capacity. This decision would enhance productivity by employing a person with higher production skills at a slightly-higher-than-average rate of pay. This is an example of considering both quality and quantity perspectives associated with labor controls.

Quantity labor expenses focus on total payroll dollars, while quality approaches focus on worker KSAAs. Smart operations managers collaborate with human resource practitioners to raise the levels of KSAAs of most positions within the workforce. As is the case with all productivity enhancement measures, decisions must be balanced between inputs and outputs. If we reduce payroll expenses to a point that compromises services levels, chances are that outputs in terms of sales will suffer. When this happens, we are actually reducing productivity levels. For this reason, it is wise to use labor ratios to measure the control of payroll dollars. Ratios give us a snapshot of efficiency measures as compared with effectiveness metrics. While efficiency measures are important, the large-scale opportunities to enhance productivity occur by examining the outputs area of the production system. It has been said that efficiency improvements result in the savings of pennies, while output enhancements attract more incremental revenue dollars.

PRODUCTIVITY OUTPUTS

We know from Chapter 8 of the text that the marketing department is in the business of acquiring and maintaining guests of the service enterprise. They do this by communicating a value proposition, which is a promise of guest experiences that become the expectations for service. When we meet or exceed these expectations during the initial guest visit, it is likely that we will generate repeat visits in the future. These become our repeat guests who may become loyal to the service enterprise as long as we continue to meet service expectations. The productivity value of a repeat guest is that this person requires no marketing expenditures, which places more dollars on the bottom line of the financial budget.

The goal of each service transaction is to maximize the volume of dollars spent by each guest of the enterprise. The casino sector of our industry exemplifies this mantra. Executives in the casino sector calculate the lifetime value of repeat guests in terms of gross gaming wins and ancillary revenues. For instance, a 40-year-old high roller (high-stakes player, also referred to as a 'whale') will spend X dollars per year at a casino property. Casino managers calculate the annual expected revenues from that guest over the next 30 years to identify the lifetime value of repeat visits from that guest. Guests who pose higher lifetime values earn higher priorities of complimentary services relative to those who spend less money at the property. The actual outputs that generate sales revenues in all sectors of the industry consist of service experiences that may be measured in terms of both quality and quantity.

The quantity of outputs is measured in terms of volume. Room nights, restaurant covers, admission tickets, number of members are all quantity measures of outputs. As we discussed in the last chapter, sales dollars are also a measure of quantity. In the lodging industry, for example, the goal is to run 100% rooms occupancy. Revenue or yield management systems assist managers with determining pricing strategies that will contribute to that goal. The occupancy level of a full-service hotel will determine the revenue and guest volume in food and beverage, as well as retail outlets located at the property.

Quantity for service enterprises may be measured by the number of units sold, as well as by dollars generated per unit. If lodging demand at a property is high, the managers will tend to charge higher room rates called 'rack rate' per room. When demand slumps, the room rates will tend to drop to encourage higher rates of occupancy. Over time, the average daily rate (ADR) will become an indicator of dollars generated for room rentals during a fiscal period. Additionally, the revenue per available room (REVPAR) will measure the dollars spent at the property as compared with occupancy levels. The lodging sector seeks to maximize occupancy and accompanying revenues on a daily basis. The ceiling levels of revenue measurements such as ADR will depend on the demand for occupancy, which is directly tied to quality perceptions on the part of guests. The ADR may also be influenced by sales dollars generated from upselling strategies. Reservation and desk agents in most full-service hotels are trained to offer room upgrades at higher-than-average room rates. The goal of this strategy is to sell the higher end of the inventory as quickly as possible.

The service levels of the lodging sector will drive the maximum guestroom rate that individuals will be willing to pay during a visit. Basic service classifications range from limited service to full-service to luxury service properties. The standards for service must be consistent with guest expectations for each of these service levels. Service expenditures will be much higher for a luxury property when compared with a limited or midrange full-service property. For this reason, the managers at the luxury property are positioned to command higher ADRs than those in the other classifications.

The lodging, attractions, air, cruise and ground transportation, as well as recreation sectors of the industry use a variable rate approach to the pricing of outputs. This is also true for certain aspects of the events and food service sectors. Examples include convention centers and catering facilities. Other sectors employ a fixed rate schedule, as would be the case with restaurants and retail outlets. Regardless of pricing structures, there is always a relationship between profit margins and volume. Lower profit margins require higher unit volume sales. Quick-service restaurants (QSRs) for example produce fast-food menu items at bargain prices. Customer volume levels are more important to these operations as compared with fine-dining establishments that operate at higher profit margins. Fine-dining establishments usually engage in limited seating hours and offer small ranges of upscale menu items. To the contrary, QSRs continuously expand numbers of menu items to entice volume customers for breakfast and dinner meal periods. Lower profit margins in these operations require higher unit volume levels to compensate for overhead costs.

As is the case with all productivity enhancement strategies, we must consider the entire model before implementing an intervention. In the case of output strategies, we would prefer to maintain the same level of expenses, which is the case with upselling strategies. Another option is to incur a minor increase in costs to

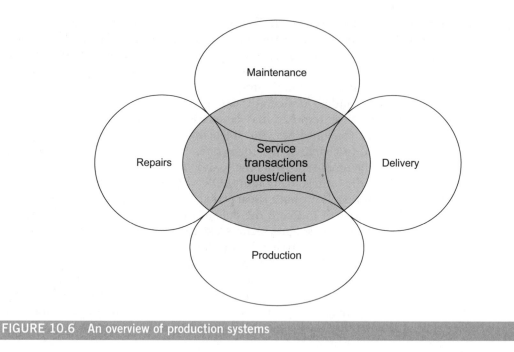

FIGURE 10.6   An overview of production systems

facilitate a quantum increase in revenues, as we highlighted with the broiler or grill cook example in the production controls section. In both cases, we are taking output-oriented approaches to enhancing productivity. The connection between inputs and outputs consists of the transformation processes, or the systems that convert inputs into outputs. Most of the opportunities for productivity enhancement interventions exist in the area of production systems.

PRODUCTION SYSTEMS

We learned about the five-service enterprise production systems in Chapter 5 of the text. We must revisit this model before discussing the transformation processes associated with various service enterprise functions. Figure 10.6 provides an overview of these production systems.

We recall from Chapter 5 of the text that service enterprises provide numerous transactions concurrently in a nonlinear fashion. This means that all of the production systems take place many times in many places throughout the enterprise. This is contrary to nonservice industries that engage in linear sourcing, manufacturing or distribution processes in a straight line that represents the supply chain moving from left to right.

Let us consider the functional departments associated with a full-service resort hotel. This will give us the opportunity to view production systems contained within each department. Figure 10.7 replicates a model we first visited in Chapter 4 of the text to assist us with this discussion.

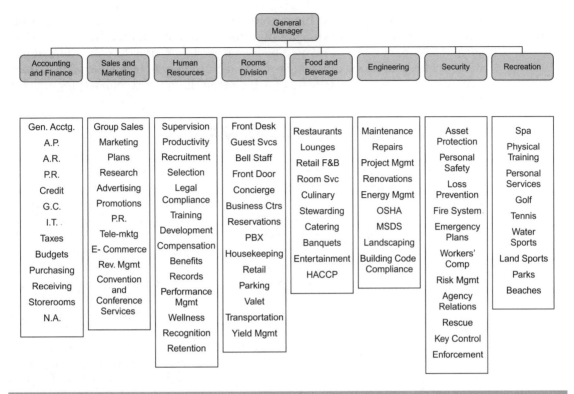

FIGURE 10.7 Hotel functions by department

ACCOUNTING PRODUCTION SYSTEMS

Accounting production systems include the entire group of ledger functions mentioned in Chapter 9 of the text. We recall these functions to consist of accounts payable, accounts receivable, payroll, credit, general cashiering, taxes and budgets. All of these functions use transaction processing activities to distribute financial information to operating departments. In many cases, the purchasing, receiving and storeroom functions will fall within the domain of the accounting office. The production systems associated with these functions are sourcing and acquiring material resources, then distributing those resources throughout the service enterprise. These systems also rely on transaction processing, but in this case they are distributing tangible products to the operating areas. The information technology department is often housed within the accounting office. These individuals distribute hardware, software and networks to the operating areas of the property. IT practitioners also engage in product production through programming activities. They repair machinery and software glitches and also maintain existing systems. We can see that the IT department uses all of the production system in the course of providing related services.

The key to enhancing productivity within the accounting office is to streamline and automate as many transaction processes as possible. Our previous discussion of Accounting Information Systems (AIS) provides examples of these forms of productivity enhancements. Input controls are implemented in areas that work with material resources to enhance inventory turnover, eliminate losses and maximize the usage of material items. The key factor influencing the enhancement productivity for accounting functions is focused on the use of technology. The current state of technology is most suited for the streamlining of record-keeping transaction processing.

SALES AND MARKETING PRODUCTION SYSTEMS

We know from Chapter 8 of the text that sales and marketing are two separate, but related functions. The marketing function drives the sales function. Marketing consists of creating value propositions about the products, price and placement of services. Marketers also create promotional materials used to disseminate information about the products and services of the service enterprise. Strategic marketing plans drive activities such as advertising, public relations, telemarketing, E-commerce and market research. Marketing production systems are similar to accounting systems in that they perform transaction processing for the purpose of communicating with prospective clients and guests. Similar to the accounting function, marketing information systems and the Internet have greatly altered the marketing and sales functions.

Sales force personnel are responsible for delivering the service proposition to potential clients and guests. They focus on group sales to corporate meeting planners, associations, government sources and other national sales niches. The first phase of the sales function is called prospecting for potential clients. This is an activity that qualifies prospective clients as being interested in doing business with the enterprise. The second phase of sales is to close specific group sales by acquiring contracts for group business from clients. The final phase is for operators to provide the contracted services to in-house groups. Convention and conference service personnel often act as liaisons between the property and the client during a visit. The sales function is also a transaction processing function to distribute product knowledge and potential clients to the property.

Both the marketing and sales functions are a bit more scientific than the record processing systems used in accounting. The outcomes of marketing efforts manifest in a large pool of qualified prospects who are interested in doing business with the organization. The output of sales consists of signed contracts for group business. Marketing and sales personnel are among the highest-paid employees within a service enterprise. Their combined function is the acquisition of new guests and the maintenance of existing clients. The goal of enhancing productivity within the marketing production process could include the streamlining of systems, but more importantly, we want those systems to continuously expand to include more potential customers. In this respect, marketing professionals use the Internet to expand the number of group and transient prospects. The sales outputs are measured in unit and dollar volumes of business. The frequency of group business during shoulder and low seasons is particularly important. Enhanced sales productivity usually involves hiring quality sales professionals and giving those individuals the tools to do their jobs. Sales managers will continually raise the bar on goals for sales productivity.

HUMAN RESOURCES PRODUCTION SYSTEMS

The human resource management function is very similar to the marketing function. In fact, human resource management is often referred to as the internal marketing function for the service enterprise. The HR function consists of the acquisition and maintenance of human capital for the service enterprise. Human resource management is completely strategic in nature. Practitioners must develop and implement strategic plans for employee recruitment, selection, training, development, retention, compensation, benefits, performance management, legal compliance, legal defenses and employee relations. The outputs of human resource management practices are visible through the levels of knowledge, skills, abilities and attitudes that are evident among the employee population. Properly executed HR strategies will yield high levels of savings to the expense side of the service enterprise budget as well as providing standards of service that enhance outputs.

The human resource information system (HRIS) is used to handle most perfunctory transaction processing. These transactions are numerous, as the HR officer is the custodian of employment records and statistics required for legal compliance issues. But the key human resource contribution to the service enterprise is in the area of professional management. Properly trained HR practitioners function as *managers' managers*. This means they provide every member of the management team with the knowledge and skills to effectively supervise and manage people. These are training and development functions, as well as a performance management systems issues. Management training and development are key strategies that enable employee retention, which results in excellent guest services and significantly reduced expenses associated with turnover. Remember that labor is the single highest operating expense in most service enterprises due to the intensity of labor required to provide high levels of service to the guests and clients.

The local labor market consists of important external variables that will affect the ability of the service enterprise to attract and retain workers with appropriate KSAAs. For this reason, HR practitioners rigidly follow the strategic planning model that we learned about in Chapter 3 of the text. They use strategic information to forecast labor market conditions as well as internal employee turnover rates. They then implement recruitment and selection strategies aimed at minimizing lag times for position vacancies. They do this by proactively maintaining pools of qualified applicants who are available for the selection process. At the same time, human resource practitioners enact programs to ensure effective employee relations strategies. The development of professional managers is the most important of these strategies. But there must also be strategies for employee counseling, progressive disciplinary due process programs, employee assistance programs, career development through training and succession plans, objective performance appraisals, incentives, recognition and compensation strategies. All of these strategies are intended to achieve the objectives for employee retention. As employee retention rates increase, fewer dollars from the human resource budget are spent, which yields enhanced productivity for the human resource department, as well as the service enterprise.

PHYSICAL PLANT MANAGEMENT

The engineering and security departments are primarily responsible for the management of the physical plant aspects of the property. The engineering function is primarily engaged in repairs and maintenance production systems, while the security department focuses on asset protection and safety issues.

We learned in Chapter 4 that the engineering department consists of trades' people such as carpenters, painters and electricians. These individuals engage in reactive repairs to malfunctioning fixtures, as well as proactive repairs through preventative maintenance (PM) programs. The engineering department also performs forecasted renovation projects on an annual basis to rejuvenate the physical plant as it begins to age. Repair production systems may be measured in terms of time and motion. A work order is generated for the repair of each fixture. The objective is for the item to be placed in working order as soon as possible. Engineering offices will dispatch trades' people to respond to work orders. A streamlined response system requires an appropriate amount of replacement parts to be on hand, as well as proficient diagnostic and repair interventions to be performed by each trades' person. The timeliness of one repair will free the trades' person to move to the next work order. They key ingredients to streamlined repair production systems include tactics for effective communication and dispatch, work order prioritization and efficient actions on the part of each worker. Preventative maintenance programs also enhance the productivity of the repair production systems by reducing the number of fixtures that will require repair. A major expense within a physical plant is the cost of energy.

Energy management systems are used to conserve the costs associated with utilities such as electricity, water and natural gas. Most energy management systems will use computer networks to monitor the use of utilities. They ensure availability of energy during peak operating hours and minimize the use of utilities during nonpeak times. The objective of the energy management system is to reduce wasted energy. For instance, guestrooms might be wired to turn off the air conditioning flow when patio doors are open. Ballrooms may include automatic thermostat controls to reduce the use of energy when the rooms are not being used. Reclaimed water may be used for irrigation purposes on the grounds of the property. The outputs of the energy management system manifest in lower utility bills for the property.

Engineering personnel collaborate with security officers to ensure that property safety systems are in place. The service enterprise has a legal responsibility to ensure the safety of guests, employees and other visitors. Workplace safety programs save many dollars in insurance premiums. Safety programs focus on environmental as well as behavioral issues.

Security personnel take the primary responsibility for asset protection and personal safety. The security production system is a distribution system. Security officers proactively monitor the property to maintain a 'security presence.' The officers must also reactively respond to safety- and security-related incidents. Surveillance technologies have greatly enhanced security monitoring functions. The key contribution of the security department to overall productivity is in the area of loss prevention. Loss prevention consists of programs used to protect assets and people. The result of effective loss-prevention programs is evident in reduced accidents, illness and asset losses. The reduction of incidents will cause insurance premiums for general liability and workers' compensation policies to go down. Also, the costs of litigation involving breaches of security will be minimized through effective loss-prevention programs.

So far, we have seen that the accounting, marketing/sales, human resources, engineering and security departments contribute in different ways to the overall productivity of the service enterprise. This is because these are staff function departments with the task of supporting the operations of the enterprise. At this point, we can focus on the heart of the service enterprise, which consists of the operating divisions and departments.

OPERATIONS PRODUCTION SYSTEMS

The operations departments of a full-service resort hotel will consist of those individuals who interact directly with the guests and clients. Most resort hotels are divisionally structured into Rooms, Food and Beverage and Recreation units. Within each of these units, we will find a number of operating departments.

ROOMS DIVISION PRODUCTION SYSTEMS

The rooms division for some hotels includes related departments such as retail and transportation. The first area most people think of is the front-office department. This department includes front desk, guest services, bell staff, parking, valet, concierge, PBX and reservations work units. All of these areas focus on distribution production systems in the form of transaction processing. Front-desk agents perform transaction processing for check-in, folio processing and checkout. The key to enhancing productivity in this area is to reduce the keystrokes and time required to process each transaction. Reservations, guest services and concierge personnel also engage in transaction processing to arrange for guest services. PBX operators handle the switching of telephone calls, which is a distribution production system. Bell staff and valet employees engage in physical distribution production systems by moving luggage, vehicles and delivering amenities. Parking personnel are responsible for maintaining parking garages and areas. Any distribution production system may be improved by diagnosing and conducting interventions to save time and motion.

The housekeeping department is often the largest in terms of employees within the rooms division. Workers in this department provide maintenance production for guestrooms, public areas and other facilities. The maintenance process involves converting used space into ready space for guest consumption. This department uses expensive equipment to perform the maintenance function. Supplies include amenities and chemicals, which are also costly. Managers seeking to enhance housekeeping productivity would take action aimed at increasing the production of clean areas over shorter periods of time. For instance, it takes the average housekeeper about 30 minutes to prepare a large guestroom for use. If we reduce that time to 25 minutes, the housekeeper will save five minutes per cleaned room. After five cleaned rooms, the housekeeper will have enough time to clean an additional room in 25 minutes. Other productivity measures include control systems for the distribution of amenities and chemical portion control systems to maximize the use of cleaning fluids and powders. Laundry services usually exist within larger properties, although some choose to contract these to outside services. Laundry facilities are capital intensive due to the types of equipment required for full-scale production. Some resorts turn the laundry facility into a revenue center by doing laundry for local area restaurants and small hotels.

Most full-service resort hotels will have a number of retail outlets available for guests to purchase various items. In some cases, these shops are concessions of established retailers, in others the retail shops will be operated within the Rooms division. Retail workers do a good deal of stocking, packing, marking and merchandising in addition to performing sales and tendering functions. The primary productivity process in retail is to maximize sales per guest. When this occurs, the percentage of wages spent on nonsales activities will decline and productivity will become enhanced.

FOOD AND BEVERAGE PRODUCTION SYSTEMS

We learned about the details of F&B production systems through an example discussed in Chapter 4 of the text. We know that food and beverage operations include product, maintenance, repair, distribution production systems that all support service transactions. These occur in restaurant, beverage, catering, meeting space and guestroom services. The culinary department handles most of the product production systems. They use large amounts of raw materials that must be controlled for waste, shrinkage, spoilage, breakage and loss. These items represent the cost of goods sold (COGS) on the income statement. Service personnel provide the distribution of finished food and beverage items to the guests. Stewards are primarily responsible for kitchen sanitation, which is an ongoing maintenance production system, with heavy cleaning performed during off-hours. Dining areas are usually cleaned by members of the housekeeping staff or outside vendors. Repairs to food and beverage equipment are performed by the engineering department and certain outside vendor specialty companies. Figure 10.8 revisits the production systems that occur within a single F&B outlet.

Product production system performance is measured through the quality and quantity of produced items. The goal for quality is zero defects, which means managers seek to have no plates returned by guests. This is a lofty goal, with a less than 5% return rate considered to be an appropriate standard. Quantity measurement identifies the volume of production that each station on the culinary line produces. Earlier in this chapter, we discussed the production levels of an excellent broiler or grill cook as compared with one who yields average production during peak meal periods. A value-added executive chef would take steps to enhance the production skills at every culinary station to establish production units that consist of talented individuals who produce maximum numbers of plates with minimal returns. This is how we improve upon productivity within a product production system.

Food and beverage distribution systems provide opportunities to generate incremental sales. Value-added managers train the service staff to use table-side mannerisms conducive to increasing sales per cover (seated guest). The average check metric monitors sales dollar volumes per seated guest. The average check may be

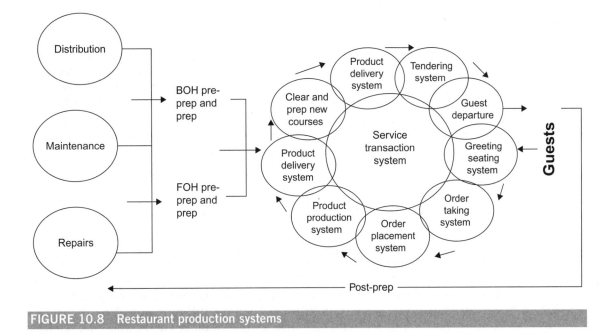

FIGURE 10.8   Restaurant production systems

increased by promoting appetizers, specialty drinks, desserts, fine wines and such. Another productivity measurement for distribution services consists of the numbers of covers that each server is able to effectively serve. This is accomplished through streamlining the distribution system and improving the abilities of service personnel to save steps by multitasking. As the ratio of covers per serve increases, the number of assigned dining room stations will decrease. Since servers are tipped employees, they seek higher levels of sales. A good server will earn between 22% and 27% of average checks in gratuities. The productivity goal for all distribution systems requires both efficiency and effectiveness of service transactions.

We already know that maintenance and repair production systems require managers to focus on time and motion activities to enhance production. Additionally, repair systems require an efficient replacement parts inventory and distribution system. Maintenance production requires the efficient use of sanitation equipment, supplies and chemicals. Managers in these areas develop job lists that indicate a listing of activities in succession along with targeted time limits for the performance of each activity. These are sometimes called checklists that permit supervisors to monitor task progression for each worker throughout the shift. Value-added managers in these departments continuously seek methods to reduce the time spent on each activity or to reduce the amount of costs incurred through each activity. For instance, a skilled trades' person may receive a work order to repair a piece of equipment. It might make sense to have a lower-paid apprentice retrieve and deliver the replacement part, while the trades' person stays at the site to disassemble the part that needs to be replaced. In this case, the repair will be completed in less time and the department does not have individuals earning high hourly wages doing tasks such as parts retrieval and delivery.

RECREATION PRODUCTION SYSTEMS

Similar to other areas of a service enterprise, the recreation facilities engage in all of the five production systems to some degree. Productivity enhancements are the same for recreational maintenance, repair and distribution production systems as they are for most other departments. Also, recreational services vary depending on the nature of the operation. Water parks differ from golf and tennis facilities, and full-service health spas are quite different from most recreational facilities. Most recreation centers employ sports professionals, trainers and licensed providers. For our discussion, let us consider all of the categories to be providers.

Most providers work on a per diem basis for services rendered. The house will charge a fee and pay a portion of it to the provider. It is common to schedule regular and on-call providers at the facility. The key to enhancing productivity is to increase the volume and frequency of guests to the facility. Repeat guests are very important as they usually prefer regularly scheduled provider sessions. As the flow of requests for services increases, the number of on-call providers will decrease. This costs the facility no money as these providers operate as independent contractors. When the majority of providers become full-time providers, the facility is in the position to accommodate unscheduled walk-in guests who seek services. Over time, each provider will establish a following of regular clients who will frequently visit the recreation facility. The facility will earn overrides for each service provided, as well as be positioned to incur incremental revenues through the sales of products.

HUMAN FACTORS AND PRODUCTION SYSTEMS

We now know that techniques exist to diagnose and conduct interventions aimed at enhancing productivity within each of the five production systems. The nature of each system provides opportunities to increase efficiency and effectiveness, resulting in value-added management practices. We learned in Chapter 2 of the text that the field of management was originally concerned with the engineering factors associated with the performance of work until the latter part of the twentieth century when human factors were added to the management repertoire. The sections of this chapter have discussed the engineering approaches that may be used to enhance productivity. But we must remember that managers who overlook the human factors in the workplace will not succeed in value-added management interventions. For this reason, we must consider the influencing factor of management when performing diagnostics and interventions aimed at improving performance.

SUMMARY

We began this chapter with an overview of tactical strategies used by managers within service enterprise work units, departments and divisions. We identified three basic strategies called run, fix and growth strategies. Run strategies are used by managers to add value to the operation through enhanced productivity interventions. Growth strategies are used to expand some aspect of current operations and fix strategies are used to turnaround troubled operations.

Managers must perform diagnostics and interventions to implement any of the strategies. Management diagnostics consist of systems investigations to identify symptoms and problems. Systems analysis is a process used to analyze symptoms to determine root problems that exist in an operation. Once the diagnostics phase is completed, managers identify and implement interventions aimed at enacting change in some area of a work unit. Systemic change aimed at organizational renewal is called organizational development. Managers act as OD interventionists when conducting diagnosis and interventions.

We know that managers follow a timeline for implementing interventions. This timeline is referred to as critical path method for plan implementation. Run strategies are productivity-enhancement interventions. We began this discussion by describing a productivity equation. Resource management requires managers to implement productivity controls. The outputs side of productivity must also be managed for quality and quantity standards.

After considering examples of production controls and outputs, we began to discuss interventions from a systems perspective. We took a look at production systems that comprise transformation processes in all of the major areas of a full-service resort hotel. We looked at the production systems that are contained within the staff functions of accounting, marketing, human resource management, engineering and security. We then considered production systems interventions as applied to the operating areas of rooms division, food and beverage operations and recreational facilities. We concluded these discussions with a few comments concerning the human factors that go hand in hand with all productivity interventions.

DISCUSSION QUESTIONS

1. During the diagnostic phase of a management intervention, what steps do we take when working with suspected symptoms and problems?
2. Describe in your own words how a manager would conduct an intervention once the diagnostics phase is complete?
3. Explain the productivity equation that is used to identify opportunities for productivity-enhancement strategies.
4. If you were responsible for an operating area of a hotel, what types of productivity controls would you implement in that area?
5. What types of interventions might you take to improve production outputs for a specific work unit?
6. Choose a functional area of a full-service hotel and describe the production systems that exist in that area.

IN THE REAL WORLD (CONTINUED)

A week has passed since you last spoke with Kelly. You run into her at school and ask about the review of accomplishments session went on her internship with Jeremy. Kelly smiles and says, 'It was awesome! I couldn't believe how many things we accomplished in just three months of work.' You smile back and ask, 'Like what?' 'Well,' she responds, 'We lowered labor expenses through cross-training and scheduling revisions. We also implemented some great controls for material resources. Another thing we did was to expedite new-hire departmental training to get workers into their positions quicker.' 'Wow,' you say, 'Those are some great accomplishments!' Kelly looks at you and says, 'That is just the beginning.' She continues, 'We streamlined a lot of our production systems to save costs and enhance outputs. Our repeat guest count went up significantly and we improved sales dollars per employee by an average of 5%.'

You smile at Kelly and say, 'You know, you are starting to sound like a seasoned veteran of management.' 'I know,' she says, 'I'm starting to feel like one. In fact, Jeremy's parting words to me were, "Congratulations, you have learned to be an effective and efficient value-added manager." '

CASE STUDY

Productivity

You are transferred to the gourmet dining room in a luxury hotel as the restaurant manager. You observe the operations for 30 days. You discover that there are well-documented steps of service and that the service levels are impeccable. The cuisine is equally excellent. The restaurant seats 140 guests. You also notice that an appropriate number of service personnel are scheduled for each shift. Your check of inventory control systems appears to be appropriate. There are appropriate levels of material resources for the restaurant.

There is very little prep, as all items were made to order. The culinary area is highly overstaffed with many culinarians holding chef titles such as chef garde-manger, chef du party and others. For these reasons, the culinary labor costs are very high. The same is true of food costs which exceeded 60%. You also observe that the table turnover is low at one turn per night, which should have been 1.5 per night, even though average checks were high.

You check with the purchasing manager who was mandated to buy ingredients from certain vendors with no competitive bids. You speak with the marketing manager only to find that no marketing plan existed to lure non-guests to the restaurant.

Conclusion Questions

1. What types of problems do you have – material resources, people resources or systems?
2. How would you work with the purchasing manager to lower food costs?
3. How would you reduce the culinary labor costs?
4. How would you work with the marketing manager to increase table turns – thus revenues for the restaurant?

ENDNOTE

1. Cummings, T.G., Worley, C.G., 2001. Organization Development and Change. South-Western College Publishers.

CHAPTER 11

Tactical Growth Strategies

OBJECTIVES

In this chapter you will learn to:

1. Identify and explain specific corporate growth strategies.
2. Describe the steps used to plan and implement tactical growth strategies.
3. Describe the strategic thinking activities that occur to ensure the success of tactical growth strategies.

ON THE JOB TRAINING

You have been working for local chain restaurants for four years while attending college. You have experience working in all of the BOH and FOH positions. As graduation time nears, you interview with the proprietor of a soon-to-be-opened bistro-style restaurant that is similar to those chain restaurants in which you have worked. The owner is interested in hiring you as an assistant manager. The owner tells you that he plans to have two additional stores open and running within one year. He entices you by suggesting that the best performing assistant managers will have opportunities to become general managers at the new stores.

Excited at the possibilities, you decide to accept an offer of employment.

To be continued...

INTRODUCTION

Directional corporate strategies will move a service enterprise toward growth, stability or retrenchment[1]. Most organizations follow a life cycle of phases from the time they are established that continually evolve during periods of many years[2].

When a firm is originally established, it is considered to be in the introduction phase of development. This is a pregrowth stage in which resources are usually quite limited and basic financial planning is required to support future growth. The operating and capital budgets are of primary importance during this phase.

Soon after the start-up, the enterprise will position itself for long-term growth on the basis of forecasting models of business demand. Demand factors exist in the environment that is external to the service enterprise. These coupled with internal factors are required to support growth-drive in the strategic direction of the firm. Eventually, the service enterprise will align the internal workings of the entire structure to proactively anticipate and implement strategies aimed at congruence with the external forces that impact the firm. This is a stage of coalignment that indicates that the service enterprise is an integrated strategic entity, which is a symptom of organizational maturity[3].

We will discuss directional growth strategies from two perspectives in this chapter. First, we will examine corporate growth strategies that are implemented from executive levels of service organizations. These are very broad strategies devised in corporate boardrooms. The second perspective consists of tactical growth strategies performed by middle- and senior-level managers within service enterprises. We will discuss techniques for conducting feasibility studies aimed at making tactical growth decisions.

CORPORATE GROWTH STRATEGIES

Corporate growth strategies include mergers, acquisitions, strategic alliances and networks[4]. Mergers are the combining of two firms into a single organization. An acquisition is the scenario in which one firm takes over another firm. This can be voluntary or involuntary. Strategic alliances occur when two firms agree to collaborate on a project or program. When three or more firms agree to collaborate, they establish a network alliance. Growth strategies are usually considered to be healthy, but can be misleading indicators of the firm's general health. For instance, an organization could be in growth mode but be masking a cash flow problem. Organizational slack is a term used to identify amounts of unused resources that could be used to resolve conflicts among divisions and departments. Almost all conflict is caused by perceived inequity of resource allocation. If the organization needs to do a turnaround strategy to overcome weaknesses, growth mode will provide resource cushions. Finally, growth strategies do provide career growth for the employees of the organization[5].

CORPORATE CONCENTRATION STRATEGIES

Two specific growth strategies are Concentration and Diversification. Concentration consists of strategies aimed at vertical growth within current product lines. This is a strategy to add various aspects of existing production and distribution channels to the organization. There are two vertical growth directions that include backward and forward vertical integration. An example of backward integration would be the acquisition suppliers and manufacturers of goods that serve the supply chain of the service enterprise. Forward integration would be procuring organizations in the distribution channel for the product or service. Vertical integration provides greater economies of scale for the service corporation. The firm acquires control of costs and distribution channels for reduced per unit expenditures and improved levels of product distribution and price.

Transaction cost economics are means for analyzing vertical growth strategies versus outsourcing strategies. The existence of certain transaction factors will serve as indicators that favor integration. These include transaction uncertainty, specialized assets, frequent occurrence of transactions between the acquiring firm and the target of acquisition[6].

There are varying levels of vertical integration. Full integration is 100% of all supplies or products are through owned entities. Taper integration is less than half. Quasi integration is partial control of the suppliers or distributors without actually purchasing them. For instance, the controlling firm could purchase 20% of the other firm's stock. Long-term contracts are agreements between two firms without actual exchange of ownership. Many companies are moving away from growth and thus vertical integration strategies. In fact, companies are downsizing by outsourcing functions, which constitute retrenchment strategies.

CORPORATE DIVERSIFICATION STRATEGIES

Horizontal growth strategies focus on expanding the distribution of products or services to new geographical locations. For instance, KLM purchased controlling stock in Northwest Airlines to gain access to American and Asian markets. If KLM purchased ground transportation to take its passengers to home destinations, this would be an example of forward vertical integration. Horizontal integration consists of working with competitors or acquiring new products.

Horizontal integration uses diversification strategies for growth. There are two categories: concentric and conglomerate diversification. Externally oriented concentric diversification consists of procuring companies that operate related businesses. An internal concentric diversification strategy would exist when a company decides to start related business within the firm. For many years, *AMR*, the parent company of *American Airlines*, made most of its money with the SABRE reservation system. It has spun off this technology to build systems for other firms in the travel/hospitality industry.

Conglomerate diversification is where a firm diversifies into unrelated areas. Tobacco companies have diversified into the food industry. This form of diversification requires strong analysis of fit between the unrelated industries. The 1980s provided opportunities for conglomerate diversification through highly leveraged financing schemes. This resulted in numerous large conglomerates with holdings that did not fit the parent company. When the conglomerates realized they had strayed from their core competencies, most large firms were forced to divest many of their holdings at huge financial losses. Many current conglomerate diversification strategies include multinational entry programs. Quick-service restaurant corporations provide numerous examples of multinational entry strategies.

The current trend for many industries is to engage in multinational entry strategies for front- and back-office operations. Production sharing is a strategy that combines highly skilled functions of a developed nation with services provided

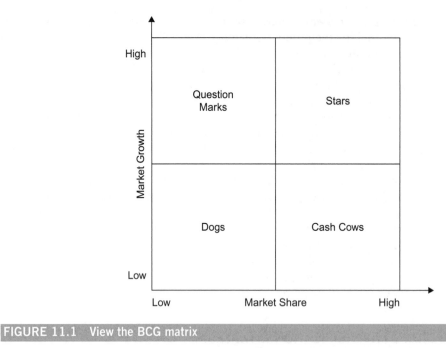

FIGURE 11.1   View the BCG matrix

by a less-developed nation. Computer programmers in India are writing most of the programs used by American software developers. The advantage is reasonably priced high-skill labor. This practice is commonly referred to as the offshoring of production units.

CORPORATE PORTFOLIO ANALYSIS

Large corporations will view the operating units as Strategic Business Units (SBUs). Portfolio analysis permits the corporate offices to review the performance of multiple SBUs collectively. Figure 11.1 provides a depiction of the BCG Growth-Share matrix.

The matrix compares levels of growth with levels of competitive position. Those SBUs that are high in position but low in growth are cash cows (reap the profits strategy). Those that are high in both categories are stars (nurture and reap strategy). Question marks are high in growth but low in market position (proceed with caution strategy). Those that are low in both categories are dogs (divest, retrench, pause and see strategies)[7].

General Electric's Business Screen is a more complex version of the BCG. A number of years ago, Jack Welch disbanded the 25-member strategic planning department soon after taking over as CEO. This model provides an example detached entity consisting of highly centralized planning specialists. This is probably an inappropriate approach in today's competitive markets, in which the individuals who interact with the customers need to participate in the firm's strategies.

Corporate Parenting is a strategy employed by highly centralized and diversified firms with large resource pools. They will use the analysis tools to add value to varied targeted SBUs on the basis of performance and potential. They do this by first identifying critical success factors (CSFs) for the SBU on the basis of its

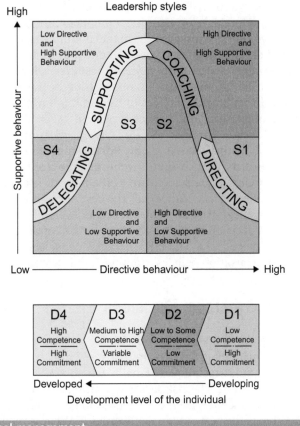

FIGURE 11.2 Situational management

industry standards. They then analyze the requirements to convert weaknesses into strengths. Finally, they determine parental fit. These criteria are used to determine the viability of absorbing the prospective SBU. Figure 11.2 shows an example of the Parenting-Fit matrix.

The category called Heartland is a perfect fit. The category called the Edge has pros and cons. The Ballast offers opportunities for limited improvement. Alien Territory companies are dogs in terms of fit. Value trap are those firms that actually could be destructive to the parent relationship due to misdiagnosis[8].

Internal Horizontal strategies provide opportunities to cut across SBUs for one of the two reasons. First is to build economies of scale for the collective group of SBUs. Second is to develop multipoint competition among SBUs. The horizontal strategy very closely resembles the parenting strategy, as resource allocation from the home office is the driving force.

CORPORATE FUNCTIONAL STRATEGIES

These are the same strategies as discussed implemented at the SBU level. The best strengths of the SBU are called Core Competencies. The absolute dominant competencies relative to the industry are called Distinctive Competencies.

The strategies at the SBU level are divided by functions. Marketing strategies may include product development (new products introduced to the market) or push strategies (promotions campaigns). Financial strategies are driven by ratio analysis. Research and development strategies boil down to leadership or imitation strategies. Operations strategies deal with material resource allocation, people and systems. While many models emphasize manufacturing operations, we already know that most current firms provide services or information. Mass Customization is applicable to the manufacturing and service sectors. It is the ability to produce customized products on demand. For instance, *Ritz Carlton* customizes the guest experience on the basis of the history of that client. Purchasing strategies include price, sourcing and inventory turns. Just-in-time inventories provide optimal turnaround time for inventory. Sourcing strategies ensure availability of need: unfinished goods, equipment and supplies. Pricing influences the cost of material resources.

A logistics strategy basically considers the levels of decentralized versus centralized operations decision making and control. Also, optimal geographical locations for operations are considered. The HRM strategy considers recruitment and selection of personnel, compensation policies, training and development and retention policies[9].

CORPORATE STRATEGIC DECISIONS

Before making corporate strategic decisions, we must visualize industry scenarios. Next, we will forecast and develop alternatives. Third, we evaluate alternatives through pro forma and other techniques. Finally, we choose an alternative and implement, evaluate and revise it. The risk factor is contingent on the stakes and the corporate culture. Analysis includes asking three questions: 1. What is the worst potential outcome? 2. What is the best potential outcome? 3. What is the likely potential outcome?

Corporate culture pressure facilitates the question: Is the current culture constructive or destructive to the mission? Needs and desires of key managers may facilitate outplacement or changing the strategy. Changing the strategy is only an option if alternative two is a close second to alternative one. Strategic choice involves group analysis, sometimes brainstorming. Devil's advocate uses constructive conflict techniques to open thinking. Dialectical inquiry brings opposing sides to the middle.

CORPORATE ENVIRONMENTAL SCANNING

From a corporate perspective, the external environment consists of two subenvironments, the general and task environments[10]. The general environment includes sociocultural forces that influence the long-term decisions of the corporation. The task environment consists of those elements or groups that directly affect a service enterprise. These groups or factors could impact both the short- and long-term strategies of a firm.

Let us discuss the many sociocultural variables included within the general external environment. Economic forces regulate the exchange of materials, money, energy and information. Sociocultural forces such as demographics, psychographics, values, attitudes and mores influence customs and normative behaviors among client groups and other service enterprise constituencies. Technological developments possess the capacity to generate problem-solving interventions, as we discussed in Chapter 8 of the text. The category called political-legal forces influences the service enterprise through the power to provide laws and regulations, which impact the efficiency and effectiveness of the corporation.

The task environment includes all the factors associated with service enterprise stakeholders. We learned in Chapter 2 of the text that these groups include employees, guests, shareholders and the community. Community stakeholders include unions, suppliers, creditors, competitors, special interest groups and others. Service enterprises must continually monitor the task environment forces in order to respond to external changes. Of particular importance is the snapshot state of the competitive environment. Most individuals think of competing firms in the same sector of the industry. While the strategies of these organizations provide important competitive intelligence, it is also important to recognize nonindustry sources of competition. For instance, creative executives at major US theme parks are attempting to compete with more sophisticated virtual reality technologies employed by the video gaming industry. Data from environmental scans tells the theme park operators that younger generations of individuals prefer the video gaming experiences to those provided by the attractions. This is causing younger teens to visit the parks less frequently, which reduces guest volumes. For this reason, creative departments at the major theme parks are spending millions of dollars to create more powerful virtual reality experiences contained within the attractions at each park.

OTHER FORCES DRIVING INDUSTRY COMPETITION

One competitive force that impacts market share levels is the threat of new entrants to a service industry sector. We commonly witness this at the local level within the restaurant sector. When new chains choose to target specific locations, the existing restaurants in the local vicinity will often lose business to the new entrants. Sometimes, this is a temporary loss of share and other times it can reduce guest volume levels permanently. It makes sense that frequent diners will seek variety in menus and environments. Hence, industry competition, particularly among standard full-service and QSR operations, will increase with new entrants to the local vicinity. Competing restaurants will develop competitive strategies to increase guest frequency through pricing, promotion and product-differentiation strategies. Of course, these strategies require resource deployment, which will negatively impact the productivity levels within competing firms.

In some competitive environments, rivalries may develop among existing firms engaged in strategies to enhance market share. The common occurrences of airline price wars provide examples of competitive rivalries. Of course, we have also witnessed alliance strategies among major airline carriers in the form of code sharing to facilitate the domination of existing markets or the penetration of new markets. Competitive environments often result in more corporate retaliation tactics than in the development of competitive alliances.

The threat of substitute products and services is another factor found in the competition area of the task environment. We see examples of product substitution displacement in the lodging sector of the hospitality industry, where the proliferation of cell phones has diminished hotel phone call revenues. Personally owned *I-pods* are the preferred means for listening to music and computer DVDs have replaced on-demand movie services. In the airline sector, recently approved executive airport routes are becoming substitutes for short-range commercial flights that were previously dominated by major carriers.

CORPORATE FORECASTING TECHNIQUES

About 70% of companies use trend extrapolation for forecasting[11]. Trend extrapolation is a simple technique – it merely involves the projection of current trends into the future with adjustments for economic conditions. However, as with other structured techniques, trend extrapolation fails to account for new and potentially disruptive information that may significantly affect the external environment. Many forecast-based planning models use historical information to make projections about the future. Other forecast and planning techniques place lower levels of emphasis upon historical data.

Brainstorming is a participative process used among groups of managers to forecast future trends and develop proposed strategies. One weakness with brainstorming is that if the sessions are not moderated properly, the discussion can digress into unimportant issues and lose focus. Statistical modeling is a quantitative technique for discovering the explanatory factors that link two or more time series together. Statistical modeling is methodologically elegant in that there is plenty of software with which models may be developed; however, like trend extrapolation, it relies on past information. Delphi technique uses panels of experts to estimate the probability of the occurrence of certain events in the future. This technique may be unbiased in that the experts are usually not informed of the decisions of their peers. Finally, scenario development and simulation techniques provide descriptions of 'what-if' environmental circumstances that could pose threats or opportunities to a firm. The advantage to using these techniques is that they can simulate levels of turbulence in the external environment. If a firm develops five scenarios containing five different responses to conditions in the external environment, it will have the flexibility to choose from among the alternative responses in the event of sudden changes.

CORPORATE GROWTH STRATEGIES

Strategic awareness provides a clear sense of grand strategy thinking on the part of corporate executives. Environmental scanning and forecasting techniques partially overcome the boundaries that commonly develop at the interfaces between internal operations and external forces that influence the corporation. These boundary-spanning activities result in sharper levels of focus on issues of strategic importance to the service corporation through an improved understanding of the dynamic forces looming within the general and task environments. Linear processes are appropriate for determining issues of importance from the task environment. The forces contained within the general environment require more qualitative and behaviorally oriented analytical techniques.

TACTICAL GROWTH STRATEGIES

So far, we have examined the broad directional growth strategies developed at the corporate level of service enterprise organizations. The broad strategies in large corporations will serve as key drivers for growth strategies to be developed at the SBU level. At this point, we should revisit the strategic planning model to understand

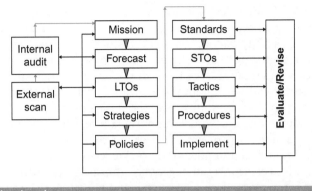

FIGURE 11.3   Strategic planning process

how to develop and execute growth strategies for work units, departments and divisions within a single service enterprise. The model is described in Figure 11.3.

The model is chunked into four activity sections. These begin with scanning and then move to audits and formulation of broad strategies. Next, we develop and implement actual tactics for the operating areas. Finally, we continuously evaluate and revise our tactical plans. Environmental Scanning represents two activities. The first activity consists of the External Scan, which focuses on situations outside of the organization. As is the case with corporate scanning, there are two subenvironments called the general and task environments that must be carefully viewed and analyzed. We learned in Chapter 8 of the text that tactical growth strategies involve the expansion of existing facilities or the development of new outlets. Factors in the external environment are examined to determine the levels of potential demand for the services to be provided by the expanded operations. In addition to demand factors, there must be consideration of limiting factors represented in the environment. These factors could include competitive barriers, government regulations, limited availability of resources and other external variables that could pose threats to the expanded operations. The environmental scanning activity concludes with an analysis of opportunities and threats to projected growth intentions. If the snapshot of external forces looks favorable, we would next take a look at the internal operations required to support expanded operations.

The internal audit requires us to look at functions within the organization. Once the factors are identified, they are analyzed. Internal factors are categorized as falling into one of the two categories: Strengths (things done well) and Weaknesses (things that could be done better). The external factors are categorized as Opportunities (things with a potential positive impact) and Threats (things with a possible negative impact). Why do we use different terms for internal and external factors? The internal factors are within the control of the organization. Therefore, they are done well or not so well. External factors are beyond the control of the organization, therefore they pose opportunities or threats. The total analysis is called SWOT (Strengths, Weaknesses, Opportunities and Threats) analysis. Its purpose is to develop strategies to convert Weaknesses into Strengths and Threats into Opportunities. This is the most important part of the strategic planning process.

At this point of the process, we should have an idea concerning the overall feasibility of the intended growth strategy. At this stage, we make the decision to fully proceed with our growth plans, proceed with caution or to postpone our intentions for growth. A high degree of confidence in the opportunities for growth and the internal strengths to support it would be the most favorable scenario. If there are potential feasibility doubts about successful growth, we may choose to proceed with caution, recognizing that we may decide to postpone our plans at a future date. If the threats and weaknesses outweigh the opportunities and strengths, our probability of success will be very low. The level of probabilities for success determines the confidence level of feasibility that the decision to grow is appropriate and timely. The reason we place so much emphasis on feasibility studies is to avoid the probability of making a poor growth decision that will be costly in terms of resources and fails to produce intended outputs. We know from our discussions on productivity that this scenario would negatively impact the performance of the service enterprise. In some cases, such a decision could put the service entity out of business.

The next category is called strategy formulation, which is a planning process. The first step is to audit the mission and vision for the organization. These provide the purpose, philosophy and core reasons for existence of the firm in its current form. The question asked here is whether or not it still makes sense to grow this business? Next, long-term objectives (1–3 years) and short-term objectives (<1 year) are formulated. Objectives are targets for performance. They are passive and just sit there waiting to be accomplished. They need action steps to be achieved. Strategies are the action steps to achieve long-term objectives. Tactics are the action steps used to accomplish short-term objectives. These result in policies, which are broad guidelines that set standards for decision making and performance.

Next is the implementation phase. These include more tactical activities such as programs, budgets, procedures and rules. Finally, it is time to compare actual performance with standards for performance in the final phase called Evaluation and Control. The Feedback/Learning loop provides for continuous evaluation and revision of the entire growth-oriented strategic plan.

STRATEGIC DECISION-MAKING PROCESS

All of the work that went into the development of a growth-oriented strategic plan was necessary to produce a grand strategy for implementation. During the implementation phase, managers must make sound tactical decisions on a daily basis in order for the plan to produce successful results. The plan provides guidelines through policies and procedures that permit managers to stay on target with intended results. The key activity on the part of managers is to continuously evaluate and revise the original plan as necessary. For instance, the initial demand for a newly developed restaurant outlet may be lower than forecasted business. In this case, managers must make decisions to increase guest volume through the creation of promotional incentives to drive new business. This is an example of executing a contingency tactical plan in response to less-than-desirable outcomes relative to the original plan. In this case, we are talking about strategic management that must occur within the operation on a daily basis.

Strategic management requires strategic thinking on the part of every service enterprise manager. Strategic thinkers use a systemic process for making decisions. The steps in this process include preliminary evaluation of the present conditions, analysis of the mission, vision, external and internal environments, planning components, implementation phase, evaluation and control and revision through the

Feedback/Learning loop. In other words, the operating manager replicates that same system used for the original growth plan when viewing the operation on a daily basis.

STRATEGIC THINKING IN ACTION

We could consider an example of service enterprise operations to demonstrate strategic thinking in action among a number of managers. Let us say the service entity is a full-service luxury resort hotel with 800 guestrooms, 11 food and beverage outlets, 4 retail outlets and a full range of recreational amenities to include a golf course. The property has the facilities to serve as a conference hotel with significant meeting, exhibition and ballroom space. Assume that the resort is located in a tourist destination city surrounded by a number of top-brand theme parks that are in close proximity to the hotel's location. The property is a chain hotel with a brand identification that is known for unique specialized services with a boutique European flair. Transient guests are composed of top-level business executives, professionals and upscale tourists. Group clients consist of executive and professional conference participants.

Consistent with the corporate policy, the property is a wage/salary leader in the area and attracts upper levels of the applicant pool for hourly and managerial positions. Also, the property attracts talented managers within the corporation who are seeking career advancement. All staff members complete rigorous orientation and guest service training programs before they may work 'on stage' or 'behind the scenes.' The executive committee is composed of a general manager (chief operating officer), rooms division manager, director of food and beverage, recreation director, security director, human resource director, engineering director, sales and marketing director, controller and retail manager. All members of the executive committee are seasoned veterans of hospitality management. At the department level, middle managers range from highly experienced to newly promoted individuals. The same is true for outlet assistant managers and supervisors at the property. As a result of the compensation strategy and work environment, there are large numbers of hourly workers with 10 or more years of seniority at the property. The median age for the employee population is 33.5 years, somewhat older than the industry average of 28.2 years for the location. This is probably due to the longevity of many hourly workers and managers with higher-than-average years of experience. There is a strong organizational culture that emphasizes superlative levels of service and professionalism among the workforce owing to the traditions of the chain affiliate and the individual property. As a result, most employees possess high levels of pride in being members of the staff at the hotel.

From a management perspective, there are equally distributed levels of responsibility and authority for the accomplishment of the property's objectives at all levels of the organization. The executive committee members engage in annual strategic planning processes that follow the steps identified in Figure 11.3. Once the analysis is complete, they agree on the long-term objectives (LTOs) for the property, with each division articulating its contributions by establishing divisional goals consistent with the overall objectives. The management team practices MBO, after establishing the LTOs.

The overall financial picture is favorable for the property, although there are areas that could improve financial contributions. ADR is very strong and REVPAR shows annual percentages that surpass industry increases, as well as increases beyond the local market. Resource allocation is fairly distributed to those departments that demonstrate proficiency in efficiency measures. Capital expenditures are also fairly allocated, allowing staff members to work with state-of-the-art technologies and durable assets in an environment that exceeds industry standards for renovation cycles.

From a sales and marketing standpoint, the property is an 'easy sell' as it is the destination of choice in the local vicinity for clients in the target markets. Discounting is a rare occurrence, since the clientele are willing to pay the price required for the status of staying at the property and hosting conferences there.

While there are rigorous standards for guest services, managers enjoy a good amount of autonomy in directing the activities of their divisions and departments. The entrepreneurial manager is nicely rewarded through generous bonus programs on the basis of unit performance. The culture among managers is a 'maverick leader' style, in which the individuals on the management team are confident and sometimes cocky people, who rebel against any form of micromanagement from above, as well as incompetence from peer managers.

The corporate office recently completed a feasibility study to determine if sufficient demand existed to warrant the construction of an additional tower at the property. From a corporate perspective, it was determined that an additional 300 guestrooms could attract significant additional occupancies at the current ADR. A situational analysis of internal strengths and weaknesses determined that an appropriate level of food and beverage outlets were in place to accommodate increased occupancy. It was further calculated that the payback on construction costs would exceed industry standards. In light of these factors, the corporate executives approved the plans for the additional tower.

With the construction of the additional guestrooms nearly complete, the executive committee at the property level is making plans to maximize the revenues from the new additions. Marketing plans were developed sometime ago and sales personnel have been actively prospecting for group business to fill the additional rooms. The human resource office is currently in the process of adding new hires to be in place prior to the opening of the new facility. Systems and structures in the rooms and food and beverage departments have been slightly modified to accommodate services to the additional guestrooms. The accounting office continues to update forecasted occupancies and rates as new information is provided from sales and marketing personnel. As the opening date approaches, the final aspects of the operational plans are completed. The executive committee has met continuously over the past year to determine contingency plans on the basis of what-if analysis of possible scenarios that could impact projections. Department managers have been briefed on the outcomes of this meeting.

We see from the example that this property is nicely positioned to expand its operations. Feasibility studies of the external environment indicate that the new tower will serve unmet demand for occupancy and rate levels. The executive committee has cautiously imagined unforeseen occurrences to devise contingency plans for future execution. The key factor at the property level that will influence potential success of the expansion lies in the profile of the management team at every level of the property. Why is this important? We know from this profile that the property had already been readied for expansion through the acquisition and maintenance of highly proficient managers at every level of the enterprise. This provides a degree of confidence that contingency strategies and tactics will be rapidly deployed by experienced managers in the event of unforeseen occurrences at the property. In short, the management team consists of strategic thinkers who possess the expertise to handle any potential situation at the resort. The proficiency of the management team at the property level may or may not have been noticed by the corporate executives. Our examination of existing property-level management proficiencies, however, gives us a very high level of confidence in the ability to manage the expanded operations. This is an example of strategic thinking in action within the operating units of a service enterprise.

STRATEGIC PERFORMANCE MEASUREMENT

We learned in Chapter 3 of the text that performance is the comparison of actual accomplishments with standards. It contains three factors: people, material resource usage and systems. Steering controls focus on future performance by measuring present performance compared with a time line. Behavior controls are influenced by policies and procedures. Output controls are objective (goal) oriented. ISO 9000 is a global standardization process for quality measurement. In the case of growth strategies, an important part of the strategic evaluation process is to continuously measure performance levels relative to the expanded operations.

The overall performance should be measured in terms of balance among responsibilities to all stakeholder groups. The mission should identify responsibility to each of the four groups. The objective is to meet standards aimed at accommodating the needs of each group. A firm could be successful in achieving fiscal responsibility for the shareholders, but at the expense of the welfare of the employees. This firm is not performing well overall. The same is true for responsibilities to the customers and the community. We know from Chapter 2 that social responsibility includes suppliers and other vendors.

If the organization is truly a strategic firm, it will have long-term and short-term objectives. They will be balanced with tactics feeding short-term objectives, feeding strategies and feeding long-term objectives. Assuming the actual operation lives up to the responsibility of objective performance criteria as established by the strategic plan, certain pitfalls will not occur. Nonstrategic firms frequently deal with misdirected or unknown objectives, a situation known as goal displacement. Behavior substitution occurs in the absence of clearly defined and articulated policies, standards and procedures. Suboptimization can only occur in unbalanced, nonstrategic environments that lack the plans and controls to ensure the maximization of outcomes. A tool called the strategic audit consists of processes used by highly experienced managers and consultants to evaluate the strategic health of organizations. This tool could have been used by corporate executives to identify the managerial proficiency levels that existed at the property in our resort example prior to the expansion process. The strategic audit process is taught in advanced strategy and policy courses at universities and executive development training programs in corporations.

GLOBAL COMPETITION AND THE FUTURE

The fact of the matter is that the driving forces of technology and globalization are so dynamic that the future is difficult to predict with precision. One thing that is true is that tourism will continue its current trend of spiraling growth and hospitality ventures will continue to operate on a global level. In the near future, expansion into the developing nations in Asia and the Pacific will continue, probably in a wave manner due to twists and turns in various economies. Middle East expansion will also continue in the near future. Latin America will probably experience spotty expansion into more tourist-friendly countries. There will be an increase in the over-65-year-old cohort to a percentage of about 25% of the world's population over the next five years. The 35–54-year-old cohort will also expand, which is good news as this group has more disposable income than younger cohorts. Developments in telecommunications technology will further enhance the demand for international travel, as high tech equates to high touch. There will likely be some new breakthroughs in the area of air transportation that will facilitate longer-range travel and fuel efficiency.

Since the half-life of technology is now about nine months, this will be the most difficult area to predict. It is likely that wireless interfaces will connect PDAs that will transmit from the traveler directly to the hotel properties, which will automate most of the administrative functions. The traditional hotel front desk will probably disappear in the next 10 years, with guest service agents greeting new arrivals at the entrance. Also, there will be breakthroughs in the implementation of new technologies that will perform periphery tasks, which will free guest service personnel to perform more core tasks of guest service.

There will be continued and enhanced emphasis on 'green' properties in the future, as global awareness of planet survival issues become more mainstream[12]. Breakthroughs will likely occur in energy management that will implement alternate energy sources that are friendlier to the environment while providing more efficient service. It is likely that many forms of 'alternate' tourism will evolve, which are difficult to predict at this time.

We can predict continuous changes in the global marketing of all service enterprise sectors to include those within the hospitality and tourism sectors. These factors will become crucial to the future growth opportunities that await these enterprises. Simply put, the customer in all service sectors currently holds the upper hand concerning product awareness thanks to the proliferation of the Internet. This caused a shift from push marketing strategies to customer relationship strategies during the 1990s. The common practice for marketers was to *push* products and services through the supply chain prior to this era. These strategies included robust budgeting for advertising and promotion over common media. In the 1990s, the value of customer relationships was fully realized, forcing service enterprise marketers to establish more intimate relationships with guests and clients over longer periods of time, as we discussed in Chapter 8 of the text. As technologies continue to further empower buyers, we can predict an evolution from customer relationships to customer advocacy. This is a slight shift in which marketers will enhance their services to the customer by helping to locate the best products and services. This practice may include locating services from a competitor. The goal of this marketing practice is to establish trust and loyalty among customers over long relationship periods. The continuously increased volumes of travel brokerage firms such as *Travelocity*, *Orbitz*, and *Expedia* are indicators of this marketing trend. Service enterprise marketers may be influenced to provide objective advice and balanced information concerning competitors in light of this trend[13].

SUMMARY

We began this chapter with a discussion of corporate growth strategies. We recognized that some of these strategies include mergers, acquisitions and alliances at the corporate level. These strategies are mostly aimed at the enhancement of corporate economies of scale and scope. We further explored corporate concentration and diversification strategies.

Concentration growth strategies include vertical growth in either forward or backward directions. The objective of all concentration is to create a larger presence in the existing market sector. Backward vertical integration involves the acquisition of corporations that exist in the supply chain. Forward vertical integration seeks to add new dimensions of the distribution channel for the firm. We identified transaction costs economics as a means to analyze vertical growth strategies. We also discussed that varying levels of integration up to 100% of direction may be acquired by the corporation.

Corporate diversification strategies include horizontal integration schemes used to place products and services into new geographical locations. We learned that there are two types of diversification to include concentric and conglomerate strategies. Concentric integration focuses on acquiring companies in related industry sectors. Conglomerate diversification consists of acquiring firms in seemingly unrelated business sectors. Many firms use diversification strategies to enter multinational markets.

We identified corporate portfolios that are composed of strategic business units (SBUs). We discussed a few different portfolio representations used to analyze the performance of SBUs within a given portfolio. Some firms choose to implement corporate parenting strategies to centralize resource allocation to enhance the strength of identified SBU portfolios. We then identified the need for corporate functional strategy analysis as part of determining portfolio performance levels. This led us to a discussion of corporate strategic formulation practices.

We learned that the first step of corporate strategic planning involves a scan of the external environment. This environment consists of the general and task subenvironments that include all of the forces that may impact the firm. After the discussion of the forces in this environment, we turned our attention to corporate forecasting techniques. We completed our discussion with final comments on corporate growth strategies.

At this point, we turned our attention to tactical growth strategies. We recognized that tactical strategies result in the expansion of existing operations and the addition of new outlets. We revisited the strategic planning model for the purpose of further understanding tactical growth strategies. We identified situational analysis techniques, mission audits, forecasting, strategy formulation, implementation, evaluation and revision practices.

We continued our investigation of tactical growth strategies by exploring the topic of strategic thinking within organizations. We learned that plan implementation, evaluation and revision are continuous processes that often require managers to employ contingency plans. We witnessed an example to further understand the practices of strategic thinking in action. We then moved toward a discussion of strategic performance measurements and concluded with some thoughts concerning the future of global growth and marketing strategies.

DISCUSSION QUESTIONS

1. Consider the discussion of corporate life cycles in the early part of the chapter. Identify companies that fit each area of a typical life cycle. In which scenarios is growth a prominent factor?
2. Describe the similarities and differences that exist between vertical and horizontal integration strategies. Identify examples of each in action.
3. Consider the Boston Consulting Group matrix. What is its purpose and how would you use this matrix to identify various SBUs contained within a specific portfolio?
4. Apply the steps in the strategic planning process to a growth strategy for a specific service enterprise. Explain what you would do at each phase of the process.
5. Consider the example used to describe strategic thinking in action. What specific symptoms do you see in that scenario that would indicate factors related to a planned growth strategy at the property level?

ON THE JOB TRAINING (CONTINUED)

It has been more than one year since you joined the restaurant as an assistant manager. No new store has been opened and you are the only remaining original management employee at the store. About six months ago, the owner, Rich, called an all-employee meeting. Here is what transpired:

Rich somberly addressed the audience by saying, 'Well, things are not going according to plan. My partners and I have underestimated our ability to expand the operation to new stores. We did not foresee rising costs of new construction, lease requirements and other overhead expenses. Further, the projected building growth in the local area was in a slow period, so new facilities are not becoming readily available.' Rich looked at each of you as he continued, 'We also did not foresee an indexed increase in the minimum wage and our operating expenses are much higher than anticipated. But the real bad news lies in sales volumes,' he said and then paused. He then started again, 'I have been trying to convince the managers in this store to promote sales. I assumed when I hired each of you that you had been trained in school to promote your restaurant.' With a serious look he said, 'We can't keep going like this. If this team can't promote this place, I will have to find one that can.' Rich concluded the meeting by saying, 'I want a plan from each of you that articulates how you are going to promote this restaurant every day starting next week.' The meeting was adjourned.

Later that day, you were having coffee with another manager, Jen. Jen says to you, 'Ya know, you are the only original manager left in this place, and I must say, right now it doesn't look good for any of us.' You reply, 'Yeah, there were big plans when I started. I should have been a GM by now.' Jen asks, 'So what are you going to do?' You reply, 'I am going to put together a tactical plan designed to bring in as many guests as I can from the local business community. All we have to do is bring them in once and they will become repeat guests. We have business offices all around us, but most people don't think to visit us because we don't have a chain brand out-front.' You conclude by saying, 'We just have to get our menus in the hands of these business offices.' Jen replies, 'I admire your spirit, I would be looking for another job if I were you.'

Fast-forward another six months. You are now the GM of the original restaurant. Jen and all the other managers have since been replaced with strategic thinkers. Your plan worked and business is good. One day, Rich approaches you for a private meeting.

You sit down for a cup of coffee and Rich says to you, 'I really thought we were going to go out of business six months ago. If it wasn't for you, we would not be in business today,' he smiles and continues, 'You are the one who grew this business, which is why you are the GM today.' Finally he says to you, 'We just closed the deal on the construction of a new store. I want you to do the marketing plan and oversee the opening. Are you interested?' The two of you shake hands on the deal knowing that Rich could only hold true to his original growth statements thanks to your marketing efforts.

CASE STUDY

The name of this company is Carribam, Inc. The organization began in the cruise industry and has grown into a diversified portfolio of casino/hotels and resorts. At one point, the firm acquired aircraft from a bankrupt air carrier, but divested that division after two years of operation. Currently, Carribam is among the top five cruise lines in the world with vessels that have a presence in most seasonal cruise markets. They are considering the pursuit of a growth strategy targeting the development of resorts in international markets.

Mission:

The mission of this organization is to provide world-class luxury service to guests in the hotel, resort, cruise and casino operations. The resort division is committed to providing upscale accommodations and service to guests on an international scale. The mission statement identifies the organization's commitment to its four stakeholder groups. Carribam is dedicated to proactive human resource management and believes that the employees are the key to achieving the guest mission. The company is committed to the selection and development of employees who possess hospitality spirit and technical abilities. The company is committed to providing sound fiscal performance for its shareholders who are stockholders on a public exchange. The company is also committed to being good community neighbors and contributing to the social responsibility associated with doing commerce in the local and international communities.

External Environment:

Carribam is expanding in Asia and the Pacific Rim. Economic conditions are currently unfavorable for capital investment, and commercial banks are not making investment dollars available to investors. At the same time, real estate is being offered at reduced prices owing to the economic conditions. Governments in these regions are somewhat open to international expansion of US hospitality chains. Labor markets are high in supply of semi-skilled and highly skilled workers. Wages are currently on a down swing due to high levels of labor market supply. Technology is widely available in these regions. However, industry-specific technology may require offshore imports. There is a shortage of qualified hospitality senior managers and professional staff in these areas.

Political systems are stable in some regions and tumultuous in others. Government officials in some of the regions are reputable. Building regulations are becoming strict in terms of code enforcement for new commercial buildings. The American dollar exchange rate is favorable. Natural resources are plentiful in most of the regions. Demand for upscale lodging is at a low point, but may rebound in the near future. Foreign destination travel is up for Western travelers due to favorable currency exchange rates. Telecommunications hardware and software is overloaded in these regions. Shipments of materials from offshore to these regions take 3–4 weeks. Import taxes are very high. Cost of domestic products is low, while import prices remain high. Local corporations have induced cost-cutting programs as a result of recent economic activity in the regions. The regions enforce tight restrictions on visa issuance for foreign workers. Potential natural disasters include earthquakes, typhoons and title surges. Private commerce operations in coastal areas must file a government-approved disaster plan in order to receive a certificate of occupancy.

Internal Operations and Administration:

Carribam has enjoyed success in domestic US markets in all of it divisions. Perhaps, the most financially successful division has been the resort division with operations on the mainland and Hawaii. The company is committed to international expansion, but comprises mostly domestic operators at every level of the organization.

The company has implemented successful marketing plans and programs aimed at attracting conventions, groups, business and leisure travelers from the United States, Europe and Japan. All offshore marketing has been done through third-party firms. The company is considered a price leader in room and function rates. Current operations have an astounding 66% repeat guest count, which has minimized marketing expenditures in the past five years. Sales forces are decentralized by individual properties with only a marketing vice president at the corporate level.

The organization is considered a leader in proactive human resource practices. All human resource practitioners are from the United States. With the exception of Hawaii operations, most employees are from North America and Europe. Human resource departments are decentralized by properties. A corporate human resource vice president handles corporate policy and legal compliance issues.

Controllers at the properties report to the property general manager. A corporate audit team inspects the accounting practices at the property level. There is no corporate coordination of controller functions. Individual budgets are submitted by each property and approved by a corporate operating committee made up of senior property general managers.

The properties have excellent Rooms division systems that are consistent among all properties. Guest history and property management systems are state-of-the-art. With the exception of systems, all Rooms divisions are independently managed at the property level.

Food and beverage is fair, but not great in terms of quality. F&B managers are mostly North American and were trained in the United States. While food and beverage products are consistent from property to property, their standards are not considered to be a five-star level. Food and beverage control techniques vary among the properties.

The resorts are self-contained as far as entertainment and recreation. A guest at one of the resorts may choose from multiple activities that run from morning until late evening. Each property has a Director of Entertainment who also oversees recreational activities. Guests do not pay extra for these activities, as they are packaged into the room rates. Each resort employs many entertainers and sports personnel.

The Resorts division has a centralized development department, which handles acquisitions, real estate and development. The staff consists of individuals with experience in domestic development only.

The Cruise division already calls on ports in the targeted development areas. This is one of the compelling reasons for resort development to capture overnight lodging of cruise passengers. Cruise division directors are not familiar with local aspects of the destinations, as their responsibilities only extend to maritime operations.

Instructions and factors for consideration

1. Conduct a thorough audit of the Mission statement. Feel free to make assumptions on the basis of inferences to the existing information. For instance, if there is reference to fiscal responsibility, feel free to determine what that means and if the division is positioned to deliver at that standard. Ultimately, show rationale for acceptance or revision of the mission statement in this section of your report.
2. Conduct a thorough SWOT analysis, listing strengths/weaknesses and opportunities/threats under each division. On the basis of your SWOT analysis, develop a grand strategy for the next three years that will get the division to penetrate and have a presence in the Asian and Pacific Rim markets. This is educated guess work based on a reasonable time line.
3. Outline the categories that would be included in a feasibility study aimed at determining a grand strategy of action concerning international expansion into a Pacific Rim host country.
4. Determine long-term objectives for each function (i.e. operations, marketing, human resources etc.) with 3–5 strategies for each objective. Determine short-term objectives with 3–5 tactics for each.

ENDNOTES

1. Enz, C., 2010. Hospitality Strategic Management: Concepts and Cases, second ed. John Wiley & Sons.
2. Hunger, J.D., Wheelen, T.L., 1999. Strategic Management. Prentice Hall, NY.
3. Cummings, T.G., Worley, C.G., 2001. Organization Development and Change. South-Western College Publishers.
4. *Ibid.*
5. Enz, C., 2010. Hospitality Strategic Management: Concepts and Cases, second ed. John Wiley & Sons.
6. *Ibid.*
7. Hunger, J.D., Wheelen, T.L., 1999. Strategic Management. Prentice Hall, NY.
8. *Ibid.*
9. *Ibid.*
10. Cummings, T.G., Worley, C.G., 2001. Organization Development and Change. South-Western College Publishers.
11. Hunger, J.D., Wheelen, T.L., 1999. Strategic Management. Prentice Hall, NY.
12. Enz, C., 2010. Hospitality Strategic Management: Concepts and Cases, second ed. John Wiley & Sons.
13. *Ibid.*

CHAPTER 12

Tactical Turnaround Strategies

OBJECTIVES

In this chapter you will learn to:

1. Identify techniques used to prevent fix strategies from being necessary.
2. Describe the steps used to plan and implement tactical fix strategies.
3. Compare and contrast similarities between small- and large-scale fix strategies.

REAL WORLD EXPERIENCES

You applied for a part-time server position with a local chain restaurant while attending college. You arrived for the interview and it seemed like the manager was desperate to hire you. After a very brief discussion, the manager asked if you could begin work that same evening. You thought this request was strange, but agreed to report for work that night.

Upon arriving at the restaurant, you quickly realized the place was in chaos. You walked to the host desk to introduce yourself. It seemed no one in the restaurant was aware you had been hired. There were no managers available at that time so the host just told you to follow one of the servers.

Josh was the server you were assigned to follow. You introduced yourself to him and began to follow as he performed his side work. As you were working, he asked, 'Why do you want to work here?' You looked a little puzzled, so he added, 'Are you aware of the reputation of this store?' 'No, I hadn't heard anything one way or another,' you reply. Josh smiles and says, 'Let me fill you in...' As the night goes on, Josh shares all of the stories of unprofessional management that exists at the restaurant. Finally, at the end of the shift you ask him, 'Why are you still working here?' He smiled and said, 'As of the end of this shift, I don't work here anymore. I took a job across the

> street and start tomorrow night.' 'Oh, you say, so you gave notice awhile back.' Josh starts to laugh and says, 'No one gives notice here – the managers don't deserve it.'
>
> To be continued...

INTRODUCTION

This will become the last chapter in Part III of the text. So far, we have investigated tactical run and growth strategies as part of this applications section. In this chapter, we will discuss the most challenging management intervention, the turnaround or fix strategy. This chapter will require us to demonstrate the ability to apply portions of all that we learned in the first two Parts of the text.

We begin the chapter by discussing the circumstances for conducting a turnaround strategy. We will consider this from the standpoint of both proactive and reactive management practices. We will also discuss the nature of diagnostic and intervention planning skills consistent with our former discussions concerning change agentry. We will recognize the need for interventionists to multitask during the diagnostic, planning and implementation phases of the turnaround intervention.

We will revisit problem-solving techniques used to identify patterns of symptoms in order to recognize and prioritize significant problems. We will also consider the nature of problems that result in the need to conduct a turnaround intervention within a service enterprise work unit. This will require us to revisit various aspects of systems and structures.

As we near the end of the chapter, we will consider the actual implementation of turnaround strategies in various work units. We will learn that these interventions require high levels of training and management experience.

PREVENTING THE NEED FOR FIX STRATEGIES

Effective managers practice professional management. Managers are primarily responsible for the performance outcomes of a work unit. Underperforming work units are the result of inappropriate management practices in most cases. For this reason, managers must possess the knowledge, skills and abilities to effectively manage each work unit. Professional management practices preclude the need for turnaround strategies.

Professional managers know that their job is to clearly articulate objective standards for performance up-front and to reinforce those standards every day. Let us revisit how those standards are developed. A simple definition for the practice of management is the accomplishment of the objectives of the organization through the activities of others[1]. Management is practiced in organizations and institutions.

Hence, an organization is a collection of individuals who meet to accomplish a common objective. An objective is a target for performance as stated in an intended result of activities. We know that the broadest objective for an organization is referred to as the mission, which is the purpose and philosophy of that organization. In essence, it is the reason that the organization is in existence. In some organizations, all decisions are prioritized on the basis of the mission. These organizations are known as 'mission-driven' organizations, in which the mission drives all of the important decision-making processes and items that are not related to that mission are considered to be minor issues. The mission values are communicated throughout the organization via the 'mission statement,' which is a brief written description of the purpose for that organization. It is the responsibility of senior managers to establish and communicate the mission for the corporation. As we discussed in Chapter 11 of the text, managers audit the mission on an annual basis to verify its accuracy, given factors from the external environment, which exists outside the organization.

After the mission audit, the senior managers develop the objectives for the organization. Some organizations practice a method called Management by Objectives (MBO), which is a process of top-down and bottom-up goal setting throughout the organization. In management, the terms goal and objective mean the same thing. The way MBO works is that the senior managers develop objectives and they share these with the next level of management below them. That level of management uses those objectives as a basis to establish their own goals. They review and revise these with the senior managers and agree on a final version of objectives. Next, this level of management works with the next level and repeats the process. Eventually, every level of the organization has participated in setting objectives that feed into the level of objectives above them. Hence, all objectives are mission-driven from the top of the organization and every person in the organization has participated in the development of their own goals. While MBO is a time-consuming process, the final result is total participation in the development of each person's goals within the organization. Hence, there is total 'buy-in' on the part of all the staff members who made their own goals, as opposed to having objectives imposed upon them from the level of management above. MBO, of course, is just one option in the goal setting process. But regardless of the process, every organization must have clearly defined objectives for performance throughout the organization.

Once the objectives are established, managers must break these down into factors that represent the expectations for performance in every department within the organization. Figure 12.1 depicts the relationship of objectives to performance expectations.

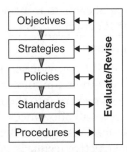

FIGURE 12.1   Objectives and strategies

255

Since objectives are targets for performance, there must be action steps that are taken to reach each objective. These action steps are referred to as **strategies**. A single objective will usually have 2–5 action steps listed below that articulate the steps to be taken to achieve the goal. Table 12.1 shows an example of an objective along with a listing of strategies.

Once the objectives and strategies are established for the organization, it is time to create **policies**, which are broad guidelines for performance. Some organizations call the collection of policies the *policies manual* or *listing of company policies* for that corporation. An example of a policy statement is listed in Table 12.2.

Once the policies for the organization are established, it is time to convert those into standards and procedures. Standards take a portion of a policy that is applied to actual performance. Procedures are the listing of steps required to satisfy the standard. For each standard, there must be listing of procedures for individuals to follow in order to meet the standard. Table 12.3 provides an example of a standard and its correlating procedures.

A comprehensive listing of standards and procedures should be available during employee training and as a reference tool for use in each department. In some organizations, the collection of standards and procedures is called the Standard Operating Procedures (SOP) manual. Notice from the example in Table 12.3 that the standard is a baseline for performance derived from the policy. The procedures,

TABLE 12.1 Objectives and Strategies

Objective #1	Increase revenues by 10% over last year's total to be achieved by December 30, 2007.
Strategy #1	Increase advertising and promotion budget by 5% over 2003 allocation to become effective by January 2, 2007.
Strategy #2	Add one new sales representative to cover missing territory by January 15, 2007.
Strategy #3	Develop salesperson incentive program for rollout by January 30, 2007.

TABLE 12.2 Sample Empowerment Policies

Guest Service Empowerment Policy

It is the objective of the *Hotel California* to provide excellent guest services as established in our Guest Service Index (GSI) rating system. One strategy to facilitate this goal is for all front-line service personnel to be empowered to handle service recovery exceptions at the moment of occurrence. The following policy is applicable to front-desk agents who have successfully completed the Guest Services Training Program (GSTP).

Empowerment Policy for Front-desk Agents

Qualified front-desk agents are empowered to provide service recovery to guests of the resort by authorizing complimentary allowances in an amount not to exceed $250 per occurrence. Each complimentary allowance requires an entry into the guest services database to justify the exception. The appointed manager reviews all allowances within 24 hours of the occurrence of authorization. The reviewing manager shall respond to the authorizing front-desk agent within the 24-hour time frame to provide constructive feedback on the action taken.

on the other hand, are listings of specific action steps to be taken to meet the standard for performance.

Professional managers subscribe to a model in which the objectives lead to policies, which convert into standards and are broken down into procedures for performance. Organizations that do not possess objectively defined and clearly communicated standards and procedures infringe upon the rights of employees to know what the expectations are for performance in the organization.

We learned in Chapter 7 of the text that human resource managers assist the operating managers with the process of job design. They perform job analysis activities for every service enterprise position on an annual basis. Figure 12.2 revisits this process.

Job analysis activities should take place for every position in the organization at least once per year. Of course, there are many organizations that have never performed job analysis, but this does not mean that the inaction is the correct

---

TABLE 12.3 **Sample Standards and Procedures**

Standard:

The standard for handling guest complaints at the *Hotel California* is to follow the procedure for complaint resolution and service recovery listed below.

Procedure:

1. Listen carefully to what the guest is articulating in the complaint. Make sincere eye contact and acknowledge/paraphrase what is being said.
2. If the guest is in an emotional state, diffuse the emotion by continuing to listen empathetically until the emotion is drained and the guest returns to a normal rate of speech.
3. Paraphrase your understanding of the nature of the complaint and ask the guest for permission to give you a chance to resolve the issue.
4. Use your knowledge of the operation to solve the guest's dilemma.
5. If the resolution involves financial remedies, refer to the standards and procedures for guest service empowerment.
6. Confirm the resolution with the guest and document the situation in the incident database.

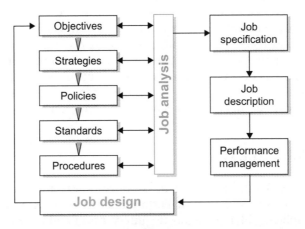

FIGURE 12.2 **Job design drivers**

way of doing business. The first result of job analysis activities is the creation of a document called job specification. The job specification (job spec, for short) identifies the knowledge, skills, attitudes and abilities that determine the qualifications for a specific position. These documents are used as part of the recruitment and selection processes. Another document resulting from job analysis is called the job description. This document articulates the tasks, duties, responsibilities, reporting relationships and sometimes the criteria for performance evaluation relative to a particular position. So, the job specification identifies the qualifications of a potential employee in specific position, while a job description articulates the activities for the jobholder. The final outcome of the job analysis process is the criteria used to evaluate actual performance as compared to standards, which is part of the performance management system. We recall that evaluations of workplace performance are known as performance appraisals.

Professional managers use job descriptions to communicate the expectations for performance for each position. These documents must be current and specific in order to effectively communicate performance expectations. The practicing manager must hold each staff member accountable for meeting performance standards. This is part of professional management. Table 12.4 provides a sample job description for a position within a service enterprise.

When professional managers supervise the performance of staff members, they ensure that standards are being met in each area of every production system. As we learned in Chapter 10 of the text, professional managers are responsible for the efficient use of material resources. There must be controls in place to ensure that standards are met for the sourcing, acquisition and distribution of resources to the work unit. Controls must also exist within each work unit to prevent waste, breakage, loss and shrinkage of material resources.

Professional managers possess the ability to design and supervise production systems. We know that maintenance, repair, distribution and product production systems all serve the hub of service transactions in our business. These are non-linear production systems that occur simultaneously and repetitively in each work unit of the service enterprise. It is the responsibility of the professional manager to ensure that each production transaction meets with established performance standards in order to maintain existing productivity levels.

We learned that production outputs are measured in terms of quality and quantity. Professional managers are responsible for meeting output objectives. They maximize business and dollar volumes by ensuring that service transactions meet the value proposition promised to their guests and clients. Outputs are measurements of service enterprise performance success. The outputs consist of guest and client interfaces that result in revenues and profits. In the absence of professional management, service enterprise outputs will also demonstrate symptoms of underperformance.

WHAT ARE FIX STRATEGIES?

Contrary to a run strategy, a fix strategy is warranted when the organization is not pleased with the current performance of an operation. Fix strategies require sound problem-solving diagnostic, intervention and follow-up skills. A person who specializes in this type of operations management is known as a 'troubleshooter.' Fix strategies are the most challenging for a manager, as they involve conflict,

TABLE 12.4 An Example of a Job Description

Position: Executive Administrative Assistant Reports to: General Manager

Department: Administrative and General Subordinates: None

Basic Function: Provides administrative support to the General Manager by coordinating calendars, handling correspondence, receiving visitors, screening telephone calls and general filing and administrative area maintenance.

Essential Duties:

1. Arrive at the work area at the scheduled time and prepare the executive offices for business within 30 minutes of arrival.
2. Handle all incoming phone calls using the standards and procedures for telephone etiquette.
3. Collect and distribute incoming mail items, place outgoing items in the mailroom.
4. Complete correspondence, filing and other administrative tasks within prioritized timelines.
5. Prepare the office for closure at the end of the business day.

Additional Duties (as assigned):

1. Accompany the General Manager to specified meetings and client functions.
2. Make administrative decisions for the administrative staff in the absence of the executives.

Qualifications:

1. Ability to process communications and computations at a level equivalent to the standards for a high-school graduate.
2. Typing speed of at least 70 wpm.
3. Ability to solve administrative problems and prioritize tasks.
4. Diplomacy skills consistent with those required of an executive-level manager.

Working Conditions:

1. Works in an ergonomically designed environment.
2. Eighty percent of working time requires sitting in an upright position.
3. Twenty percent of working time requires mobility to various areas within the organization.

Measures of Effectiveness:

1. Measured to the standards articulated in the Standard Operating Procedures Manual for Executive Administrative Assistants.
2. Demonstrated willingness to make sound administrative decisions and show flexibility in work routine.
3. Demonstrated efficiency and effectiveness in the prioritization and completion of administrative tasks in a timely manner.

change agentry, negative human emotions, difficult decision-making scenarios and a definite need for an impartial strategic mind-set on the part of the manager. Operational 'chess players' are most suited for this type of work, which requires the planning and execution of operational interventions. The good news is that troubleshooters are among the highest-paid operational managers and some individuals really enjoy 'fixing' operations from an intrinsic perspective. A review of problem-solving techniques will serve us well here.

The first step in performing a fix strategy is to diagnose the situation within the department. It is likely that the manager appointed to conduct a fix strategy

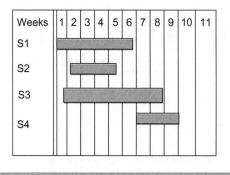

Weeks	1	2	3	4	5	6	7	8	9	10	11
S1											
S2											
S3											
S4											

FIGURE 12.3   Turnaround intervention CPM

will be new to the department, since the last manager apparently could not fix it, or he/she would still be there. Also, timing is of the essence in a fix strategy. The new manager should be prepared to work many hours until the 'fix' is complete. The manager will notice some obvious symptoms and will have to use experience and intuition to detect those symptoms that are not obvious. We should note that a troubleshooter is viewed by the existing staff as a threat, so they will try to hide things from him/her. The manager will place symptoms in one of the three categories: people, materials and systems (a single symptom can be placed in all the categories in some cases). When the symptoms are categorized, the manager then determines where the real problems are and prioritizes those in order of importance to the operation, as is shown in Figure 12.3.

If a fix strategy involves reworking the department, it is considered to be a turnaround strategy. For instance, if the only problem is the lack of training for assistant managers, this would be a quick-fix intervention by providing training for those individuals. In most cases, however, by the time the troubleshooting manager is called in, the little problems would have escalated to complicated problems. For instance, if the manager does not provide training for the assistants, then communication problems start to arise. Next, organizing activities start to fail and staff schedules become a mess. Then, customer complaints start to increase. After a while, employee morale starts to suffer. At this point, some of the more experienced hourly staff start to take advantage of the untrained assistants, by upwardly delegating their work to the managers. Soon, the good hourly staff members start to quit and the new hires are friends of those same hourlies who take advantage of the managers and so on until the manager gets fired or quits and the organization hires a troubleshooter.

Fix Strategy Diagnostics

Internal problems in service enterprises sometimes go undetected until they impact the outputs of the organization. The first place a troubleshooter will look for symptoms will be in the output area of each production system. Table 12.5 displays some symptoms found in the outputs area.

The troubleshooter will view output symptoms objectively, by viewing those issues that warrant further investigation. This is the data-collection phase of diagnosing the factors to later be addressed through the intervention. The troubleshooter will

TABLE 12.5 Samples of Symptoms and Problems

Customers:	Service Enterprise:
• Slow distribution of service	• Insufficient staff levels
• Long lines	• Slow transaction processing
• Lost items	• Inaccurate transaction processing
• Returned items	• Lack of inventory management
• Overbooking	• Lack of service delivery
• Inattentive service	• Negative staff behaviors
• Negative service attitudes	• Inferior production
• Billing disputes	• Inaccurate preparation
• Subpar quality of products	
• Running out of products	

work backward through the production systems and inputs areas to identify further symptoms that could be indicators of substandard performance in the outputs area. The troubleshooter will observe the operations, interview staff members, conduct small focus groups, view documents and in large operations, possibly administer surveys to collect data about the operation. Most troubleshooters will compare empirical observations with other forms of information to identify areas of consistency and inconsistency. The troubleshooter will also collect information on historical management practices that may shed insight on current symptoms.

A troubleshooter seeks causal relations between service enterprise practices and symptoms that appear in the output area. For instance, numerous guest complaints concerning the slow distribution of service could be matched with service enterprise output symptoms such as insufficient staffing levels and slow transaction processing. When the troubleshooter identifies a match among these three symptoms, he/she will seek additional information concerning the root causes of these symptoms. He/she will ask, 'Why are there insufficient staffing levels in this work unit?' This question will lead the troubleshooter to review scheduling practices, rates of absenteeism and tardiness, recruitment and selection of new hires, training programs and progressive disciplinary actions on the part of managers. Of course, the very first sources of information sought by the troubleshooter will be documented policies, standards and procedures for the work unit. It will be likely that these documents do not exist, are outdated or just ignored in that work unit. If this is the case, there will be an immediate suspicion on the part of the troubleshooter that one of the causal symptoms is mismanagement in that work unit.

As the troubleshooter begins to uncover causes of the output systems, he/she will place those in categories. We already know that the three categories of causal symptoms are people, systems and material resources. For instance, if the cause of insufficient staffing levels is an unrealistic labor budget, the troubleshooter will consider the cause to be insufficient financing, which we know is a material resource. If the cause lies in inferior scheduling practices, we will have a systems cause. And if the troubleshooter detects the cause to lie in human resource practices, he/she will assume there is a people situation to deal with. In most cases, the troubleshooter will identify a small number of causal factors that influence the output symptoms. Once this is established, the troubleshooter has identified the major problems that exist in the work unit.

Let us say for instance that the troubleshooter learns that the insufficient staffing levels are due to a chronic shortage of staff members employed with the work unit. The troubleshooter would dig deeper by visiting with human resource office to determine information gained from personnel requisitions, exit interviews, recruitment and selection practices, as well as training programs. It is likely that the troubleshooter would learn that individuals are simply not interested in working for that work unit. This could be verified through exit interview information, as well as absenteeism and tardiness rates. If this is the case, the troubleshooter knows there is a mismanagement problem on his/her hands. If he/she does not detect flaws in the payroll budget and transaction processing systems, he/she will plan to do a management turnaround intervention to solve the staffing shortage.

FIX STRATEGY INTERVENTIONS

So, our troubleshooter intends to plan an intervention to solve the problem of insufficient staffing levels within a work unit. The experienced troubleshooter would understand that chronic staffing shortages occur in departments or enterprises that are unprofessionally managed. Such a negative work environment begins to experience high levels of employee turnover. In most cases, the most proficient staff members will be the first to leave the work unit, leaving lesser-qualified workers behind. Newly hired employees will be trained by these less-qualified staff members and quickly recognize the difficulties associated with working in a poorly managed unit. It will not take long for newer workers to seek new positions with other departments or firms. The turnover will continue for a short while and over time, qualified individuals will stop applying for positions within the work unit owing to its poor public reputation. At this point, the remaining workers will have leverage over the managers, who have become desperate to retain even the worst performers. This situation will require the troubleshooter to plan and perform a complete turnaround intervention in the work unit. Once the intervention begins, the environment in the work unit will become disruptive and eventually stabilize over a short period of time. This intervention will require competent strategic thinking on the part of the troubleshooter.

Prior to commencing with intervention implementation, the troubleshooter will meet with senior-level managers to present the plan. Troubleshooters know that turnaround interventions will not work without top-management support. The interventionist will clearly articulate the types of disruptive behaviors that will occur during the interventions and describe the tactics that will be employed to minimize these occurrences. An experienced troubleshooter will not proceed with an intervention without senior-management support and commitment to the project.

The troubleshooter will begin the intervention by establishing specific policies, standards and procedures for each position within the work unit. At the same time, he/she will file personnel requisitions intended to overstaff the operation. The troubleshooter will contact individuals within his/her professional network to apply for jobs. The interventionist will meet with assistant managers, leads and supervisors to roll out her plan. He/she will sternly articulate the need for compliance on the part of these individuals. He/she will establish a very short timeline for the supervisors to memorize the new policies, standards and procedures. It is likely that one or more assistant managers will resign at the beginning. This generates an opportunity for the troubleshooter to bring into the work unit a trusted assistant through his/her professional network. By this time, the interventionist will have a list of qualified applicants for work unit positions and will begin to hire and train them. The next step is for the interventionist to present his/her new set of performance expectations to the workers on each shift. He/she will clearly articulate compliance requirements and specify progressive disciplinary actions for noncompliance. The experienced troubleshooter will have already identified the informal leaders among the staff members and will watch them closely, looking to make an example out of those who do not comply with the new standards. There will likely be a certain level of fallout among staff members due to voluntary and involuntary separations over a short period of time. It will become clear to the workers that the managers may not be held hostages owing to an overstaffed work unit. During this phase, there will be strong pockets of resistance to the management changes and the troubleshooter will micromanage the work unit and the environment begins to stabilize.

After the first 30 days or so of the intervention, the work unit environment will begin to stabilize and new standards for performance will have become habituated among the remaining workers. Natural attrition rates will cause staffing levels to reach par as well. The remaining leads, supervisors and assistant managers will have learned to manage performance to the new standards. The operation will be completely turned around in 60–90 days and negative output symptoms will significantly decrease over this time.

When the operation begins to perform to established standards, the troubleshooter will begin to implement run strategies to enhance current productivity levels. Over a period of about 6–9 months, the majority of output symptoms noted in Table 12.5 will have been fixed.

In this case, the work unit experienced chronic shortages of appropriate staffing levels, which are almost always symptoms of poor management practices. The turnaround intervention provided by the troubleshooter targeted both staffing levels and professional management practices within the work unit. Over a short period of time, staff levels were stabilized. We learned that the transaction processing problems were not systems oriented, but instead tied to the low staffing levels. This also seemed to be the cause of inaccurate transaction processing, poor service delivery and negative staff behaviors. These output problems as well as most of the customer complaints were addressed during the first 30 days of the intervention. The remaining problems are likely to be systems oriented and would have been addressed within 60–90 days.

Our experienced troubleshooter has solved all of the output symptoms within a 90-day window. About four months into the intervention, the troubleshooter would have started to groom one of the assistant managers to take over as the new manager of the operation. The troubleshooter will move on to his/her next project after a stay of nine months to one year.

SYSTEMS THINKING AND TURNAROUND STRATEGIES

We have already seen how a troubleshooter takes a systems approach to diagnosing causal problem areas within a work unit in this chapter. To clarify this approach, we will revisit the systems model presented in Figure 12.4.

We learned in Chapter 6 that this model represents a single restaurant outlet. However, the systems model may be applied to any service enterprise work unit. We remember from this chapter that the troubleshooter begins looking for symptoms at the right of the model and works backward to diagnose causal relationships in the production systems and resources areas of the productivity system.

If the interventionist detects a symptom in the profit margin area of the model, there would be a suspicion of a causal problem in both the revenues and resource control areas of the service enterprise. If revenue symptoms appear, but profit margin percentages have not declined, the immediate suspicion will focus on the service transaction and related production systems. Guest complaints and revenues go hand in hand. If guest complaints are not addressed, the revenues of the enterprise will eventually begin to decline. If a number of guest complaints are detected with no impact on revenues, the troubleshooter will know that an opportunity to perform an early intervention exists.

Troubleshooters know that the cause of guest complaints could stem from back-of-the-house as well as front-of-the house operations systems. In our earlier example, we dealt with mostly FOH operations, as the nature of the symptoms appeared to occur during guest transaction processing. If, however, we see symptoms indicating substandard delivery of products, or the delivery of inferior products resulting in returned items, we would suspect a BOH causal problem. The nature of this problem would vary with the nature of an operation. In a restaurant, the cause could lie within product production systems. If the symptom is related to guestrooms in a lodging establishment, we would look at housekeeping and engineering functions at the hotel. Sometimes, the troubleshooter will trace the cause of a symptom back to the inputs area of the productivity model.

For instance, in our earlier example we identified the symptom of insufficient staffing levels. The interventionist systematically worked back through the supply chain to collect data concerning the potential cause. The troubleshooter learned

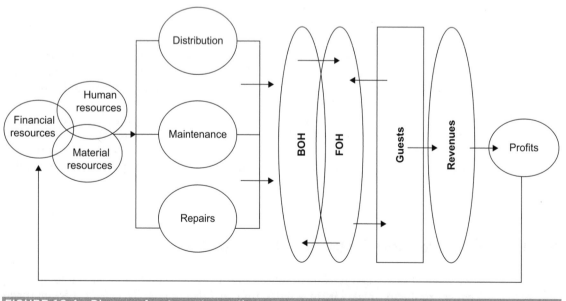

FIGURE 12.4   Diagram of restaurent operations

that the work unit was chronically understaffed, which eliminated suspicions of a scheduling problem. Additionally, it was learned that the labor budget was sufficient to provide appropriate staffing levels, which precluded the probability that a lack of financial resources existed. Finally, the interventionist looked at human resource management practices, only to learn that recruitment and selection practices were in place to fill personnel requisitions in a timely manner. Finally, it was detected that the work unit had a poor reputation resulting from unprofessional management practices that discouraged qualified individuals from applying for positions within that work unit. Once the troubleshooter generated professional management practices, the reputation of the work unit became positive and qualified people began applying for positions once again. This happens in the restaurant sector of the industry all the time.

LARGE-SCALE TURNAROUND STRATEGIES

In some cases, there are symptoms that indicate that an entire service enterprise is in need of a turnaround strategy. When this happens, the interventionist will be an experienced senior operations manager, who may recruit a team of senior-level specialists to assist with the intervention. The timeline used to implement large-scale interventions is usually slightly longer than those implemented within specific work units. Similar to work unit turnarounds, the critical path method (CPM) chart for large-scale interventions will include both concurrent and consecutive strategies and timelines. However, the scale of service enterprise turnaround must include both macro- and microdiagnostics and interventions requiring a longer period of time to complete the overall intervention. Figure 12.5 revisits the systems viewpoint of a large-scale troubleshooter.

As is the case with all large-scale strategies, service enterprise turnaround tactics require a functional view of the organization. The original set of symptoms will occur in the outputs area of the enterprise. The outputs area is much more complex

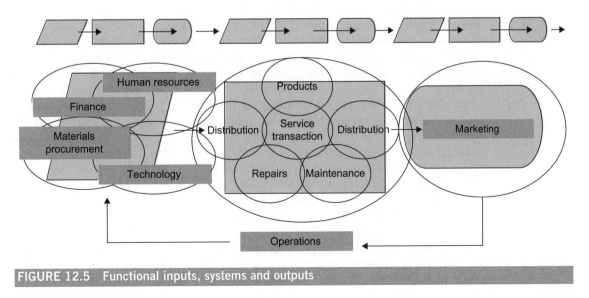

FIGURE 12.5 Functional inputs, systems and outputs

at the organizational level due to the operations of multiple work units occurring simultaneously. Interventionists working at this level must start with macro viewpoints and work down to the micro aspects of specific work units.

The complexity of large-scale turnaround diagnostics and interventions requires a systematic process for data collection and analysis. One method consists of conducting a strategic audit once the outputs systems have been identified and prioritized on the basis of levels of impact to the overall performance of the enterprise. A strategic audit is a functional diagnostic tool used to determine situational analyses within every department and division of the enterprise. The comparison base of a traditional strategic audit is an existing strategic plan. However, in actual practice, it is likely that such a plan would not exist or be used in practice within an enterprise requiring a turnaround strategy. In such cases, the interventionists would devise a strategic plan on the basis of pro forma expectations of the shareholders for the property. That plan will become the diagnostic benchmark. In other words, the interventionists will devise a hypothetical strategic plan that would have been appropriate for the enterprise at the beginning of the present year. This plan will render benchmark objectives, strategies, policies, standards and procedures for the enterprise.

The strategic audit is used to compare actual performance to the now constructed strategic plan. This process includes an audit of each functional department in terms of mission fulfillment, responses to external opportunities and threats, as well as internal strengths and weaknesses relative to the objectives, strategies, policies and procedures. The audit will provide a snapshot of current departmental and work unit operations. The findings of the audit will then be analyzed in view of the symptoms discovered in the first phase of data collection. The findings of this comparison will render causal relationships among all departments and the outputs of the enterprise. Once these are identified and prioritized, the troubleshooters will construct an intervention plan for each department within the enterprise.

In most cases, the strategic audit will uncover a small number of dysfunctional departments, as well as many professionally managed departments. The intervention plan will target the weakest departments as priorities for the intervention. It will simultaneously provide support to those departments that are operating consistently with performance standards. The primary focus of an intervention will vary on the basis of the causal problems identified during the diagnostic phase. In most cases, interventionists find that primary causal problems exist within operations departments, which perform production systems that directly influence service transactions. If primary causal problems are detected in the resource departments, however, these areas must be fixed before attempting to address issues within the service operations. For instance, a poorly performing human resource office will adversely influence the KSAAs and staffing levels within the operations. This function must be fixed in order to generate a critical mass of qualified workers before attempting to perform operations-oriented interventions. The same would be true of poorly performing material resource acquisitions areas. Experienced troubleshooters realize that the tools required to do the job must be in place before attempting to fix operating areas.

The troubleshooter will act in the capacity of general manager or managing director for the duration of the turnaround strategy. The average period of time will be between one and two years for such an intervention. During that time, the interventionist will replace targeted executive committee members with qualified senior managers. The troubleshooter will begin to train a replacement COO during the latter phase of the intervention. This person will eventually assume control of the enterprise when the turnaround intervention is completed. At that time, the new COO will be charged with implementing enterprise-wide run strategies aimed at enhancing organizational productivity levels. The troubleshooter will move on to a new assignment.

WHY DO TROUBLESHOOTERS MOVE ON?

Experienced troubleshooters are a unique breed of managers. Most effective operating managers are considered to possess a traditionalist mind-set, while successful growth-oriented managers are often referred to as visionaries[2]. Turnaround interventionists seem to get an intrinsic sense of satisfaction through troubleshooting or fixing operations. In fact, some say that troubleshooters will begin to fix things that are not broken when they get bored[3]. For this reason, most troubleshooters make careers out of fixing operations, while visionaries do the same with growing operations and traditionalists tend to be satisfied by running operations. Also, experienced troubleshooters earn higher than average salaries. In addition to being very experienced managers, they are highly trained in organizational development (OD) techniques. We learned in Chapter 10 of the text that OD consists of diagnostics and intervention implementation that generates systemic change aimed at organizational renewal. When a corporation realizes the need to perform a turnaround strategy, it will seek the KSAAs of a proven troubleshooter. Desperate times call for desperate salaries, which is why proficient turnaround interventionists earn high salaries.

SUMMARY

We began this chapter with an introduction to the final of the three major strategies emphasized in the text. The turnaround or fix strategy is perhaps the most challenging of the three main strategies presented in the text. Fix strategies are applied to underperforming work units, departments, divisions and in some cases, entire service enterprises.

The need for turnaround strategies is usually preceded by unprofessional management. We discussed the components of professional management in an early portion of the chapter. We recognized that professional managers clearly articulate expectations for performance. They also hold all staff members accountable for achieving performance measures. Professional managers establish objectives, strategies, policies, standards and procedures for each work unit. The human resource function assists by developing job descriptions from job analyses activities. We identified examples of these activities and related documents throughout this topic of discussion.

There are times in which fix strategies are required within work units. We described the nature of these strategies in the relevant section of the text. We learned that turnaround strategies consist of diagnostics and interventions aimed at fixing underperforming work units.

We revisited problem-solving techniques as part of our discussion of diagnostics. We recognized that diagnostics consists of data collection and analysis. We usually find symptoms that may lead us to causal problems in the output areas of a work unit. We work backward through the production systems and input areas to identify causal relationships with those symptoms. This led to a scenario used to highlight examples of output symptoms and the diagnosis of causal relationships.

Upon the completion of the diagnostics phase, troubleshooters will begin to formulate intervention plans to solve the causal problems. We walked through the steps of a sample intervention to witness these steps in action. Next, we investigated systems approaches to conducting turnaround interventions. This led to a discussion of large-scale interventions.

We recognized that large-scale interventions deal with turning around entire service enterprises. This is a complicated task that requires highly trained troubleshooters. We identified the steps of the strategic audit, which is a tool used during the diagnostics phase of large-scale interventions. We learned the intervention steps taken to complete this type of turnaround strategy.

We concluded the chapter with a discussion on the nature and training of turnaround interventionists. We compared these managers with other management personalities.

DISCUSSION QUESTIONS

1. Consider a situation in which an operation that you are familiar with needs to be fixed. What factors have caused this situation? How could the enterprise have avoided such a situation, specifically?
2. Does the human resource function of a service enterprise play a role in the development of professional management practices? What specific activities should they provide?
3. When are fix strategies warranted? What do we specifically mean when we discuss diagnostics and interventions? Please give examples of these.
4. Please identify the systems approach to turnaround diagnostics and interventions. Be specific.
5. Please identify the similarities and differences between work unit and large-scale turnaround strategies. Be as inclusive as possible in your answers.

REAL WORLD EXPERIENCES (CONTINUED)

After just one month from taking the job at the restaurant, you realized you made a big mistake. Every night was a nightmare. There were call-offs on every shift. Those workers who did show up did not seem to care much about the operation. The managers were never on the floor. They did show up at the end of the shift to party with the staff. Scheduling preferences were based on personal favorites. It seemed over time that business was getting slower and slower. The kitchen commonly ran out of menu items and guest complaints were unbelievably high. There were insufficient tools to do the job, which created an environment where everyone would fight over limited resources.

Every time you mentioned the restaurant to your friends at school they would say, 'I can't believe you work there. The reputation on the street for that place is horrible.' Finally, you decide to give one week's notice of your resignation. You arrive to work ready to resign, when you are met by a new general manager, Kristen. She greets you and introduces herself as the new manager. You take the opportunity to hand her the resignation letter. She reads it and says, 'I understand completely why you don't want to work here and I commend you for giving notice.' She continues, 'I am here to turn this place around. If you like the changes that you see over the next week and decide to stay with us to help fix the restaurant just let me know.' With that you went about setting up your station.

You arrive for your shift on the next night and notice a bunch of new servers doing side work. You ask the host what was going on. The host mentions that Kristen had a meeting with all the full-time staff members and laid down an ultimatum of improved service standards. After a bunch of servers walked out, she brought her new staff out from the kitchen. She also introduced her new assistant managers who were charged with training all the new workers. You thought to yourself, 'This seems kind of drastic.'

Over the past week, the environment of the restaurant has completely changed. The floor is flooded with assistant managers, the tools to do the job suddenly appeared, incentives were bringing in new customers and the service systems were greatly simplified. You had your best money night since joining the restaurant.

At the end of your shift, Kristen approached you. She said, 'According to my records, this will be your last night of work here. Are you sure you want to leave us?' she asks. You think for a moment and then respond off the top of your head, 'I can't believe the changes you made here in just one week. If it's okay with you, I would like to hang around to see what happens next.' Kristen gives you a smile and says, 'I don't think you will be disappointed with this decision.'

CASE STUDY

A national chain hotel located on the beautiful Gulf Coast had performed exceptionally well in comparison to its nearby neighbors. Thanks to legalized gambling that had come into the local county, all hotels were performing better than anyone could have ever expected. With occupancy rates running over 92% annually, this 80-room, beachfront property was a 'star' in the eyes of its guests, owners and national franchising company. However, a villain was hidden in the guestrooms, the linen closets and the laundry room – this villain was that of prejudice – prejudice held by the housekeeping director.

It was summer of 1999 and the general manager, Mr. Lee Wilson, had just received his end-of-month financial report for the month ending June. He was astonished to find that his hotel not only achieved a 152 on yield index, but that both his occupancy and rate indexes were both above 130 as well. These are both very high indices. He decided to take a walk down to the assistant general manager's office and show her the good news. Cathy (the AGM) was in her office with Betsy, the housekeeping director. They were discussing the day's issues. When Lee shared with them the great news, Cathy said it was of course her doing since she added such great features to the continental breakfast bar. Betsy, always a stand-up-for-your-rights type of person, exclaimed, 'Heck, no! It has all to do with the way my ladies clean the rooms – they're spotless from top to bottom – and everyone knows that cleanliness is what attracts people to a hotel!' Lee knew that they were *both* correct, and congratulated them. Before he left the office, Cathy reminded him that she was leaving for her week's vacation to Mexico the following morning and that Betsy would, as usual, fill in as Manager on Duty during her absence.

On Cathy's first day of vacation, Lee often called on the radio for Betsy and relied upon her knowledge and skills. Indeed, as his comanager, they were both quite busy during this time period. At one point in the day, Betsy said, 'It's easier for you just to stop by my office instead of using the radio for the next half hour or so. If you need me for anything, I'll be in here reviewing housekeeping applications anyway. As a matter of fact, why don't you definitely stop by and we'll look at some of these applications together.'

When he entered her office, Betsy was handling a guest lost & found issue on the telephone. Betsy was always so professional with guests – she often received 'outstanding' in her annual reviews. As a matter of fact, she was employed at the property since its opening 12 years prior and had never had a single write-up or day of absence for any reason! It had become a 'running joke' around the property that the only time Betsy would miss a day of work would be for her very own funeral. Additionally, the property remained in the top 10% (as measured by guest satisfaction with housekeeping issues) of all similar hotels in the national chain with which they were a franchise.

Betsy hung up the phone and promised the guest a return call within five minutes. She politely asked Lee to review the applications on her desk while she went down to the locked cage in the lost & found office to look for this particular guest's lost item. While she was away, a horrible situation unfolded before Lee's very own eyes – but he did not yet realize how awful the situation would become. He read through a stack of six applications on Betsy's desk and, when turning to get more comfortable in his seat, noticed three applications in the garbage pail. As a matter of both national chain and ownership policies, applications were to be held on file for a period of no less than six months, even if the candidate was not qualified for the current opening.

At first, he just though this was a mistake and that the applications must have fallen into the wastebasket by accident.

Betsy returned, with the guest's item in hand and quickly returned the call to the now very happy guest. She promised that the items would be mailed out C.O.D. as soon as she finished her brief meeting with the general manager. When she hung up the phone, Lee innocently told her that he had reviewed the applications on her desk and that he had found three applications in the trash can, which must have been an accident.

Betsy immediately became fidgety, seemed angered and turned red in the face. It was obvious that she had become uncomfortable. Lee asked her what was wrong. She became very irate and said, 'How dare you go through my trash can while I'm working on company time!' Not understanding what caused this outburst, he asked, 'Betsy, calm down, what's wrong? I just simply said these must have fallen off your desk and that I want to review them with you.'

Betsy, now both visibly angry and shaken, replied, 'You know darn well why those are in the trash.' Honestly, he did not. As the story unfolded, Betsy went on to explain to him that all of the applicants in the trash were black. He quickly corrected her and said, 'These applicants are African-American.' Even more heated, she yelled, 'You know exactly what I mean. They're black and blacks don't clean as well as whites. I refuse to hire 'em and you can't change me to believe or do otherwise.' With that, she stormed out of the office muttering obscenities.

It became obvious to Lee, with a few minutes of reflection, that indeed his entire housekeeping staff (laundry attendant, room attendant and housepersons) consisted of white (Caucasian) individuals. While he had never considered this 'odd' or 'strange,' it now became quite apparent that Betsy had probably made these hiring decisions without his input. Since he was the general manager of this hotel for only three years, he had no idea that an all-Caucasian staff in the housekeeping department had been the 'norm' since the hotel's opening (12 years ago) and that Betsy would have it no other way. As a matter of fact, Betsy had never indicated any signs of being a racist or having an issue with diversity on any previous occasion.

With feelings of rage, frustration, betrayal and nausea, he rushed out of the office and confronted Betsy. He said, 'I want you to meet with me in my office right now!' By this time, Betsy realized that she had made a grave mistake, not only by throwing away the applications, but also by her hiring practices. After a lengthy two-hour conversation, she had agreed to attend diversity training, she agreed to a formal write-up for her behavior, she agreed to interview the three candidates who were just as qualified on paper as the other six applicants she had in her files and, lastly, she agreed that she was in the wrong.

As Lee dialed the management company's director of human resources to set up an immediate face-to-face meeting with Betsy and schedule her for the very next diversity training session, he still felt quite unsettled over the entire matter. For certain, he believed, someone who just told him a few hours before that 'blacks don't clean as well as whites' would certainly not be able to be changed through just a reprimand, coach and counsel or diversity training.

His day had been so great – the STAR report was excellent, his guest satisfaction scores were perfect, his AGM was away on a much-needed vacation and the hotel was operating beautifully. Now, his day had been shattered. How could he have not noticed in three years that his entire housekeeping department consisted of only Caucasian employees? Maybe he overlooked it because he had Hispanics, African-Americans and other minorities employed in other areas of the hotel? Maybe he was just a terrible general manager? Maybe he was a racist himself? After all, he was Caucasian and never noticed the ethnic backgrounds of his housekeeping staff? Would his regional vice president be more irate with him than with Betsy? Would he be fired for his inaction?

With a sinking feeling in the pit of his stomach, he began to dial the phone number of the corporate office. 'Human resources,' he muttered, as the receptionist answered the phone.

Questions

- Who is at fault in this situation? Betsy? Lee? Cathy? The owner? The management company?
- Did Lee take the correct course of action thus far? Would you have proceeded in the same manner? If not, what would you have done differently?
- How do you think the owner will respond? The management company? The national chain? Further, should all of these parties be informed of what has occurred on the property?
- If you were a minority employee working at the hotel in a different department, would you have noticed that there were no employees working in housekeeping? If so, why? If not, why not? Is it quite possible in day-to-day operations that some departments may have more ethnic diversity than others?
- What are some logical procedures or policies to ensure ethnic and racial diversity in your place of employment? Are these policies and procedures necessary? Why or why not?
- What about the long-term success of the hotel, especially when rated by guest satisfaction with cleanliness – which is a direct result of the housekeeping department's efforts? Can this fact be overlooked?

ENDNOTES

1. Tesone (2003), Tactical Strategies for Service Industry Management: How to Do It. Pearson-Prentice Hall: Boston.
2. Kearsey Bates Temperament Sorter.
3. Ibid.

PART 4

Leadership Applications

Leadership Awareness

In this chapter you will learn to:

1. Understand the relationships of leaders, followers, and the environment (situation).
2. Identify the characteristics associated with leadership traits.
3. Recognize types of interactions that are associated with transactional and transformational leadership.
4. Identify a few theories of employee motivation.
5. Apply motivational strategies to managing workers.
6. Recognize differences in individual motivators.

IN THE REAL WORLD

You are working in the human resource office for a large branded chain hotel at the property level. The director of human resources invites you to attend the local Hospitality Human Resource Association chapter meeting after work. You realize this is a good opportunity to network with other HR practitioners. You arrive at the meeting and are introduced to the other attendees who include directors, as well as HR specialist (compensation, employee relations, training, labor relations) managers.

The topic of the meeting is leadership strategies. A guest speaker provides a presentation on leadership development programs. After the presentation, there is an open forum discussion session. Since you want to learn as much as you can about HR practices, you pay close attention to the interactions of the discussion session. You start to notice after awhile that these HR managers, while somewhat knowledgeable, seem to be lacking some quality that your director has.

At the office the next morning you are having coffee with the training manager. You start to tell him about your experience at the association meeting. You then mention, 'Is it me? Or is there some quality that our HR director has that the other practitioners don't have?' He just smiles at you.

To be continued...

INTRODUCTION

In this chapter we will discuss **leadership** awareness and motivation theories. We will learn that leadership and motivation go hand-in-hand when it comes to managing people. Leadership is one area of management that has not received a great amount of attention in actual practice. One simple description of leadership is the power of influence to generate the authentic desire on the part of others to act in a certain way. So, leadership is all about the 'power of influence over others.' While the body of research has attempted to describe this power in terms that are consistent with the **scientific method** of analysis, to this date there is really very little agreement of the definitions of the terms leadership, **leaders**, and **leading**[1]. Leadership in the field of management seems to be the power of influence that creates a willingness to accomplish the objectives of the organization. Most managers are familiar with this description of leadership; but why do they spend so little time trying to really understand the phenomenon associated with leadership power?

One reason many managers are not well versed in the practice and theory of leadership is that such a practice is contrary to the traditional functions of management, as we learned in chapter 2 of the text. Most managers are trained in the functions and processes of organizational management. The nature of management practice is focused on administrative and coordinating activities, which are contrary to the activities of leadership to a certain extent. This is not to say that management practitioners disregard leadership concepts; in actuality the opposite is true. Many organizations have replaced the job title of 'manager' with the word, 'leader.' In some organizations the wording of, 'department' or 'work unit' has been replaced with the title of 'team'. The use of these titles is certainly a step in the right direction as far as creating general awareness of leadership and teamwork within organizations. However, most anecdotal reports indicate that units and managers within these organizations are doing nothing other than traditional management practices. This is not to say that there is anything wrong with traditional management practices, as many individuals in possession of the title, 'manager' have yet to learn these concepts and it is certainly one major task of human resource practitioners to train these managers in these practices. Leadership, however, goes beyond management practices. Many case studies concerning great moments in management are centered on individuals who demonstrate both leadership and management skills in the process of achieving greatness. Leadership is one area of research that is still in its infancy, so there is much to be learned about this phenomenon.

Proactive managers take every opportunity to train themselves in the comprehension of the leadership phenomenon. They seek to become leaders within their own management practice. Finally, they pursue the grand strategy of imparting leadership development training to protégés and other willing managers. It is possible for a person who is not a manager to teach management. For some reason, however, it seems impossible for a person who is not a leader to teach leadership practices.

Any experienced leader will tell us that as managers of people we must know as much as we can learn about applied human behavior. Certainly our discussion of leadership awareness would be worthless if we did not move into an understanding of the underlying factors that influence individuals to behave in certain ways, which is the purpose of this section.

We know that managers must know as much as can be known about human motivation. No management development program is complete without motivational training seminars. While it is true that many managers in organizations studied motivation as part of their curriculum at school, it is apparent from anecdotally watching them in the 'real world' that many have missed out on how to apply it to the management of people. Those managers who do learn the applications of these concepts become very powerful leaders.

THE PRACTICE OF LEADERSHIP

Leadership is a common topic of discussion in organizational and institutional settings. Curricula in schools of business administration, and hospitality/tourism management include courses, seminars, or cross-curriculum infusion of topical areas that are related to leadership concepts. The word, 'leadership' is commonly used in the course of daily conversations in professional and administrative settings. Printed literature includes articles and advertisements for professional development workshops on the topic of leadership. Also, employers rank leadership skills toward the top of desired abilities of candidates for supervisory employment. Finally, a good deal of academic research has been conducted to develop leadership paradigms.

While the concept of leadership is much discussed, it still remains difficult to describe. Individuals seem hard-pressed to provide agreeable descriptions of what leadership really is. This factor may contribute to the many definitions that have been provided to describe the many aspects of leadership.

WHAT THE RESEARCHERS SAY ABOUT LEADERSHIP

The old **Machiavellian** belief that leaders are born, not made, remains present in modern day thought among certain individuals. Others contend that leadership may be learned by anyone with a desire to lead others. If this is true, the question for trainers and educators seems to be, 'How do we teach people to become leaders?'

One study provides comparisons between leadership and management in organizations to determine differences between the activities of leaders versus managers[2]. Another investigation discusses characteristics and qualities of leaders as means to provide case study examples of leadership situations[3]. One researcher provides a developmental model as a means for teaching leadership relations[4]. Some studies identify leadership credibility factors as determined by the perceptions of others to describe leadership qualities[5]. Other academic investigators take research-based model approaches to present paradigms to develop an understanding of leadership phenomena[6]. Finally, recent research provides focus on the transformational leadership paradigm to describe leadership dimensions[7], as well as universal systems models[8].

It would seem that regardless of the approach taken to understand and teach leadership, three **interdependent** factors must be considered. First, we must observe the behaviors and attempt to identify the characteristics of leaders. Second, we should gain an understanding of the perspectives of followers. Third, we must analyze contributions of the environment or **situation** to leader/follower interactions. This view may seem simplistic; however, when attempting to understand complex concepts, simplification may be the means through which we clarify our understanding.

It is apparent that those who have been mentored or exposed to dealing with great leaders possess a clear snapshot of leadership in action. Therefore, it may be possible that an experiential approach to learning is appropriate in the study of leadership topics.

LEADERSHIP AND MANAGEMENT

People often confuse leadership and management, when in fact they are two different concepts. One illustration of this is the advice provided by many authors that instructs supervisors to manage 'things' and to lead 'people.' This suggests that leadership is an influencing activity while other aspects of management refer to planning, organizing and controlling functions[9]. It is important to note that not all managers are leaders and not all leaders are managers. Think for a moment about people with supervisor titles that just don't come across to you as leaders. Now, consider those with no formal authority who seem to influence co-workers to follow their lead.

Some experts speak of leadership from the standpoint of the support role owed to the followers, which are referred to as '**stewardship**' qualities of leaders[10]. Ancient philosopher, Lao Tzu proclaimed that leaders must learn to follow, which is one of the signs of stewardship[11]. One tendency of effective leaders is their willingness to share the role of leader and follower in appropriate situations. Leaders also demonstrate the capacity to provide simplified interpretations of complex issues[12].

EXAMINING TRADITIONAL MODELS AND THEORIES OF LEADERSHIP

There are sufficient amounts of traditional models and theories concerning the topic of leadership. Consideration of traditional models reviewed by the experts seems to provide evidence that research is not the key to developing a practical understanding of leadership. A number of research articles are available for review. Yet, the data seem to provide ineffective knowledge for the purpose of imparting leadership skills. This, once again, seems to provide evidence that the concept of leadership is phenomenal in nature.

Organizational theory frames provide us with categories of leadership strengths. However, no single frame provides a holistic picture of an actual leader. Instead, leaders are categorized as having conceptual strengths in structure, relations, political skills, or facilitative skills. Most widely acclaimed leaders possess strengths in all these categories.

A number of studies have been conducted to identify characteristic and response theories to explain leadership[13]. **Trait** theories cite personal characteristics which help us determine to what extent leaders will gravitate toward transactional versus transformational leadership styles. Behavioral theories focus on internally motivating factors of task and relations, while contingency theory considers the same tendencies from external motivating aspects. These traditional theories assume an objective viewpoint of interactions between leaders and followers. Other research departs from this tradition by identifying means used by leaders to elicit follower participation. These are basically focused on communications skills. The underlying inference is that leaders manipulate followers through symbolic gestures such as rites and rituals, or that leaders create mythical perceptions in the minds of the followers. Regardless of the focus, the technique seems to involve the construct of perceived realities consistent with the beliefs, attitudes, and values of the followers.

In actual practice, it may be true that leaders possess and employ the ability to communicate in terms identifiable with followers' cultural systems. This activity might be viewed as the ability of the leader to **empathetically** communicate with followers through an innate understanding of the internal value systems of individuals and groups. While this may be labeled as a form of manipulation, it may be more accurately described as effective managerial communication to achieve common and constructive outcomes.

ETHICS AND LEADERSHIP

Is there a moral component in the leadership paradigm? An interesting departure from the traditional viewpoint associated with the achievement of transformational leadership through power and influence, is the diminished moral connotation within the model. Some of the research indicates that the moral aspect has evolved into a code word for innovative and motivational leadership. It would be hard to imagine a true leader who did not create an image of personal morality in the minds of his or her followers. Even leaders in illicit environments portray a code of personal values in their behaviors and communications.

Regardless of the semantics, most researchers and practitioners agree that credibility is the key to a leader's ability to influence people. This credibility evolves from perceptions of the leader by peers, followers and other leaders. Credibility is attained by peoples' perceptions of a person's behavior and expression of thoughts. The leader, by nature of her or his relationship to others is highly scrutinized in this regard. Therefore, it seems likely that the credibility factor is greatly influenced by the moral and ethical value systems of the person occupying a leadership position.

Finally, discussions concerning leadership diversity provide a departure from traditional views which is different than those presented by other authors. In this case the word, 'traditional' refers to the white male leader, as opposed to the non-traditional leader of different gender or color (to include National Origin). While it is certainly true that cultures have provided limitations to the achievement of legitimate power possessed by repressed classes of people, it is unlikely that differences exist as to the inherent ability of these individuals to lead. It appears that these writings are concerned more with cultural challenges as opposed to actual leadership concerns. This may be a limitation associated with the perspectives of social scientists engaged in leadership diversity studies.

EMERGING THEORIES AND MODELS

Emerging theories in leadership seem to reflect the dynamic environment in which organizations and institutions currently function. Less focus seems to be placed on narrow models of leadership. Holistic leadership paradigms are now emerging. Visionary aspects of leadership are becoming a dominant consideration in discussions of leadership effectiveness. **Change agentry** is also a prominent concern. It stands to reason that today's leaders need to be skilled visionaries capable of enacting change. Organizations are rethinking, restructuring, and revitalizing the types of work that are done and processes aimed at the achievement of outcomes. Therefore, it is appropriate for effective leaders to possess skills in supporting the followership in these environments.

The leader of today deals with such diversity as to require much more advanced levels of sophistication than former leaders. Emphasis in emerging leadership models provides focus on the dynamics of the followership. Individuals in today's organizations possess stronger values of individualism and sophisticated convictions with regard to quality of lifestyle issues. Also, today's workforce is comprised of individuals who are knowledgeable and adamant in the preservation of individual rights in the workplace. This impacts the ability of leaders to provide effective influence over others and further enhances the moral component of leadership influence.

PURPOSE, MISSION AND VISION

Certain environments provide what one might call, 'motivating missions'[14]. In such cases, people seem to be naturally motivated to perform at peak levels. Usually, these scenarios are project based. Common examples would be special events that occur in organizations that challenge and energize workers to work toward a common purpose and to achieve a common set of goals. During these events, the job of leadership is somewhat simplified. Also, during these times, unsuspecting leaders tend to temporarily emerge. The unfortunate aspect of this scenario is that it seems to be unsustainable. That is, it is temporary and when the inspiring mission is fulfilled, the performance levels and enthusiasm seem to drop to 'normal' (sometimes mediocre) levels.

The challenge for leaders is to provide sustainable purpose and mission that motivate the workforce. The reason this is challenging is that most institutions and organizations do not serve a naturally glamorous or exciting purpose. Therefore, it becomes the challenge of the leader to embrace and communicate the mission and purpose in ways that impassion others.

The current trend in organizations and institutions goes beyond purpose and mission to include vision statements. Unfortunately, when the word 'statement' is added, the bureaucrats become licensed to turn visioning into a paper and pencil (disk and keyboard, these days) exercise. One expert draws contrasts and comparisons to approaches taken by managers versus leaders to develop and communicate visions[15]. The managers have a tendency to formulate administrative representations, similar to what is taught in strategic planning sessions. The leaders bring the vision to life. They depict the vision in terms that are consistent with the value systems and description preferences of the people in the organization. In essence, leaders bring visionary concepts to life.

BUILDING AND SHARING POWER

According to some researchers leaders possess the ability to use informal means to align people[16]. They do this by developing informal networks within various areas of the organization. Bureaucratic managers rely more on formal lines of communications such as written reports and job descriptions. These formal documents do have their place in an organization or institution. However, bureaucrats rely more heavily on these tools than their leader counterparts.

Leaders seem to be highly skilled communicators. Whether these skills are acquired or inherent, the leader recognizes the power behind effective communications. They seem to use all means of communication available to them. Their mannerisms, body language, appearance, posture, and examples seem to be orchestrated to drive home the message being sent to people. Leaders also seem to possess the ability to convert complex concepts into simplified strings of messages. This probably is attributable to a thorough understanding and rapport with people in the organization. Finally, leaders seem to recognize the importance of active listening. They realize that by listening effectively, they can better understand the people with whom they are dealing. Leaders seem to be keenly aware of the importance of information gained through informal interactions.

SELF-ANALYSIS AND CONTEXTUAL RELATIONS

More than one person has proclaimed that prior to leading, one must learn to follow. In the same way, before one can know others, she or he must know him/herself. This may be the basis of the understanding of human behavior that many leaders seem to possess. Leaders seem to take time for introspection and creative thinking. Popular phrases for this activity might be meditation or focused reflection. No matter what the format or title, it is believable that leaders spend a good portion of time in contemplative silence (day dreaming might be another label for this activity). It is possible that this quiet time permits an individual to analyze the self and interactions with others. This activity may help to create a certain type of wisdom within an individual. Sometimes we call these people 'worldly'.

One expert reminds us that leaders see individuals as holistic beings[17]. People are more than their positions, accomplishments, and status. They are fully developed human entities with all of the experience, knowledge, and emotions possessed by our beings. Leaders take the time to consider the human factors of people. They are also capable of identifying individual talents, preferences, motivational factors, and feelings. The researchers also remind organizations to be on the lookout for corporate entropy[18]. In organizations, there are signs that indicate the settling-in of bureaucratic thought processes. As these processes take hold, the organization begins to decline. One sign is when individuals begin to lose sight of the purpose, mission, and vision for the organization. These symptoms, if left unaddressed, may lead to cultural shifts in organizations in which leadership values may ultimately decline, only to be replaced by bureaucratic values, which may be detrimental to the survival of those corporations.

DEVELOPING AND IMPROVING LEADER RELATIONS

Leaders seem to be self-developing people. Also, leaders, being people who self-analyze, usually become aware of their strengths and areas for assistance. Someone once said that great leaders have great weaknesses[19]. This may be true. Regardless, leaders appear to be aware of those areas in which they need assistance. For this reason, the leader would have a tendency to enlist the support of individuals who may assist the leader in specifically required areas. The leader might also have a tendency to appropriately empower or align with others to facilitate accomplishment of the overall mission. In this sense, leaders are sensible. They seem to recognize that none of us is as good or smart as all of us.

In addition to possessing an awareness to select human capital to increase overall strengths, leaders seem to have the ability to energize individuals toward achievement. It is likely that they do this in a manner that provides personal satisfaction to people as well as benefit to the organization or institution. Therefore, leaders seem to maximize relations with others for the common welfare of all.

TRANSACTIONS AND TRANSFORMATIONS

Transactional leaders seem to be those who possess the ability to influence others through highly developed interpersonal relations skills. The power of influence is certainly a key skill shared among all leaders. In some organizations, leaders may rely more heavily on this set of skills depending on the specific organizational structure. Often, in these organizations individuals are provided legitimate power through the attainment of positions, such as division or department director. However, in some settings workers may tend to resist people who have been given titles. One factor, which may contribute to these types of attitudes, may be the tendency by senior managers to appoint individuals who do not possess credibility

with the workers to positions of power and influence. Thus, lack of c
usurp acceptance of formal authority.

However, people who possess appropriate levels of credibility with tu
in these organizations seem to be unaffected by the overall lack of respect for pc
ple with formal job titles.

THE NATURE OF CHANGE

For years now, students of management have been told about the impact of external environmental factors on organizations. Models are provided to assist managers with identifying and predicting external events, for the purpose of making
decisions to limit threats and embrace opportunities looming outside the organization. Being good students of management, they have learned to perform auditing, scanning, forecasting, and analytical activities. A factor that seems to be
overlooked is the importance of making decisions to modify how the organization operates to remain congruent with its environment. At the same time, we
are entering an era in which those external factors of influence are becoming more
dynamic at exponential proportions. As the world around us changes, people must
also change. For this to happen, people must accept responsibility and accountability for changing their lives. Evolutionary change involves personal growth.
Leaders who pursue paths of personal growth for themselves and their followers
are practicing the highest level of interaction called **transformational** leadership.
In today's business environment both transactional and transformational leaders
are considered to be change agents.

CHANGE AGENTRY

Most of us have met individuals who are natural troubleshooters. We learned
about these people in chapter 12 of the text. These individuals are always seeking challenges that require implementing change. Some personality tests identify
people who prefer to work in troubleshooting capacities. Troubleshooters who possess training and skills in effective change implementation may be referred to as
change agents.

This is not to say all change agents are troubleshooters. In the same sense, not
all troubleshooters are effective change agents. Some are muck stirrers. While
they mean well, they lack the ability to systematically implement change that is
accepted by others. An organizational aspect that change agents and troubleshooters undoubtedly face is conflict. As a matter of fact most of us deal with conflict on
a regular basis. We have a tendency to consider conflict to be negative. However,
there are forms of conflict in organizations that are constructive. This type of conflict may be entitled 'managed conflict'. A leader who recognizes the synergistic
outcomes of creative idea generation might welcome this form of conflict. When
constructive conflict is present, the threat of groupthink phenomenon is reduced.
This type of conflict fosters multiple viewpoints to generate outcomes greater than
those that may be established by a single individual working alone.

MOTIVATION

Motivation may be defined as a willingness to do something. Managers are interested in motivation applications because they want workers to be willing to perform tasks and activities aimed at the accomplishment of the objectives of the organization[20]. Workers who are willing to do the work do better jobs. Willing workers also permit the manager to act as leader instead of manager. Motivated people do not need to be managed. They simply require leadership to remain focused on the collective attainment of objectives[21].

Various factors motivate individuals in different ways. This is because motivation is based on the perception of unfulfilled wants, needs, and desires[22]. These perceptions vary among individuals. For instance, most people agree that money is a motivator. The experts indicate that, for most people, it isn't the money that motivates, but the unfulfilled material needs associated with having money[23]. Some people are definitely motivated by the opportunity to earn unlimited incomes. These people have a tendency to work in commissioned sales positions. Other people value earning the most income in the shortest period of time spent working. These people may have a tendency to work for gratuities or large bonuses. Another group of people may prefer to work in pleasant surroundings with specifically scheduled work hours and standard work routines. These people may prefer administrative positions. Managers are often motivated by challenging work, achievement, recognition, and a personal sense of accomplishment as an important member of an organization. Managers usually perceive the need to make a decent income but often choose management positions over more lucrative positions such as commissioned sales jobs. For many managers, a performance bonus is primarily a measurement of accomplishment, with the actual dollar amount representing the reward for achievement.

Individuals have varying needs and priorities of needs. For this reason, there is no general rule concerning motivators for different people. The manager does not possess the ability to motivate another person. This is because motivation comes from within a person, not from external sources. Therefore, the best a manager can do is to get others to motivate themselves. Managers accomplish this by identifying unfulfilled perceived needs and wants for each individual. Once needs and wants are identified, the manager makes every attempt to combine need fulfillment with performance outcomes. This combination results in motivated workers.

MONEY

For most workers, money (in the form of salaries and hourly wages) is not an effective motivator. Instead, it is a potential dissatisfier[24]. This may be partially due to compensation structures in organizations; most people are paid for time worked. Organizations have limited resources concerning the amount of money that can be paid to workers. When a worker receives a pay raise, that person is content for a few weeks. After that time period, the amount of the paycheck becomes the expectation and the worker feels that more money is deserved. However, there are ways to structure compensation practices to attach financial rewards to performance achievements. In these cases, money (or at least its intrinsic meaning to the worker) can serve as a strong motivator.

THEORIES OF MOTIVATION

Over the years, many researchers have developed theories concerning motivation of individuals and groups of people. This section presents a few popular concepts. The theories that describe the 'whys' of human motivation are referred to as **content theories**. Those that explain 'how' to motivate people are considered to be **process theories**. In this section we start with content theories and conclude with process theories of motivation.

HIERARCHY OF NEEDS

Perhaps the most popular motivational content theory among managers is the Hierarchy of Needs theory. Figure 13.1 provides a model of this theory.

Psychologist Abraham Maslow developed a model that depicts unfulfilled wants and needs as motivating factors[25]. Maslow contends that five categories of needs exist in a hierarchy that ranges from lower-level needs to higher-order needs. As one set of needs becomes mostly fulfilled, the set of needs on the next level become motivators. Maslow indicates that individuals who mostly fulfill lower-level and higher-order needs will seek fulfillment of the highest possible need. That need is called the need of Self-Actualization. Self-Actualization occurs when a person seeks to be all that a person can be in a holistic sense. This person is at peace with the self, having attained a self-perceived level of spiritual, material, and personal contentment. In the past, most people began to pursue self-actualizing needs in later adult years. However, current generations of adults start reaching for self-actualizing goals in their mid-to-late 20s due to higher levels of evolution among newer generations[26]. According to Maslow, less than 2 percent of the world's population attains the level of being completely self-actualized.

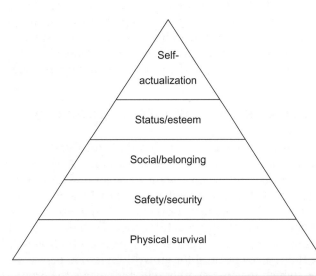

FIGURE 13.1   Hierarchy of needs

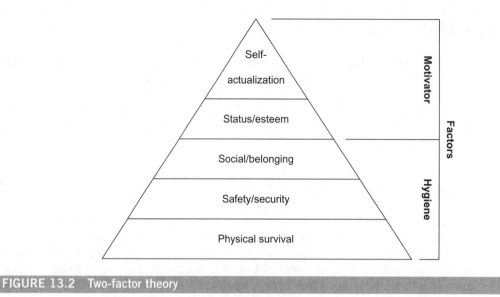

FIGURE 13.2   Two-factor theory

TWO-FACTOR THEORY

Researcher Frederick Herzberg was a disciple of Maslow for many years. Eventually, Herzberg generated a new content theory of motivation based on Maslow's work. Figure 13.2 provides a comparison of Herzberg's theory to Maslow's.

Herzberg agrees with Maslow that there is a hierarchy of lower-to higher-order needs. Herzberg suggests that the lower order-needs are extrinsically (external) based, while the higher-order needs are intrinsic (internal)[27]. According to Herzberg, lower-order needs are not motivators; rather, they are hygiene factors. By this, Herzberg implies that lower-level needs do need to be satisfied for individuals to pursue higher-order needs. However, the potential satisfaction of the lower-level needs does not motivate people to perform work. Instead, the absence of needs fulfillment, such as pay, working conditions, and safety, will make workers dissatisfied. Dissatisfied workers will not be motivated by higher-order needs. Maslow and Herzberg provide two of the most popular content theories of motivation.

OTHER CONTENT THEORIES OF MOTIVATION

Some theories contend that Maslow and Herzberg provide theoretical constructs that are not conducive to empirical studies. Additionally, some motivation scholars contend that core motivators may be altered more subtly by immediate workplace experiences. Clayton Alderfer reworked Maslow's Hierarchy into three core needs categories that include: E-existence, G-growth, and R-relatedness. Appropriately, he named this theory the **ERG** model[28]. Let's say that two individuals are competing for promotion to a single position. Both would be motivated at that time for the G-need or need for growth. Only one person will be promoted to the position, which means the other will not receive the promotion. The person who earns the promotion will continue to be motivated by growth. The individual who does not receive the promotion will revert to another core needs group, such as related-ness (R-need) as a means to cope with the disappointment resulting from not being selected for promotion. So, while this person may have not socialized very much with coworkers, that person will return to higher socialization levels to feed the R-need, which that person uses to compensate for the inability to satisfy a growth need. When another promotional opportunity occurs, that person will once again shift into growth orientation.

Another focus of needs development ties motivators to personality preferences for certain individuals. David McClelland and associates developed a model called the 'Theory of Needs'[29]. Similar to the ERG theory, the theory of needs focuses on three needs categories. These include A-Achievement, A-Affiliation, and P-Power. One interesting way to identify varied dominant needs is to observe the office or work spaces for individuals. High achievement work areas will be decorated with plaques, trophies, diplomas and certificates. While, high Affiliation work areas will be adorned with social symbols such as, pictures of friends, family, and pets; favorite coffee mug, plants and home style touches and the like. The power office, will be designed with dark colors that are often contrasted with red shades, large desk with high-back (throne-style) chair, decorations may include mid-evil weapons or other power symbols. One executive was reported to have his desk on top of a platform, with very low chairs about three-feet in front of it.

All of the content theories have some applications in organizational settings. For this reason, managers must be well versed in the substance of the theories and work to apply them to the practice of understanding the 'whys of human behavior' for members of the staff.

PROCESS THEORIES OF MOTIVATION

Process theories of motivation describe how people respond to motivators through behavior. While the content theories described previously discuss the 'whys' of human behavior, process theories focus on 'how' to motivate workers to enhance their performance levels.

BEHAVIORAL MODIFICATION

The behavioral science school of thought focuses on reinforcement and punishment associated with stimulus and response to explain motivation. Behaviorist B.F. Skinner provides a model of reinforcement of desired behaviors as a form of motivation[30]. Reinforcement occurs in response to a desired behavior. For instance, praise for a job well done will reinforce future positive performance. Those who subscribe to this reinforcement philosophy believe that only positive actions should receive a response; punishment does not provide a sustainable change in a person's behavior or attitude. Therefore, some individuals contend that undesirable behavior should be ignored. This theory is called extinction. However, as discussed in former chapters, managers are responsible for addressing all incidents of performance related behavior. Therefore, managers must provide reinforcement for desired behaviors and other appropriate responses for undesired behavior. It is important to remember that workers, unlike pigeons, are cognitively and emotionally developed individuals.

Reinforcement always rewards desired behaviors. It does this in two ways. **Positive reinforcement** attaches something pleasant to the performance of desired behaviors. **Negative reinforcement** takes away something considered to be unpleasant as a reward for desired behavior. For instance, a worker does a particularly good job on a project and receives a nice bonus. This is positive reinforcement. Or the supervisor could remove an unpleasant task (like side work for a restaurant server) in response to the good job on a project. This is an example of negative reinforcement. Both are approaches to providing rewards for desired behaviors. Therefore, negative reinforcement is not a bad thing; it is just another way of providing a reward.

OTHER PROCESS APPROACHES

While behavioral modification is perhaps the most widely used process motivational tool for supervisors, there are other theories that are relevant to managers above the supervisory ranks. One process theory is called the **Expectancy Theory**, which deals with structuring rewards that hold value relative to the amount of energy expended by the worker to earn the reward; this is coupled with the expectation that the reward will actually be received by the worker upon achieving the stated goal[31]. For instance, the supervisor may be empowered to award a $50 bonus to the restaurant server with the highest amount of wine sales. If this is worth the up-selling effort to the server and if the server trusts that the bonus will be paid at the end of the shift, this may result in additional wine sales.

Another process theory that is relevant to compensation practices is the **Equity Theory**[32]. This concept is based on perceived fairness in pay and treatment among the workers in a department. Individuals who believe they are paid less than others performing similar work are likely to lose motivation to perform. Managers should keep this in mind when designing compensation structures.

One powerful motivational tool is shared goal setting from the top of the organization through every level of the organization. This technique is called **Management by Objectives** (MBO)[33]. In organizations that do not implement this strategy, supervisors may choose to provide it on the departmental level. They do this by establishing department goals and sharing those with the workers. Based on these goals, each worker contributes with his or her objectives for performance. Supervisors and workers agree on these goals and use them to evaluate performance. The advantage to this process is that workers feel a sense of 'buy-in' to the objectives for the department. This generates a sense of 'ownership' and 'empowerment' on the part of each worker. When we 'own' a goal, we usually strive to make it happen.

OTHER FACTORS THAT CONTRIBUTE TO MOTIVATION

Motivation concepts are certainly important for understanding the dynamics of workers' attitudes. Attitudes have to do with the willingness of workers to perform tasks and activities. A motivated workforce does not necessarily guarantee productivity. Productivity depends on psychological factors as well as engineering factors. Work area layout, division of tasks, tools to do the job, technology, and other factors are within the scope of workplace engineering. A combination of engineering design and management of behaviors is required to impact worker satisfaction and enhance productivity.

JOB DESIGN AND MOTIVATION

Job rotation is a management technique of providing different forms of work with equal levels of responsibility. This technique is sometimes used to break the monotony of doing a single fragmented task. While this may offer variety, it is not necessarily a motivational technique for improved performance.

In these times of corporate downsizing, **job enlargement** is a popular alternative. Job enlargement involves adding more duties to an existing job. The additional duties do not usually include added compensation, responsibility and authority. Therefore, job enlargement is not a motivational technique. Sometimes managers inadvertently penalize good workers by adding additional responsibilities to their jobs. Managers do this because they know that the worker will be able to handle the additional assignments. However, the manager who does this actually discourages workers from becoming top performers.

Job enrichment (also known as job enhancement) is a technique of restructuring a job to provide added autonomy, responsibility, and authority[34]. Job enrichment is a motivational job design method because it provides benefits to those workers who prove they are capable of more important positions based on their performance. This technique may be combined with succession planning programs that lead to promotional opportunities. When this happens, achievement oriented workers will be motivated to demonstrate high levels of performance.

SUMMARY

We engaged in discussion aimed at presenting an overview of leadership and motivation in this chapter. The purpose has been to generate a general awareness of these issues as they impact the influencing skills of managers in the workplace.

In this chapter we have identified the characteristics of leaders, which are considered to be leadership traits. Interactions among leaders, followers and a given situation (environment) are the basis of transactional leadership. Transformational leadership considers these same factors in addition to the evolutionary growth of all participants in the interactions.

Leadership influence among individuals requires perceived credibility on the part of leaders; thus leaders are viewed as possessing qualities associated with personal and professional integrity. Transformation is preceded by the enactment of change. Leaders are change agents who systematically develop individuals to grow with the dynamic external environment. While the topic of leadership has been widely considered in research settings, the best way for practitioners to become skilled leaders is to model and engage in mentorship relationships with those established leaders in the workplace.

Managers prefer to work with motivated employees. Leaders must possess an understanding of human motivation. When workers are motivated, managers may perform fewer tasks associated with 'people management', which provides opportunities for the supervisor to focus more on leadership tasks. It is much easier and more fulfilling to lead people than it is to manage them.

We discussed both content and process theories of motivation to generate an awareness of the why's and how's of motivating workers. We learned that content theories focus on the psychology of people in the workplace. We also discovered that process theories help us to understand the relationships of workers and leaders. Process theories identify likely responses to workplace environments and leadership practices. We noticed that both intrinsic and extrinsic needs are impacted by most motivational processes.

We know that more than motivation is required to impact productivity. Workplace engineering issues must be combined with managing people to provide enhancements to productivity.

Some managers believe that demonstrating favoritism to certain workers will provide motivation for others to improve performance. We learned from the Equity theory that the opposite is true. The individuals receiving preferred treatment will feel uncomfortable interacting with peers. The other workers will resent the preferential treatment and usually become less than constructive in their behaviors. Managers who are perceived by workers as playing 'favorites' will eventually alienate all of the staff members in a work unit.

DISCUSSION QUESTIONS

1. Some people say that leadership is a natural ability and others say that these skills may be learned by anyone who wants to be a leader? What do you think?
2. If you were to analyze your leadership style and come to the conclusion that you are mostly task oriented (focused on what needs to be accomplished), what style would you look for in your assistant? Would she be just like you or different than you? Why?
3. Think about great leaders in history or in your personal experience. What qualities do you think made them so great?
4. Now, consider those individuals who may not be classified as good leaders at all. Where were they deficient? Is there anything to be learned from their examples?

IN THE REAL WORLD (CONTINUED)

Finally, you say to the training manager, 'Are you going to just smile at me? Or are you going to explain why I am sensing a difference between our leader and the other members of the association?' He laughs, 'You just answered your own question.' 'What are you talking about?' you say. He replies, 'The difference is leadership. Our director is a leader.' He continues, 'I have worked with her for sometime now. When I started with her, she used to drive me crazy by never giving me direct answers to my questions. She seemed to take almost sadistic pleasure in watching me try things and fail. Some days, she would be very nurturing and on other days, she would be a hard-driving task manager. I thought she was "schizo" in the beginning.' The training manager pauses in his own reflection of the past, 'Then it dawned on me—she was a leader who was teaching me (in her own twisted way) to become a leader just like her.' He smirks a little, and then continues, 'As soon as I achieved that awareness, she told me that I was now "getting it". It was like she was reading my mind.' He concludes, 'She and I have been leadership partners ever since.'

'Wow' you, say to him. 'How do you get that way?' He replies, 'I don't know, but if she takes you under her wing, you will know you have reached leader status when she no longer appears to you to be the director from hell.' he laughs.

CASE STUDY

You have just been hired as a supervisor for a security department at a large resort. You notice that the staff appears to be lax, with many of them failing to meet standards for performance. During your assessment of the work unit you learn that former supervisors were somewhat apathetic and failed to provide solid supervisory techniques such as communicating standards for performance and training new staff. Now you have inherited a group of individuals who are unfamiliar with the standards and have never been trained. While you really can't blame them for their sub-standard performance, you must turn this work unit around. This will require firmly communicated and enforced standards for performance and re-training of the existing staff.

Question

What will be your leadership style during this intervention? Will you act as a transactional leader or a transformational leader?

Hint

Is it too soon to use one of these, given the nature of this situation?

ENDNOTES

1. Tesone, D.V., 2000. Leadership and motivating missions: a model for organizations from science literature. J. Lead. Stud. 7 (1), 60–69.
2. 2002. Management and Leadership Should Not Be Confused, vol. 249. ENR, New York, p. 76.

3. Whetten, D.A., 2002. A social actor conception of organizational identity and its implications for the study of organizational reputation. Bus. Soc. 41 (4), 393, 22.

4. Mahon, J.F., 2002. Corporate reputation: a research agenda using strategy and stakeholder literature. Bus. Soc. 41 (4), 415, 31.

5. Brockmann, E.N., 2002. Tacit knowledge and strategic decision making. Group Organ. Manag. 27 (4), 436, 20.

6. Ibid.

7. Alban-Metcalfe, R.J., 2000. The transformational leadership questionnaire (TLQ-LGV): a convergent and discriminant validation study. Lead. Organ. Dev. J. 21 (6), 280.

8. Quay, J., 2002. Leadership and the New Science: Discovering Order in a Chaotic World, 2nd ed., vol. 13. Consulting to Management, Burlingame, pp. 59, 3.

9. Maxwell, L.M., 2002. The Challenge of Front-Line Management: Flattened Organizations in the New Economy, vol. 55. Personnel Psychology, Durham, pp. 244, 4.

10. Cavanagh, G.F., 2002. Virtue as a benchmark for spirituality in business. J. Bus. Ethics 38 (1/2), 109, 9.

11. Yaeger, T.F. 2002. Leading OD through linkage: Meet Dr. Phil Harkins. Organ. Dev. J. 20 (1), 53, 3.

12. Ibid.

13. Kezar, A. Expanding notions of leadership to capture pluralistic voices: positionality theory in practice. J. Coll. Student Dev. 43 (4), 558, 21.

14. Brewer, G.A., 2000. Why elephants gallop: assessing and predicting organizational performance in federal agencies. J. Publ. Admin. Res. Theor. 10 (4), 685, 27.

15. Ibid.

16. Ibid.

17. Ibid.

18. Ibid.

19. Smith, A.D., 2002. From process data to publication: a personal sensemaking. J. Manage. Inq. 11 (4), 383, 24.

20. Tesone, D.V., 2003. Tactical Strategies for Service Industry Management: How to Do It. Pearson Custom Publishing, Boston, MA.

21. Ibid.

22. Jackson, B.G., 2001. Art for management's sake? Manag. Commun. Quart. 14 (3), 484, 7.

23. McConnell, C.R., 2002. The manager and continuing education. 21 (2), 72, 12.

24. Ibid.

25. Eustace, B., 2002. Hospitality, London, pp. 34, 3.

26. Ibid.

27. Ibid.

28. Grimes, D.S., 2002. Challenging the status quo? Manag. Commun. Quart. 15 (3), 381, 29.

29. Sussman, L., 2002. Organizational politics: tactics, channels, and hierarchical roles. J. Bus. Ethics 40 (4), 313, 17.

30. De Souza, G., 2002. A study of the influence of promotions on promotion satisfaction and expectations of future promotions among managers. Hum. Res. Dev. Quart. 13 (3), 325, 16.

31. Whetten, D.A., 2002. A social actor conception of organizational identity and its implications for the study of organizational reputation. Bus. Soc. 41 (4), 393, 22.

32. Heugens, P.P.M.A.R., 2002. The confines of stakeholder management: evidence from the Dutch manufacturing sector. J. Bus. Ethics 40 (4), 387, 17.

33. Ibid.

34. Tesone, D.V., 2006. Human Resource Management in the Hospitality Industry: A Practitioner's Perspective. Pearson Prentice Hall.

CHAPTER 14

Leadership Practice

OBJECTIVES

In this chapter you will learn to:

1. **Identify leadership behaviors.**
2. **Identify the characteristics associated with leadership traits.**
3. **Identify leadership styles.**
4. **Identify transactional and transformational leadership practices.**

IN THE REAL WORLD

Your friend, Katie, began a school internship with an event planning company last year. You have not seen her for some time and finally run into her at school. You caught up on what has been going on.

Finally, you ask her about that internship. Katie says, 'That internship was a wonderful experience. I learned so much more than just event planning there. As a matter of fact, I still work there part-time and have an offer to go full-time after graduation.' 'Wow,' you respond, 'That's not what I hear from others about their internships.' Katie laughs, 'I just got lucky I guess. I hooked up with this very powerful leader named Dan. Today he is my mentor.'

To be continued...

INTRODUCTION

We will begin this chapter with a discussion about leadership behaviors in service enterprises. We will learn that observable leadership behaviors generate information used to develop attributes associated with successful leadership practices.

Next, we will identify the skills required to practice effective leadership. This will lead us to answer the question of whether leadership skills may be learned. We will consider the aspects associated with leadership training. With this information, we will be positioned to engage in a discussion of leadership styles and evolution. This information will be used to identify leadership practices in action. We will discuss behaviors associated with the work life development model.

We will conclude the chapter with a discussion concerning leadership relationships. We will identify transactional leader relationships. We will then discuss transformational leadership in action.

LEADERSHIP BEHAVIORS

A number of leadership studies have been performed by social and behavioral scientists, with focus on the relationships among leaders, followers and environmental situations[1]. Leadership behaviors involve an engagement in processes. Hence, we could say that leadership behavior is a continuous process[2]. What does this process involve? From a management perspective, leadership involves a continuous process of relationships through which individuals are influenced to attain the objectives of the service enterprise. Behavioral and social scientists focus on the **observable qualities** of leadership. Observable qualities are those aspects of an individual that are observable to a third party through behaviors.

The initial studies of leadership used observable qualities to identify leadership traits associated with successful leaders. **Traits** include personality tendencies within an individual that may be observed by others through behaviors. When we combine the culmination of observed qualities and traits, we may identify personality **characteristics** of leadership. Of course, the problem with trait theories of leadership is their exclusive focus on leaders. These types of observations were successful at describing the qualities of leaders. However, this approach was single dimensional in that it focused solely upon leaders without consideration of followers or situational environments. Later approaches to understanding leadership focused upon **interactions**, which include the communication exchanges among individuals and groups. A prominently cited instrument used to empirically test leadership interactions is called the Leader/Member Exchange instrument (LMX)[3].

OBSERVABLE LEADERSHIP BEHAVIORS

We know that observable behaviors are evident in themselves. The causes of those behaviors are much less certain as they require us to make judgments on the basis of some form of science or intuitive thinking. It is commonly known that human behavior is **unpredictable** for the most part in that many behaviors do not follow a logical flow according to most observers. One behavior that is evident among effective leaders is the practice of **self-leadership**. Self-leadership involves the discipline of objective self-awareness to ensure congruence with internal leadership models. In other words, we know that leaders learn first to manage themselves before they engage in leadership relationships with others. Another term for this would be 'leadership through example.' The way leaders practice self-discipline is by engaging in a practice of **internal dialog**. Internal dialog involves self-talk, perception and reflection attained through a practice of guided contemplation.

Another common behavior among effective leaders is the granting of authority, autonomy and responsibility to other deserving individuals. At the same time, leaders have been observed to engage in behaviors that entail possible negative consequences. This is a behavior that embraces **risk**-taking activities. This is a practice of delegation. Those managers who may be considered control freaks are the antithesis of a leader. Another commonly cited behavior among leaders is the practice of **stewardship**. Stewardship is a form of servant leadership in which the welfare of the followers is the primary directive of the leader[4]. This set of behaviors is particularly important for leaders within service enterprises. A final commonly observed leadership behavior is called **integrity**. Integrity consists of behaviors that are congruent with one's words. Leaders say what they mean and do what they say because they are always acting from integrity or congruency. The appearance that actions are congruent with mental models is what creates the phenomenon known as **charisma**. Charismatic leaders demonstrate congruence among thoughts and actions.

TRAITS ASSOCIATED WITH LEADERSHIP BEHAVIORS

Certain traits are assumed to generate the leadership behaviors we have just learned. We know that leadership is a process of relationships that influence individuals to willingly accomplish the objectives of an organization. Willingness comes from positive emotional states in the minds of followers. It has been said that leaders generate **passion** in the minds of followers. Passion is a positive emotional yearning to perform a task at hand. Leadership requires a sense of confidence, which generates a positive sense of self that is referred to as **pride**. Pride should not be confused with overconfidence or cockiness. Instead, it should be viewed as a healthy sense of self within an individual. The test as to whether the leader's pride is healthy versus dysfunctional will be the demonstrated behavior of **humility** on the part of the leader. Humility consists of a grounded sense of self relative to others.

LEADERSHIP SKILLS

So far, we have learned that effective leaders demonstrate specific behaviors that may be caused by certain internal character traits. This suggests that some individuals possess a leadership **personality**, which consists of preferences of response to external stimuli. In essence, effective leaders are individuals who chose to engage in leadership relationships. Effective leaders seem to demonstrate an enhanced sense of **awareness** relative to other people. This means they have the ability to possess an objective sense of self in given moments. In the case of leadership, effective leaders are aware of who they are being when they are being leaders. Leadership awareness is an **internal process** that occurs within the mind of the leader that is not observable to third parties. Successful leaders provide self-reports concerning these processes. The collective memories of continuous internal processes comprise the **leadership being** of an individual. Leadership being is an internal self-awareness of who an individual is relative to the dogma of leadership and who that person is being during leadership moments. Leadership being is a heightened state of self-awareness that becomes established through certain practices.

One daily practice among successful leaders is the engagement in a process of **self-examination**. This involves internal observation and comparison to the standard for personal being that lies within the leader's intention. The leader learns to become an **objective witness**, who possesses the ability to conduct internal observation from the standpoint of objectivity that is similar to a third-party witness. In other words, effective leaders learn to observe themselves as others might observe them. Most successful leaders understand the relationship of congruence among their being, their actions and their words. We already defined this as personal integrity, the integration of being and acting. These leaders would advise a protégé to simply **be your word**. Finally, the tool that practicing leaders use to support these other skills is a daily practice of **introspection**. Effective leaders enhance their abilities to objectively examine their own levels of self-awareness. This practice creates a level of awareness called metacognition.

CAN LEADERSHIP BE LEARNED?

We learned in Chapter 13 of the text that experienced individuals who think leaders are born and not made are subscribing to a Machiavellian belief system. The fact is that most inexperienced individuals do believe this is true. After gaining a number of years of experience, the majority of people change their views to believe that leadership may be **natural** or **learned**. Learned versus natural leadership refers to knowledge and skill acquisition, as opposed to innate gifted abilities. Another observation tells us that nature and nurture are sometimes misunderstood. Nature refers to genetic predispositions, while nurture refers to learned behaviors. It is probably true that some individuals would desire to become leaders on the basis of genetic codes and may even be in possession of some natural leadership instincts. However, neuroscientists tell us that individuals make choices concerning neural pathway selections during early formative years. Some individuals that we believe to be natural leaders may have chosen pathways conducive to leadership behaviors on the basis of a survival strategy during early childhood. If this is true, we could say that natural leaders are those who choose to learn leadership strategies unconsciously.

Neural pathways consist of electrochemical patterns of energy emitted at juncture points in the brain called synapses. The same is true of **chemical interactions** that occur during moments of interactions in which patterns of energy are exchanged. These are emotional triggers. When leaders exude passion and elicit like responses from followers, emotional exchanges are taking place. For this reason, all effective leaders are considered to be excellent communicators. **Communication** is the exchange of ideas and meaning among individuals and groups. Leaders learn to appeal to the meaning systems of followers, which provides a positive emotional state used to energize each follower into constructive action. The important skills of leadership lie below the surface of observable behaviors. They are intrinsic skills that may be developed by any individual as long as that person has a motivating desire to lead others.

Leadership training is the process of imparting leadership knowledge and skills. Leadership knowledge may be extracted from the social, behavioral and neurosciences. The development of leadership skills requires practice, introspection and awareness. The acquisition of leadership skills is often facilitated through **mentoring**, modeling and trial and error. Mentoring consists of relationships between protégés and senior leaders engaged in informal development relationships. The engagement in mentor relationships results in young leaders with skill sets that makes them appear to be wise beyond their years. **Leadership development** occurs when leaders engage in practices that result in higher levels of leadership ability. It is a process of personal and professional transformation. We will discuss the concept of leadership development in detail in Chapter 15 of the text.

WHAT IS LEADERSHIP STYLE?

Prior to discussing leadership style, it is important for us to note that there is a difference between individuals in leadership positions and actual leaders. A leader is a person who possesses the behaviors, traits and skills we have talked about in this chapter. There are many individuals who occupy leadership positions who do not meet the criteria for being a leader. It is also true that these individuals may not possess the qualifications to be called professional managers, even though they have been bestowed with management titles. So, there is a difference between possessing a title and demonstrating the skills associated with that title. There is also a difference between management and leadership styles.

Management styles describe a person's preference for managing an operation. Autocratic managers are individuals who tend to horde power, authority and decision-making activities. Micromanagers are autocrats with a compelling need to control every activity within their jurisdiction. The antithesis of the autocrat is the delegating manager. These individuals prefer a style of hands-off management and tend to delegate authority, responsibility and accountability to others. Democratic managers have a tendency to engage in participative decision making. These individuals are sometimes referred to as participative managers. Laissez faire managers are solely concerned with the social aspects that come with their job titles. They demonstrate little concern for the operations and tend to completely delegate all aspects of the operation and will empower those individuals who socialize with them. We can see that management styles have nothing to do with leadership. There is no one correct style, and professional managers have an awareness of their style preference for the purpose of shifting their behaviors on the basis of various situations. The same is true for leaders, who tend to possess a preferred focus on either task orientations or relations orientation.

A task-oriented leader tends to focus on tasks, duties and responsibilities associated with the positions within a span of authority. The opposite is the relations-oriented leaders who place emphasis on employee relationships. Neither focus is right or wrong. But there are advantages and disadvantages to each focus. For instance, the task-oriented leader may cause hard feelings by failing to establish rapport with followers, which could be a mistake when dealing with people with high needs for socialization. By contrast, the relations-oriented leader may tend to lose sight of the mission, objectives and strategies. When we discuss style preferences, we should think of them as extreme points on a continuum. In this case, we could place task orientation to the left of a straight line and relations focus at the right end of the line. These would be the two extremes associated with each style. In reality, only few people are extremists. Most individuals will gravitate toward the middle of the continuum. However, individuals will tend to have preferences slightly to the left or right of the middle. This is how we determine our style, or preference of focus. Consistent with all of our discussions concerning leadership, awareness of our preferences is important. If we know our preference between task and relations orientations, we will possess the ability to shift our styles on the basis of circumstances within the operation. This awareness will also influence our decisions concerning empowerment. If a manager knows he/she tends to be task oriented, he/she should promote his/her assistants with a relations orientation. This way, there will be balance among the leaders in the work unit. This must be a conscious act, as we have a tendency to promote like-minded individuals. Hence, the absence of task-oriented awareness would result in a leadership team comprising task-oriented managers. This would be a mistake. With our new knowledge of management styles and leadership focus, we are ready to discuss the topic of leadership styles.

We can determine a person's leadership style by observing his/her behaviors during stressful leadership moments. We can also conduct testing by placing individuals into distressing leadership scenarios and logging their responses. Leadership styles are based on unconscious psychological strategies referred to as action-logic rationale[5]. Figure 14.1 provides a depiction of seven action-logic reasoning preferences.

The first three strategies are low-level survival modes that have more to do with political power within the organization. Many nonleaders who find themselves in leadership positions will gravitate toward one or all of these strategies during leadership interactions. Trained leaders will be familiar with the lower-level survival strategies and use them for organizational politics. However, when it comes to leading, these trained leaders will use transactional or transformational leadership styles.

The Opportunist views other people as means to an end. They tend to seize opportunities by exploiting others. They are manipulative, controlling and treat others as if they are expendable. Autocratic and micromanagers are usually driven by opportunistic strategies. Trained leaders only call upon this strategy when doing political battle with peers or during turnaround strategies that require discharging destructive informal leaders.

The Diplomat pursues a congeniality strategy. This strategy is commonly adopted by junior managers seeking to gain political favor at all levels of the organization. This will serve these people for a time. But many managers continue to employ this strategy when they find themselves in leadership positions. This is a mistake. Diplomats are highly liked, but seldom are they respected. Diplomats

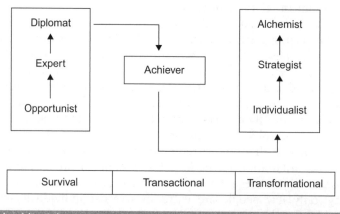

FIGURE 14.1 Leadership styles

will avoid conflict at any cost. They favor relations over task orientations and continuously seek consensus and approval. Trained leaders know to use this strategy solely for the purpose of acquiring political alliances with peers and senior managers. This is also a wise strategy for newly appointed younger supervisors to initially and temporarily employ with members of the work unit. Experienced leaders will only use this strategy with followers during times that require consensus and high levels of relationships.

The Expert is a person with highly proficient technical skills. Sometimes, the expert gets promoted into management positions and continues to manage from the perspective of technical expertise. Experts have value, as they continuously learn the technical aspects of their craft. For instance, IT professionals usually rely heavily on their expertise levels. The problem with experts in leadership positions is that they tend to be control freaks who demand unconditional compliance with their own techniques for performing tasks. They tend to discount the value of employees, feeling they know more than any other worker. Autocratic managers often rely upon the expert strategy. Trained leaders will use the expert strategy to earn the respect of the followers in a work unit. They will demonstrate technical proficiency and perform tasks along with the workers from time to time. They will particularly take on the less desirable tasks to show the followers that they would not ask them to do anything that the leader would not do. It is important for younger individuals in service enterprise supervisory positions to possess a certain level of technical expertise concerning the tasks, duties and responsibilities performed within the work unit. They should have performed these functions prior to accepting a supervisor or lead position.

The three lower-level survival strategies have nothing to do with effective leadership skills. Yet, unaware individuals find themselves stuck in these strategies after assuming leadership positions. Over time, some of these people may become aware that they are ineffective leaders and choose to adopt a higher-order strategy to fuel their leadership style. However, this is the exception to the rule. Many individuals in leadership positions spend their entire careers employing lower-order survival strategies in the management of workers. Many require an awareness intervention to evolve into higher-level strategies. This is the job of the human resource managers within a service enterprise. It is their duty to act as 'managers' managers' to ensure that professional management and leadership practices are adopted within every work unit.

Successful transactional leaders employ an Achievement strategy. In many cases, this strategy is an outpouring of their natural drive for achievement. This is the classic leadership-by-example scenario. Of course, these leaders must possess the influencing skills we learned earlier in the text and use them as part of their leadership repertoire. These leaders learn to project their own achievement orientation onto the followers. They use their conceptual skills to generate a big picture and show each follower the part they will play in achieving an objective or outcome. Achievers tend to be task oriented, so they wisely surround themselves with relations-oriented assistant managers. Leaders who embrace this strategy exhibit high-energy behaviors and the desire to pull as many followers as possible to the top levels of achievement. Over time, the achievement-oriented leader will begin to attract other achievement-oriented people to the work unit. Eventually, the entire staff unit will become composed of workers who are achievement oriented. When this happens, peak performance becomes the standard within the work unit. There is an intrinsic euphoria associated with the energy levels of pursuing achievement strategies. This becomes a difficult habit for the leader to break. However, those who become stuck in achievement mode will eventually dissipate more energy than they can regenerate. For this reason, achievement mode is not sustainable because an achiever will eventually demonstrate symptoms of job burnout. Aware achievers realize that they must evolve into transformational styles of leadership before this happens.

As leaders breach the cusp of transformational leadership, they will demonstrate characteristics attributed to the style of an Individualist. This is a volatile time in the leader's transformation, as that person could experience feelings dissolution with the corporate values, attitudes and beliefs. We learned in Chapter 1 of the text that the corporate culture contains these variables. When a conflict arises between the personal values of an Individualist and those of the corporate culture, that person enters a mental state of cognitive dissonance. A person in this phase of leadership evolution may engage in a major career change after seeking, but not finding compatible cultures among alternate service enterprises. The Individualist may be described as a moralistic leader who cherishes his/her own sense of personal and professional morality. This leader will focus more on the career development of others rather than levels of professional achievement. Servant leaders are usually in this phase of their leadership transformation. These leaders find themselves being challenged by lesser-developed managers within an organization. This is a defense tactic that indicates that the strong will of the Individualist is a threat to lesser-developed individuals who hold positions of power. Leaders in the Individualist stage often become corporate mavericks who are tolerated by higher levels of management owing to the performance levels they are able to elicit in their work units. Like the Achiever, the Individualist will become drained of energy in a corporate environment because of the challenge to overcome resistance from lesser-developed managers. The only way to sustain an Individualist leader is to place him/her in a full-time mentoring or coaching role. There are very few corporate positions for these activities. In order to sustain a corporate career, the Individualist must evolve to a higher level of leadership transformation.

Few leaders fully embrace Strategic leadership as a dominant style. The Strategist is capable of playing 'management chess,' always thinking a few moves ahead of other managers. This leader is an internal change agent within the service enterprise. The Strategist is a master communicator, especially when it comes to listening skills. This leader has learned to empathize and communicate effectively with those who subscribe to each of the other leadership styles. Strategists possess the ability to simultaneously direct multiple run, fix and growth strategies in various work units throughout a service enterprise. They possess the capability to comprehend and communicate shared futuristic visions for the people within the organization. They demonstrate a unique talent for reframing negative issues into potential positive opportunities. These leaders have acquired a very high level of self-awareness. They attract highly talented workers seeking professional transformation. Yet, they know when to limit their relationships for those who respond solely to leadership transactions. Strategists have the ability to convert their experiences into knowledge compartments for future recall. This provides them with the capability to use parallel brain processing to formulate new proactive and reactive strategies. Parallel brain processing permits them to respond intuitively to situations that require intense concentration on the part of lesser-developed leaders. Strategists convert reactive organizations into proactive operations. This reduces chaotic events. However, the Strategist becomes energized during chaotic scenarios, seeing these as ultimate challenges to test the leader's strategic skill set. These leaders conserve energy by reducing the levels of reactive interventions through strategic thinking. In fact, the primary motivator of the Strategist is to teach strategic thinking to others within the organization. Every topic discussed within this text has been presented from the strategic frame of reference. Strategic leaders are at the high end of transformational leadership practice.

The ultimate stage of leadership evolution occurs when a leader chooses to become an Alchemist. This is a very rare breed of leader. The Alchemist possesses the ability to become an organizational chameleon, in that they intuitively and strategically behave as though they have multiple personalities. They are the corporate equivalent of storybook wizards who appear to perform magical leadership transformations. They act as leaders of leaders. This is possible due to their extreme level of self-awareness. Their awareness levels are so developed that they have the capacity to witness their leadership interactions from the reference of a third-party witness as they are happening, or shortly after. We already learned that this is a process called metacognition. In this sense, the Alchemist transcends the self. This gives these leaders the ability to be themselves and see themselves at almost the same time. This goes beyond transformational leadership. This might be called transcendental leadership, in which the Alchemist is able to transcend the self. The Alchemist is a master of personal and professional reinvention. In fact, they engage in a practice of personal renewal that causes them to continuously reinvent themselves. If we were to meet an Alchemist today and revisit that leader in one year, we would meet with a noticeably different person. This process of personal reinvention results in continuous organization renewal for areas within their management jurisdiction. Alchemists are excellent organizational development (OD) practitioners. They intuitively practice OD just as they practice personal and professional reinvention. In fact, they naturally perform incremental OD interventions in the course of doing everyday business. A powerful reflective practice transforms the Alchemist into a transcendental leader. As a result, the Alchemist is a very powerful and charismatic leader. However, as charismatic as this leader may be to some, he/she is equally scary to those managers who are stuck in the survival levels of leadership style.

In the absence of blended knowledge and self-awareness, most managers do not engage in leadership style transformations. They usually settle into a comfortable style based on personality and stay with that style for their entire career. There are instances in which career or life-altering events may spark the desire for leadership transformation. But, these are rare. Service enterprises with proactive human resource practitioners may require participation in leadership style transformations. However, few practicing HR workers possess the knowledge and skills to deliver such programs. There are instruments available for leaders to enhance an awareness of their styles, such as the Leadership Development Profile[6].

In actual practice, leadership transformation is a lifelong journey that should last throughout the career of a professional manager. Leadership development requires daily practice; a topic we will address in Chapter 15 of the text.

How Do We Practice Leadership?

Now that we know a little about leadership styles, it is appropriate for us to revisit the work life development model to learn about leadership practice. Figure 14.2 presents the model.

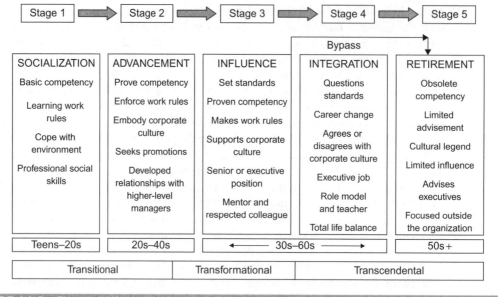

Stage 1 ⟹	Stage 2 ⟹	Stage 3 ⟹	Stage 4 ⟹	Stage 5
			Bypass	
SOCIALIZATION	**ADVANCEMENT**	**INFLUENCE**	**INTEGRATION**	**RETIREMENT**
Basic competency	Prove competency	Set standards	Questions standards	Obsolete competency
Learning work rules	Enforce work rules	Proven competency	Career change	Limited advisement
Cope with environment	Embody corporate culture	Makes work rules	Agrees or disagrees with corporate culture	Cultural legend
Professional social skills	Seeks promotions	Supports corporate culture	Executive job	Limited influence
	Developed relationships with higher-level managers	Senior or executive position	Role model and teacher	Advises executives
		Mentor and respected colleague	Total life balance	Focused outside the organization
Teens–20s	20s–40s	← 30s–60s →		50s+
Transitional		Transformational		Transcendental

FIGURE 14.2   The work life development model

Many service enterprises attract younger workers when compared with traditional manufacturing industries. For this reason, the work life development model addresses the psychology of younger and older workers alike. One advantage of working in service enterprises is that promotional opportunities to leadership positions occur more rapidly than they do in other industries. The result is individuals who are presented with managerial positions in their early 20s. As can be imagined, this is both a blessing and a curse.

The blessing, of course, is the opportunity for rapid career advancement. The downside is that younger managers report high levels of resistance to authority on the part of same age and older workers. This is particularly true for first-time supervisors or leads. As we already discussed, it would be a mistake for an individual to accept a position of authority absent the possession of the technical skills employed by the workers. So, let us assume the new manager or supervisor has had some line experience associated with the tasks, duties and responsibilities performed by staff members within the work unit. There are two ways for the promotion to happen. The supervisor could be hired from outside the department or could be promoted within the department. Each of these scenarios poses different actions for the supervisor to take.

If the supervisor comes from outside the department, he or she will diagnose the operation by using the steps we discussed in Chapter 10 of the text. This will involve observations, individual discussions and group meetings. The direct conversations should be focused on what the supervisor can do to support each staff member. At the same time, the supervisor should get a feel for the culture within that work unit and also identify potential individuals who may resist the authority of the supervisor. If the person is promoted from within the department, no diagnosis of the working situation is required, as the supervisor is already intimately familiar with the operation. However, the supervisor should expect that attitudes toward the appointment will change from prior working relationships. Hopefully, the supervisor did not engage in personal friendships with coworkers prior to the promotion. Personal friendships create opportunities for finger-pointing about playing favorites in the work unit. Also, in many cases, the supposed friends of a newly promoted individual will be the first ones to resist that supervisor's authority. After a short period of time, the newly promoted supervisor should identify individuals who embrace the promotion, those who are agnostic and those who will become resistant.

Once the initial diagnoses are completed, the supervisor should set in place a strategy to earn the respect of the workers. The supervisor should demonstrate the behaviors of working harder than any other staff member, to include performing less desirable tasks, as we already discussed. The strategy should aim at developing 'small wins.' A small-win strategy works in baby steps to earn respect from one individual at a time. The supervisor should begin with the most agreeable staff member who should also be one of the top performers in the work unit. The goal is to provide support for that person by making the job easier than it was before the promotion. Once the supervisor wins the first person over, he or she will move on to the next. After a short period of time, the word will get out that it is better to work with the supervisor than against him or her. At this point, individuals will volunteer to collaborate and the supervisor will have begun to earn the respect of the majority of the staff.

The strategy employs three survival styles as applied to establishing a leadership position. A person pursuing a small-win strategy is acting as a constructive Opportunist. They are aligning with a compatible individual to earn their respect and demonstrate to others that they are worthy of respect. The work harder tactic demonstrates technical expertise to the staff members. The part where the supervisor seeks knowledge about how to help the workers and the demonstration of doing less desirable tasks is a diplomatic gesture to win over the favor of the workers. So, in the first month of a new position, the supervisor has already applied the leadership styles associated with Opportunists, Diplomats and Experts in a manner that produces win/win outcomes. Once the supervisor establishes rapport and earns respect, it is time to shift into the use of the Achievement leadership style.

OTHER APPLICATIONS OF THE WORK LIFE DEVELOPMENT MODEL

As a manager or supervisor, we must understand the psychology of the staff members. Most work units are composed of workers of various ages and from diverse backgrounds. The model provides some guidelines to help managers diagnose the mentalities of the workforce.

Workers in the first stage of work life development are motivated by socialization factors. This is a recently discovered scientific fact. Neuroscientists tell us that the decision-making frontal cortex of the brain continues to develop into the mid-to-late 20s. This portion of the brain is responsible for linking with emotional centers to produce the desire for self-actualization, as we discussed in Chapter 13. The portions of the brain that provide the desire for socialization are already fully developed. Socialization needs tend to decrease as self-actualization needs increase. Hence, individuals in their 20s are pretty much at the end of their peak need for socialization. Visit a nightclub some time if you require anecdotal proof of this assertion. Recognition and incentive programs with a social twist appeal to workers in their twenties. Pizza parties, picnics, movie nights, pep rallies and such are more appealing to those with higher social needs.

Sometime between the late-20s and early 30s, the socialization need declines for most individuals and begins to be replaced with the need for self-actualization. When this occurs, an individual enters the advancement stage of work life development. Self-actualizing people begin to seek promotions, autonomy, professional recognition, awards and such. It is at this stage that certain leaders will decide to engage in transformational relationships with select achievers.

At some point between the 30s and early 40s, many individuals will discover they have reached the third stage of work life development called the Influence phase. By this time, they have many years of experience and occupy either professional or higher-level management positions. They are experienced decision makers and begin to influence the strategic direction of the service enterprise. They engage in mentoring relationships with younger advancement-stage workers. They may choose to engage in many transformational leadership relationships. Some, but not most have mastered the Achiever leadership style at this point. Many service enterprise managers remain in this stage until retirement from their careers. They bypass stage four and go directly to stage five.

A small, but growing number of people will experience one more stage before retirement. This is called the Integration stage of work life development. Managers who experience the symptoms associated with this stage have usually mastered the Individualist leadership style. As we discussed earlier, this stage could be volatile for a manager's career in the event of cognitive dissonance, which often results in changing organizations and in some cases produces major career changes outside of the industry.

It is possible for managers at any level of the service enterprise to encounter individuals who represent each of the five work life development stages. The veteran restaurant server could demonstrate characteristics attributed to the influence stage through informal leadership practices. The veteran concierge could be an accomplished artist in his/her spare time and pursuing motivators associated with becoming an integrated person. There are numerous anecdotal reports of individuals who have retired long before they choose to actually leave the workplace. Laissez faire managers provide examples of these people.

By now, we have realized that there are three components that influence leadership practice. They are the leader, the followers and the environment or situation. All three of these will influence the success of leadership transactions.

TRANSACTIONAL LEADERSHIP IN ACTION

We have discovered that leadership is a process of relationships used to accomplish the objectives of the service enterprise. There are two types of leader relationships with followers. These are transactional and transformational relationships. Transactional relationships comprise the majority of leader relationships. Transformational relationships are usually reserved for select individuals.

Transactional leader relationships consist of the transactions that occur between the leader and followers in the course of doing business. They are present-moment interactions and are temporary in the sense that when the task is complete, the interactions end. They take place numerous times on a daily basis. They are usually based on a management function theme that could include planning, organizing or controlling activities. They always include the influencing function of management because that is what leadership is really all about. Even though the transactions are temporary, they do register in the memories of the followers. Those memories will accumulate over time to represent a picture of the leader in relationship to each follower. Those collective memories will determine levels of respect, loyalty and responsiveness on the part of each follower toward the leader. Leadership transactions are always moments of truth in the eyes of followers[7].

The collective body of transactional leadership memories constitutes the leader's reputation from the followers' perspectives. This and accomplishing the objectives of the organization are all that really matter to the professional leader. As is the case with any reputation, one mistake will remove many successful interactions in the followers' memories. This is not to say that leaders do not make mistakes in their transactions. They do so all the time, as human relationships are not based on any exact cause/effect science. But, professional leaders do score many more transactional wins than they do mistakes. And they produce more wins and fewer mistakes consistently as they gain additional experience and continue in their own personal transformations.

In order to successfully engage in transactional relationships, leaders must possess self-awareness, as well as an acute awareness of the psyche of each follower. Leaders must be aware of both the follower's general disposition and those issues that are influencing a transaction in the present moment. General disposition characteristics include the follower's motivational needs, personality, knowledge, skills, abilities and attitudes. The factors that influence individuals during moments of transactional interactions include considerations such as mood, stress levels, current personal issues and the like.

Successful transactional leadership relations are more about the leader earning respect and loyalty rather than being liked by the followers. There are numerous ineffective leaders that could easily win popularity contests. The highest compliment paid to a professional leader is that he or she is 'firm but fair.' Transactional leadership is about honesty, passion, integrity, communication, support, recognition, responsibility, accountability, motivation, discipline, calculated risks, vision, mission, tenacity, knowledge and skills.

The key indicator of professional leadership is the degree to which that person is willing to accept responsibility for issues that are beyond his or her control. Strategic leaders are first to accept blame for things that go wrong, whether or not those things were within the realm of personal control. They also share deflect recognition for success to the followers. These are the two symptoms of a strategic leader in action.

SITUATIONAL LEADERSHIP

We already know that leadership style is a preference for ways of leading followers. We also know that leaders must possess an awareness of their leadership styles. We have discussed alterations made by transactional leaders on the basis of the general and circumstantial disposition of each follower. Another factor that will influence a leader's chosen approach will be environmental factors, otherwise known as situations that occur within the work unit. This practice is called situational leadership[8]. Figure 14.3 provides a depiction of situational leadership in action.

The model is based on two factors that we have already discussed. The first factor is the degree of task abilities that will be required to perform an activity. The second factor considers the degree of leader relations required to perform the task at hand. If the task requires high task skills and low levels of relations, the leader might consider

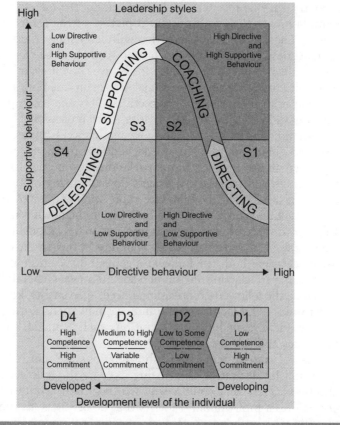

FIGURE 14.3 Situational leadership

telling the followers what to do. If the task degree is high and relations levels are high, the leader would be positioned to sell the idea to the followers. If task requirements are high but relations requirements are low, the leader may choose to use persuasive skills with the followers. Finally, if both task requirements and degree of relations are low, the leader could delegate responsibility for the tasks to the followers.

The model provides an oversimplification, but the message is clear. Transactional leaders must consider themselves as leaders, the followers and the situation at hand when choosing to adopt a leadership style. For instance, if there is an urgent crisis at hand, it is probably time for the leader to assume control and tell the followers how to respond. However, if the work unit needs to produce an important project that requires teamwork along with an urgent deadline, the leader would tend to sell his/her ideas to the followers. If the work unit needs to brainstorm ideas to generate a participative solution to a problem, a persuasive style might work. Finally, if there are few consequences associated with performing a service transaction, the leader could choose to delegate those procedures to the followers.

The key concept to remember about transactional leadership is that it consists of strings of short-term interactions that occur in the present moments of performing tasks, duties and responsibilities. Transformational leader relationships, on the other hand, are future-based long-term committal relationships between leaders and selected followers.

TRANSFORMATIONAL LEADERSHIP IN ACTION

There is some confusion among certain practitioners and scholars on how transformational leader relationships actually work. Some contend that leaders who manipulate followers into believing that accomplishing the objectives of the organization are in their best interests constitute transformational leader relationships. This really is not true. Also, transformational leader relationships are not right for all followers. In many cases, transactional leader relationships are sufficient to enable effective leadership. However, there are times in which leaders must be aware that transformational leader relationships are healthy for certain individuals.

Thinking back on the work life development model, there are occasions when a leader will acquire a follower pursuing the advancement stage who may be labeled as an overachiever. Symptoms include the intention to pursue a fast track to promotions; an intrinsic sense of satisfaction on the part of a follower from achieving challenging objectives and the desire for increased levels of autonomy, responsibility and authority. When a leader identifies these symptoms, he/she knows he/she has an overachiever on his/her hands. The positive aspect associated with over achievers is that they thrive on challenges that result in high-level accomplishments, which is a professional leader's dream. The risk associated with these individuals is that they could become bored in the absence of such challenging work and may seek opportunities with another department or service enterprise. The appropriate response of a professional leader to such a follower is to offer the opportunity to engage in a transformational leader relationship.

Transformational leader relationships are based upon a 'triple win' paradigm. The follower wins because he or she seeks challenges and a string of accomplishments. The service enterprise wins because it reaps the benefits of this individual's achievements within the work unit. The leader also wins because she or he has acquired a high achieving protégé who will be groomed for a future management position of influence within the organization. Professional leaders gain an intrinsic thrill from enabling other future leaders.

Transformational leader relationships differ from transactional interactions on the basis of the duration, futuristic orientation and level of commitment on the leader's part to the success of the follower as a future leader. In fact, there have been transformational leader relationships with followers who never intended to be leaders. Take for instance a manager of an entertainment department within a theme park. This manager could be working with an excellent performer who desires national recognition. The entertainment manager may choose to assist this performer in reaching that goal by stretching the talent and exposure to a variety of audiences to include talent agents. This is a form of transformational leader relationships. However, most relationships evolve from the desire of followers to become professional leaders within the service industry.

Short-term-oriented executives sometimes berate managers for engaging in transformational leader relationships. Take for instance an HR director who engages in transformational leadership relations to groom HR managers for positions as directors at competing firms. The myopic executive may believe that he/she is funding the training and development of future leaders for the competition. A professional leader, however, would understand that the HR director is building a network of collaboration among the competition, which will result in future healthy competitor relationships.

There is a tendency among professional leaders seeking continual personal transformational leadership evolution to seek additional transformational leader relationships with followers. This makes sense given the universal law of reciprocity. Strategic leaders know how to make this happen. The strategy involved with increasing the numbers of transformational leader relationships is consistent with the 'small win' strategy presented earlier in our discussion concerning newly promoted supervisors.

The professional leader acquires a single overachiever as a follower within the work unit. They engage in a transformational leader relationship. The follower experiences successful outcomes. Another high achiever witnesses the interaction and seeks a similar relationship with the leader. They engage in such a relationship and that person becomes successful. Other staff members in the department begin to consider a path of high achievement and leadership success. Those workers that do not subscribe to such aspirations begin to feel uncomfortable due to mounting peer pressure to become an overachiever. Those people begin to leave the department. Other workers within the service enterprise have heard about the power of transformational leadership relations based on the success stories of their peers. They begin to seek transfers into that department. Over time, the entire department consists of overachievers seeking future leadership opportunities under the tutelage of the transformational leader. This is how we develop a department of full of peak performers. When multiple like-minded leaders from various departments engage in such relationships, they start to form collective peak leadership experiences within that service enterprise. This is one way to positively impact an organizational culture.

SUMMARY

We began this chapter with a discussion about leadership behaviors in service enterprises. We learned that observable leadership behaviors generate information used to develop attributes associated with successful leadership practices.

Next, we identified the skills required to practice effective leadership in organizations. This led us to answer the question of whether leadership skills may be learned. We learned that some innate talents are available in leaders, but that all leaders require some form of training to effectively lead others. We considered aspects associated with leadership training. We realized that the key components include knowledge and awareness levels. With this information, we engaged in a discussion of leadership styles and evolution. There are seven different leadership styles. The lower three are really political survival strategies that some people in leadership positions adopt as styles. The upper four styles serve the effectiveness of leaders. A leader has the potential to transform to higher-order styles over time.

We discussed leadership practices in action. We identified how newly promoted individuals might behave to earn employee respect as leaders. We then discussed behaviors associated with the work life development model. We realized that leaders must understand the psyche of each follower. The model helped us to identify general tendencies among various individuals in the workplace.

We concluded the chapter with a discussion concerning leadership relationships. We identified transactional leader relationships as those that are temporary in nature and occur in the present. We also learned that transformational leader relations are future-oriented long-term interactions. These relationships are based on a triple win paradigm.

DISCUSSION QUESTIONS

1. What traits or characteristics do you believe are demonstrated by effective leaders?
2. Please provide an example of effective leadership behaviors in practice.
3. Please describe each of the seven leadership styles and identify the ones that pertain to your leadership abilities.
4. Use examples to compare and contrast transactional and transformational leadership relations.
5. After reading the conclusion of the In the Real World vignette, describe the current leadership relationship between Dan and Katie. Was this the case when she began the internship? What changed?

IN THE REAL WORLD (CONTINUED)

Katie sees your level of interest and decides to share her story about the internship that turned into a job. She begins, 'I felt really lucky to land that internship because I wanted to be a meeting planner. But I didn't expect the level of training I received there. When I was paired with Dan, he was intimidating at first – he seemed sort of stern. He is a senior manager in charge of an entire division for the company. I was amazed that he didn't just have me shadow some junior person.' 'Wow,' you say, 'I guess he likes working with younger people.'

Katie replies, 'That wasn't my first impression of him. In fact, I think he was going to dispatch me to someone else after our first conversation.' 'What happened there?' you ask. 'Well,' Katie begins, 'We sat down and he started firing questions at me about who I am, what I want to accomplish, what did I know about the company and so on. I thought I was really blowing it. When the conversation was over, Dan told me to report to his office at eight the next morning and to be prepared to learn.' Katie finishes.

You tell Katie, 'That guy does sound intimidating.' 'He was at first,' Katie responds, 'But after watching him in action, I realized he is a powerful leader who is very respected by the followers. I think that's why he has the best division in the company. At the end of my internship, we had a wrap-up interview.' You ask Katie, 'What happened there?'

Katie looked embarrassed as she responded, 'He told me I am a high achiever and that I have earned the opportunity to stay on as a part-timer while I finished school. He gave me a development plan to be completed by the time I graduate. He told me that the successful completion of that plan could lead to a full-time job with the firm.' 'Wow!' you respond. Katie continued, 'Yup, I feel like I have been transformed by my working relationship with Dan. I graduate in two months and I completed my action plan last week. When I showed my accomplishments to Dan, he just smiled and said that I had just earned a full-time position.' As you look at Katie telling her story, you eventually say to her, 'Ya know? You do seem different. You don't seem like a kid anymore. You seem kind of worldly all of a sudden.' Katie smiles and says, 'Thanks, I feel that way too.'

CASE STUDY

You are a supervisor for a small work unit consisting of five workers. The previous two supervisors were fired for poor performance. Needless to say, the workers are doubtful about whether you will be any more successful than your predecessors. It is interesting that the work group has sort of bonded as a result of poor leadership and is pretty self-sufficient when it comes to doing the job. You know that the first thing you must do is to earn their respect. Once this is done, you will want to build a team.

Question

How will you earn their respect and then build a team?

Hint

Setting a good example and demonstrating stewardship could help with both objectives.

ENDNOTES

1. Hersey, P., Blanchard, K.G., 1969. Life cycle of leadership. Training Dev. Eric Education Government.
2. Kouzes, J., Posner, B., 2007. The Leadership Challenge, fourth ed. John Wiley & Sons Inc.
3. Graen, G.B., 1976. Role-making processes within complex organizations. In: Dunnette, M.D. (Ed.), Handbook of Industrial and Organizational Psychology. Rand McNally, Chicago, pp. 1201–1245.
4. Depree, M., 1986. Leadership Is an Art. Doubleday, New York.
5. Rooke, Torbet, 2005. 7 transformations of leadership. Harvard Bus. Rev. April.
6. *Ibid.*
7. Albrecht, K., Zemke, R., 1985. Service America! Dow Jones-Irwin, Home-wood, IL. Carlzon.
8. Hersey, P., Blanchard, K.G., 1969. Life cycle of leadership. Training Dev. Eric Education Government.

CHAPTER 15

Organizational Behavior and Leadership Development

OBJECTIVES

In this chapter you will learn to:

1. Demonstrate a basic comprehension of Organizational Behavior concepts.
2. Identify self-actualization concepts relative to transpersonal psychology.
3. Describe the processes used to provide leadership development.
4. Apply these concepts to the earlier chapters in the text.

IN THE REAL WORLD

Graduation is just a few days away. Everyone, including you, has senior-itis. A group of friends are sitting at a table in the student union, when your friend, Adam, bursts in all excited. 'I just got the best job offer,' he exclaims. 'I am going to be a department manager at a large resort.' Everyone shares Adam's excitement. Your friend Shannon asks Adam, 'How did you land that one?' Adam replies, 'Well, let me tell you how I handled the interview.'

To be continued...

INTRODUCTION

This chapter will provide theoretical foundations to support the practical practices we have discussed throughout the text. It will begin with an overview of organizational behavior (OB) as related to leadership practices. We will then move on to a discussion of earlier research in the area of emotional labor to help us understand the basic concepts associated with emotional intelligence. Emotional intelligence is the ability of leaders to identify and respond to mental states in other people. It is a powerful knowledge base for practicing leaders.

Next, we will engage in a brief discussion of historical aspects of OB to gain an understanding of the transpersonal psychology movement and theoretical constructs associated with self-actualization as a motivator in the workplace. This will take us into a discussion of how the brain influences leaders and followers.

At this point, we will learn a little about developmental models that support some of the figures we have used in the text. Then, we will discuss the processes involved in leadership development. We will conclude the chapter by reviewing key concepts learned throughout the text.

ORGANIZATIONAL BEHAVIOR

Organizational behavior is the study of individual and group applied psychology to understand behaviors in the workplace. Organizational behavior concepts are certainly important for understanding the dynamics of workers' attitudes. Attitudes have to do with the willingness of workers to perform tasks, duties and responsibilities, which require them to expend energy[1]. Many service enterprises consist of workers who interact as hosts with visiting guests or clients. These customers have come to expect employees to display certain hospitable behaviors that include emotional expressions during service encounters[2]. This is not the case with assembly line workers and others affiliated with manufacturing or distribution enterprises[3].

EMOTIONAL LABOR

Most positions in service organizations require workers to expend both physical and emotional energy in the course of performing job functions. These employment scenarios led earlier scholars to engage in an area of research called 'emotional labor' in order to investigate concepts related to the management of emotional displays through normative behavior in organizations[4]. It has been anecdotally noted that some service industry managers believe in hiring for 'attitude' and training for knowledge and skills. Researchers in the field of emotional labor seem to focus on attitudinal factors from the standpoint of employee recruitment, selection, organizational policies and incentives[5]. Certain investigations have placed emphasis on relationships between internal mental states and displayed emotional behaviors with mixed results, similar to earlier work in the field of cognitive consonance/dissonance[6]. Other attitudinal studies presented findings concerning positive and negative 'affective responses' to emotional labor expectations within organizations[7]. Still, other investigations considered 'coping' strategies that were reported by workers who experienced states of emotional dissonance in business enterprises[8]. It would seem that one major contribution of the emotional labor perspective is the acknowledgment that workers are emotive beings.

EMOTIONAL INTELLIGENCE AND ORGANIZATIONAL BEHAVIOR

Studies from the field of emotional labor seemed to foster interest among organizational behavior (OB) researchers to pursue broader investigations concerning the emotional aspects of people in organizations[9]. It seems as though this interest has accelerated over the past decade or so[10]. Sometime ago, the concept of emotional intelligence was introduced to the literature[11], with the notion becoming popularized just a few years later[12]. The new century brought forth numerous books and articles that applied aspects of emotions and emotional intelligence to workplace behaviors[13]. Newer versions of OB textbooks appear to be providing coverage of the emotional aspects of workers as well[14]. Also, researchers from the fields of social and personal psychology have demonstrated a renewed interest in the area of emotions over the past 10 years[15]. As might be expected, the findings from these studies have begun to migrate to those concerning workplace cognition and behavior.

Intrinsic needs theories of motivation have always inferred a sense of emotional energy created from within an individual that serves as a catalyst for performance-based behaviors. The recent 'affective revolution' in organizational behavior research seems to permit more open discussion around the emotional aspects of motivating workers[16]. Some studies demonstrate linkages between emotional motivation and enhanced enterprise profits[17]. Others suggest a relationship between worker emotional satisfaction levels and effectiveness/efficiency improvements[18]. Still others focus on positive changes in organizational climates resulting from emotionally motivated individuals[19].

HISTORICAL PERSPECTIVES OF BEHAVIOR AND AWARENESS

There seems to be a historical pattern that indicates behavior and motivation as being related to transpersonal experiences and awareness[20]. It is apparent that certain schools of philosophical thought ranging from reductionism to monism are somewhat consistent with developments in the field of psychology[21]. The first prominent thinking in psychology was the school of psychoanalysis, which focused on unconscious drivers of behavior. The antithesis of psychoanalysis is the behaviorism model with exclusive focus on empirical observations of environmental influences. The commonality between both schools of thought lies in the therapeutic objective for individuals to control and regulate their own behaviors. Two more modern approaches focused on humanism (valuing the self) and transpersonalism (transcending the self)[22]. Transpersonal psychology was first presented in the 1960s and more precisely described in 1992 by Lajoie and Shapiro[23].

In the decade prior to the discovery of transpersonal psychology, Abraham Maslow was responsible for popularizing humanistic psychology, which became prominent in 1954. The *Journal of Humanistic Psychology* was established in 1958, resulting in the formulation of the American Association for Humanistic Psychology in 1964[24]. The *personal growth* and *potentiality* focus of humanistic psychology was a broad departure from previous paradigms (psychoanalysis and behaviorism) that were preoccupied with pathology. Humanism was based on the assumption that individuals possess a propensity toward self-actualization that could be achieved through experience and reflective practice, as opposed to therapies aimed at correcting pathological behaviors through logical analysis or behavior modification[25]. Humanistic thinking spawned numerous studies in the late 1960s that resulted in popularizing broad interests concerning states of human consciousness among behavioral scholars and practitioners for many years[26]. In more recent times, consciousness studies have been embraced by some researchers within the domains of neuroscience and physics[27].

Transpersonalists seem to have an interest in understanding consciousness from the viewpoints of both the intrinsic self (humanistic) and transcendent self (transpersonal). The concept of human transcendence was originally described as nonlocal information that exists in a state called the 'collective unconscious' by psychoanalyst C.G. Jung (1953)[28]. If it is true that Maslow could be recognized as the 'father' of humanistic thinking, he and Jung should be considered as the 'forefathers' of transpersonalism. One reason the doctrine of humanism is only discussed from a historical perspective could be that transpersonal psychology encapsulates the concepts of self-actualization and human potentiality as well as transcendental mental states as constituting the mind/body relationship[29].

SELF-ACTUALIZATION AND ORGANIZATIONAL BEHAVIOR

Most managers view self-actualization as the highest-order need within the context of Maslow's 'Hierarchy of Needs' model, which is a broad generalization used to describe needs-based motivation theory. It suggests that individuals possess an intrinsic propensity toward achieving their potential and that 'healthy' work environments might assist in unleashing this tendency among workers within organizations[30]. It has even been reported that leaders possess the duty to create environments conducive for followers to self-actualize in the process of doing their jobs, a concept that we learned to be transformational leader relationships in Chapter 14 of the text[31]. Some suggest that self-actualization is closely related to ego or identity needs and that according to Maslow, neither one could ever be fully satisfied[32]. Others contend that individuals possess an innate and compelling drive to realize their own potential by directly quoting Maslow, who said, 'What man [or woman] can be, he [or she] must be.'[33] It seems that all of these descriptions imply the intrinsic need for humans to grow or evolve on personal levels. Maslow further provided direct applications of fulfilling this need within workplace environments.

Maslow was mostly focused on humanistic psychology throughout his career. Interestingly, his experience with industrial psychology was limited to a summer of observation in a factory. This led to the publication of Maslow's only book on workplace psychology entitled *Eupsychian Management: A Journal* in 1965[34]. The book advised managers to treat workers as holistic human beings who possess varied emotional needs and levels of self-awareness. It further suggested the ultimate goal of leadership motivation as being the creation of workplace environments aimed at facilitating the self-esteem and self-actualization needs of individuals. Toward the end of his career, Maslow joined the faculty at the Esalen Institute in Big Sur, California, to lecture and conduct research in the areas of self-actualization, peak experiences and states of consciousness. Many of his colleagues were leading scholars in the emerging transpersonal psychology movement.

CONSCIOUSNESS, EMOTIONAL INTELLIGENCE AND THE BRAIN

Recent advances in technology have facilitated the capacity for researchers to observe brain functions during various states of consciousness[35]. Magnetoencephalography (MEG) machines are used to monitor brainwave activity, while functional magnetic resonance imaging (fMRI) is used to view activated regions of the brain during responses to stimuli. These technologies have lured researchers from the field of neuroscience to conduct studies aimed at understanding brain activity that processes emotions and feelings[36]. Some suggest that feelings are states of emotional awareness[37]. Most researchers agree that emotional awareness is the result of synaptic connections between the emotional and cortical frontal regions of the brain[38].

Certain scholars suggest that self-actualization is a state of cognitive and emotional awareness of the self in relation to an individual's perception of the world[39]. The brain process for self-actualization involves synaptic connections to bring stored memories and emotions from the hippocampus and amygdale into the frontal cortices to generate cognitive awareness of the self. The physical process involves some form of contemplation (reflection, meditation or biofeedback, for instance) used to access and process thoughts and feelings of an individual relative to worldly experiences[40]. An individual who uses this information for the purpose of evolving toward potentiality would be considered to possess a high need for self-actualization.

Anecdotal observation might suggest that individuals mentally and emotionally evolve more rapidly with each successive generation over time. If this were true, it could be hypothesized that individuals self-actualize at younger ages than those of previous generations. Earlier brain researchers might have supported this notion on the basis of the belief that the human brain becomes fully developed by the age of 18 years or so. However, recent research has determined that this is not the case. The last region of the brain to develop is the frontal cortex, which does not complete its growth until the mid-20s or so[41]. Decision-making centers reside in this area of the brain. The need for self-actualization is a personal decision that is made in this region of forebrain in response to emotional needs that are emitted from limbic system synaptic transmissions. Since self-actualization requires processing through the frontal cortices, it would seem unlikely that younger individuals would report a high need in this category, even though they may have evolved more rapidly than prior generations in other ways. For instance, neuroscientists seem to agree that one of the primary functions of childhood brain development is in the area of socialization[42]. Perhaps, young adults experience more rapid social maturation relative to previous generations. This understanding of brain processes for the awareness of self-actualizing needs became the theoretical grounding of an empirical five-year study[43]. The study demonstrated a correlation between the perceived importances of self-actualization and socialization with age. The findings were consistent with the neuroscience's discovery of frontal cortex brain development. Individuals in their 20s scored significantly higher in socialization needs and significantly lower in self-actualizing needs than those over 30 years of age. For the older cohort, as self-actualizing need priorities increased, the need for socialization decreased at an equal rate.

There have been other studies linking frontal cortex brain development to behaviors in younger people to include traffic accidents, risk-taking propensity and suicide. However, there are no known studies that have attempted to use brain research to explain socialization and self-actualization needs within individuals up until this point. Even though each of the survey categories is mutually exclusive, it seems as though the perceived need for social/belonging declines with age, while self-esteem and self-actualization needs appear to increase. It is possible that these perceptions could be influenced by frontal cortex brain development that impacts the levels of self-awareness.

The ideal way to empirically study the linkage between regions of the brain and self-actualization would be to scan the forebrains of subjects while they are engrossed in thoughts of self-actualizing experiences. This of course would require a laboratory setting. The scope of this study was narrowly focused on individuals associated with hospitality and health care professions. As such, the evidence pertains to those specific industries. The findings of the study do seem to support the first two stages in a work life developmental model that was first posited 10 years ago and later published[44]. The model is revisited in Figure 15.1.

The model applies the findings of classical developmental scholars to the stages of development experienced by individuals throughout their working lives[45]. It suggests that younger individuals assimilate to the social climate of the workplace (*Socialization*) before moving toward achievement opportunities (*Advancement*). Many achievement-oriented workers find themselves in positions of Influence by the time they approach middle age. A number of individuals might settle into the

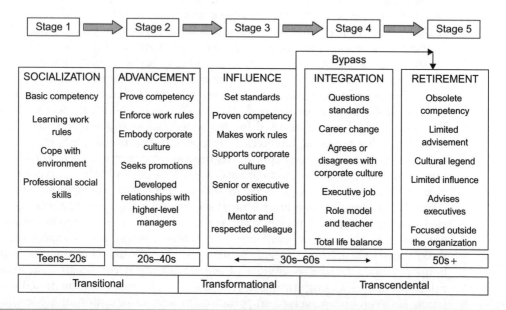

FIGURE 15.1   The work life development model

Influence stage until it is time to retire. Others, however, may evolve into higher levels of self-actualization in which they seek balance among the varied aspects of the self. This *Integration* stage may lead an individual to experience a career crisis if the professional position or organization limits a sense of meaningful work in that person's mind. The bottom of the model depicts suggested leadership and motivational styles for managers ranging from transactional, through transformational and ending with a self-leadership style that could be called *transpersonal* or *transcendent*.

The model might be an accurate depiction of work life development, if systems scholars are correct in their thinking about self-actualization. Systems scholars appear to describe self-actualization in more organic terms than OB researchers. Albert Szent-Gyoergyi (Nobel Prize winning biologist) describes self-actualization as a 'drive in all living matter to perfect itself' and another eminent biologist George T. Ainsworth Land describes it as the 'unifying principle of growth.'[46] These comments suggest the natural tendency for lifelong development. The work life development model is based on the same assumptions.

LEADERSHIP DEVELOPMENT FOR MANAGEMENT PRACTITIONERS

Leadership development is the process we use to continuously transform ourselves into higher-order leadership styles throughout our management careers. It is a process of lifelong learning from experiences and knowledge. Leadership development requires daily reflective practice on the part of each manager. From a systems thinking perspective, learning may be considered to be the enactment of permanent change within an individual[47]. Thus, it is a transformational process in that new learning imposed on a person changes him/her from a prelearning state to a postlearning state. That change must take him/her to a higher level of self-awareness, which results in personal evolution through development. Hence, learning facilitates self-development. And reflection upon that development transforms us from who we were before the learning process to who we are after the learning process. The relationship of these factors is depicted in Figure 15.2.

When it comes to learning an applied practice in a formal organizational setting, the two reception points for the individual's learning system seem to be knowledge and experience. Knowledge may be defined as information that is cognitively assimilated by an individual[48]. On the other hand, experience may be considered to be a person's visceral representation of an event or collection of related events[49]. Hence, a single learning loop consists of both knowledge and experience that is interpreted through reflection (contemplation), which enhances self-awareness on the part of the learner[50].

The triangle represents two types of learning by the arrows that originate at the top and then loop through the bottom and return to the upper point for infusion into self-reflection concerning what was learned. An experiential learning loop moves in a clockwise direction from the right to left sides of the triangle, in which an individual practices a function then assimilates information about the function and returns to a state of reflection. For instance, a front-office manager for a resort is working with the staff on a particularly hectic day. The nature of the situation causes the manager to personally handle guest check-ins along with the front-desk agents; a unique situation, as most of the agents had never seen the manager actually perform desk functions.

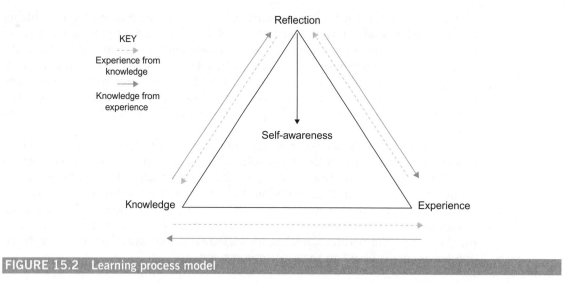

KEY
- - - ▷
Experience from
knowledge
——▶
Knowledge from
experience

Reflection

Self-awareness

Knowledge

Experience

FIGURE 15.2   Learning process model

When the operation returns to normal, the front-office manager might return to his/her office and reflect upon the experience to draw a number of conclusions as a result of that thought process. These thoughts might include the fact that the agents were impressed with his/her desk skills, a sense of bonding with the agents, a sense of recalling the feelings of working on the line and other random thoughts. If the manager chooses to take this reflection into his/her self-awareness as a leader, he/she might pledge to him/herself to work the desk one day per month as a staff rapport-building practice. In this case, an experiential circumstance has enhanced the self-awareness of a leader, who decides to add a new practice to his/her existing inventory of leadership practices as an outcome of the new awareness. Hence, the manager has become a better leader through the experiential (e-loop) processing of a single experience. In essence, this is an example of the process performed by a person to gain 'knowledge from experience.'

Conversely, a knowledge loop (k-loop) reverses this order by functioning in a counterclockwise fashion (left to right) around the triangle (knowledge, then experience) to return to the reflective state. In this scenario, a recent graduate from a hospitality school may be working as a newly appointed front-desk supervisor. When the check-in volume exceeds limits of the operation, the supervisor will search his/her memory of knowledge training for a solution to this situation. He/she may handle it well, or he/she may not. In any event, his/her actions will create an experience for comparison to whatever abstract knowledge of supervision he/she used to respond to the situation. During that reflective state, he/she will generate a visceral feeling for the application of some aspect of his/her knowledge base, giving that new supervisor a snapshot of experience to add to his/her own leadership self-awareness. In this case, new knowledge is being applied experientially for the first time. The comparison will cause the individual to possibly validate the knowledge, determine it to be useless or draw some conclusion in between. This is where a mentoring relationship becomes a powerful force. In this scenario, the discussion of an incident with a mentor assists the neophyte with a 'big picture' comparison of experiences to knowledge. This serves to expedite the benefit of the reflective process, resulting in efficient leadership development. The absence of a mentor could cause an individual to have the same experience multiple times before useful conclusions are drawn on the part of the learner.

A SYSTEMS APPROACH TO LEARNING LEADERSHIP

The tripartite approach to understanding systems extends back to the days of Socrates, when he introduced the three parts of personality to describe human nature. Certain systems scholars present models suggesting a triple-loop learning approach to describing learning processes. For instance, Argyris and Schon (1978) differentiated among single-, double- and triple-loop learning, although they are commonly credited with the double-loop approach[51]. They suggest that the first loop provides information (knowledge), the second results in altered 'values-in-use' (experience) and the third involves reflection on the whole learning process (reflection or metalearning). Perhaps, one reason the third loop is not widely reported in the literature is that the reflective process is considered to be a natural contemplative response to experiential stimuli, or that common perception is to blend knowledge and experience. In any case, triple-loop learning seems to go mostly unreported, while double-loop learning is a common reference when addressing organizational issues. Senge (1990) takes a fivefold approach to organizational learning, but provides a single attribute to individual learning within the noted discipline of 'adapting mental models' that include multiple loops[52]. There is an inherent problem with these theories as applied to the practice of leadership development in that nobody teaches metalearning or adaptive mental model processing to individuals. The few individuals who discover this process on their own are considered to be 'natural leaders,' while the majority are deemed to lack leadership potential. This is an injustice, since most individuals will embrace leadership development once they are taught the proper 'brain technique' for doing so.

A number of additional multiple-loop learning process theories exist to support reflective learning techniques[53]. Each provides a variation on the core themes that have already been mentioned. While discussion of these is best reserved for the academic literature, it is important to note that the key contribution of these theories correctly supposes that the relationship of knowledge and experience exist 'interdependently' within the mental processing of individuals[54].

This interdependency among knowledge, experience and reflection provides the rationale for the triangular impression of the model presented in the figure. This is a departure from mainstream education and training paradigms that work under the assumption that knowledge and experience are two independent states of mind among learners. This is a common deficiency associated with the leadership training provided in hospitality management schools. Formal academic programs focus on the teaching of knowledge to individuals who often lack practical experience as supervisors and managers in the industry (single-loop learning). These individuals often come away with abstract theoretical concepts that possess no direct application to the 'real world' of working in the industry. Conversely, industry practitioners who return to school in their adult years seem to readily assimilate the knowledge-based concepts into their daily work activities. The difference between the two cohorts exists not in the delivery of the content, but in the processing by the learners.

In both cases, the educators are delivering single loops of knowledge to the students, with the expectation that the knowledge will be transferable to working in the industry. There is no experiential base of comparison for traditional learners; hence, the knowledge is not connected to anything concrete in the right hemisphere of the brain, which renders the information as meaningless in the minds of those learners. This is not the case with industry practitioners who return to school. In their case, a single bit of knowledge information that is processed by the left hemisphere of the brain will trigger a visceral representation stored from experience in the brain's right hemisphere. This is an example of the actual application of double-loop (whole brain) learning within a training process that may be used for leadership development[55].

SINGLE- AND DOUBLE-LOOP PROCESSES

It is apparent that the e-loop process contains more power in terms of learning than that possessed by the k-loop, which indicates that the simplest learning process exists when experience precedes knowledge. However, there are cases in which the intent is to develop leadership skills among individuals who possess very little actual experience, such as newly hired graduates from hospitality schools. In these cases, the trainer may wish to add the second e-loop as reinforcement for the original k-loop. An example could be to present a foundational concept, then apply it to a 'live' situation. Pause for reflection, then present another 'live' situation and have learners choose and apply the appropriate foundational concepts. An astute trainer might recognize that this example is the 'case study' method of learning, which is true; except in this scenario, the 'cases' are actual situations that a manager would deal within the organization. This is in contrast to what might be presented in a Harvard Business School case study for analysis from an executive viewpoint, which is utterly abstract in reference to the base of experience possessed by the inexperienced manager. Table 15.1 provides a suggested sequence of learning activities for trainers who use the whole brain–learning model of leadership development for newly appointed practicing hospitality supervisors.

HOW CAN WE INFORMALLY ENGAGE IN LEADERSHIP DEVELOPMENT?

If we choose to pursue a path of lifelong learning that includes our own transformation as leaders, we need simply to follow the steps and model presented above. One powerful tool is to engage in a daily reflective practice. To do this, we need to choose a time of day or night when we are at our peak mental states. Some individuals are morning people and others are evening people. This is concept called circadian rhythm. Identify your peak time of the day. Next, place yourself in a relaxed state. We can do this by closing our eyes, listening to quiet slow tempo music through earphones or any other technique that will make us feel relaxed. For those who practice a form of yoga or meditation, these provide excellent states for guided reflection.

The next step is to quiet our minds. This sometimes takes some practice. We want to sort of daydream. When we daydream, we are in a quiet contemplative state in which the alpha brain waves are dominant. This is a learning state. It is one

TABLE 15.1 Leadership Process Model

	Activity	Example	Process	Model Loop
1.	Presentation	Leadership style preference	Interactive Discussion	K-loop
2.	Practice	Style preference surveys	Survey completion	E-loop
3.	Awareness	Identification of style preference	Review	Reflection
4.	Practice	Practice from style preference	Application within the work unit	E-loop
5.	Awareness	Record observations	Mentor's discussion/ journaling	K-loop
6.	Contemplate	Identify style preference strengths and limitations	Mentor's discussion/ journaling	Reflection
7.	Self-awareness	Who was I before? Who am I now?	Journaling, self-talk	Change in self-awareness

of parallel brain processing, which is very different to beta brain waves we use for concentrated activities. This is why relaxation is very important. We want to parallel process events in our brains. As we reach a state of relaxation and our minds begin to settle down, we could replay the last 24 hours or so of our lives in our minds. Some people like to vision a television screen in the center of the forehead when they engage in guided reflection. We just want those memories to replay in our minds without judging them. Eventually, we will begin to replay our work activities. These have been opportunities to have performed in leadership moments.

As these thoughts enter the mind, simply view, hear or feel them and keep two questions in the back of our minds. The first question when witnessing a leadership memory is to ask, 'Who was I being in that moment?' We follow this question with, 'Who do I want to be in future moments?' Chances are we will not receive any answers, which is okay. We are just processing our memories within the context of who we were being and who we want to be. The brain will do the processing unconsciously.

As we continue to perform a guided reflection process at about the same time every day or night, we will begin to get 'aha' thoughts seemingly out of nowhere. We will know that our brains have made some new sense out of leadership practices when these thoughts begin to come to us. When we continue our daily practice for about three weeks, our brains will have become habituated to reflect without us consciously thinking about it. As long as we remember to be in a relaxed state, our brains will feed us new ideas about practicing leadership. Remember that leadership is all about self-awareness of who we are being during leadership transactions.

PUTTING IT ALL TOGETHER

We most recently learned a few basics about organizational behavior as it is applied to leadership and motivation. We also learned a few practical techniques for engaging in leadership development activities. We know from earlier leadership chapters that leadership is a process of relations and that we may choose to engage in leader relationships that are transactional or transformational. We know that leadership in service enterprises consists of influencing others to willingly accomplish the objectives of the organization. Some of us may have already made a personal commitment to use leadership practices in the management of service enterprises.

We learned how to perform the diagnostics and interventions associated with three major tactical strategies in service enterprises. These include run, growth and fix strategies. We know that run strategies require us to view the operation from systems perspective. In particular, we look at the inputs, transformation processes and outputs associated with each system. Our industry is unique and complex. We have many nonlinear systems in play simultaneously many times through each working day. Most of us will be required to lead maintenance, repair, distribution and product production systems that support the core competency of the service enterprise called service transactions. We incrementally enhance the productivity of the production systems on a daily basis when acting as value-added managers. This is done through controls on the inputs side of the system, as well as quality and quantity improvements within the outputs side of the system. We continually see ways to tweak the transformation process to enhance both effectiveness and efficiency.

We learned that growth strategies require careful planning to determine feasibility to make a go or no-go decision concerning some form of expansion. We know that growth strategies may include expanding existing operations or adding additional outlets. We revisited the strategic planning model from Chapter 3 of the text to assist us with growth strategy planning, implementation, evaluation and revisions. We learned that corporate growth strategies are broad in nature and that tactical growth strategies take place at the property level of the service enterprise. We viewed growth strategies through the lens of product life cycles.

We know that fix tactical strategies are the most challenging of the three major strategies. They require individuals who are highly experienced at management diagnostics and interventions. Managers that perform these strategies are referred to as troubleshooters. Troubleshooters earn higher than average salaries because desperate times call for desperate dollars. We learned that troubleshooters are called in to turnaround underperforming operations. This process often involves certain levels of conflict within the underperforming work unit for a short period of time. Troubleshooters establish critical path method (CPM) timelines for the execution of these turnarounds, just as other managers do with growth and run strategies.

We learned there are three levels of management in most service enterprises. These include senior, middle and junior management levels. Junior managers occupy titles such as assistant manager, lead or supervisor. These individuals spend most of their time enabling the control function of comparing actual performance to standards for performance. Middle-level managers spend the majority of time organizing activities within and among departments. They rely heavily upon their interpersonal relationship skills to perform this function. Senior-level managers use conceptual skills to plan and implement the strategic direction of the service enterprise. All managers must become highly trained in influencing skills, which led us to discuss leadership and human resource management. Managers must also become well versed in understanding technologies that provide inputs and systems used to produce outputs.

We know that service enterprises consist of structures and systems designed to permit them to efficiently and effectively perform service transactions. We learned the organizational structures and functions of each department within a typical medium-size service enterprise. We also identified the systems associated with each operating department. We also identified staff business functions that include marketing, human resource management, information technology, security, accounting and finance, purchasing and receiving. We know that these support the line functions that comprise the operations of the service enterprise. We learned about operating departments in full-service lodging, resort and restaurant service enterprises.

We identified the stages associated with the evolution of management from the early 1900s through current practices. We recognized that we include scientific management, management science, human relations, behavioral management and systems thinking in the current-day practice of management. We learned all the things discussed in this section to help us accomplish the objectives of the organization through the activities of others, which is the definition of management.

Summary

This chapter began with discussion of various theoretical constructs that provided a foundation for the many practical aspects of management and leadership discussed throughout the text. We began our discussions with a look at organizational behavior (OB), which is a discipline that uses applied psychology to understand workplace behaviors. We realized that service enterprises require emotional interactions with guests and clients. This led to the discovery of earlier studies in the field of emotional labor.

Emotional labor studies were the forerunners to a growing field of intense interest known as emotional intelligence. Leaders must become skilled in the foundations of emotional intelligence for the purpose of understanding the emotional bases of behaviors in the workplace.

We then took a look at historical perspectives of OB to identify the scholarly grounding of motivational topics. We focused in particular on the development and sustainability of the concept of self-actualization, which was first identified by scholars associated with the humanistic movement of management. We witnessed the transformation of this movement into the transpersonal psychology movement, which is vibrant to this day.

Modern theories associated with awareness and leadership are being developed within the fields of neuroscience and physics. We have current technology that permits us to witness brain functions during varied states of consciousness. This topic is of interest for those who wish to understand leadership and the brain. We identified a few studies that used the findings from neuroscience to support the work life development model used extensively throughout the text.

We used the foundational information to engage in discussions concerning leadership development. We recognized that leadership development is a continuous transformation process for leaders to attain higher-order leadership styles through enhanced self-awareness. We provided information for implementing leadership development programs within service enterprises. We also shared an informal leadership development practice that will enhance the individual transformation of practicing leaders.

We concluded the chapter with a virtual trip through prior chapters of the text. We discussed highlights of what we have learned about management and leadership. We inventoried certain areas of knowledge for the practice of management and leadership.

DISCUSSION QUESTIONS

1. Identify five of the most important concepts learned from the text and describe how you would use them as a practicing manager.
2. Describe the relationship of organizational behavior to our understanding of motivation and leadership.
3. If you were a human resource manager, what steps would you take to establish a leadership development program for managers within a service enterprise?
4. What do you plan to do to transform your leadership style in the future?

IN THE REAL WORLD (CONTINUED)

Adam grabs a soda and starts to tell you all about his job interview. He says, 'After I got through the human resources screening, I went to a number of interviews with the operators.' He pauses to back up, 'As you guys know, I have been working line and supervisory jobs at resorts for four years now and I think those experiences really paid off.' He continues, 'So, this intimidating manager asks me, "If you were to come to work with us as a manager, what activities would you pursue during the first 30 days of employment?"' Adam says, 'I looked him square in the eyes and said, "In the first 30 days, I should have the opportunity to complete a complete diagnosis of the operation's performance relative to the established standards." Adam continues, "This answer blew the guy away. Next, the guy asks, 'Once you have done the diagnostics, what would you do in the course of running the operation?'" Adam continues, 'I said to the guy, I would perform small incremental interventions to the systems to enhance productivity levels everyday.' Adam just stares at you all just beaming and finally finishes with, 'The guy looks at me and simply says, when can you start? The next thing I know, I have an offer letter in my hand.'

CASE STUDY

You are working in the human resource office for a large branded chain hotel at the property level. The director of human resources invites you to attend the local Hospitality Human Resource Association chapter meeting after work. You realize this is a good opportunity to network with other HR practitioners. You arrive at the meeting and are introduced to the other attendees who include directors as well as HR specialist (compensation, employee relations, training, labor relations) managers.

The topic of the meeting is leadership strategies. A guest speaker provides a presentation on leadership development programs. After the presentation, there is an open forum discussion session. Since you want to learn as much as you can about HR practices, you pay close attention to the interactions of the discussion session. You start to notice after awhile that these HR managers, while somewhat knowledgeable, seem to be lacking some quality that your director has.

Preliminary Questions

1. Is there a difference between those who possess leadership knowledge and those who actually practice leadership? What specific behaviors would indicate such a difference?
2. Do you think hospitality companies give the title of 'lead' or 'leader' to individuals with no leadership skills? Provide a specific example of this in practice.

Conclusion

At the office the next morning, you are having coffee with the training manager. You start to tell him about your experience at the association meeting. You then mention, 'Is it me? Or is there some quality that our HR director has that the other practitioners don't have?' He just smiles at you.

Finally, you say to the training manager, 'Are you going to just smile at me or are you going to explain why I am sensing a difference between our leader and the other members of the association?' He laughs, 'You just answered your own question.' 'What are you talking about?' you say. He replies, 'The difference is leadership. Our director is a leader.' He continues, 'I have worked with her for sometime now. When I started with her, she used to drive me crazy by never giving me direct answers to my questions. She seemed to take almost sadistic pleasure in watching me try things and fail. Some days, she would be very nurturing and on other days, she would be a hard-driving task manager. I thought she was bipolar in the beginning.' The training manager pauses in his own reflection of the past, 'Then it dawned on me – she was a leader who was teaching me (in her own twisted way) to become a leader just like her.' He smirks a little, and then continues, 'As soon as I achieved that awareness, she told me that I was now 'getting it.' It was like she was reading my mind.' He concludes, 'She and I have been leadership partners ever since.'

'Wow,' you say to him. 'How do you get that way?' He laughs and replies, 'I don't know, but if she takes you under her wing, you will know you have reached leader status when she no longer appears to you to be the director from hell.'

Conclusion Questions

1. Why did the leader act like a schizophrenic when she first started developing the training manager?
2. Was the leader really being sadistic, or was she trying to get the training manager to think for himself? Provide a specific example of how this might work.
3. Was the leader really reading the training manager's mind, or was she just tuned in to leadership thinking? How can this be so?

ENDNOTES

1. Tesone (2005).
2. Ashforth and Humphrey (1994).
3. Krebs (2005).
4. Hoschild (1983).
5. Ekman and Friesen (1975), Goffman (1959), Rafaeli and Sutton (1987).
6. Morris and Feldman (1996), Watson and Clark (1984), Wharton (1983).
7. Eisenberger, Fasolo and Davis-LaMastro (1990), Eisenberger, Armeli, Rexwinkel, Lynch and Rhoades (2001), Shore and Wayne (1993), Watson, Clark and Telegen (1988), Weiss and Cropanzano (1996).
8. Aldwin (1994), Lazarus and Launier (1978), Moos and Billings (1982), Pearlin and Schooter (1978), Snyder and Dinoff (1999).
9. Ashforth and Humphrey (1995).
10. Barsade, Brief and Spataro (2003).
11. Salovey and Mayer (1990).
12. Goleman (1995, 1998).
13. Brief and Weiss (2002), Fisher and Ashansky (2000), Lord, Klimoski and Kanfer (2002), Payne and Cooper (2001), and others.
14. Fineman (2003), Robbins (2004).
15. Damasio (1994).
16. Barsade et al. (2003).
17. Milliman, Czaplewski and Ferguson (2001).
18. Ashmos and Duchon (2000).
19. Mitroff and Denton (1999).
20. Fontana and Slack (1996).
21. Ajaya (1997).

22. Strohl (1998).
23. Lajoie and Shapiro (1992).
24. Boss (1980).
25. Bugental (1965).
26. Cleary and Shapiro (1995).
27. Zohar and Marshall (2000).
28. Jung (1953).
29. Strohl (1998).
30. Schrage (2000).
31. Townsend and Gebhardt (2002).
32. Brenner (1999).
33. Chasse (1997).
34. Linstead (2002).
35. Zohar and Marshall (2000).
36. Damasio (1994).
37. Damasio (2003).
38. Damasio (2003), LeDoux (2002), Pert (1999), Zohar and Marshall (2000), and others.
39. Zohar and Marshall (2000).
40. Pert (1997).
41. Pert (1999), Zohar and Marshall (2000).
42. Damasio (1994), LeDoux (2002).
43. Tesone, (2005).
44. Tesone (1995, 2005).
45. Dewey (1895), Kohlberg (1976, 1981), Maslow (1965), Piaget (1932).
46. Stonefield (1992).
47. George (1999).
48. Theodore (1998).
49. Dougal and Caren (1999).
50. Tesone (2003).
51. Argyris and Schon (1978).
52. Mohr (2002).
53. King (2002), Gunasekara (2003).
54. Senge (1990).
55. Argyris and Schon (1974, 1978).

PART 5

Sustainability

CHAPTER 16

Sustainable Hospitality Marketing Management

In this chapter you will learn to:

1. Identify and explain the role of marketing and sustainability.
2. Identify sustainable marketing strategies and the role that E-marketing is involved with.
3. Differentiate between marketing and sales functions.
4. Identify the four Ps that comprise marketing.
5. Describe market segmentation and the role of marketing managers.

INTRODUCTION

Many hospitality organizations are seeking sustainable competitive advantage. Maintaining sustainability presents varying challenges to all areas of operations. Additionally, large conglomerates are expanding their businesses to a global range. Two particularly important management functions associated with such expansion as well as sustainability are marketing and human resource management.

This chapter addresses sustainable marketing initiatives and strategies. We touched upon the electronic marketing support function in the E-business segment of Chapter 8. This chapter presents an overview of the marketing function from a global perspective.

The first issue of importance is to note that marketing and sales are two different functions. Marketing departments support both operational and formalized sales departments within hospitality enterprises. Sales generate revenues, which impact the outputs of the organization. In its simplest term, sales personnel, just like all operational personnel, are responsible for the acquisition and maintenance of guests/clients. Marketing management is a strategic process that brings these tasks to fruition. A marketing department is responsible for promotion, product, place and price. These four areas of the function support the needs of all stakeholder groups. The objective of marketing strategies is to generate competitive advantage for the enterprise within a specific market.

PROMOTION

The marketing function is charged with creating strategies that create an awareness of products and services to the generalized population or specific target markets. This is primarily accomplished through advertising. Historically, advertising was restricted to print media and television. However, electronic advertising has replaced a good deal of the strategy. This is one reason that marketing managers must work closely with IT professionals to create enticing and widely available Internet-based information. This form of advertising should lead a member of a target audience to a well-maintained and easily navigational website. Each site should entice the viewer to peruse aesthetic representations of products and services offered by the enterprise. The purpose of each site is to entice the visitor to make a purchase decision. When this occurs, the viewer should easily navigate to a transaction-processing link. For this reason, marketing managers would work closely with centralized or localized reservations systems. Should a purchase transaction occur, the information concerning the future guest/client would be placed into a customer relationship management (CRM) database. This provides opportunities with the enterprise to interact with the guest/client before and after they have used the products and services. In a sense, this becomes a mailing list for future promotional information to be sent to the guest/client. The goal of CRM is to generate repeat business and is practiced in numerous hospitality sectors.

PRICING

Many hospitality conglomerates consist of multinational operations. Lodging and food service companies possess portfolios of brands that range from limited to full service to upscale and luxury operations. Pricing strategies vary among brands and are commonly decided on the basis of perceived differentiation and competitive environments. Also, there are changes in the demand for products and services from time to time. For this reason, revenue management (formerly known as yield management) is practiced in many sectors.

For instance, in the lodging industry, pricing strategies may be to charge what competitors charge or charge higher rates on the basis of differentiation perceptions. Other strategies may include follow-the-leader strategies (charge the same rates as industry leaders) or discount pricing (charge less than the competition). All of these strategies are determined by volume forecasting. Because of the developments of the Internet, many travel agencies have been replaced by travel brokers.

These firms offer discounted rates by purchasing blocks of hotel rooms, flights, cruises etc. Obviously, it is the responsibility of marketing and hospitality operations managers to maximize revenues.

PRODUCT

As already discussed, there are various brands that serve different missions for diverse travelers. An example would be the deregulation of the airline industry in the United States that created a market in which anyone is able to fly to destinations. In the past, flights were restricted to those willing to pay premium dollars to use an air carrier. In the lodging sector, signature hotels are developing, which provide limited amenities beyond a limited service property at a pricing that is below full-service lodging facilities. The key for marketing managers is to differentiate their brand from equal competitors to lure traveler bookings and loyalty. This is perhaps the most creative aspect of marketing management.

PLACE

The destination plays a key role in this function. Also, convenience factors such as airport access and proximity to preferred locations are also important. The lodging sector provides urban properties to suburban properties to remote bed and breakfasts. All of these appeal to various market niches. Some destinations are restricted to seasonal operations, while others are appealing on a year-long basis. Beyond the role of destination, it is the job of a sales manager to place the guest/client with their enterprise.

THE ROLE OF MARKETING MANAGERS

The marketing manager is responsible for all of the items discussed above. They must cultivate awareness of products and services, demonstrate how they are differentiated from the competition, recommend pricing strategies and promote the enterprise to potential guests/clients. The role of the sales force is to book clients and guests and ensure they receive expected services. This is called the value proposition, which is the job of both sales and marketing managers. The goal of both teams is to maximize revenues while being fiscally responsible.

It is the job of the marketing manager to analyze the needs of potential guests/clients and make strategic decisions about promotion, product, place and pricing. This activity is referred to as marketing research. Marketing research includes analyses of demographics, psychographics and the competitive environment. Third parties accredit the success of hospitality entities. For instance, in the lodging sector, the two most prominent US agencies are the published guides from AAA and Mobile travel service sectors. AAA awards 1–5 diamonds, while Mobile awards 1–5 stars for a specific enterprise. A five-star or diamond award indicates a top-notch luxury property.

MARKETING SEGMENTATION

There are various sources of marketing segments. As already mentioned, the Internet and brokers are the fastest growing areas. Travel agents book business on the basis of commissions. Event planners book conventions, functions and festivals, which include lodging, food and beverage as well as entertainment. On an individual or family level, the segments include business and leisure travelers.

CUSTOMER RELATIONSHIP MANAGEMENT

As mentioned earlier, the ultimate goal is to generate guest/client loyalty. This requires communicating the seriousness with which the enterprise values its clients. Examples of activities include sport outings, complimentary entertainment, gifts and appreciation events. For instance, the airline industry reserves private upscale relaxation facilities for its most valued clients.

STRATEGIC MANAGEMENT

Marketing managers follow the same systems for strategic management as every other operating area. These include competition analysis, environmental scanning, internal audits and future market forecasts. The next phase is to develop a strategic marketing plan that includes objectives, strategies, policies, standards and procedures. A marketing budget must be developed to ensure fiscal accountability. Finally, a set of evaluation criteria must be established.

E-MARKETING

Let us recap some of what was discussed in Chapter 8. All enterprises must have online reservation systems with linkages to global distribution systems (GDS). Enterprises must provide access to travel agencies for direct bookings.

Additionally, there are considerations for website design. Websites should be interactive and easy to navigate. They should provide for online bookings and have links to appropriate companion sites. Sites should have mechanism for easy updates of guest/client rates. They should accumulate prospects' information in a way that does not intrude on their privacy. The sites should provide multilingual capacities and domains should be easy to remember. Delta.com is an example of this for Delta Airline. Email is an inexpensive and powerful tool for retaining guest/client relationships. It is also a way to easily mass mail potential clients.

SUSTAINABILITY

Sustainability may be summed in a single word, 'coalignment.' This is the practice of closely monitoring the global external environment from every aspect of the operation. In order for hospitality organizations to be competitive, they must both internalize a market-driven environment as well as align every aspect of the corporation with the marketing strategies. They must demonstrate the ability to be agile in changing competitive times.

As we will see in the following chapter, the concept of sustainability becomes quite complex as organizations venture into multinational operations. The chapter presents a human resource management perspective, which really does not differ from marketing functions. In fact, it has been noted that HRM is really internal marketing aimed at maximizing human capital. A firm that operates in a state of coalignment will meet or exceed the expectations from all of the stakeholder groups to include shareholders, employees, clients/guests and the community. This is the type of differentiation that creates competitive advantage.

SUMMARY

This chapter began with the concept of sustainable competitive advantage as well as global expansion. While we recognized that all operations are crucial to achieving both objectives, two in particular are the marketing and human resource management functions.

We began the chapter with references to the E-business systems noted in Chapter 8. We continued by differentiating marketing and sales functions. We learned that marketing is the support function of sales and reservations systems. We identified the four Ps of marketing that include promotion, product, price and placement and went on to discuss each of these functions.

We went on to discuss the role of hospitality marketing managers. It was determined that marketing is truly a strategic function. We concluded with brief discussions of market segmentation, customer relationship management, strategic management and additional information concerning E-marketing.

We concluded with a discussion of coalignment within organizations as a means to attain sustainable competitive advantage.

QUESTIONS FOR DISCUSSION

1. Would you consider a career in sales or marketing? Why or why not?
2. Do you believe that developments in the field of telecommunications will further advance as a part of marketing strategies? How so?
3. Do you believe that hospitality enterprises may use marketing strategies to develop and maintain competitive advantage? Why?

CHAPTER 17

Development of a Sustainable Tourism Hospitality Human Resources Management Module

OBJECTIVES

In this chapter you will learn to:

1. **Identify two educational approaches to learning human resource management.**
2. **Describe the role of sustainable human capital in multinational firms.**
3. **Complete the objectives for each of the modules listed in the chapter.**

INTRODUCTION

It would seem that two methods of concept delivery prevail within hospitality and tourism management programs at institutions of higher learning. The first method is to provide specific courses designed to cover topics that fall within an appropriate concept and the second would be to deliver those topics 'across the curriculum' (infusion into the content of various courses).

Most hospitality and tourism educators would agree that concepts associated with sustainable tourism practices are crucial components that should be included in programs intended to develop the knowledge and skills of future industry leaders. One group called BEST – Business & Entrepreneurial Sustainable Tourism – is composed of academics and industry practitioners representing various sectors of the tourism industry, worldwide. The leaders of this group are guided by a strong belief that sustainable tourism principles should be practiced in all aspects of tourism operations on a daily basis. The leaders and volunteers of BEST gathered on several occasions over a number of years in 'think tank' formats to develop frameworks for programs of study aimed at the teaching of sustainable tourism 'across the curriculum' of coursework offered in Tourism programs at institutions of higher learning.

The following module on sustainable tourism practices in hospitality/tourism human resources (HR) management is the outcome of the first think tank that was conducted in Bongani, South Africa. The author developed this first module in conjunction with the leaders of BEST, who provided formative and summative reviews. It is intended for infusion into hospitality/tourism HR courses and to serve as a template for future modules of sustainable tourism practices, as applied to other courses.

MICRO-MODULE 1

ORGANIZATIONAL STRUCTURE AND CONTEXT

OBJECTIVE

At the end of this micro-module, the readers will be able to:

- Appreciate that sustainable principles should be a part of corporate goals and an organization and the organizational structure should be appropriate to local culture.

INTRODUCTION

It is common knowledge that the practice of human resource management (**HRM**) is prevalent in most organizations ranging from small- to medium- to large-scale corporations. The current-day human resource (**HR**) manager has direct influence on the strategic direction and thinking of both private and public sector organizations.

Tourism is the broad umbrella that drives related indicators within local and national economies. Hospitality organizations are driven by public (governmental) and private (institutional) sector tourism policies and practices. The proliferation of telecommunication technologies along with the development of multinational hospitality organizations has generated an awareness of tourism policies on a global level. Sustainable tourism is a long-term collaborative systems approach to establishing and maintaining harmonious relationships among hospitality/travel-related organizations and the social, cultural and environmental aspects associated with tourist destinations.

While the process of sustainable tourism involves the establishment and maintenance of harmonious relationships, the goal (desired outcome) is the creation of continued viability and development of tourism-related entities. Hence, proponents of sustainable tourism engage in a process of creating a mutually beneficial balance between the macroenvironment (social, cultural and environmental aspects) and the microenvironment (internal workings of a specific organization). The objective (goal) of this process is the institutionalization of the tourism industry as a contributor to the sociocultural welfare and development of each and every destination. In essence, this goal seeks what might be called a 'triple win' outcome. Successful sustainable tourism initiatives result in positive outcomes for consumers (guests, travelers and customers), organizations (commercial enterprises) as well as the society (indigenous people and cultures). But how does the practice of hospitality human resource management fit into this picture?

CAREER PATHS

As part of the commitment to the social environment of the community, human resource practitioners in sustainable tourism-based organizations (STO) must determine the career goals and desires of host country citizens. While certain individuals will exist who do not possess progressive career aspirations, there will be others who will view the organization as a means to pursue professional development activities. For this reason, job design processes should provide a clear snapshot of knowledge, skills, abilities and attitudes for every position within the organization through job descriptions and job specifications.

The job descriptions and job specifications provide foundational information to track logical paths of career progression among the many disciplines found within the operations and administrative areas of a medium-to-large hospitality enterprise. Once these paths are discovered, human resource practitioners may engage in career counseling activities aimed at communicating activities to attain the necessary job requirements for internal promotions. Human resource practitioners may choose to take this one step further through formal succession planning programs coupled with training development activities.

Many cases of global expansion within hospitality organizations include the placement of expatriate managers from home nations into positions at host country locations. STO strategies might be aimed at the temporary placement of such individuals until citizens of the host nation are adequately prepared to assume senior management positions. An advantage to this strategy would be the assimilation into the mainstream culture of the host nation by establishing a representation of senior management positions that are held by qualified host nationals.

PROPORTION OF LOCAL STAFF MEMBERS

It makes good business sense for human resource practitioners to scan the external environment of the host nation to determine the statistical representation of various groups of individuals by ethnicity, age, sex, race, national origin and in some cases religion. Once the demographics for the locale are discovered, the human resource manager would enact strategies aimed at a statistical representation within the organization that is somewhat similar to those evident within the region.

Some reactive hospitality organizations might claim to have sufficient numbers of represented groups within their companies. Upon further inspection, however, it could be determined that the representation exists exclusively for lower-level position holders. This would not be the case for an STO, as the human resource

FIGURE 17.1 Organizational stakeholder groups

practitioners in such an organization would possess objectives for appropriate levels of group representation among all levels of the organization. In this case, career path objectives would become one strategy used to balance the representation of various classes of individuals in middle- and senior-level positions. Other strategies would exist within the established plans for recruitment and selection of staff members.

Policy and Governance from an External Context

Who are the stakeholders or 'constituents' served by human resource management practitioners? In actuality, HR practitioners have the same responsibilities in the area of stakeholder service as any other corporate manager. The stakeholder group consists of shareholders (stockholders in publicly traded firms), employees, customers and the community. The trick here is 'balance.' In a healthy organization, the needs of each stakeholder group will be satisfied more or less equally. On the other hand, dysfunctional companies will serve the needs of one stakeholder group (the shareholders, for instance) at the expense of another group (such as the employees). When this happens, the senior HR manager is at odds with the value system of the organization (or at least the CEO) and will attempt to stabilize the imbalance in the interests of both groups. In organizations that are committed to the practice of sustainable tourism, the role of the human resource practitioner as a shareholder group stabilizer is particularly crucial. Figure 17.1 provides a description of the stakeholders as the people who the HR practitioner and every other manager in the sustainable tourism-oriented organization should serve in balanced proportion.

Shared Ownership

In cases of organizational expansion strategies, it is common for corporate entities to engage in partnerships that result in multiple ownership of an operation. Usually, this strategy is based on cost of capital and shared risk taking in unproven markets. For instance, a start-up project may include limited partners such as real estate developers, construction firms and multinational investment bankers. A proven STO ownership strategy is to include organizations and individual investors that exist within the targeted host country, if the legal environment permits such collaboration. In some cases, it is permissible for certain government agencies of the host nation or republic to possess an ownership interest in a hospitality enterprise.

Similar to the case stated in favor of group representation among an organization's employees, shared ownership interests held by host country nationals help the parent corporation assimilate into foreign national cultures. Additionally, successful enterprises contribute to the local economies through returns on investment to host national private and public entities.

Employee ownership strategies take the form of profit sharing and stock acquisition in some nations. This is not appropriate in all nations; however, in those countries with economies that lean toward individual accumulation of assets, employer ownership strategies may serve to motivate individuals to achieve organizational success factors such as growth and profit.

In some cases, it may be appropriate to focus on 'psychological' employee ownership through programs such as participative decision-making and team-building activities. While these would not be well received in all social environments, certain 'collective-thinking' cultures would expect this type of psychological ownership to exist within the organization.

ORGANIZATIONAL STRUCTURE AND MANAGEMENT

Human resource practitioners within STOs recognize the fact that organizational cultures should become micromirrors of the culture within the local and national societies. A number of factors external to the organization should be considered prior to establishing internal structures and management practices. Typical considerations from the 'external environment' include social/political, economic, competitive, technological and cultural factors.

Human resource managers working in sustainable tourism-based organizations will construct job analysis processes on the basis of the social and cultural factors that exist in the surrounding environment. The findings of job analysis activities are used to determine the managerial structure of the hospitality organization. That structure will drive the spans of authority that exist for each manager. For instance, in cultures that value 'authority' relationships, organizations will tend to possess a tall management hierarchy with multiple layers of management and narrow spans of management authority. Other nations may design the organization to be structured in a flat pyramid style with wide spans of management authority to facilitate decision-making activities on the part of most employees. Nations that value 'individualism' may find this organizational structure to be appropriate.

We know that the key driver for any organization is its mission. The mission describes the purpose for the organization's existence, which includes the values and philosophies for that enterprise. The mission is the broadest objective that drives the firm. Missions that include the values of perpetuation and evolution drive sustainable organizations. An STO is a 'mission-driven' organization, which means that the mission is the key driver for all of the management objectives for the enterprise. Hence, 'sustainable objectives' or targets for performance direct an STO.

THE GLOBAL-TO-LOCAL MIND-SET

One way to describe the mind-set of STO human resource practitioners would be to say, 'They think globally and act locally.' This describes the mental approach that is taken to establish a balance between the macrocosm and the microcosm. For instance, a group of host country enterprises could be said to each represent a subsystem of a larger system called the multinational corporation. That corporation could be considered to be a subsystem of a larger system called the hotel industry and that industry would be a subsystem of global tourism. When human resource managers frame their thinking in this manner, they see each entity as a node within a much larger pattern. Sustainable tourism views these patterns as an evolving ecosystem.

Multinational firms engaged in sustainable tourism will empower human resource practitioners at the property level to balance performance factors with the sociocultural needs of each respective host country. This practice is driven by a philosophy that healthy local operations contribute to performance on a global level.

PEOPLE AND COMMUNITY MANAGEMENT

A hospitality organization is only as good as its people and the management of those people should take place in close cooperation with local community activities. The human resource manager must take steps to align closely with the needs of the local community through social assimilation to ensure that the practices within the organization are consistent with the values of that society. The human resource practitioner should become a participant with those agencies in the community that promote initiatives such as social welfare, education and community service. There is a twofold benefit to this practice. First, the human resource manager acts in the capacity of 'ambassador' to the community. Second, the human resource manager uses what is learned through these activities to enhance the level of community awareness among the managers of the organization.

QUESTIONS FOR DISCUSSION

1. Do you think hospitality organizations should become STOs? Why or why not?
2. When you think about the stakeholder group called 'the Community,' would this group be considered to be more or less important for an STO? Why?
3. If you had a choice of becoming an HR practitioner for a regular hospitality organization or one that includes sustainable tourism practices, which would you choose? Why?

MICRO-MODULE 2

STO RECRUITMENT AND SELECTION STRATEGIES

OBJECTIVE

At the end of this micro-module, the readers will be able to:

- Realize that a local focus and equitable approach should be used in recruitment, and sensitivity to local cultures and local community needs is important.

INTRODUCTION

The key factor that differentiates human resource management from personnel administration is the strategic nature of acquiring, developing and maintaining human capital. Since the break from personnel administration, human resource managers have been included in the overall strategic direction of a firm, which places the HR manager within the senior management of the organization. The strategies for recruiting and selecting employees for a sustainable tourism-based hospitality organization must balance the human capital needs for the business with a long-term approach of community citizenship with the host nation.

The key driver for recruitment and selection strategies from the external environment is the labor market for all hospitality organizations. The labor market consists of individuals who possess knowledge, skills, abilities and attitudes that are consistent with the tasks, duties and responsibilities required of employment positions. These, as well as the volume of individuals needed in each job classification are determined through the process of job analysis, which is the key activity within the process called job design. The job design process yields a number of positions in each job classification that must be filled through recruitment and selection activities.

The human resource manager for an STO that is operating in a secluded area within a developing nation would be faced with even more daunting recruitment and selection challenges. A reactive organization would be tempted to place needed skilled positions with expatriates from more developed nations to solve this dilemma. However, this strategy would be in contrast with a mission that is based on sustainable tourism principles. The HR manager for an STO would devise strategies to develop the skills base within the local population to provide career opportunities to members of the host nation. An outside shareholder could argue that this strategy would be cost-prohibitive. However, the skilled HR practitioner would counter this argument by demonstrating that the exorbitant costs associated with expatriate placement could be better invested into the development within the local community. From a cost/benefit analysis perspective, the human resource manager could easily show how the same investment in the community could yield a greater return on investment, relative to the short-term benefit of the huge level of expenses associated with expatriate placement.

LOCAL FOCUS AT ALL LEVELS OF THE ORGANIZATION

STOs may be said to 'think globally and act locally.' This saying is particularly true of recruitment and selection activities for an organization that operates in a host nation. Factors such as language, culture and management must reflect the local norms for acceptability. Multilingual employees may be preferred in hospitality organizations that cater to guests from eclectic national origins. The hospitality organization should attempt to assimilate the internal workings of the company with the cultural values of the host nation. In some cases, the 'local flavor' will become part of the marketing and promotional strategies to attract guests to resorts located in host nations. Human resource practitioners must ensure that procedures for attracting and hiring applicants are consistent with the local laws and customs.

EQUITY ISSUES AND DISADVANTAGED GROUPS

While many developed nations legislate equality in hiring practices, some developing nations may not have these protections for workers. However, the STO would perceive an ethical responsibility to build equality safeguards into all of its policies concerning workers. One particular advantage of doing business in some developing nations is the opportunity to provide economic stability to disadvantaged groups within the society. Hospitality operations are often labor intensive, which means that large numbers of employment opportunities exist within the local vicinity of such a business. While the community may appreciate the decline in unemployment levels that may result when large numbers of people are hired, the STO would take this responsibility further by providing progressive career development opportunities for workers.

IMPLICATIONS OF SEASONAL/MIGRATORY LABOR

While certain industries engage in employment practices that may be construed to exploit the labor available to them, this is not an option for hospitality STOs. Since the STO is a good community citizen, it would be inappropriate to engage in practices that take advantage of the host country workers. The same would be true for migratory workers from other nations.

The nature of the hospitality industry calls for certain percentages of the total workforce to include part-time workers. The definition of part-time workers varies across cultures. But a traditional definition of less than one full-time equivalent could be applied on a global basis. Another employment option is to hire 'on-call' or casual workers to perform functions on a project basis. Regardless of the mix of workers involved in an STO, the key consideration is to treat all employees with the respect and dignity that would be expected by the leaders of the community for its citizens.

CULTURAL SENSITIVITY

On a positive note, certain developing nations possess populations that naturally exude a spirit of hospitality, which provides a natural transition into service-oriented positions. On the other hand, the people of some developing nations confuse the concept of service with the notion of 'servitude.' STOs in these nations are faced with the challenge of providing attitudinal training to those individuals who are selected for service-oriented positions. Such training initiatives as well as all interactions concerning the recruitment and selection processes require excellent skills in the area of interpersonal relations and communication.

MISSION AND POLICIES

The key differentiating feature of an STO is a mission statement that articulates a commitment to sustainability principles. If the mission drives the organization, the activities associated with recruitment and selection must also support sustainability. The result of this thinking will be manifested in practices associated with skill analysis that will focus on recruitment and selection functions aimed at long-term sustainability for the organization.

> ## QUESTIONS FOR DISCUSSION
>
> 1. In an STO, which function is more complex, the recruiting or selection process? Maybe you think they are equally intricate? Which is more important? Why?
> 2. Think about a scenario in which you have a choice of using expatriate managers versus those from a given host country. What would be the cost/benefit of each choice?
> 3. If you were a human resource manager, would you prefer to work for a reactive hospitality organization or an STO? Why?

MICRO-MODULE 3

STO ORIENTATION PROGRAMS FOR NEW EMPLOYEES

OBJECTIVES

At the end of this micro-module, the readers will be able to:

- Comprehend local environmental and cultural issues in relation to orientation.
- Apply training that is ongoing; supporting progression, including to managerial levels for locally recruited staff; sensitive to local culture and incorporating the understanding of the application of sustainable tourism practices.

EMPLOYEE ORIENTATIONS

New employee orientations fall within the category of knowledge training. For this reason, the sessions are conducted in a classroom setting with a training facilitator, who is often the training manager him/herself. This process is an exchange of the custody of the new employees from the domain of the employment manager over to the training manager. Most organizations benefit from two types of new employee orientation. The first may be referred to as a general orientation session(s), with the second phase referred to as the department orientation session(s). In many cases, the department manager will act as the facilitator for department orientation programs.

The primary objective of orientation programs is to assimilate new employees into the organization. This means that the new employee should be made to feel comfortable with the new position by learning a little about the organization and the people who work there. The reason for assimilating new employees into the organization is to familiarize them with a strange and new work environment. Think about the first day you spent in a new job or at a new school. The experience is almost hostile because you are entering an unknown environment that is full of people who are strangers to you. The first immediate psychological response for most people in this situation is to refrain from returning to the uncomfortable environment. If they are persistent, however, the environment becomes comfortable to them in a short period of time. The purpose of the new employee orientation is to ease this transition into the organizational environment, by sharing information that explains the 'whats, whys and wheres' in an effort to make the new workers comfortable in their new positions with the organization.

NEW EMPLOYEE ENGAGEMENT

STO Training Managers are adept at transitioning new staff members into the organization through orientation techniques that fully engage the participants as members of a new microcommunity. The psychology of newly acquired employees is based on the understanding that people bring a host of mental and emotional backgrounds with them into the organization. Human resource managers view individual employees as 'holistic beings,' which impacts the methods used for interpersonal communications. The goal of all managers is to fully engage an individual into the workplace by using communication methods that are consistent with each person's psyche to ensure that each person will understand his or her role as a member of the organization. At the same time, each person is reassured that organizational membership does not require loss of personal identity.

FOCUS AND BACKGROUND ON SUSTAINABLE TOURISM PRINCIPLES AND PRACTICES

One of the effective learning outcomes for orientation programs is to instill a sense of personal pride on the part of an individual for becoming a member of the organization. Sustainable tourism-based organizations are naturally aligned with this inclination since they are acutely aware of their role as corporate citizens of the host community. It would be an appropriate strategy to base a thematic approach to each orientation session on the sustainable tourism objectives for that organization. This is a conceptual approach in which the Training Manager paints a 'big picture' of sustainable tourism and articulates how each principle and practice within the organization fits into that landscape.

LOCAL ENVIRONMENTAL AND CULTURAL AWARENESS INTEGRATION

An elegant induction program will continuously infuse comparisons of the organization's culture with that of the local environment to emphasize the similarities that make the two systems seem as one. This has a twofold benefit. First, it enhances and reinforces cultural awareness on the part of each participant. Second, it reassures each individual that the leadership of that organization respects the psychological validity of personal cultural values. The goal of this orientation process is to fully embrace group similarities and respect individual identities.

CREATING A STRONG SENSE OF COMMUNITY ATTACHMENT

Training managers who represent STOs will take extra care to ensure that orientation sessions are consistent with the values of the host community. This is done through language, gestures, meeting formats, attire and proxemics (space/distance/ formality issues). The goal of an STO orientation should be the appearance that the values of the organization reflect those of the host community. The overriding theme of this orientation approach should be to reinforce the concept that the organization is a composite of the community and exists as a contributing citizen of that environment.

LOCAL SPECIFIC CORPORATE CULTURE

Most operations within host countries are part of larger corporate entities, with some being multinational in scope. One strategy employed by sustainable tourism-based organizations is the creation of 'hybrid' corporate cultures at the operations level within specific host countries. In addition to creating a relationship of positive corporate citizenship at the community level, this strategy facilitates a local identity that is consistent with the values of most host country nationals. Again, the articulation of the relationship from local community to a global scale requires a conceptual approach on the part of the Training Manager. Inductees should be assimilated into a local corporate identity in terms of values, attitudes and beliefs and then be shown the ripple effect of that identity on regional, national and ultimately global levels within the corporation.

QUESTIONS FOR DISCUSSION

1. One task of the training department in an organization is to conduct orientation programs. Is this particularly important for an STO? Why?
2. It is no secret that there is a labor crisis in the hospitality industry as well as certain other service sectors. Could orientation training play a role in lessening the crisis? How? Could the practice enhance community relations? How?

MICRO-MODULE 4

STO TRAINING AND DEVELOPMENT STRATEGIES

OBJECTIVES

At the end of this micro-module, the readers will be able to:

- Comprehend local environmental and cultural issues in relation to orientation.
- Apply training that is ongoing; supporting progression, including to managerial levels for locally recruited staff; sensitive to local culture and incorporating the understanding of the application of sustainable tourism practices.

LOCAL TRAINING FOCUS THROUGHOUT THE ORGANIZATION

The key to providing training programs within an STO is to ensure that all processes are consistent with the social norms of the host nation. For instance, corporate training documents may be developed in the local language of the home company and should be converted to the most popularly used languages of the host nation. Facilitators should possess fluency levels of the languages spoken among the majority of trainees. Also, training program design and delivery should meet with the educational customs of the local culture. Seating arrangements and other layout formats for training rooms should resemble educational settings that are familiar to host nationals. Other factors of cultural relevance that should be incorporated into training design would be levels of formality, group dynamics and types of role-play scenarios.

The organization should provide an articulation of progressive training and education policies and opportunities that are made available to various levels of employees. These policies should be made available through employee handbooks, bulletin board postings and meeting announcements. The company should convey an interest in the personal and professional development of its employees. When possible, alliances should be made with appropriate education and social agencies from the local community. Training programs should seek to expand beyond knowledge and skills for the workplace through the offering of 'life-enhancement' training options.

INCORPORATION OF LOCAL VALUES AND CULTURE

Since training initiatives are crucial for STOs, one strategy is to employ 'tandem' training managers (one from the host nation working with one from the home nation of the corporation). At first glance, this appears to be a duplication of salaries. However, this temporary placement strategy could yield the equivalent of five years of assimilated cultures in a period of 1–2 years. With this strategy, the primary directive for the home country trainer would be a process of emersion into the culture of the host country, while the opposite would be the directive of the host nation representative. Within a short period of time, a 'hybrid' training culture would emerge within the STO, resulting in seamless assimilation of all trainees into the new culture, which represents a blending of home and host nation values, attitudes and beliefs. This is a very powerful strategic technique that forms a solid bond between the STO and the host nation community.

DEVELOPMENT PROGRAMS FOR PROMOTIONAL OPPORTUNITIES

Sustainable tourism-based organizations will make every effort to prioritize the development training of local employees who are seeking management positions. In keeping with the 'human capital' aspect of the employment relationship, proactive organizations take steps to identify talented workers for potential career advancement with the organization. The identification process occurs through performance appraisals. Performance appraisals are just one aspect of performance management systems, which combine strategic planning initiatives with performance evaluation criteria. One aspect of this process is to identify individuals within the workplace who possess the desire and potential to pursue career advancement with the organization.

Development programs may be conducted within in the organization (in-house) or through external training activities. Most organizations provide for a combination of internal and external training development programs. There are other aspects to development training in addition to management development programs. In keeping with the 'human capital' approach to worker development, any set of competencies that enhances the worker as a holistic being may be considered to be a form of development. Some organizations refer to these types of programs as human development programs. For instance, certain quick-service restaurants that hire very young workers will assist those workers in earning college degrees. While those college degrees may not be in the field of restaurant management, these programs are offered as employee retention strategies, with the organization benefiting from the human development aspects attributed to the workers, as they progress through their academic training. STOs that provide for human development training are viewed as contributors to the host community, while benefiting from the employment of 'self-actualizing' individuals, even though they may not be ultimately pursuing careers in our industry. These types of programs at the local level encourage a process of lifelong learning for all members of the organization.

IMPLICATIONS OF TRAINING FOR SUSTAINABILITY

While all training processes should be consistent with the local cultural value systems, training content would not be restricted to the local norms. Instead, the local cultural customs training could be used as a benchmark of comparison to the cultural aspects associated with other cultures to provide a holistic sense of cultural diversity training for all members of the staff. This awareness presents opportunities to incorporate principles and practices in sustainable tourism as part of the training process. For instance, skills training in the areas of service and guest relations would be provided from the perspective of global awareness. At the same time, management development programs should include programs aimed at the development of skills in the areas of conflict resolution, leadership and crisis management.

All training should be customized to suit the cultural values of the local community. However, this does not suggest that training programs should be designed in a subjective manner. All training must be standardized to ensure that all employees achieve the same learning outcomes. A significant portion of the training budget should be allocated to management development programs aimed at training for careers rather than specific jobs.

QUESTIONS FOR DISCUSSION

1. Is it possible to run an STO without a serious commitment to training programs? Why?
2. Why is it important for STOs to provide training for careers as opposed to training just for specific jobs?
3. Most operations managers think that training is a waste of money. How might you convince them otherwise using a sustainable tourism-based organization argument?

Micro-module 5

Sustainability Through Performance Standards

Objectives

At the end of this micro-module, the readers will be able to:

- Perceive the importance of participation in developing ethical, adaptable and negotiated performance standards that are appropriate to local context and sustainable principles.
- Know the importance of providing employee support during employment and postemployment through such policies as opportunities for job growth, good quality of personal life (including family) and skills training to aid with future employment.

Professional Management

Professional managers within STOs know that their job is to clearly articulate objective standards for performance up front and to reinforce those standards everyday. Performance standards should reflect the values of the local community as well as those that are consistent with sustainability. Since sustainability exists within the core values of an STO, these organizations tend to operate 'mission-driven' corporations, in which the mission drives all of the important decision-making processes, and items that are not related to that mission are considered to be minor issues. The mission values are communicated throughout the organization via the 'mission statement,' which is a brief written description of the purpose for that organization. It is the responsibility of senior managers to establish and communicate the mission for the corporation. The managers audit the mission on an annual basis to verify its accuracy, given factors from the external environment, which exists outside the organization. The mission should clearly articulate the posture of an organization as possessing the core values of sustainability that ultimately become evident in daily management practices.

Training for Careers Rather than Jobs

While job training will certainly be an important factor in most cultures, the goal of the STO human resource practitioner is to train for careers. A career is a life-time progression of jobs that are more challenging, yet professionally fulfilling. All career development programs should be consistent with the norms for professional life subscribed to within a host nation. For instance, some countries respect positions of authority, so management careers may be acceptable in such an area. In collectivist cultures, most individuals may prefer team-oriented contributory positions. The intended and achieved positions throughout a person's professional life constitute a 'career path' for that person. Human resource practitioners may find it appropriate to develop the career paths of those employed within the STO. In such cases, the practitioner would arrange for development training and succession planning for each interested worker.

ADAPTABLE PERFORMANCE STANDARDS TO LOCAL CONTEXT AND SUSTAINABILITY

One practice that is common among centralized organizations is to establish and enforce consistent standards for performance for all hospitality locations. This may not be suitable for sustainability within a given locale. STOs seek to blend within the local and national environments. Hence, adaptability is the way to do business when it comes to performance expectations and evaluations.

EVALUATION OF HUMAN RESOURCE OPPORTUNITIES

Human resource practitioners scan the environments for resources as part of the planning process for doing business in multinational locations. In the case of human resources, managers are seeking knowledge, skills and abilities that are consistent with the needs of a hospitality organization. STO managers look at this issue from two perspectives. First, they seek those talents that are valued by the organization. The second practice includes providing opportunities for individuals within the community that would not exist in the absence of the hospitality organization. This two-way approach is intended to balance the needs of the organization with those of the local community.

CULTURALLY RELEVANT MOTIVATIONAL AND EVALUATION TECHNIQUES

When applied to the workplace, human motivation is defined as the willingness to perform in a professional capacity. Motivation is influenced by factors such as personality, experience and culture. It is important for human resource practitioners to understand the psychology of individuals and groups of workers. Since the social environment influences motivation, it is necessary for the HR practitioner to understand the cultural norms within the host nation and local communities. Each culture seems to demonstrate behavioral patterns based on value systems concerning issues such as authority figures, formality of interactions, collectivism, individualism and others. Human resource practitioners within STOs strive to create organizational cultures that resemble the community environment through the creation of culturally sensitive policies.

QUESTIONS FOR DISCUSSION

1. Do you think a manager who acts unprofessionally while working in one nation will act differently when transferred to another nation? Why or why not?
2. Are the people in a given community aware of the management practices within the hospitality organizations that do business in that community? Could this have an affect on the reputation of the tourism industry among members of that community?

Micro-module 6

STO Performance Appraisals

Objectives

At the end of this micro-module, the readers will be able to:

* Perceive the importance of participation in developing ethical, adaptable and negotiated performance standards that are appropriate to local context and sustainable principles.
* Appreciate that participation in developing ethical, adaptable and negotiated appraisal standards that are appropriate to local context and sustainable principles are of significant importance.

Introduction

This micro-module presents a systems approach to performance standards and appraisals. When STOs determine performance appraisal criteria at the same time as the development of standards and procedures, the result is a holistic performance management system. A performance management system provides planning, identification and encouragement through the communication of standards, as well as the process for the evaluation of actual performance. The performance management approach is the practice of proactive managers to ensure objective standards and performance evaluation criteria. Reactive organizations often succumb to the negative outcomes of low morale, high employee turnover and decreased productivity associated with subjective management practices. Supervisory subjectivity is the antithesis of the professional management standards subscribed to by sustainable tourism-based organizations.

The purpose of performance measurement is to provide feedback to employees about their performance and to take actions to facilitate improvement, as well as provide recognition of successful performance levels by giving rewards. Actually, this is not a stand-alone process, as some managers would have us believe. Instead, it is a multidisciplinary approach to people management that requires daily observation and communication through coaching, mentoring and disciplinary warnings on the part of the supervisor. The effectiveness of these practices is related to the levels of awareness on the part of the supervisor concerning the service perspective, leadership practice, worker motivation and work life development.

Performance Appraisals

STO human resource practitioners recognize the need for sensitivity to the cultural norms that exist within the host nation and local community. For instance, in some cultures, it may be the expectation for performance standards to be established by the senior managers of the organization and mandated to the staff at large. In other settings, individual employees may possess the expectation of having input to the process of setting organizational standards. To ensure sustainability, it is a generic practice to negotiate certain standards for performance at the host nation organizational level. This is not to say that guidelines established by the home corporate office will be negated, but to some extent it may be appropriate to modify those standards at the local operating level. For instance, in some Polynesian cultures, tattooing is a common practice among individuals of all generations. The corporate home office for the hospitality organization may subscribe to a grooming policy prohibiting tattoos that are visible while wearing a uniform. At the property level in a Polynesian nation, it may be appropriate to disregard this policy in the interest of demonstrating an authentic local appearance by members of the staff.

Savvy human resource practitioners will engage the services of an individual or group of people of high-level social acceptability from the host nation to assist with establishing a set of performance standards that are culturally relative. In most cases, the hospitality enterprise possesses an interest in preserving local cultural customs as part of the 'guest experience.' Hence, a hybrid set of culturally acceptable practices serves the business interests of the enterprise, while providing for cultural sustainability – a double 'win' for the organization and the host community.

In many cases, employees expect to gain performance feedback directly from the immediate manager. However, this is not true in all cultures. In certain societies, it is extremely important for individuals to 'save face,' or maintain levels of dignity in social settings. In such instances, business negotiations follow protocols that preclude person-to-person interactions to avoid potential embarrassment on the part of a given individual. Negotiators in these countries use third-party intermediaries to present messages in an effort to save face for all individuals involved in the business deal. The issue of saving face may be true for performance appraisals as well. Human resource practitioners in certain host nations may elect to provide third-party individuals to share performance feedback on behalf of a given manager, in order to save face for both parties.

STAFF OWNERSHIP OF THE APPRAISAL PROCESS

In certain cultures, the concept of 'psychological ownership' is achieved through participative decision-making activities, such as Management by Objectives. However, participative schemes are not welcomed by the standards of all societies. Absent the practice of participative management, acceptance levels of the appraisal system by the majority of the workers within the organization could create a sense of psychological ownership. Workers seem to be motivated to attain peak performance levels in a work environment that fosters a sense of ownership on the part of the employees.

STAFF PROBLEMS AND GRIEVANCES

As can be expected of any system, employees will occasionally perceive problems with the performance appraisal process. Sometimes, these problems are communicated as perceived unfair treatment, which constitutes workplace grievances. Reactive managers sometimes work from the assumption that all grievances are without merit or frivolous in nature. This is a mistake, since proactive managers know that perception is reality in the mind of the perceiver. Hence, individuals with complaints or grievances must be heard. A performance appraisal process should have a mechanism for the lodging of grievances via a 'due process' policy. STOs are likely to have such a mechanism that provides for third-party hearings, multiple-level reviews and rapid notification of determinations to employees regarding such matters.

In nations that hold 'saving face' as an important value, formal grievance systems may be considered to be contrary to the social norms for behavior. In such cases, the grievance procedure could be replaced with alternative communication processes, such as third-party mediation.

QUESTIONS FOR DISCUSSION

1. Some hospitality organizations provide centralized formal appraisal processes that are applied to all operating properties to ensure consistency throughout the corporation. Would this be an appropriate strategy for an STO? Why?
2. Should an STO human resource practitioner always implement participative decision-making processes within the organization? Why?

MICRO-MODULE 7

STO COMPENSATION AND MOTIVATION

OBJECTIVE

At the end of this micro-module, the readers will be able to:

- Integrate an ethos associated with sustainable tourism into the workplace with critical elements that include such principles as equitable and transparent pay, noncash benefits and empowerment.

INTRODUCTION

As we know from our human resource training, the organization spends a good deal of financial resources to recruit, select, train and develop its employees. Some organizations throw these investments down the drain by failing to realize that simple management activities are required to maintain a staff of satisfied employees. When employees become dissatisfied, they find jobs in other organizations. They sometimes realize later that they had better work lives with the former employer, but by that time it is too late to return to the former place of employment. The particularly sad fact is that the best employees will be the first to leave. In such a case, the organization has spent large dollars in staffing and training activities only to realize later on that they are retaining mediocre workers at best.

When this happens, the shareholders put pressure on the organization to limit its allocation of recruiting and training budgets, since it becomes evident that the managers are wasting money on selecting and developing the skills of employees who simply go to work for the competition. How many times have general managers been heard to say, 'Why should we spend money on employees to prepare them to go work somewhere else?' This is dangerous thinking that serves as an incentive for talented human resource practitioners to seek positions with more proactive organizations. This spiral continues as the HR personnel are replaced with cut-rate semitrained practitioners. In such a case, the company controller proudly notifies the shareholders that expenses in the human resource office have been cut in half and that the training budget has been eliminated altogether.

The scenario is not possible within a sustainable tourism-based organization, since an STO remains focused on the 'big picture' by balancing shareholder interests with those of the community constituents. STOs attract highly trained proactive human resource practitioners, who possess knowledge and skills in the area of employee retention strategies. Further, these practitioners recognize that practices associated with effective employee exit procedures serve as both learning systems for the organization and positive relations vehicles with the community at large.

FAIR COMPENSATION

In typical organizations, compensation practices are primarily driven by labor market variables and competitive practices. There are three basic strategies within this realm of doing business – to become the wage leader, wage 'meeter' or wage laggard. Compensation policies within STOs, however, require more creative thinking on the part of human resource managers to include an overriding mission of enhancing the standard of living for hospitality workers. The opposing force to this type of thinking falls within the realm of organizational labor costs, and the solution lies within the domain of productivity. As workers in hospitality organizations develop the capacity of producing higher levels of outcomes (products and services) by using fewer resources (costs), the result is the ability to 'do more with less.' Over time, the organization will require fewer numbers of individuals in certain positions to accomplish outcomes that meet established quality and quantity standards. When this happens, it is feasible to appropriately compensate more productive workers, which enhances the standard of living for those individuals. These types of organizations encourage 'value-added' managers who continually seek to enhance productivity levels of the workforce.

While productivity improvements would be good for the financial standing of the organization, this strategy could be viewed as being in contrast with local economic interests of a host country. Certain developing nations would expect STOs to provide full employment levels through job opportunities for unemployed individuals. This appears to be in contrast with enhanced productivity strategies, as it could be argued that higher levels of efficiency and effectiveness would cause the elimination of positions within an organization. This scenario produces two strategic opportunities for the STO.

One option would be to enact a strategy aimed at providing employment opportunities to as many individuals as can be supported by the hospitality organization. Since the result of this strategy would be inflated labor costs, the organization would seek to support those expenses through increased pricing or reductions in material resource expenditures. The justification for such a strategy would be the appeasement of local and national employment interests.

Another option could include productivity enhancement strategies coupled with retention policies, such as a commitment to refrain from employee layoffs. In this case, the goal would be to train workers who are displaced by productivity improvements for higher levels of work. Improved systems usually yield new demand for higher-level positions. For instance, an STO could find a way to reduce the number of individuals required to provide room attendant services. The individuals who are displaced by this system could be trained to provide butler services to guests, which would be a higher level of work that provides enhanced 'value' from the guest perspective. Improved guest value perceptions drive justifications for pricing increases. In this case, the organization is able to retain high employment levels with enhanced productivity and higher average daily rates. This type of thinking generates 'spirals' of productivity enhancement that benefits workers and guests, as well as the organization and the economic needs of the local community.

FAIR FINANCIAL BENEFITS

The reason employers offer benefits to employees is to compete with other organizations in the industry and geographical location in terms of creating employee loyalty to the organization. The importance of benefits seems to vary with age groups. For instance, younger workers seem to place less emphasis on retirement benefits than older workers. Workers with families place higher emphasis on family benefits, as opposed to individual benefits, and so on. Also, benefit packages vary dramatically among different global locations on the basis of the perceived role of employers as providers of certain individual and social needs. The main intent of employee benefits is to reward individuals for membership within a specific organization.

The importance of benefits also varies among individuals within various cultures. For instance, social structures that emphasize individual independence may weigh the value of benefits differently than those espousing social collectivism. The perception of 'fairness' of benefit distribution will also vary across cultures. For example, some societies value equal pay and benefits despite length of service or performance levels, while others support seniority and merit differential systems. In some locations, it may be permissible to alter remuneration on the basis of family needs, such as numbers of dependents, while such a consideration could be considered to be preposterous and even illegal in other nations.

JOB STATUS AND PRESTIGE

From a motivational perspective, it is important to note that compensation means different things to different people. The obvious meaning of pay systems is the economic ability to obtain the necessities and perhaps a few luxuries in life. Beyond that, there is a psychosocial aspect of compensation that equates to social status, a means of keeping score with the 'Joneses,' or feelings of psychological self-worth. For those individuals who value personal achievement, growth may be a motivational factor associated with compensation levels. When the scholars tell us 'money is not a motivator,' what they are really saying is that the meaning of money motivates people beyond the money in and of itself.

Certain positions within hospitality organizations possess natural levels of social status and prestige. Most of these are management and professional positions, with compensation levels that exceed those of lower-level positions for the most part. For instance, hotel General Managers are often noted as pillars within a local community and often find they are involved with upper strata social circles. In some developing nations, certain nonsupervisory line positions possess levels of social prestige, usually based on the earning potential of the jobholder or the prominence of the clientele directly served by that jobholder.

PARTICIPATION IN DECISION-MAKING AND SHAREHOLDING ACTIVITIES

It is true that participative decision-making practices enhance employee 'buy-in' to organizational standards and procedures. One exception would be in host nations that have the expectation of high power/distance and low tolerance for the ambiguity that goes hand in hand with decision-making activities. The trick is for human resource practitioners to be aware of the social values of individuals from the local community. Alternative strategies through motivational compensation practices may be employed in those areas where participative processes are not desired by most employees.

In some nations, it is permissible for employees to participate as organizational shareholders through benefits such as employee stock option plans, profit sharing and gain share programs. These forms of compensation can motivate workers to enhance productivity if they clearly understand the relationship of their job duties to the financial outcomes of the organization. In localities that do not condone this form of employee benefit, alternative performance-based incentives such as commissions and bonuses may serve as motivational tools for performance enhancement.

DISCOUNTING AND LIVING CONDITIONS

Astute managers will conduct orientation sessions that demonstrate the overall value of compensation for a jobholder. Using visuals, such as pie charts, the workers are made to realize that direct wages represent just a small portion of the overall earnings when factors such as medical benefits, other insurance and perquisites are added together. In remote locations, it is a common practice to provide staff housing units for employees. Also, meal benefits are commonly provided at nominal or no cost to the workers. These types of benefits significantly reduce living expenses and may be used to attract and retain lower wage–earning workers. It is important to provide safe and comfortable living communities when providing staff housing. Amenities such as laundry facilities, low-cost restaurants and entertainment facilities enhance the quality of life in these communities.

WORK ENVIRONMENT/CONDITIONS

One advantage to working in hospitality organizations is that the environment is usually pristine and luxurious. STOs should take care to ensure that the 'back of the house' reflects the guest areas in terms of sanitation, safety and ambience. Some STOs permit employees to use recreational and entertainment facilities as a benefit of employment. For some workers, these are truly appreciated as they are permitted to use amenity areas that most individual pocketbooks could not afford. These types of benefits are sometimes bundled with wellness programs, which demonstrate that the organization cares for the welfare of its employees.

OTHER FACTORS ASSOCIATED WITH COMPENSATION PRACTICES

Family values are also a very high concern in certain host communities. Human resource practitioners in STOs should consider the impact of employee job duties on family life in these localities. This consideration may lead to a variety of creative employment scenarios such as job share, flextime and day care programs.

A large number of employees within a hospitality organization provide guest services that warrant service charges or gratuities. In some cases, legal regulatory agencies possess jurisdiction over this form of compensation; but most nations leave the regulation of gratuities to the discretion of the hospitality enterprise. As is the case with every other human resource practice, care should be taken to ensure that gratuities and service charges are distributed in a culturally defined fair and consistent manner. A variety of systems such as tip pooling, distribution based on hours worked and station rotation policies may be used to provide equal distribution of gratuities.

Cost-of-living issues are always a concern when constructing compensation strategies. The infrastructure associated with hospitality enterprises in some developing nations could cause shifts in local economies by inflating the overall cost of living, limiting housing supply, increasing demand for leisure industries and other impacts. It is likely that certain economic impacts will be positive, while others may be detrimental to the local population. Compensation managers must consider the big economic picture when forecasting the compensation needs of workers over time.

QUESTIONS FOR DISCUSSION

1. Consider an example of a large resort hotel in a developed nation's metropolitan area versus one located in a remote area of a developing nation. What compensation strategies would be required of the latter that would not be issues in the former?

2. All compensation strategies must be considered with a degree to sensitivity to the host community. How does this potentially impact the motivation of workers from the host nation?

MICRO-MODULE 8

STO EMPLOYEE RETENTION

OBJECTIVE

At the end of this micro-module, the readers will be able to:

- Integrate an ethos associated with sustainable tourism into the workplace with critical elements that include such principles as equitable and transparent pay, noncash benefits and empowerment.

INTRODUCTION

While recruitment and selection activities are aimed at attracting individuals to vacant positions within a hospitality organization, retention strategies focus on keeping talented workers as company employees. A number of human resource substrategies feed into retention outcomes. Compensation practices, for instance, are designed to reward employees for organizational membership and performance. Other strategies include employee relations, recognition programs and career development. Human resource practitioners in STOs should pay close attention to the symptoms that indicate the overall 'health' of the workplace in terms of worker impressions concerning 'quality of work life.'

A number of techniques are used to measure the 'organizational climate,' which consists of the general perceptions of employees concerning the work environment. One indicator of organizational climate is employee morale. Human resource practitioners should continually interact with work groups on an informal daily basis to observe levels of employee morale. A more formal method of identifying worker satisfaction levels is to administer 'attitude surveys' with the majority of the staff and to analyze the findings in terms of workplace strengths and weaknesses. Most sustainable organizations conduct formal surveys at least once per year to identify areas of employee morale that require management interventions. However, it should be noted that some cultures find the activity of questionnaire distribution to be offensive, which could result in poor levels of response, as well as a lack of reliability concerning survey findings.

Another indicator of worker satisfaction is employee 'turnover rates.' By dividing the total number of voluntary and involuntary employee separations by the total employee population, human resource practitioners can calculate turnover rates. While the total rate of turnover may indicate a trend of workplace problems, more succinct analysis is required to pinpoint management intervention areas. Human resource practitioners will identify turnover statistics by position and department to localize specific problem areas within the organization. Perhaps, the most succinct tool for identifying workplace problem areas is through the practice of 'exit interviews,' which are conducted with those individuals who are leaving their positions. A human resource practitioner will meet with an exiting employee prior to the final date of work to engage in a candid and confidential conversation concerning the perceptions of that worker concerning her or his position, department and the overall organization. Of course, this practice should be modified or even eliminated within certain cultures. But in the event the practice is conducive to the local environment, the information would be collated and analyzed to identify trends that may adversely affect employee retention within the organization.

As is the case with all multinational sustainability initiatives, it is possible that the issue of employee turnover may not have merit in certain cultures. For instance, in a nation that values and subscribes to 'lifetime' employment, rates of employee departure are very low. In these cases, employee turnover cannot be considered as a measure of the organization's well-being.

COMPLAINT AND GRIEVANCE PROCEDURES

In certain cases, human resource managers will be surprised to learn that the reason individuals are leaving their positions is due to the perception that they did not have an internal vehicle to voice opinions and concerns about their work activities. For instance, an individual may have encountered problems with other workers that could have been easily solved had the supervisor been aware of the situation. This is an example of a worker 'complaint' about the work environment. Human resource practitioners in STOs proactively establish employee 'Complaint Procedures' for these types of scenarios.

One form of complaint that focuses on the perception of 'unfair treatment' in the workplace is called a 'grievance.' An employee may lodge a grievance in the event that he or she feels is being treated differently than others within the job classification. Again, the human resource department should articulate an established 'Grievance Procedure' for these types of complaints.

Sustainable-based tourism organizations take steps to provide complaint and grievance procedures on different levels from informal to formal activities. On an informal level, all supervisors and managers in the organization are encouraged or required to practice 'open door' policies. This is a mechanism in which individuals with grievances or general complaints may feel free to discuss their situation with the immediate supervisor at the time of occurrence.

On a more formal level, employee handbooks should list the steps in voicing complaints and grievances to third parties within the organization. Usually, employees will be encouraged to pursue this process only after an attempt has been made to resolve an issue at the departmental level. However, in some cases, such as harassment, it may be appropriate to seek the counsel of a third party immediately. In these cases, the third party consists of designated human resource practitioners who are trained in the practice of employee counseling.

While at first face it may seem that complaint and grievance procedures provide focus on the negative aspects of work, they are valuable tools for managers to diagnose perceived injustices in the workplace. It is the duty of human resource practitioners to safeguard retention efforts by continually learning about individual perceptions of the work environment – both good and bad.

Consistent with all of our discussions, local cultural compatibility is the key concern with all STO practices. In the case of grievances, formal processes may not be effective. For instance, in collectivist societies, informal grievances through third parties are more effective than those commonly used in the United States or Europe, as discussed in a previous module.

QUALITY OF LIFE ISSUES

It has been said that hospitality workers live to work, while those in other industries work to live. It is true that the nature of the industry does create a subculture lifestyle owing to hours of operation and the social nature of the business. However, human resource practitioners must realize that each individual possesses a life outside the organization. STO managers are trained to be sensitive to the personal needs of workers in areas such as family responsibilities, health and welfare, rest and relaxation, human development as well as social and economic status. Collectively, these issues and more comprise a topic called 'quality of life.' From a workplace perspective, job positions should provide for the pursuit of life quality through things such as paid vacations, paid holidays, health and welfare benefits, reasonable scheduling practices and human development initiatives. From a holistic perspective, work comprises a large portion of an individual's lifestyle (approximately 2,000 hours per person per year for a full-time worker). This is why human resource practitioners in STOs seek to know the 'whole person' by identifying their life situations, needs, wants and ambitions. They seek to strike that balance between providing quality of life within the workplace and having the workplace contribute to external quality of life issues.

QUALITY OF SUPERVISION

Perhaps, the most important person in the work life of an individual is the direct supervisor. The professional demeanor of that supervisor is the difference between stimulating work and drudgery within a position. It has been said that people do not quit jobs, they just quit other people. This refers directly to the way individuals are treated by their immediate supervisor. For this reason, the hospitality organization possesses an ethical duty to provide 'professional management' within the workplace.

Professional managers are those who are thoroughly trained to perform in the capacity of leadership. These managers must possess the technical, relational and conceptual skills associated with leading other people. In STOs, management training should also include applied psychology, interpersonal communication skills as well as team-building and leadership skills. Sustainable-based tourism organizations ensure that an individual is thoroughly trained to act as a professional manager before placing that person in a supervisory position. This is in contrast to the haphazard promotion of individuals who have demonstrated good technical skills to simply fill a supervisory vacancy. In the case of the latter, the hospitality organization is contributing to its own increase in employee turnover.

COMPANY POLICIES

The executive management team must support all activities within the organization. The way this is done is through corporate missions that feed into objectives and strategies for direction of the hospitality enterprise. At the operating level, these strategies are converted into policies, standards and procedures to guide every worker within the hospitality organization.

In STOs, the general policies of the organization take into account the strategies for sustainability. These strategies are then converted into human resource policies similar to those mentioned above. Mission-driven sustainable hospitality organizations will ensure that all human resource policies feed into the ultimate objective of social and cultural assimilation. In practice, this involves professional people management within a holistic paradigm that balances the needs of the organization and the individuals who interact with the enterprise.

QUESTIONS FOR DISCUSSION

1. What are the benefits of professional management within an STO?
2. How should a human resource practitioner from the United States modify retention practices for an STO doing business in Japan?

Micro-module 9

STO Employee Exit Process

Objective

At the end of this micro-module, the readers will be able to:

- Recognize the impacts on individuals, families and vulnerable local communities of separation in less-privileged societies.

Introduction

Human resource practitioners spend most of their time and energy attracting and retaining quality workers. However, they must also practice professional procedures for employee exit from the hospitality organization in order to preserve sustainability as good community citizens. While the goal of every good human resource practitioner is to minimize employee turnover, it is not desirable to bring that statistic to a level of zero. The reason for this is that individuals from the outside environment reenergize those who have been with the corporation for a while. For instance, if all senior managers within a hospitality operation are promoted from within the organization and stay in place for many years, the scope of thinking among that group would begin to become closed, since all members are from the same internal environment. If new members are added to that group once in awhile, ideas from outside the organization are introduced. New ways of looking at issues revitalizes the thinking process within groups of decision makers. The same dynamic is true at every level of the organization. So, reasonable levels of employee turnover are actually rejuvenating for the STO. Since employee turnover is a fact of organizational life, the human resource practitioner must become adept at providing professional exit procedures for those seeking new opportunities with other organizations.

Voluntary Exit

Individuals who chose to leave the organization on their own free will are considered to be 'voluntary separations.' In most cultures, it is appropriate for these people to give reasonable notice of the intent to leave their positions within the organization. This gives the managers of the organization time to replace the vacated position. One of the finalization procedures for these individuals is a formal meeting with a human resource representative to discuss the reasons for leaving the organization, as well as to find out the perceptions of that person regarding the experiences of being employed with the organization. This is really a fact-finding process, in which the human resource practitioner follows a pattern of open-ended questioning used to ascertain the thoughts and feelings of the exiting individual.

A secondary purpose of the exit interview meeting is to generate positive final impressions on the part of the exiting employee concerning the organization. This is important because the departing individual will become a spokesperson as an alumnus of the organization. One goal of sustainability is positive public relations within the industry and the general community at large. Hence, the goal of the human resource practitioner is for people to exit the organization with positive impressions to be shared with other individuals outside the organization.

Immediately upon the completion of the exit interview, the human resource practitioner will record all observations to include actual quotes from the interviewee as well as intuitive impressions from the interaction. This information could be entered into a database for an analysis of trends that indicate the positive and negative perceptions of separating employees about their experiences with the organization. Human resource practitioners will use the information to reinforce those positive impressions (strengths) and correct negative perceptions (weaknesses), in an effort to improve the workplace environment.

As mentioned in a previous module, exit interview procedures are only effective in those nations that find the practice to be appropriate for workers and organizations. Some cultures find this practice to be embarrassing and offensive. In such cases, the exit interview process should be modified or abandoned by the STO. The key to all STO functions is compatibility with the value system of the host nation.

Involuntary Exit

There will hopefully be few cases in which individuals will be asked to leave their positions with the hospitality organization. These cases result from either chronic poor performance or incidents of misconduct on the part of that employee. While such a scenario is unpleasant for the exiting worker, human resource practitioners realize that these cases support the overall welfare of the organization and those people who do perform in accordance with expectations.

Human resource practitioners in STOs realize the severity of such an action in the mind of the person being separated. That person is being released from a microsocial environment, which is like being banished from a society. Also, that person is losing a source of financial income, which equates into an economic survival issue. The goal of the human resource practitioner in such cases is to mitigate the sense of loss and to maintain that person's sense of dignity. It is important for practitioners to remember that the person being released is not a 'bad person.' He or she was simply unable to comply with the standards for employment.

In some nations, involuntary exit from an organization is not an option. Certain societies subscribe to 'lifetime' employment values where losing a job would be considered to be an unbearable disgrace to an individual. Cases of performance problems in some of these cultures require managers to move individuals into positions that are consistent with the worker's abilities. Some social value systems support the movement of a worker into a position with no responsibilities at all. While this scenario will cause the worker to 'lose face,' it is still preferred to the level of disgrace associated with involuntary separation from the company.

The exit interview in these situations should include an opportunity for the separated employee to share his or her impressions concerning the organization prior to the incident that caused separation, as well as to voice their impressions of the situation leading to termination. Prior to this point, there should have been an opportunity for the employee to provide testimony in his or her defense. This is referred to as 'due process,' which should be provided to employees as part of a 'covenant of good faith and fair dealing' on the part of the organization. The purpose of giving one more opportunity to voice a defense on the part of departing employee is simply for that person to be heard once again by a human resource practitioner. If the due process was handled correctly, the employee should understand the issues resulting in the separation. Why do practitioners invest this time and energy into an involuntary separating employee? The objective here is for that person to leave the organization with a sense that he or she was listened to and that the organization was fair in dealing with the situation. Where appropriate, the human resource practitioner may offer to assist with outplacement services in such cases.

GRIEVANCE PROCEDURES

Sustainable organizations should uphold a policy of providing procedures to hear employee complaints and grievances. One of the questions that should be asked of employees with negative perceptions of their experience with the organization is whether they pursued these procedures prior to deciding to leave the organization. Sometimes, the employee will experience a less-than-favorable decision regarding a grievance. The STO should ensure that such matters result in a clear and convincing description as to why a grievance was not upheld. This determination should be a matter of record that could be reinforced at the exit interview. In cases where a person did not use the procedure, it should be clarified that the procedure was communicated clearly and that the organization wishes that the person had used the vehicle for articulating the nature of their discontent.

As discussed in a previous module, grievance procedure format and formality levels will vary across cultures. STO human resource managers should be prepared to modify or even abandon such practices in localities that do not support such policies.

SUMMARY

Some managers may contend that exit procedures are a waste of time and money. Managers in STOs realize the importance of positive community relations. It should be remembered that all employees are members of that community and will share their perceptions of employment experiences with other citizens. For these reasons, the hospitality organization must be viewed as being fair, uniform and consistent in all dealings with its employees. It would be unrealistic to expect that all individuals will leave the organization with positive opinions. However, if the organization does business in a fair and impartial professional manner, the majority of personal opinions will be positive in nature. These opinions collectively impact the status of the organization as a member of the community. Positive community relations contribute to organizational sustainability.

UNCITED REFERENCES

Clarke, J., 2002. A synthesis of activity towards the implementation of sustainable tourism: ecotourism in a different context. Int. J. Sustain. Dev. 5 (3), 232–239.

Hobson, K., Essex, S., 2001. Sustainable tourism: a view from accommodation business. Serv. Ind. J. 21 (4), 133–146.

Risko, V.J., 2002. Preparing teachers for reflective practice: intentions, contradictions, and possibilities. Lang. Arts 80 (2), 134–145.

Tesone, D.V., 2003. Human Resource Management for the Hospitality Industry: How the Practitioners Do It. Pearson-Prentice Hall, Boston, MA.

Glossary of Terms

180 degrees model	A review system that includes subordinates review of the supervisor.
360 degrees model	Holistic appraisal feedback from subordinates, supervisors and peers.
Acceptance	Accept challenges, accomplishments and failures as learning opportunities.
Accountability	Measurement of authority and responsibility exercised through actual performance.
Accounting information systems (AIS)	Computer networks that are used to report business transactions and economic events that occur within a hospitality enterprise.
Accounts payable (AP)	A journal that tracks the payment of bills owed to suppliers of material resources such as goods, equipment and supplies.
Accounts receivable (AR)	A journal that tracks entries pertaining to credit transactions with clients who owe payment to the hospitality enterprise at some future point in time.
Action research	An informal process of data collection, analysis, alternative solution generation, intervention selection, implementation and evaluation to solve organizational problems.
Altered status	An internal state resulting from change.
Alternatives	Viable options for selecting problem solutions based on analysis.
An organization	A collection of individuals brought together to achieve a common goal.
Applicant pool	The pool of individuals demonstrating interests in seeking vacant positions who are placed into the selection process to determine fitness for hire based on KSAAs.
Assimilate	Adapt to an environment and its people.
Authority	The right to perform or delegate tasks, duties and responsibilities.
Autocratic management	Centralized decision making by senior level managers without input from others in the organization.
Awareness	A phase during contemplative practice that transcends self-awareness temporarily to gain insights from non-local sources of information.
Awareness	An objective sense of self in given moments.
Balanced scorecard	An X and Y axis representing qualitative and quantitative performance criteria.
Bandwidth	Speed of transmission over telecommunication channels as measured in bits per second.
Basic leadership styles	Categories that include, but are not limited to, autocratic, participative, telling, selling, persuasive, delegating and laissez-faire leadership styles.

Behavioral approaches	Appraisal method that focuses on specific observable behaviors.
Behaviorally Anchored Rating Scale (BARS)	Behavioral approach using standardized practices.
Being your word	Congruence among being, acting and preaching.
Beyond physical senses	Invoking a 'mental eye' to access non-local sources of information.
Booking transactions	Reserve space for future use, which may include a confirmation deposit rendered to a hotel, or full payment for a cruise or flight at the time the reservation is transacted.
Brainstorming	Group decision-making activity used to generate creative ideas to solve problems.
Business ethics	A branch of normative philosophy applied to business decisions and behaviors.
Business strategies	Strategies initiated by specific business units.
Camaraderie	Like-minded individuals working as teams.
Capital intensive	Large amounts of capital dollars are spent on the assets of each hospitality enterprise.
Cash management	The balance of receipts and disbursements of cash flows for the organization.
Category rating method	An appraisal model listing items by categories.
Celebrate accomplishments	Be good to yourself and let others be good to you for all that you learn and all you do.
Central tendency	Forcing individuals into a normative grouping.
Centralized decision making	Decisions are made at the top of the organization and passed down; common within tall organizations.
Change	Keep in tune with the environment, it is always changing.
Change agentry	The process of enacting systematic change.
Change agents	Internal (inside the organization) and external (outside the organization) change interventionists.
Characteristics	The culmination of observed qualities and traits.
Charisma	Appearance and actions that are congruent with a mental model.
Charismatic leadership	A congruence of appearance with external mental models that foster positive emotional states among potential followers.
Checklist methods	An appraisal method in which the reviewer checks appropriate categories.
Checks and balances	A procedure of separating the order and entry points for purchases.
Chemical interactions	Electro-chemical patterns of energy exchanged during moments of interaction.
Classical management	Early engineering approaches that did not consider human factors involved with work.
Climate	Includes present worker attitudes, management proficiency and transformational systems.
Closed system	An entity consisting of related parts that is not influenced by outside forces.
Codes of ethics	Formal statements providing guidelines for ethical behavior.
Cognitive dissonance	An internal value conflict in response to an environment representing those ideologies that are contrary to an individual's self-awareness.
Collaborative teams	Cohesiveness of interdepartmental workers collaborating to achieve mutually beneficial and synergistic outcomes.

Communication	Sharing information and meaning with other individuals.
Communication	The exchange of ideas and meaning among individuals and groups.
Communication	The sharing and understanding of information among individuals.
Community	Outside stakeholders who are not within other stakeholder groups.
Comparative methods	An appraisal method that compares individuals with their peers.
Competencies	Combined knowledge, skills and abilities of human resources.
Complexity	Large number of variables influencing a problem.
Complications	A state of internal disorder arising from reflection of complex issues.
Conceptual skills	The ability to articulate and influence workers toward achieving the mission and vision of the organization.
Congruence	Sameness of appearance, manner and words.
Constructive conflict	Divisive interactions yielding positive outcomes.
Content theories	Theories describing what might motivate individuals.
Contingency leadership	The recognition that environmental factors must be considered during leadership moments.
Contingency planning	Pre-planned interventions based on 'what-if' analysis.
Contrast error	Comparisons to subjective criteria.
Control	Tasks that ensure that actual performance meets established standards for performance.
Control function	The comparison of actual performance to standards for performance.
Corporate strategies	Broad strategies for the overall organization.
Credit transactions	Sales are posted to an account that includes terms and conditions for future cash payment.
Critical incident method	A method of recording important observations for later formal appraisal recollection.
Critical path method	The concurrent and consecutive steps to implement an intervention, with duration determined by the single longest step.
Customer loyalty	A measurement of the strength of an ongoing customer relationship.
Customer relationships	Continuing patterns of interactions with new and repeat guests and clients.
Customer relationships	Interactions and transactions that result in relationships among customers and members of the staff.
Customer service	Interactions between workers and customers measured in terms of intimacy (levels of service) and duration (length of service).
Customers	A stakeholder group consisting of those who purchase products and services.
Data collection	The process of accumulating facts and assumptions as the first phase of an intervention or planning process.
Databases	Systems with storage, manipulation and query interfaces that convert data into useable information.
Decentralized decision making	Individuals share authority and responsibility for decisions; common within flat organizations.
Decision making	Choosing from alternative problem solutions.

Delegation	The granting of authority, autonomy and responsibility to another.
Delegation	The process of assigning both authority and responsibilities to individuals.
Delphi technique	A panel of experts who anonymously respond to question-naires until consensus is reached.
Department managers	Managers with spans of authority over a division as deter-mined by function, product, geographic location, brand or project.
Departmental collaboration	Shared efforts to coordinate activities among department managers.
Dependence	Reliance of a sub-system on a system.
Development	Provides abilities required for future promotional opportu-nities within the organization.
Development	The process of growth into new evolutionary mental and emotional states of self-awareness.
Diagnosis analysis	The process of analyzing facts and assumptions accumu-lated during data collection for the purpose of identifying core problems.
Diagnostic interviews	Discussions with individuals to identify symptoms.
Diagnostics	Consist of identifying and prioritizing symptoms that ultimately fit into a pattern that defines a problem.
Diagnostics	Data collection and analysis to identify personalities, moti-vators and emotional triggers residing within the psyche of others.
Differences	The interactions that occur when individuals with diver-gent or conflicting mental and emotional models attempt to collaborate.
Disciplinary warning	A documented warning notifying a worker to alter behaviors.
Discipline	Training to achieve desired behaviors.
Disorganization	Failure to coordinate activities around a department.
Distress	Individual negative reactions to stressors.
Effectiveness	Metrics used to evaluate outcomes in terms of quantity and quality.
Effectiveness	The process of enhancing the quality and/or quantity of produced outputs.
Efficiency	Metrics used to evaluate inputs in terms of costs of goods sold.
Efficiency	Results when outputs are achieved using fewer inputs.
Electro-chemical communication	Projection and reception of energy patterns.
Electronic commerce	Systems that permit business-to-business (B2B) and business-to-customer (B2C) interfaces for the purpose of conducting commercial transactions.
Empathetic	The ability to communicate with the same emotional sensibility of the individual who is the recipient of the communication.
Empathy	The ability to internally identify with emotional states that exist within another individual.
Employee relations	Strategies aimed at improving the retention and lessening the turnover of employees.
Employee relations	Workplace practices aimed at ensuring the integrity of agreed upon terms, conditions, rights and privileges associated with employment and enhancing employee development.

Employee retention	Employees who remain with the company over a period of 1 year.
Employee retention	Those employees who choose to remain with an organization during an annual metric period.
Employee turnover	Voluntary and involuntary separation from an organization.
Employees	A stakeholder group consisting of the workers for an organization.
Energy exchanges	Projection and reception of electro-chemical communication on subconscious levels.
Energy patterns	Sensations of resonance that are experienced during deep contemplative states, sometimes appearing as swirls of multi-colored light impressions.
Environmental scanning	Data collection from the environment outside the organization.
Equity theory	Process theory that indicates individuals will behave in various manners when there is an inequity of treatment in the workplace.
ERG	Existence, relatedness and growth needs.
Essay appraisal	A written narrative describing strengths and areas for improvement regarding performance.
Ethics committees	Employees from multiple departments who create and maintain codes of ethics and hear ethical complaints.
Eustress	Individual positive reactions to stressors.
Evaluation and revision	A process of measuring progress and taking corrective actions based on the timelines established by a strategic plan during the implementation phase.
Expectancy theory	A process theory that considers the task, the effort, the reward for performance, the value of that reward and the likeliness of the worker receiving the reward.
Experience	Visceral engagement in environmental stimuli that results in knowledge after a period of reflection that influences self-awareness.
External change agents	Consultants brought in from outside the organization.
External customers	Those individuals who choose to purchase products and services from an organization.
External forces	Influencing factors from the external environment that are beyond the control of the organization.
Extranets	Proprietary systems replicating Internet structures to permit access to an organization for invited external entities.
Extrinsic rewards	Rewards of a material nature that come from sources external to the individual.
Factors of influence	The leader, the followers, the situation (environment), individual differences and emotional triggers are all factors that influence leadership effectiveness.
Feasibility studies	Data collection and analysis of pro-forma growth probabilities.
Financial management system (FMS)	Uses mathematical models to analyze and report on the financial planning aspect of the hospitality enterprise.
Fix strategies	Objectives and actions aimed at problem solving in organizations.
Fix strategy	Interventions to turnaround a work unit that is experiencing significant problems.
Fix strategy	Turnaround an underperforming department.
Forecast	A process to determine likely future scenarios.
Formal appraisal	Systematic written performance evaluation and feedback.
Formal groups	Groups established by the organization.
Functional organizational structure	Departments and reporting relationships are categorized by functions (accounting, operations, marketing, etc.)

Functional strategies	Strategies implemented by functional units.
Gangplank	Means for individuals to interact laterally across departments without having to run up and down the scalar chain.
Gatekeepers	Individuals who guard access and influence opinions of executive managers.
General ledger (GL)	A journal that consolidates data received from other journals that contain data from specialized accounting functions.
Gigabytes	Ten times the capacity of a megabyte.
Goals and objectives	Targets for performance.
Grapevine	A type of informal communication also called the rumor mill.
Graphic rating scales	Numerically scored appraisals.
Groupthink	Overly cohesive groups that believe they are invincible and members stop questioning processes and decisions.
Groupthink	Phenomena of group invincibility perception resulting in lack of challenges to ideas and poor decision-making activities.
Groupware applications	Shared application programs.
Growth strategy	Expand current operations.
Growth strategies	Objectives and actions aimed at organizational expansion.
Growth strategies	Plans for expansion.
Halo effect	A focus on a single issue that influences an entire rating.
Harmonic waves	Energy pattern compatibility.
Health	General state of well-being that is free from dysfunction.
Hierarchy of needs	Theory that there exists an order of needs from low to high, requiring portions in lower order needs to be satisfied prior to higher order needs and acting as motivators for an individual.
Historical research	Theoretical descriptive constructs identifying trait, charismatic, contingency, situational, other forms of transactional and transformational leadership concepts.
Human capital	Human resource management thinking that suggests workers are worthy of the organization's investment in development to become corporate assets.
Human capital	The belief that the development of workers will add value to an organization.
Human resource management	Area of management focusing on human capital enhancement within organizations.
Human resource strategies	Objectives and actions aimed at the maintenance and development of human capital levels within an organization.
Humility	A grounded sense of self relative to others.
Implementation	The execution of a strategic plan.
Independence	Free-standing sub-systems with no reliance on any other system.
Individual motivation	Unfulfilled wants, needs and desires along with emotional perceptions within an individual.
Individuality of followers	Personalities, emotional triggers and perceptions within individuals who comprise a follower group.
Informal appraisal	Informal feedback on performance.
Informal communications	Communications that do not have a business purpose.
Informal groups	Groups that naturally develop without organizational design.
Information loops	Patterns of interfaces used for communication among individuals and groups.
Information systems	Interrelated systems that convert data into useable information.
Integrity	Behaviors congruent with one's words.
Interaction	Communication exchanges among individuals and groups.
Interaction	Verbal, non-verbal and emotional exchanges among individuals and groups.

Interdependence	Patterns of relationships that are neither reliant nor independent.
Interdependency	A state of mutual dependence and independence existing at the same time.
Interdependent	The highest level of relationship with sub-systems that is achievable by an individual or other sub-system. It is beyond the levels of dependence and independence.
Interfaces	Unconscious mental attachment to non-local sources of information.
Internal audits	Data collection process of variables inside the organization.
Internal change agents	Managers of change who work within the organization.
Internal customers	Workers within an organization who use the products and services of other workers to interact with external customers.
Internal dialogue	Self-talk, perception, reflection through contemplation.
Internal process	Processes occurring within an individual that are not observable to third parties.
Internal processes	The contemplative process of quieting the conscious mind in a state of relaxation to permit entry into non-local sources of information.
Intervention implementation	A stepwise critical path of intervention activities.
Intervention planning	Strategic problem-solving approach.
Intervention strategies	Objectives and actions aimed at solving organizational problems through initiating a critical path of successive changes.
Internet	Interconnected public domain systems linking servers throughout the world, using Internet service providers (ISPs) and search engines.
Intranets	Private Internet-like programs for organizations.
Intranets	Proprietary systems replicating Internet structures for internal use within an organization or institution.
Intrinsic knowing	Non-local information coming into self-awareness.
Intrinsic rewards	Rewards or meaning of rewards generated from the internal perspective of an individual.
Introspection	Ability to objectively examine self-awareness.
Job analysis	Part of job design that analyzes tasks, duties, responsibilities, work environment and confidentiality requirements associated with a position of employment.
Job analysis	The systematic process of data collection and analysis of tasks, duties, responsibilities and working environments for each position within the organization.
Job description	A document containing general and specific tasks, duties and responsibilities, work environment, legal accommodation and specific performance measurement criteria.
Job descriptions	The listing of tasks, duties, responsibilities and reporting relationships of the job holder for each position within an organization.
Job enlargement	Giving a worker added responsibilities or duties.
Job enrichment	Giving a worker more status, autonomy and authority.
Job enrichment	The granting of autonomy, authority, along with responsibility at higher levels for individuals.
Job rotation	Moving people among various similar jobs.
Job specifications	The listing of qualifications for a position based on KSAAs.

371

Kilobytes	1,026 bytes of data.
Knowledge management system	A formalized system of accumulating and disseminating new knowledge throughout the organization.
Knowledge, skills, abilities and attitudes	KSAAs, those qualities possessed by employees
KSAAs	Knowledge, skills, attitudes and abilities; those qualities possessed by potential and current employees.
Labor intensive	Payroll expenses are extremely high relative to other service industry providers.
Labor law	State and federal regulations and tort doctrines applied to employment relationships.
Labor relations	A body of law with focus on the right of individuals to elect union representation and engage in collective bargaining processes.
Lateral communication	Horizontal communication channels within a level of the organization chart.
Leaders	Individuals who possess the power to influence others.
Leadership	The ability to influence others to willingly follow.
Leadership	The demonstrated ability to influence others to willingly participate in activities.
Leadership	The power to influence others to willingly take action. In management it is the willingness of individuals to accomplish the objectives of the organization.
Leadership being	An internal self-awareness of who an individual is relative to the dogma of leadership and who that person is being during leadership moments.
Leadership development	The evolution to higher levels of leadership ability.
Leadership flexibility	The ability of the leader to assimilate to changes in the environment. The 'chameleon' approach to leadership.
Leadership style	A leader's preferred approach to leading under normal circumstances.
Leadership style preference	A leader's preferred approach to leadership given normal circumstances.
Leadership training	The process of imparting leadership knowledge and skills.
Leading	Leaders in the practice of exercising power to influence others.
Learned versus natural leadership	Knowledge and skill acquisition, as opposed to innate gifted abilities.
Learning	The enactment of enhanced self-awareness through reflection upon new knowledge and experiences.
Learning	The enactment of permanent change within an individual.
Learning system	Feedback loop that converts shared experiences into knowledge that is used to further enhance production.
Learning systems	Collective intelligent capital possessed by workers in the organization used for process improvement.
Legal compliance	Strategies that use the knowledge of the legal environment and employment law to protect the assets of an organization from potential legal damages.
Like-minded thinking	Interactions that occur when two or more individuals of similar mental and emotional awareness models collaborate.

Limited power	Restricted availability of power-bases used to influence others. For instance, the limited ability to motivate another person requires offering a catalyst for an individual to become motivated from within.
Line and staff managers	Operations managers (line) and support managers (staff).
Line and staff workers	Line workers produce products or services and generate revenue. Staff workers support the line workers.
Line authority	The right to direct operational activities that generate products or services or revenue.
Local area networks (LAN)	Small interconnected systems in limited physical locations.
Locus of control (higher)	The mental belief that one is able to influence self-destiny.
Locus of control (low)	The mental belief that one is not in control of self-destiny.
Long-term objectives (LTO)	Organizational goals that will take 1 year or more to accomplish.
Machiavellian	The belief that leaders are born and not made.
Macro-system	External environment that surrounds a system.
Management	Accomplishing the objectives of the organization through the activities of others.
Management	The accomplishment of an organization's objectives through the activities of others.
Management by objectives (MBO)	Top/down, bottom/up goal setting at every level of the organization.
Management communication	The process of exchanging meaning among individuals and groups.
Management control	The use of metrics to compare actual performance with standards for performance in an organization.
Management development	Training to enhance the current levels of management skills in preparation for improved management ability and higher levels of responsibility within the organization.
Management diagnosis	Identifying symptoms in an organization to determine significant problems.
Management functions	Planning, organizing, influence and control.
Management responsibility	Assuming responsibility for an area of authority.
Management risk	Engaging in behaviors that may be detrimental to a manager's standing in an organization.
Management rites and rituals	Informal and formal cultural norms for celebrations and recognition.
Management style	The overall approach that an individual uses in the performance of management activities.
Management training	Imparting knowledge and skills in the areas of management functions and practices to enhance the ability for managers to accomplish the objectives of the organization through the activities of others.
Management training	Imparting skills in the functions of planning, organizing, influence and control.
Management turnover	Managers who voluntarily and involuntarily separate from positions with an organization.

Management universality	Premise that management is an art and a science that has applications across all industrial boundaries.
Manager's handbook	Responsibility reference guides for managers.
Marketing	Function of acquiring and maintaining guests and clients.
Meaning system	The organizational culture that generates unwritten norms for behavior in the workplace.
Meaning systems	Interpretation of the organizational values combined with internal value and belief systems of workers that influence workplace motivation.
Mechanistic lifecycles	The path of inception through non-existence associated with mechanistic systems.
Mechanistic systems	Systems comprised of mechanical mechanisms and structures.
Megabytes	Ten times the capacity of a kilobyte.
Mental and emotional growth	The evolution to higher levels of awareness concerning the mental and emotional models of the self.
Mentoring	Coaching relationships between mentors (experienced professional managers) and protégés (learners of management) aimed at developing management skills.
Mentoring	Protégés and senior leaders engaged in informal developmental relationships.
Mentoring	Protégés working with more senior leaders for coaching on leadership development.
Metropolitan area networks (MAN)	Broad interconnected systems in unlimited physical locations.
Micro-managers	Managers who closely observe the actions of the workers, while refusing to delegate autonomy or authority to them.
Middle management	Management level below the senior executives and above the supervisory managers.
Mismanagement	Negligence in managing to a reasonable standard.
Mission	The purpose and values of the organization based on its current existence.
Modeling	Emulating the visible behaviors of professional managers.
Motivation	A willingness to take action to satiate unfulfilled needs, wants and desires.
Mutual outcomes	Multiple party benefits from collaboration.
Negative reinforcement	Removing something unpleasurable in response to a desired behavior.
Networks	Interconnected systems with multiple users.
New science	Quantum investigation of phenomena beyond empirical scientific method.
New science management	Quantum theories applied to organizational systems thinking.
Nominal group technique	A form of brainstorming that assures equal participation in consensus decision making.
Non-programmed decisions	One-of-a-kind decisions that lack structure.
Objective	A target for performance.

Objective witness
Internal observation from the standpoint of objectivity that is similar to a third party witness.

Observable qualities
Those aspects of an individual that are observable to a third party through behaviors.

Open system
An entity consisting of related parts that is influenced by outside forces called the external environment.

Opportunities and threats
Categories for listing external variables based on potential consequences to the organization.

Organic systems
Natural systems comprised of biological/chemical entities and cellular structures.

Organization charts
Representations of spans of authority, responsibility and reporting relationships within an organization.

Organizational behavior
The study of individual and group behaviors within organizations.

Organizational climate
Opinions of individuals concerning the organizational culture.

Organizational climate
Perception of workers concerning the general state of the organization.

Organizational culture
Shared attitudes, values and beliefs among members of an organization.

Organizational development (OD)
A process of systematic change aimed at continuous organizational renewal.

Organizational development
An approach of systemic change interventions aimed at organizational renewal.

Organizational mission
The purpose and values of the organization based on its current existence.

Organizational vision
The potential purpose and values of the organization at some point in the future.

Organizing
Coordinating activities within and outside the department.

Organizing function
Coordinating activities within and outside the department.

Outside consultants
Management experts hired from outside the firm.

Paradigm shift
A change in foundational mental models.

Passion
A positive emotional yearning to perform a task at hand.

Pay for performance
Merit compensation systems that reward objective measurements of performance in organizations.

Payroll (PR)
An account used to monitor the payment of salaries and wages, as well as deductions that are placed in accounts to pay federal, state and local payroll taxes and benefit contributions.

Perception
Objective witnessing of non-local phenomena during deep contemplative states. Sometimes they include facial impressions of unknown individuals.

Performance appraisal
Comparison of actual performance to standards for performance.

Performance assessment
Compare actual performance to standards (same as evaluation).

Performance assessment
The metrics used to evaluate actual performance to standards for performance.

Performance management system
Clearly established expectations for performance and honest, objective feedback on how well an employee meets those expectations.

Performance standards	An objective and measurable list of performance criteria used as the benchmark for comparing actual performance with outcomes ranging from 'does not' to 'exceeds the standards'.
Permanent change	The intrinsic result of learning, in which the individual has altered the thinking process on a permanent basis.
Personality	Preferences of response to environmental stimuli.
Piece-rate compensation	Pay per unit of work produced (outputs).
Planning	A strategic approach used to achieve future objectives.
Policies	Broad guidelines for performance
Positive reinforcement	Giving something pleasurable in response to a desired behavior.
Post-change stabilization	The return to a state of organizational equilibrium after the disruptive stages of change interventions.
Practice it right away	If you don't use it, you will surely lose it.
Pride	A positive sense of self.
Primary storage	Hard coded information residing on machine chips such as read only memory (RAM) and random access memory (RAM).
Proactive	Strategic thinking used to prevent problems from occurring.
Problem	A negative gap between actual performance and performance standards.
Problem analysis	Identifying causal relationships involving of potential problems.
Problem categories	Classification of problems to include material resources, people and transformation systems. All problems fall within one, two or all three categories, with the majority being systems problems.
Problem identification	Analyzing symptoms to determine real problems.
Problem identification	The analysis of symptoms used to determine core negative gaps between actual performance and standards for performance in an organization.
Problem solution	The selection of the most viable existing alternative for problem resolution based on measures of effectiveness and efficiency.
Problems	Negative gaps between actual performance and standards for performance in an organization.
Procedures	Daily action steps used to meet standards.
Process improvement	Dissection and revision of subroutines to improve overall processes.
Process theories	Theories describing how managers might motivate employees.
Productivity	A linear system of inputs (resources) placed into a transformation process to yield outcomes in the forms of products and services. The linear process is surrounded by non-linear, invisible factors to include meaning and learning systems, which serve as dynamic feedback loops.
Productivity	The linear system of inputs that flow into transformation processes to yield outcomes in the form of products and services that is surrounded by non-linear, invisible meaning and learning loops.
Productivity process	A process of tracking activities from input through output stages to improve the learning and meaning systems influences.
Programmed decisions	Highly structured routine decisions.
Purchase order (PO)	Authorization for accounts payable to pay for a specific invoice after the goods are received by the hospitality organization.
Purchasing agents	Individuals responsible for acquiring material resources.
Purchasing managers	Individuals responsible for acquiring material resources.
Put it into practice	Practice while you learn. Practice while you earn. Practice it for free. Just practice constantly.

Quality of life	Perception of a positive lifestyle.
Quality of work life	Perception of positive existence in a work environment.
Quality standards	Specifications for each service or product produced.
Quantity standards	Number of outputs produced in a timely manner.
Quid pro quo	Something of value exchanged for something of value.
Ranking method	An appraisal method in which all employees in a work unit are rated from first through last.
Rater bias	Personal attributes influencing the rater.
Rater error	Statistical error on the part of a rater causing an appraisal instrument to lose its validity and/or reliability.
Receiving agent	The person in charge of receiving purchased items.
Recency effect	Recalling a small portion of the appraisal time frame.
Recognition	Extrinsic and intrinsic acknowledgment of accomplishments.
Recruitment	The process of developing a sufficient pool of qualified applicants for vacant positions.
Recruitment	The process of generating qualified pools of applicants for positions.
Recruitment and selection	Human resource activities to attract and hire applicants for positions.
Redirecting behavior	Revised behaviors toward constructive practices.
Relationship patterns	Connections among sub-systems and systems.
Resource categories	Materials, people, technology, finances, equipment and supplies used as inputs for the productivity system.
Risk	Behaviors that entail possible negative consequences.
Run strategies	Maintenance objectives and actions aimed at continuous productivity enhancement during times when organizational problems are minimal or non-existent.
Run strategy	Enhance productivity levels within a department that is meeting standards for performance.
Run strategy	Value-added management practices.
Sales transactions	Payment for products and services rendered by the organization.
Scalar relations	Identify chain of command (reporting relationships).
Scientific method	A method used in management science based on hypotheses, data collection and analysis to prove original assumptions.
Secondary storage	Any read/write storage device such as magnetic disks.
Selection	The process of choosing the best applicant for each position.
Selection	The process of determining those individuals who are best suited for vacant positions from a pool of applicants.
Self-awareness	Internal objective consciousness within an individual.
Self-examination	Internal observation and comparison to the standard for personal being.
Self-leadership	The discipline of objective self-awareness to ensure congruence with internal leadership models.
Self-managed teams (SMT)	Teams that require little or no supervision.
Self-motivation	The willingness to take action to satiate unfulfilled wants, needs and desires without external influence.
Self-transformation	The practice of individual mental and emotional evolution through self-induced contemplative exercises to enhance self-awareness.
Shareholders	A stakeholder group consisting of the investors or owners of a company.
Short-term objectives (STO)	Organizational goals that will take less than 1 year to accomplish.

Situation	The environmental factors influencing a leadership style at a given moment.
Situational analysis	Identifying and analyzing factors of influence that exist in internal and external environments.
Situational leadership	Demonstrating flexibility in leadership style to suit given environmental situations.
Solution optimization	Providing the best possible solution to a problem.
Span of authority	The number of individuals who directly and indirectly report to a manager.
Span of management	Measured by the number of direct reports to a single manager.
Staff authority	The right to advise members of the organization.
Staff relations skills	The ability to influence the staff to meet performance standards.
Staffing	The practice of ensuring appropriate levels of workers within an organization.
Stakeholder group	Groups of constituents for an organization.
Stakeholder groups	Constituency groups of an organization (customers, employees, shareholders and the community).
Standards	Expectations for performance.
Stewardship	Self-sacrificing service by a leader to the followership.
Stewardship	Servant leadership in which the welfare of the followers is the primary directive.
Strategic business units (SBU)	Divisions within a corporation.
Strategic control	A pre-determined mechanism for performance appraisal built into the strategic plan, such as a performance management system.
Strategic planning	Attaching strategies and tactics to each goal as action steps used to achieve objectives.
Strategic thinking	Thinking in terms of objectives and strategies.
Strategies	Action steps used to accomplish long-term (greater than 1 year) objectives.
Strategies	Broad range action steps to accomplish objectives.
Strategy formulation	The development of a plan to conduct an intervention or implement an organizational master plan.
Strengths and weaknesses	Categories of internal data based on potential consequences to the organization.
Subjective management	Appraisals of performance based on non-objective criteria resulting in evaluations that are determined from the personal value system of the manager.
Sub-system	A smaller system within a system.
Supply chain	A continuum of sequential steps that occur in manufacturing and distribution of products that ranges from the original point of manufacture to the end user (customer).
Supply chain transactions	Part of the procurement processes used to acquire material resources for use within the hospitality enterprise.
Sustainable tourism	A long-term collaborative systems approach to establish and maintain harmonious relationships among hospitality/travel related organizations and the social, cultural and environmental aspects associated with tourist destinations.
SWOT analysis	The process of analyzing strengths (S), weaknesses (W), opportunities (O) and threats (T) to the organization.
Synergistic outcomes	Scenarios in which the total outcome from a specific unit exceeds the sum of its parts.

Synthesis	The ability to apply abstract concepts in a realistic setting.
System	A network of relationships.
Systems management	Views the organization as an entity that consists of interdependent relationships with internal and external sub-systems.
Systems theory	A theory that describes patterns of interdependent relationships among all systems and sub-systems.
Systems thinking	A practice related to theories from science and philosophy that describe patterns of collaborative energy called relationships.
Systems thinking	A view of parts and sub-parts as possessing interdependent relationships culminating in an entire system.
Tactics	Actions steps used to accomplish short-term (less than 1 year) objectives.
Tactics	Narrow action steps that occur daily, weekly, monthly or annually to accomplish strategies.
Tasks, duties, responsibilities	Items in a job description articulating activities of employees.
Team	A group of individuals who produce outcomes greater than the sum of its parts (synergy).
Teambuilding	The development of combined energies and activities that yield synergistic outcomes from a specific unit.
Technical skills	The actual skills required to perform a line or staff function.
Tendering or cash settlement transactions	After-the-fact payment for products and services rendered
Terabytes	Ten times the capacity of a gigabyte.
The big picture	The ability to reach stages of awareness that are beyond the self to envision holistic models of leadership interactions.
The next step	Draw your own conclusions on what works for you.
Theory of needs	Achievement, affiliation and power needs.
Total quality management (TQM)	A process of continuously improving inputs and processes used to achieve quality and quantity standards.
Total quality management (TQM)	A process of measuring quality achievement and shortfalls to produce processes for continuous improvement as determined by customer oriented criteria.
Training	Provides knowledge and skills required for employees to perform in current positions.
Training and turnover expenses	Costs associated with recruitment, selection and training of replacement employees.
Training evaluation	Measuring training outcomes to training objectives.
Training reinforcement	Habituating new behaviors resulting from training.
Training reinforcement	Habituate the learning in all that you do.
Trait	Characteristics or personality factors possessed by an individual.
Traits	Personality tendencies within an individual which may be observed by others.
Transactional congruence	Interactions that are consistent with the leader's sense of integrity.

Transactional leadership	Interactions among leaders, followers and others.
Transactional leadership	Leadership that focuses on the moment of leading only.
Transcendence	A temporary evolution to unnatural awareness attained through contemplative reflection practice.
Transcendental leadership	A leadership practice in which the leader engages in a regular practice of reflective contemplation concerning leadership phenomena during states of unnatural awareness.
Transformation	A permanent change toward personal growth.
Transformation	Evolutionary growth through learning and reflection of the growth process used to enhance self-awareness.
Transformation process	The linear process that converts materials and human capital and technology into products and services for customers, guests and clients.
Transformational leadership	A leadership practice that affords individuals with a process of enhanced self-awareness through the exercise of activities aimed at achieving organizational objectives.
Transformational leadership	Leadership that focuses on the intrinsic desires of all involved parties that is applied to leading those parties.
Trial and error	Learning from actually practicing management scenarios.
Troubleshooter	Individuals who exclusively implement turnaround (fix) strategies.
Turnaround strategies	Interventions designed to alter the overall performance of a work unit.
Turnaround strategies	Performance in an operating area is completely fixed to meet standards for performance.
Turnarounds	The collective 'troubleshooting' interventions conducted throughout an organization.
Uncertainty	Limited amounts of total information due to complexity.
Uncontrollable forces	Any force beyond control regardless of which environment the factor resides in.
Unfulfilled wants and desires	The perception that intrinsic or extrinsic factors require satiation.
Unity of command	Individuals who directly report to one boss.
Unpredictable	Behaviors that do not follow a logical flow according to most observers.
Value-added	Workers engaged in continuous productivity enhancement add value to the organization and to themselves.
Value-added management	Managers who practice continuous productivity enhancement.
Value-added managers	Add value to the organization by enhancing productivity levels in small increments every day.
Value-added workers	Workers engaged in continuous productivity enhancement add value to the organization and to themselves.
Value dichotomies	Conflicts among internal values represented by two or more individuals engaged in an activity. The same as cognitive dissonance; it is more descriptive of the conflict that occurs between two individuals in leadership roles.
Value proposition	Inferred promises made to potential guests concerning our standards of service.
Wide area networks (WAN)	Larger interconnected systems in physical locations measured by a few miles.
Willingness to follow	Desires manifested within individuals to follow the leader.
Win, win, win outcomes	Triple 'win' outcomes are results that benefit an organization, the leader and the followers through transformation.

Win/win	An outcome in which both the individuals and the organization benefit from an intervention.
Worker 'buy-in'	A state of commitment to work related processes.
Worker outputs	Units of production completed by each worker.
Working the plan	Making components of the strategic plan key drivers of performance in the organization.
Workplace reputation	The perception of outside parties concerning the practices within an organization.

Index